THE CARTULARY OF THE ABBEY OF MONT-SAINT-MICHEL

Edited by K. S. B. Keats-Rohan

Frontispiece to the Cartulary of Mont-Saint-Michel,
Avranches, BM, ms. 210, fol. 4v, the Vision of St Aubert.

THE CARTULARY OF THE ABBEY OF MONT-SAINT-MICHEL

edited by

K. S. B. KEATS-ROHAN

SHAUN TYAS
DONINGTON
2006

Typeset from the disc of the author by the publisher

Published by

SHAUN TYAS
1 High Street, Donington
Lincolnshire
PE11 4TA

ISBN
1 900289 69 5

Printed and bound by Woolnoughs of Irthlingborough

In loving memory of my husband
John Lyttleton Lloyd
this book is dedicated to our son
Anthony

ACKNOWLEDGMENTS

This edition has been in preparation for just over ten years. During this time I have benefitted greatly from the generosity of several French scholars in discussing or commenting upon aspects of the work, especially François Avril, Mathieu Arnoux, Pierre Bouet, Véronique Gazeau and Jacques Le Maho. Particular thanks are due to the late Hubert Guillotel, a very dear friend and colleague whose own work was a source of inspiration to me over many years. Working at different paces in different countries made an initial plan for a joint edition unworkable, but I profited nonetheless from regular discussion and consultation with him until a few months before his untimely death earlier this year. I hope that in some small way the many references to his work in the pages that follow might be seen as both testimony and a lasting tribute to the inspiration of a most remarkable historian.

I am grateful to Pierre Bouet and Pierre Bauduin for the opportunity to present somewhat controversial ideas on the abbey's history at conferences held at Cerisy-la-Salle in 2000 and 2002, to Christopher Harper-Bill and the Battle Conference for the first opportunity to present my work on the Cartulary in 1998, and to Michael Clanchy and David Ganz for subsequent opportunities to discuss the historical background at seminars in London. These have all been invaluable in helping me to shape some firm ideas about some very complex and rather treacherous data. All responsibility for opinions expressed and any errors committed here is mine.

No manuscript collection has a more devoted, sensitive and conscientious guardian than M. Jean-Luc Leservoisier, *conservateur* of the manuscripts of Mont-Saint-Michel at Avranches, who has been unstintingly generous with his time during my visits to Avranches. My thanks also to Mme Danielle Leservoisier for her friendship and hospitality. In the past two years my visits have been greatly facilitated by the meetings of the *comité scientifique* of the projected *Centre des manuscrits* at Avranches, on which I have been privileged to serve at the kind invitation of *M. le Maire* and the *Conseil municipal* of Avranches.

A special vote of thanks is reserved for my editor and publisher, Shaun Tyas, for the saintly patience he has exercised since first accepting this book.

Unhappily, instead of finishing with heartfelt thanks to my family for the different ways in which they have supported this work, I have instead to dedicate the book to our son in memory of my husband, who died just as work on the book's index began. John was an outstanding scientist and a wonderful person who needs no monument beyond his own achievements. His is an irreparable loss for me and Anthony. In dedicating this book as a testament to our love I hope that we may all stay together a while longer on its pages.

K. S. B. Keats-Rohan
December 2004

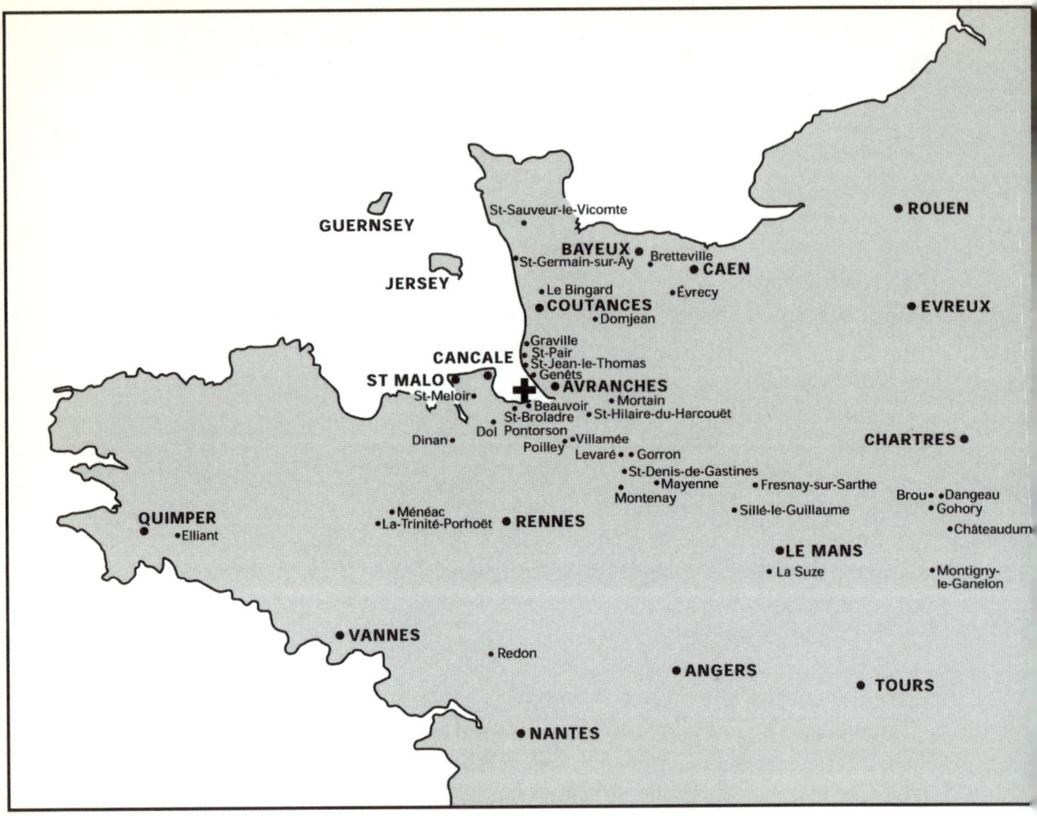

Map illustrating the location of places in north France mentioned in the Cartulary.

CONTENTS

The 'foundation' of 966,
Avranches, BM, ms. 210, fol. 19v.

Grant by an unidentified king, probably William I,
duke of Normandy and king of England,
Avranches, BM, ms. 210, fol. 25v.

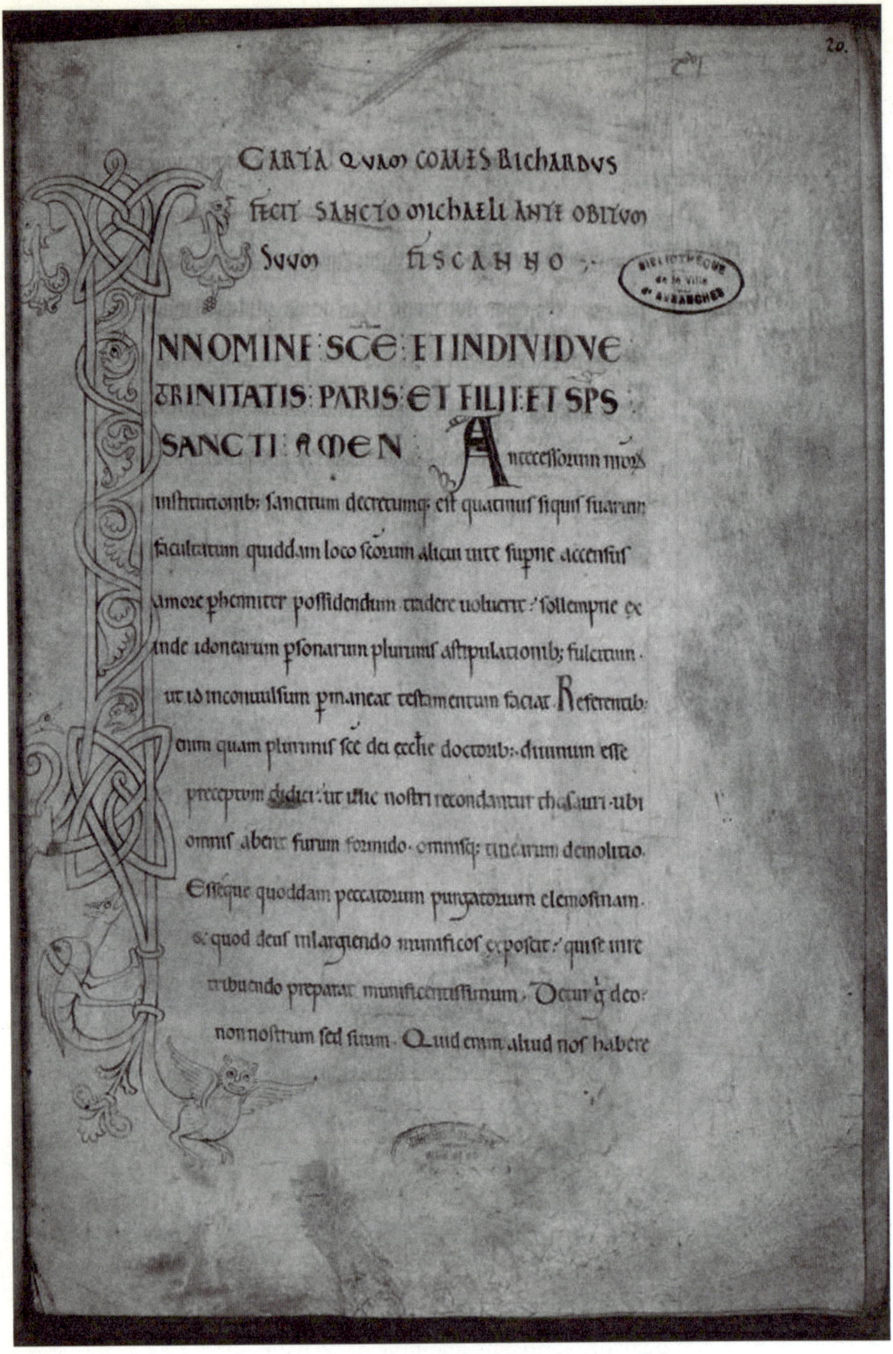

Historiated initial 'I',
Avranches, BM, ms. 210, fol. 20r.

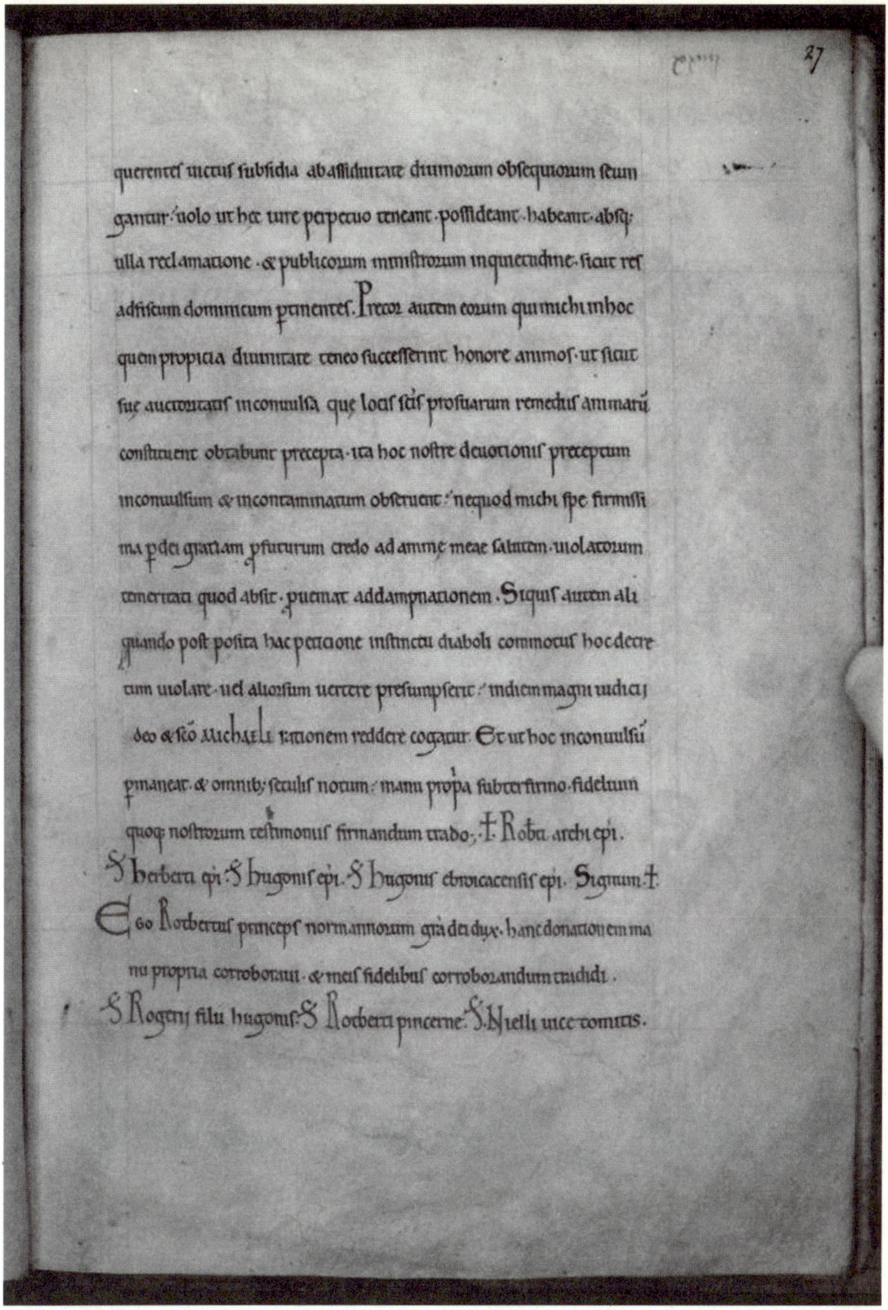

Full text page
Avranches, BM, ms. 210, fol. 27r.

INTRODUCTION

A manuscript cartulary is at once a unique artefact and a unique written text behind which will lie a specific purpose related to, and revealed by, the moment in an institution's history when it was written. It can only be understood through a dual study of the manuscript as artefact and as a single text, which will consist of a series of separate texts arranged to form a whole.

In a perceptive study of the origin and functions of cartularies, in the context of 'Archival memory and the destruction of the past', Patrick Geary wrote: "Traditionally, diplomatists have given low priority to the study of cartularies as such, using them primarily to reconstruct texts of lost originals with little regard to the nature, function and history of this genre. Examination of their contents focuses on the identification of genuine, forged, or interpolated texts which, properly categorized by the techniques of diplomatics, can then be exploited as though they were originals. When editing cartularies, most nineteenth- and twentieth-century editors have ignored the organization of the cartularies themselves, attempting instead to present all the charters and documents of a given institution in a chronological order, regardless of provenance and organization in the cartularies or tradition books themselves. In other words, most scholarly attention has focused on eliminating the cartulary itself in order to provide transparent windows into the original archives of an institution. This process was considered legitimate because each cartulary was considered a self-evident attempt to preserve the contents of the institution's archives".[1] Unhappily, based though they are on a thorough misconception of the cartulary, such attitudes are still common and have even been enshrined in an otherwise excellent modern handbook on medieval diplomatic: 'Le cartulaire ... a pour but d'assurer la conservation et de faciliter la consultation d'un ensemble bien précis de documents relatifs à une personne physique ou morale. Les actes qu'il contient, ayant été retranscrits par l'intéressé lui-même, ne présentent en principe aucune présomption de sincérité ou d'authenticité. D'autant que, parfois, les scribes ont omis systématiquement de reproduire tantôt les listes de témoins, plus souvent les marques extérieures d'authenticité. Editer tel quel un cartulaire ne se justifie que dans les cas exceptionnels, lorsque le classement

1 Patrick J. Geary, *Problems of Remembrance. Memory and Oblivion at the end of the First Millenium*, Princeton 1994, 83. An earlier version of some sections of this Introduction was delivered at the Battle Conference in 1998 and has been published in *Anglo-Norman Studies*, XXII (1999), 95–112.

des actes est en lui-même intéressant'.[2]

Of course, such elimination of the cartulary is wholly indefensible, being nothing less than the destruction of a unique written work, analagous to setting fire to the autograph of Orderic's *Historia Ecclesiastica*. To the maker of a cartulary or a *Traditionsbuch* the value of his archive material was its import for his institution at the time of writing; the diplomatic was of no account in itself, though it could receive detailed attention and transformation as the cartularist accomplished his task. For even in the case of genuine cartularies, where the deeds were all copied from originals and not turned into the third-person *reportages* of the *Traditionsbuch*, or massaged into the formats required by the *cartulaire-chronique*, the *Urtext* of the original could be modified to bring it in line with the practices, needs and requirements of the cartularist's own time. An editor seeking to undo the work of the cartularist in order to achieve some specious notion of 'the original' will in the process destroy the precious and unique original that it must be his duty to preserve.

Part of the problem has been a lack of understanding about the nature and function of cartularies. Like all medieval books, they tend to be varied in form and content and to vary over time and place of origin. It is nevertheless increasingly clear that early- and central-medieval cartularies are self-consciously histories of their communities, their benefactors and their estates.[3] The organization of many cartularies reveals their function and utility as records relating to the composition, management and preservation of great estates, but they were not created or used as legal documents *per se*. Legal documents are public documents. A cartulary is essentially private, produced by and for a community for specific reasons relating to its self identity.[4] The purpose was memorialization, the committing to written memory of key information relating to rights in and over their estates (including, where it suited the required purpose, forged material), and to the ways in which those estates had been built up or acquired.[5] By writing a cartulary, the monks aimed to claim or enforce certain cherished rights by showing that they had been granted or acquired a long time ago and had been exercised ever since. Memorialization, especially the commemoration of the dead in liturgical

[2] Olivier Guyotjeannin, Jacques Pycke, Benoít-Michel Tock, *Diplomatique médiévale*, Brepols 1993, p. 414; cf. pp. 277–281.

[3] Patrick Geary, 'Entre Gestion et Gesta', in O. Guyotjeannin, L. Morelle, M. Parisse, edd., *Les cartulaires. Actes de la table ronde (Paris, décembre 1991)* Paris, Ecole des Chartes, 1993, pp. 13–26, and *ibid.*, Jean-Philippe Genet, 'Cartulaires anglais du moyen age', pp. 343–361; see also Genet's article, 'Cartulaires, registres et histoire: l'exemple anglais', in B. Guénée ed., *Le Métier d'historien au Moyen Age*, Paris 1977, pp. 95–138.

[4] See Monique Zerner, 'L'élaboration du grand cartulaire de Saint-Victor de Marseille', in *Les Cartulaires*, pp. 217–246; Rolf Grosse, 'Remarques sur les cartulaires de Saint-Denis aux XIIIe et XIVe siècles', *ibid.*, pp. 247–260.

[5] Hubert Guillotel, 'Cartulaires bretons médiévaux', *ibid.*, pp. 325–432.

offices such as Chapter, using lists of names written into necrologies, was a key monastic obligation and a core part of the monastic ethos. Cartulary records of acts of donation or restitution commemorated key benefactors in non-liturgical fashion. The same records reveal much about the success or failure of individual abbots as heads of their community and guardians of its interests; formally or informally they function as *gesta abbatum*.[6] Whatever else a cartulary could be, the commemorative and historiographical functions were primary and inseparable.

Few manuscripts illustrate better the value of cartularies than MS 210 of the Bibliothèque municipale d'Avranches, now known simply as the Cartulary of Mont-Saint-Michel, because it contains the only one of at least two cartularies of the abbey to remain extant.[7] It is one of the most celebrated manuscripts of the Middle Ages, chiefly on account of an illuminated drawing of the Archangel Michael appearing in a vision to the sanctuary's founder, Bishop Aubert of Avranches, at a date early in the eighth century.[8] Illustrated cartularies are extremely rare and are always an indication of their *sui generis* nature. The drawings in particular stress the singularity of the work: the iconography is not intended to be recopied and is highly specific to the cartulary it illustrates.[9] Nonetheless, this marvellous manuscript has not been well served by modern historians. Until my article was published in 1999, no competent documentary historian had ever published an account of a serious codicological examination of the manuscript, but a long series of art historians had offered opinions on all manner of issues on the basis of a total of four drawings, one of them the famous illumination of the Vision of Saint Aubert.[10] The contents of the manuscript have for the most part been published in bits and pieces in various guises; discussion of the items contained in the manuscript have received equally piecemeal treatment.[11] None of them is any substitute for the complete Cartulary text, an unique

6 Cf. Dominique Iogna-Prat, 'La confection des cartulaires et l'historiographie à Cluny (XIe–XIIe siècles)', in *Les Cartulaires*, pp. 27–44.

7 For a basic description see Henri Omont, Catalogue général des manuscrits des bibilothèques publique de la France t. x, 1–125, manuscrits de la bibliothèque d'Avranches, Paris 1889, following the account of Mont manuscripts in *Catalogue général des manuscrits des bibliothèques publiques des départements*, 7 vols, Paris 1849–85, t. iv, 427–562.

8 Abbé Lelagard, 'Saint Aubert', in *Millénaire monastique du Mont-Saint-Michel*, 2 vols, Paris 1967–93 [hereafter *Mill. mon.*], t. i, 29–52.

9 Patricia Stirnemann, 'L'illustration du cartulaire de Saint-Martin-du-Canigou', *ibid.*, pp. 171–178.

10 See references in notes 24, 26, 70 and 72 below. Cf. François Avril, 'La décoration des manuscrits du Mont-Saint-Michel, xi–xii siècles', *Mill. mon.*, ii, 203–238.

11 See the excellent *Bibliographie générale* in Dom Jacques Dubois, 'Les dépendances de l'abbaye du Mont Saint-Michel et la vie monastique dans les prieurés', *Mill. mon.* i, note 1 on pp. 620–624.

compilation of truly outstanding importance, which is published here in full for the first time.

It has been stated several times in various notices of Avranches 210 that it contains one complete work, the Cartulary proper, on folio 5r to folio 112r. On folio 112v through to folio 118, there is a register of *acta* produced in the first five years of the abbacy of Robert de Torigny, from 1155–9. This register was published as an appendix to Delisle's edition of Robert of Torigny's Chronicle.[12] It is followed by further additions of documentary material from Robert's abbatiate, as well as later documents, mostly of the thirteenth century but also of the fourteenth. In this edition of the Cartulary of Mont-Saint-Michel all the additional material has been excluded as an undesirable distraction. It is crucially important to focus upon the Cartulary as a written work produced before 1155. Study of the codicology of the manuscript underlines this point. Attention to the history of the abbey around the time the cartulary was produced and later, and to the history of its archives, brings further useful understanding to Avranches 210. Each of these matters will be considered in turn in sections I–III below, and in the Notes on Persons Occurring in the Cartulary. Section IV will look in detail at the Cartulary text(s) and explain the significance of the texts printed here as an Appendix. The Cartulary is a cardinal witness to the abbey's history both because it preserves a large collection of important charters and because the circumstances in which was compiled can be reconstructed. One of the best-known parts of the Cartulary is its introductory matter, the so-called *Historia*. A composite work uniting several texts for the first time, the *Historia* presents a version of the community's early history that circulated widely and has been accepted virtually unchallenged until the present day. Unfortunately for those who have uncritically accepted the *Historia* during the past 700 years, the full-scale investigation of a wide range of sources required for a full understanding of the *Historia* traditions reveals that those traditions are thoroughly unreliable. Such an investigation was undertaken for the benefit of the present work, but the results have so far outstripped it that only an introduction to the problems can be given here, found in section II. A full discussion of the abbey's history will be treated at length in a book currently in preparation which will contain editions of the Mont's necrologies and other texts.

I. PALAEOGRAPHY AND CODICOLOGY OF MS AVRANCHES 210

At one time numbered 80, Avranches 210 acquired its present form when it was rebound by the Congregation of Saint-Maur, established at the Mont in 1622. The numbers 80 and then 210 were assigned at the library at Avranches to which the manuscript went at the time of the French Revolution. An

12 *Chronique de Robert de Torigni ... Suivie de divers opuscules historiques de cet auteur*, ed. L. Delisle, 2 vols, Rouen 1872–3, ii, 237–260.

earlier pressmark, 'M[entio]ne C', is written in ink in the top left of the paste-down on the Maurist binding. It was described, without a pressmark, in an inventory of 1639 by the monk Dom Le Michel as *cartular[ium] niger*, a junior partner of a now lost *major cartular[ium] albus*.[13] It contains 11 leaves and 138 folia; folia 5–134 average 361 x 255 milimetres in size. The folia are written on membrane, doubtless parchment. The quality is variable, and nowhere is it especially high. Signs of frequent handling are visible in the bottom and outer margins. None of the annotations made by readers predates the late Middle Ages. There are two sets of foliation in the manuscript's main body of 138 folia; the first, in Roman numerals, belongs to the fourteenth, or possibly fifteenth, century, the second is modern, probably of the nineteenth century. The original manuscript of the cartulary begins on the folio numbered 5r in the modern foliation and 1r in the late medieval foliation. It is preceded by a flyleaf and seven folia of paper numbered in Roman numerals, containing two tables of contents for the codex. The first of these is a gathering of four folia written and pasted into the codex in the nineteenth century; the second contents table, on folia vi–vii, is written in a seventeenth-century hand, perhaps belonging to one of the Maurist historians of the abbey, such as Dom Thomas Le Roy; the latter is headed 'Table des matieres contenues en ce livre'.[14] These are followed by a binion, two folia of membrane which at one time were flyleaves to the codex; the first recto is blank except for a large capital V at the top, the word *Veritas* in the bottom left and the phrase *Veni creator spiritus* halfway down the right side, all of which is written in green ink.[15] The first verso and second recto contain fourteenth-century acts in several different hands.[16] There follows a second

13 Printed as an appendix to G. Nortier, 'La bibliothèque du Mont Saint-Michel', cited in note 26 below, pp. 163–68. The references to the lost cartulary and to Avranches 210 read: *Major cartular. albus. Item alter niger*, indicating that *cartular.*, presumably an abbreviation for *cartularium*, is not being used as a neuter noun, as would be usual.

14 Eugène de Robillard de Beaurepaire, *Les curieuses recherches du Mont Saint-Michel par Dom Thomas Le Roy*, Caen 1878.

15 Perhaps this is the origin of the otherwise inexplicable description of Avranches 210 as *livre vert*, a title used in the catalogue descriptions of Delisle and Omont (note 7 above). Possibly this manuscript was confused with the Livre vert of the bishopric of Avranches, now Bib. mun. Avranches 206 (*Chartularium ecclesiae Abrincensis*) (cf. Omont, *Catalogue*).

16 [Fol. 1v:] L'an de grace mil troyscent lxxii le jour de la feste S. Nichol de Mei les Angleis vindrent a Tombe Heleinie. | Mention que la chartre [sic] de Cauge est a lxxii en nombre. Item carta de Bouceyo est a iiii xx xiii en nombre. | [Fol. 2r:] Anno domini millesimo trecentesimo lxxii die lune in festum Beati Georgii item arripuit Johannis de Squ'tot [...] famulus bailliui die hanc sequenti dictum festum. | Item eodem anno in festo translationis Beati Nicolai uenerunt Anglici apud Tumbam Helenam causa ibi morandi. | Anno millesimo clv Henricus Rex Anglorum et dux Normannorum confirmauit dona possessiones alia pertinentiis

binion, also composed of two folia of membrane; the first of these, numbered 3r, contains documentary texts of the second half of the thirteenth century. On folia 3v and 4r there is a fragment of a *Translatio Sancti Maglorii*, written in a thirteenth-century hand on membrane ruled in dry point below top line, which would normally indicate a date before before 1220.[17] At the bottom of folio 4 recto is written: 'Bastien Ernault Religieux en ceste abbaye'. Dom Jean Huynes identified him as the prior, Sebastien Ernault, who died in 1570.[18]

On folio 4 verso, now forming the frontispiece to the Cartulary, is the celebrated drawing of the Vision of St Aubert. There are a number of tenth- and eleventh-century parallels in manuscripts of the Mont for a frontispiece.[19] All of them are found on what is now the first verso of the first quire, suggesting that the recto was intended as a blank guard. There is no doubt that the Vision relates to the first text in the cartulary, the so-called *Revelatio*, which describes the place of St Aubert's vision in the founding of the sanctuary. The fact that details in the drawing are left unfinished further links it to the cartulary text, as will be seen, so we may assume that it was designed as the original frontispiece. It is unlikely, nonetheless, that the use of gold-leaf to paint part of the Vision is coeval with the production of the cartulary since a thirteenth-century copyist, using a good black ink and a firm ductus, completed his fragment of the *Translatio Sancti Maglorii* on the back of the Vision (folio 4r). It is clear that this binion was intended as a guard to the original codex; folio 3, the original flyleaf, is of poor quality, scarred, membrane. Whether anything else was intended for what must have been two blank rectos and one blank verso of a binion separate from the first written quire, we cannot know. The arrangement can be compared to a late twelfth-century Mont manuscript, now BN lat. 14832, in which a binion (now folia A–B) precedes the regular eight-leaved quires of the codex. In this case the principal original scribe also wrote the first of three contents tables for the

---

abbatie de Sauigneyo et dicte abbatie et hominibus tenentibus ab ipsam donauit et concessit priuilegia franchisia et libertates quas habent [4 words here, reading uncertain]. | In isto caterio continetur ista primo Reuelatio Sancti Micaelis postea fondationem istius ecclesie in pagina ii, iii, iv, v, vi, et vii. De ducibus Normannie viii, ix et x Qualiter monachi ibi sunt constituti et priuilegiis ducum Normannie regemque Francie Domini Pape archiepiscopi Rothomagensis et episcopi Abrincensis omnibus predictis consentientibus ut patet x, xi, xii, xiii, xiiii, xv. Carta de Sancto Paterno | Ancien livre. The slash is used to indicate a change of hand in the manuscript.

17 On the *Translatio Sancti Maglorii* see Hubert Guillotel, 'L'exode du clergé breton devant les invasions scandinaves', *Mémoires de la Société d'histoire et d'archéologie de Bretagne* lix, 1982, 301–316.

18 Dom Jean Huynes, *Histoire générale de l'abbaye du Mont Saint-Michel au péril de la mer, publié par Eugène de Robillard de Beaurepaire*, 2 vols, Rouen 1872–3, ii, 232. He was remembered on 24 May in the abbey's Martyrology-Necrology, Avranches Bib. mun. 214, part I, p. 74.

19 Bib. mun. Avranches MSS 50, 59, 75, 76, 115.

manuscript on folia A verso and B recto.[20]

With folio 5r we come to the original codex, which consists of 14 regular eight-leaved quires, ruled in lead-point and rubricated throughout. One leaf was cut out between fol. 39v and 40r.[21] The work of one north-French scribe writing in a protogothic *litera textualis media-formata* script of the first half of the twelfth century, it contains two-, three- and five-line decorated initials in alternating patterns in red and blue, as well as fifteen-line major initials. Some of the major initials are unfinished, with decorative flourishes having been drawn in ink but left unpainted; e.g. on folio 110v a four-line initial H would have become seven-line if the detail on an ink-sketched descender had been painted. Major headings in the text are written in uncial capitals. Lesser headings – the *invocatio* of each charter or the first word or phrase of a major section of text – and key personal- or place-names are written in rustic capitals. For most of the work, up to about folio 76, the scribe always picked out the name of the archangel Michael in rustic capitals. A key feature of his script is the leftwards sweep of the descender on his 'g', which becomes more dramatic as the work progresses. He always uses a very competent form of the ampersand for *et*, but was unable or unwilling to fix a standard for the æ diphthong. He uses *ae*, *æ*, tagged e (e *caudata*), and *e* indifferently from folio 5 to folio 80, with two forms possible within the same word and more within a sentence. After folio 80, where the signs of haste are accumulating, the form *e* is preferred, with only an occasional use of *ae*. His use of abbreviation was light. Capitalization of *nomina sacra* and place-names is normally absent. His work was generally careful and he corrected most of his few mistakes as he worked.

There are three major drawings in ink on folia 19 verso, 23 verso and 25 verso. Much of 48 recto is blank, all of 48 verso and two thirds of 49 recto. The size of this gap suggests that it was intended to be filled with an additional text or texts, and possibly another drawing. There are frequent gaps of up to nine lines between charters occurring between fol. 26r and 66v (all of them have been noted in the edition). These are clearly intended to separate charters relating to different priories. All of this indicates that the layout of the cartulary was carefully thought out in advance. None of the quires of the original codex seem ever to have been signed. But on the verso of first folio in the seventh and eight quires, were later added a letter 'c' and 'ab' respectively in the left of the lower margin. The dimensions of the written space are fairly regular, typically (as on folio 13) 19 lines of text in an area 245mm by 156mm. There are top and bottom margins, 27 and 26 mm respectively; outer and

20 BN MS lat. 14832, a manuscript produced at and for Mont-Saint-Michel before *c.* 1220, some time after which it went to Saint-Victor in Paris, was discussed by M. F. Columbaluzier, 'Le Pontifical dit d'Avranches', *Mill. mon.* i, 383–398, who showed that Delisle's account of this manuscript is erroneous.

21 There is no indication that the loss is textually significant and it was probably due to damage to the parchment.

inner margins are 8mm wide. The fourteenth quire, on folia 108r–115r, is the last 8-leaved quire of the original codex. The final original writing was an unfinished act on fol. 112 recto. The fifteenth quire, also eight-leaved, on folia 116 to 123, is a later addition, on poor quality membrane. Folia 124–9 are a later addition, apparently forming a trinion. Folia 130–134 are additional leaves intercalated with the trinion. There is a break in format after fol. 134v, with the addition of four further leaves which are rather smaller than the other folia. Some of the added folia from 124–134 have suffered small losses of text in upper and outer margins (eg. fol. 128v and 129r).

Given the presence of medieval foliation from the fourteenth or fifteenth century continuous from modern folios 5 to 138, and the addition on each flank of the original codex of documentary material relating to the fourteenth century, it is likely that the manuscript was bound in or around that century. In fact, there is clear evidence of one and perhaps two bindings earlier than the present seventeenth-century one; the first was in or shortly before 1372, as indicated by notes on fol. 1v and 2r relating to the English presence on Tombelaine in that year (quoted in note 16, above). The present binion fol. 1–2 was evidently once used as flyleaves and there are clear traces of paste on folio 1 recto. This is mirrored on folio 134 verso, which also shows the outline of a former pasting-down. Revealing also is the deep wrinkle on the lower half of folia 3 and 4, the binion of the original manuscript, which postdates the drawing of the Vision on fol 4v. The wrinkle is matched by one on fol. 129v, which contains a number of texts, mostly of *c.* 1360. When the codex was bound *c.* 1372 it is unlikely that either binion now forming modern folia 1–4 had previously been formally bound with the fourteen regular eight-leaved quires of Avranches 210, because the late medieval foliation started at 1 recto with the original cartulary text on folio 5 recto, i.e. the first recto of the first regular quire. Since the late-medieval foliation was applied to all of folia 116–138 (112–134 in the late-medieval foliation), it becomes apparent that an earlier binding of the leaves up to folio 134 was replaced by one that incorporated the four intercalated leaves, fol. 135–8. At any rate, a binding of *c.* 1372 was apparently modified so as to permit the addition of folia 135–8. This modification was accompanied by the late-medieval foliation. None of the texts thus assembled is later than the fourteenth century. Possibly, therefore, the modification or rebinding was done during the abbacy of Pierre Le Roy (1384–1411), who famously reorganized the abbey's archives and ordered the production of another cartulary, the now lost *Maior cartular[ium] Albus* (*sic*, see note 9), *c.* 1400.[22] According to a life of the abbot written at Mont-Saint-Michel, Abbot Le Roy went through the archives personally, so he would certainly have known

22 Michel Reulos, 'L'organisation et l'administration de l'abbaye à partir de l'abbé Pierre Le Roi jusqu'à l'application du Concordat', *Mill. mon.* i, 191–209.

what he was doing if it was indeed him who put Avranches 210 together. The illumination of the Vision on folio 4v perhaps belongs to the same date.

II. DATE, HISTORICAL CONTEXT AND PURPOSE OF THE CARTULARY

a. Date

The nineteenth-century table of contents is headed *Table des Matières contenues dans le grand cartulaire du Mont-Saint-Michel, rédigé par Robert du Mont, abbé au 12e siècle*. Note that with the loss of the Pierre Le Roy's *maior cartular[ium] albus* or *Livre Blanc*, Avranches 210 has become 'le grand cartulaire'. This heading is the sole documentary basis for the assumption of all modern commentators, without exception, that the cartulary owes its existence to Robert de Torigny.[23] The importance of the cartulary as a unique written document is such that the attribution of its 'authorship' is a matter of some consequence, demanding detailed consideration. We should be clear at the outset that the cartulary, written by and for a community of monks, was a corporate enterprise. I shall refer to their collective decisions about the content of their cartulary as being those of 'the cartularist'. In seeking to identify the commissioning abbot the personal identity of the abbot will matter less than the circumstances of his abbatiate.

Let us return again for a moment to the famous drawings in the cartulary. The most recent commentator is Monique Dosdat who observes that the cartulary was the work of a single scribe, but that the drawings were the work of two separate artists, possibly laymen.[24] In her view, this indicates that the abbot wanted the work done quickly and to that end he spared no expense. For her it goes without saying that the abbot is Robert of Torigny. She states as fact, as others have done, that the Cartulary results from one of the earliest decisions taken by Robert as abbot. Abundant evidence yielded by the cartulary text shows that it predates Robert's abbatiate. The cartulary was not only hastily executed, it was abandoned. It may be that the only

23 For example, André Dufief, 'Vie monastique au Mont pendant le XIIe siècle', Mill. mon. i, 121; M. Bourgeois-Lechartier, 'A la recherche du Scriptorium de l'abbaye du Mont Saint-Michel', *ib.* ii, 171–200; Avril, 'La décoration des manuscrits', *ib.*, ii, 203–238. J. J. G. Alexander, *Norman Illumination at Mont-Saint-Michel, 966–1100*, Oxford 1970.

24 Monique Dosdat, L'enluminure romane au Mont Saint-Michel xe–xiie siècles, Rennes/Avranches 1991, discusses the cartulary on pp. 72–81. Other commentators, notably M. François Avril, 'La décoration des manuscrits du Mont-Saint-Michel, xi–xii siècles', *Mill. mon.*, ii, pp. 203–238, detect the presence of a sole artist. Avril has suggested that this artist, a monk, was associated with Le Mans. At the time the Cartulary was composed the priory of Saint-Victeur-au-Mans was one of its most important. A charter possibly forged at the time of the Cartulary's composition (no. 62), related to Saint-Victeur.

completed part of the work was the illustrations – which were undoubtedly coeval with the main work of the scribe, though the size of the gap between fol. 48r and 49r is a possible indication that one other drawing was projected. The scribe of the cartulary completed his work to the foot of folio 112 recto, in the middle of the fourteenth quire, ending with an apparently incomplete quitclaim by William Goion dating to a period between 1100 and 1131. The act contains an *intitulatio* and dispositive clauses (*linquo et trado*), but lacks full validation clauses – no witnesses, seals or evidence of a chirograph form; the final *x. sol.* is left unspecific – and hence lacks legal force. At the top of folio 112 verso a scholar's hand begins a record of the acts of Robert of Torigny with the words: 'In the year 1155, in the second year of the reign of Henry II of England and the year in which Robert was called to direct the monastery of St Michael, the said abbot purchased the land of Rualend, provost of Genêts.'.[25] This lapidary statement introduces a register of the abbot's acts relating to abbey property. The register is a set of administrative annals. The work of a bureaucrat, not a historian, it gives not the slightest hint of any concern whatever with or for the abbey's archives. Geneviève Nortier's study of the manuscripts of the abbey led her to observe that there was a tendency under Robert of Torigny for the monks to use blank folia in their manuscripts to copy acts or important documents, of which she cites Avranches 82 as an example; another is Avranches 128.[26] Clearly, Avranches 210 is yet another. Finally, Nortier repeats Boinet's observation that Avranches 210 is exceptional among Torigny manuscripts for being decorated.[27] All this points to a single conclusion: great abbot though Robert de Torigny undoubtedly was, the production of the first cartulary of Mont-Saint-Michel was not among the achievements of his abbatiate.

The clearly unfinished state of the original cartulary, combined with the subsequent use of its unfinished final quire for an annalistic register of Robert's early years as abbot, is in itself an eloquent statement that the Cartulary predates his abbatiate. The abrupt abandonment of what was obviously intended as a very fine manuscript suggests either that the monks tired of their project or that the work was interrupted by external events. The scale of the original intention, betrayed principally by the provision made for illustrations, excludes the former possibility and leads directly to the

[25] Anno ab Incarnatione Domini MCLV Regni uero secundi Henrici regis Anglorum. Primo eodem etiam anno quo Robertus abbas uocatus est ad regimen monasterii Sancti Michaelis, idem abbas emit terram Rualendi prepositi de Genez, Avranches 210, fol. 112v, printed in Delisle, *Torigni*, ii, 237.

[26] G. Nortier, 'La bibliothèque du Mont Saint-Michel', in *id.*, *Les bibliothèques médiévales des abbayes bénédictines de Normandie. Fécamp, Le Bec, Le Mont Saint-Michel, Saint-Evroul, Lyre, Jumièges, Saint-Wandrille, Saint-Ouen*, Caen 1966 (reprinted from *Revue Mabillon* 1953, 135–171, with same pagination), here p. 144 note 56.

[27] Nortier, 143.

conclusion that the work was abandoned when the abbey suffered some trauma. The years leading up to Robert's election in 1154 were indeed notoriously traumatic for the abbey. In 1138 the abbey was attacked and burnt by men from the Avranchin loyal to King Stephen.[28] Since 1131 the abbey had been led by Abbot Bernard, a former monk of Bec and friend of Henry I, whose daughter Matilda he supported at the old king's death in 1135. Bernard was one of the Mont's great abbots, condemned unfairly by modern historians to live permanently in the shadow of his historian successor Robert.[29] He had energetically worked to have restored to the abbey lands usurped from it by local laymen. He reorganized some of the abbey's holdings into new priories at Brion, Tombelaine and St Michael's Mount. He was the first abbot seriously to exploit the relics of the founder St Aubert and, of course, as a former monk of Bec, he was an important influence on the growing intellectual reputation of an abbey that had had an active scriptorium since the late tenth century. The fire of 1138 was a blow to the very great achievements of Bernard, who had reversed the fortunes of a semi-derelict and almost bankrupt institution since his accession seven years before. But Bernard's work continued notwithstanding and it was a financially sound and well-administered house that he abandoned at his death on the night of 8 May 1149. It was a blow for which the monks were probably well-prepared. The very next day they elected Bernard's successor, Geoffrey, from one of their own number. Geoffrey very probably had been closely associated with Bernard before his death. He was possibly the monk called *Gaufredus Episcopus* – Geoffrey L'Evêque – who attested two of Abbot Bernard's charters as found in the cartulary. Later documents in the material added to the Cartulary after 1155 show that the L'Evêque family came from a region between Coutances and Avranches.[30]

Geoffrey's election was a highly significant event for the abbey. The monks had exercised their right as Benedictines freely to elect their own abbot, but they did so in the teeth of established Norman ducal opposition to such free elections. The result was a fine so punitive that much of Abbot

28 Thomas Le Roy, *Les Curieuses recherches*, pp. 157–8; *Chronique de Robert de Torigny*, II, p. 234; cf. Orderic Vitalis, vi, p. 492, recounting an attack in 1137 led by Gelduin of Dol, who drowned trying to escape the tide.

29 André Dufief, 'Vie monastique', 92–101.

30 Cartulary, no. 68 (fol. 81), re Esquay, Abbot Bernard and monks, including *Richard de Musca* and *Gaufredus Episcopus*, and *ib.*, no. 85 (fol. 91). On folio 113 of the Cartulary, published in *Torigni*, ii p. 239, there is an item referring to 'Ricardus archidiaconus Constanciencis, qui cognominatur Episcopus, qui habebat ad feudi firmam terram de Estreis'. A later document refers to an accord concerning rents made between the abbey and Jordan Bertin fitz Bertin Leuesque de Goi, MS Avranches 211, fol. 123v, relating to the priory of Saint-Germain-sur-Ay. A Peter Episcopus attested items in the register of Robert de Torigny's early years, Delisle, *Torigni*, ii, 242–3.

Bernard's work in restoring abbey finances was undone overnight. To the monks, it was a price worth paying. Abbot Geoffrey eventually sought and obtained a papal bull from Eugenius III that confirmed the abbey's possessions, extended to it the protection of St Peter, and, most importantly, confirmed the Benedictine right of free election of its abbot (**Appendix, ii.11**). This great triumph occurred on 15 December 1150. Fifteen days later Abbot Geoffrey was dead.[31] His death was a catastrophe that could have led to a far greater one. The monks waited over a year before proceeding to a second election of one of their own number, this time Richard de La Mouche, a kinsman of Bishop Richard of Avranches, by whom he was consecrated as abbot. Ironically, as *Ricardus de Musca*, he occurs as a witness for Abbot Bernard in one of the two Cartulary charters also attested by Geoffrey L'Evêque. Henry of Normandy was furious. He insisted upon a second election, which produced an abbot from Fécamp in Robert Hardy. Eugenius III intervened and, in a writ of 7 July 1152, insisted in his turn that Richard de Musca be restored. On 17 July 1153 both abbots and the bishop were summoned to Rome, and Henry – now married to Eleanor of Aquitaine – was threatened with excommunication and interdict. All round disaster was averted by the death of both rival abbots and the bishop in Rome, towards the end of 1153, and by the subsequent election, on 27 May 1154, of Robert of Torigny, prior of Bec, as an abbot acceptable to monks and Henry alike.[32]

Clearly, then, there was drama a-plenty to account both for the abandonment of the Cartulary of Mont-Saint-Michel at the time of writing, and for why it was never subsequently finished in more stable times. It remains to determine precisely which part of all this drama underlies the Cartulary and hence which of Robert's predecessors was responsible for commissioning it. This is a question that must be answered with reference to the contents of the Cartulary, because they will clarify what, if anything, was its specific purpose and hence why and when it is most likely to have been commissioned.

The Cartulary contains a total of 119 items, of which 117 are individual acts. Of that 117, two are duplicates, so that there are really 115 separate acts

[31] Dom Huynes, *Histoire*, i, 171: *Chapitre douziesme. De Geoffroy, quetorziesme abbé.* L'abbé Bernard n'estoit encore ensevely que les religieux desireux d'avoir un abbé selon leur choix esleurent Geoffroy, religieux de ce mont, lequel tout après fut beny à Saint Georges de Bauceville par Hugues archevesque de Rouen. Et ce afin d'empescher par cette hastiveté le duc de Normandie de leur en donner un autre, mais cela ne leur servit de gueres, car ce duc pour les affliger les contrignit de luy bailler une grande somme de deniers qu'on fut contrainct d'emprunter pour luy satisfaire. Et la mort sembla favoriser l'abbé Geoffroy, qui estoit fort marry de ces troubles lors que l'an mil cent cinquante le quatriesme de janvier elle le vint enlever de ce monde. Son corps fut inhumé au bas de la nef de cette eglise aupres de son predecesseur.

[32] Delisle, *Chronicle of Robert de Torigny*, i, pp. 282, 284–5.

relating to abbey property recorded in the Cartulary. One item is a record of property lost to the abbey during the eleventh century (no. **115**). The first 11 documentary items relate primarily to members of the eleventh-century Norman ducal family, including the English king, Edward the Confessor.[33] A handful of later charters by lesser Normans follows, after which the items occur in a rather crude order which, broadly speaking, presents the foundation of each of the priories in turn with a roughly chronological presentation of key charters. Geographically, the charters range over Normandy, Brittany, Maine and the Touraine, all in north-west France. There are six genuine acts of the late tenth or early eleventh century, and 62 from the eleventh century.[34] The bulk of the material from no. **71** onward relates to the twelfth century; of 46 charters from the twelfth century, 29 belong to the period of Bernard's abbacy, i.e. 1131–1149. The bulk of the material antedates Bernard's death on 8 May 1149, though in no. **78** he is mentioned as already dead; none of it dates before the death of Abbot Geoffrey – who is never mentioned – on 29 or 30 December 1150. Few of the Bernard charters are precisely dated, but most can be roughly divided into two groups according to whether the attesting prior was Peter or his successor Hugh, who first occurs in a charter dated 1142.[35]

This overview of the contents of the Cartulary establishes beyond doubt the date of its composition as 1149–50, during the brief abbacy of Geoffrey. The charters themselves cover the period from *c.* 982 to late 1149. Inevitably, they will be valuable witnesses to the abbey's history in that period. The burning issue of the period of composition was the monks's right freely to elect their own abbot. The same period was also significant in terms of the ongoing struggle between the heirs of Henry I, notably the consolidation of the Angevin hold on Normandy. Examination of the Cartulary contents should allow us to understand how the monks responded to the momentous events of this period and even earlier periods.

33 See S. Keynes, 'The Aethelings in Normandy', *ANS* xiii, 1991, 190–94, who shows that the charter is genuine, and explains its context.

34 On abbey property see Dom Jacques Dubois, cited above note 11, and André Dupont, *Essai d'un catalogue critique des églises et chapelles dont le patronage appartenant à l'abbaye du Mont Saint-Michel*, Saint-Lô 1979.

35 We can be confident that the two priors did not serve at the same time. The Cerimonial of the abbey gives the order of seniority among the monks as abbot, prior, subprior, *presbiter misse*, cantor and subcantor; MS Avranches 214, part ii, pp. 202. Cf. the charters printed in Delisle, *Torigni*, ii, pp. 305, 322, 327, 328, 331, 333, where the distinction between prior and subprior is clear.

b. The Historical Context

In providing the cartulary of Mont-Saint-Michel with a prefatory foundation history, the cartularist was doing nothing unusual: what is unusual is the degree to which he thereby became the architect of all subsequent historiography of his community. His *Historia*, which occupies folia 5 to 16, is the earliest version of a work that continued to be copied and embellished in abbey manuscripts, and was exploited by abbey historians from the seventeenth-century Maurists until the present day. The *Historia* is a composite work broadly consisting of two works, the *Revelatio* and the so-called *Introductio monachorum*. The various parts of this 'official history' are well-known, though they have been poorly understood as texts. Fortunately, however, work by Professor Pierre Bouet on new editions has led to more accurate dating of the texts and opened the way to new interpretations.[36] The first and earliest text in the *Historia* is the *Revelatio*, dated by Bouet to *c.* 820, soon after the Council of Aix (816/7) sought to impose the Rule of St Benedict as a monastic norm throughout the empire of Louis the Pious. In part a hagiography describing the foundation around 708–715 of a sanctuary of St Michael Archangel by Bishop Aubert who established prebends for twelve canons to serve it, the *Revelatio* is also a serious attempt at a history of the sanctuary written by one of the canons. The *Revelatio* was subsequently adopted by the Benedictine monks of the later abbey, who (with minor modifications) continued to use it as an eight-lesson lectionary for the feast of the Dedication of St Michael's Basilica on 16 October. The earliest extant copy of *Revelatio* is the copy now bound in MS Avranches 211, which forms the basis for the new edition. The scribe has been identified as the monk Heriward, who was active *c.* 995 to 1015.[37] The Cartulary version is one of many later versions which differ only slightly from the earliest one.[38] The most significant difference is the addition of a short phrase indicating that the archangel's impatient poking of the slumbent bishop actually perforated his skull: 'Interea tercia admonitione uenerandus episcopus pulsatur austerius [apparente in eiusdem presulis capite usque in hodiernum diem in testimonio foramine] ut, qui non adquieuerat bis admonitus';[39] The additional phrase is found in the Cartulary version, and

36 The *Revelatio* is being re-edited from some thirty surviving manuscripts by Pierre Bouet and Olivier Desbordes. See Pierre Bouet, 'La *Reuelatio* et les origines du culte à Saint Michel sur le Mont Tombe', in Bouet et al., ed., *Culte et pèlerinages à saint Michel en Occident. Les trois Monts dédiés à l'archange* (Rome, 2003). I am very grateful to Professor Bouet for an advance copy of this paper.

37 J. J. G. Alexander, 'A Romanesque copy from Mont Saint-Michel of an initial in the Corbie psalter', *Mill. mon.* ii, p. 241 note 10.

38 Detailed in Hourlier, 'Les sources écrites', p. 125, note 9.

39 The same story, with similar phrasing is recapitulated in the *Prouincia Lugdunensis secunda* paragraph with which the *Introductio* compiler of *c.* 1086 opened his work.

echoed in the introduction to the second of the *Historia* texts, the *Introductio*, written around 1086. It is a clear reference to the relic of St Aubert's trepanned skull, which can still be seen today in the treasury of the church of St Gervais at Avranches. The modification to the text was therefore made after the rediscovery of Aubert's skull, in the time of Hildebert I.[40] The need to explain the skull's appearance indicates that this particular relic at least had been missing for a considerable time before its rediscovery.[41]

The next literary production known to survive from the abbey is a compilation of related pieces written at different dates in the eleventh century and welded together as a whole some time around 1086.[42] An abridged version of this work was appended to the *Revelatio* by the cartularist of 1149 to form the *Historia*. Known from a nineteenth-century publication as *Introductio monachorum*, the title describes accurately only that part of the compilation used by the cartularist.[43] According to this work, in the mid-tenth century the canons at the Mont were examined for laxity and found wanting. As a result, Richard I of Normandy, with the advice of Archbishop Hugh of Rouen and the blessing of Pope John XIII and King Lothar, decided to replace the canons with Benedictine monks, offering the canons the choice of becoming monks or being expelled. The author inserts a section describing, with some virulence, how disaffected canons hid St Aubert's relics, which were rediscovered in the time of Abbot Mainard II. In so doing he contradicts the more authentic version of the *Miracula*, in which this incident occurs later, in the time of Hildebert I.[44] The story is embellished with texts ascribed to John XIII and King Lothar. The author of this account was the compiler of the whole collection of texts published by Beaurepaire as *Introductio monachorum*. He was not, however, the forger of the bull or the diploma, nor the author of the powerful, yet strangely lyrical, passage beginning *Perpendant igitur* (which the cartularist misplaced – it should follow the Lothar text), nor

40 See Lelegard, 'St Aubert', *Mill. mon.* i, pp. 47–9.

41 It may have been the discovery of the skull (during building works?) that prompted the struggle for the control of all Aubert's relics between the canons and the monks. Although St Aubert is only evidenced in *Revelatio*, there is no reason to doubt his historical authenticity. There has long been doubt over whether the trepanned skull still at Avranches could be that of an eighth-century bishop since the skill to have performed trepanning seems to have been lost long before. There is no doubt, however, that the skull is the one discovered by the monks *c.* 1010/1014 and believed by them to be that of St Aubert.

42 I am deeply grateful to Professor Bouet for his advice on the dating of the *Introductio* texts. It must be emphasised that my account of them is based upon my own extensive investigations of the historical context of the Cartulary documents, which lead me to reject a small part of Professor Bouet's dating, as will appear below.

43 Edited by E. de Beaurepaire, *Les curieuses recherches du Mont Saint-Saint par Dom Thomas Le Roy* (Caen, 1878), i, 407–19.

44 Cf. M. Lelegard, 'Saint Aubert', in *Mill. mon.*, i, 29–52,

was he the original author of the *Miracula* (omitted in the Cartulary version), a text or collection of texts from the early eleventh century which he rewrote.

The preamble to the author's tale is his account of Norman history from Rollo to Richard I, an account firmly based upon Dudo of Saint-Quentin's *De moribus*, as was all Norman historiography from the early eleventh century onward.[45] This in itself an indication that we should hesitate to accept the *Introductio* author's story. Dudo's work is the earliest source to mention any involvement of a Norman ruler at Mont-Saint-Michel and it alleges merely that Richard I (d. 996) rebuilt the church and enforced strict monasticism there.[46] Nowhere does Dudo mention canons at the Mont. The *Introductio* author was typical of many writers of his time in eleventh-century Normandy and elsewhere. By the late eleventh century, when he compiled *Introductio*, it was an article of faith among Benedictine monks that the new vigour that their vocation had enjoyed throughout the century stemmed from the sweeping away of corrupt canons during the tenth century. This was a grave distortion of the reality of the tenth-century reforms, in which corrupt canons figured very little in general; in Normandy neither of the two communities which saw canons replaced by monks – Saint-Ouen de Rouen, *c.* 950/50 and Fécamp, 1001 – could fairly be described as corrupt, though in both cases texts condemning their tenth-century predecessors were written in the eleventh century.[47] As Jacques Hourlier pointed out, the late-tenth-century scribe of the version of *Revelatio* found in ms Avranches 211, the history of St Aubert's canons, made no attempt to insinuate criticism of the canons into his copy, nor any allusion to the arrival of Benedictines.[48] For Hourlier, who accepted the *Introductio* tradition, this might imply a date before 966 for the manuscript, but Alexander's work on the scribe Heriward is conclusive as to its date. Heriward's copy of what was a liturgical text in use at the abbey is evidence of the harmonious co-existence of the monks and canons throughout the tenth century.

Nothing in Dudo's text or the later *Introductio* is historically accurate, though, somewhat ironically, Dudo's brief description of what happened exactly fits the rôle of Richard II of Normandy (996–1027), who exercised genuine influence at the Mont from 1009 onward. Richard II appointed Abbot Hildebert I as the ageing Mainard II's successor in 1009 (no. **52**), he

45 Mathieu Arnoux, 'Les premières chroniques de Fécamp: de l'hagiographie à l'histoire', in *Les Saints dans la Normandie médiévale (Colloque de Cerisy, 26–29 septembre 1996, Caen, 2000)*, ed. Pierre Bouet and François Neveux, pp. 74–6; id., 'Before the *Gesta Normannorum* and beyond Dudo: some evidence on early Norman historiography', *Anglo-Norman Studies* 22 (2000), 29–48.

46 Dudo de Saint-Quentin, *De moribus et actis primorum Normanniae ducum*, publié par Jules Lair, Caen, 1865, p. 164.

47 See Mathieu Arnoux, 'Les premières chroniques', p. 71–82.

48 Jacques Hourlier, 'Les sources écrites de l'histoire montoise anterieure à 966', *Mill. mon.*, ii, p. 125.

helped finance a rebuilding of the abbey, and both he and his mother were benefactors of it (nos. **2**, **3**, **4**). It was he who, in 1023, appointed Abbot Thierry (of Jumièges) to bring the reforms being pioneered by Abbot William of Fécamp to the Mont. Despite the rapidity with which the Dudo story spread throughout Normandy and beyond, none of the charters of the Norman rulers or their kinsmen (including Gunnor, relict of Richard I) from Richard II onward ever gave any hint of the rôle he assigned to Richard I. The rapidly changing circumstances in which the monks found themselves after 1009, when the Norman rulers established a clear and in many ways unwelcome presence in their affairs, led to a version of the story becoming accepted at the Mont itself. The first sign was the interpolation of Richard II's charter (no. **2**), between 1028 and 1058; the *Introductio* of *c.* 1086 was the elaborated final version of a myth-making process that can be traced in other ways.

Taken as a whole, as the Cartularist intended, the *Historia* of St Michael's sanctuary tells of its foundation by the bishop of Avranches in 708, served by twelve canons, and its subsequent refoundation by the count of Normandy as an abbey served by Benedictine monks in 965. This gives the impression of a single community whose history fell into two distinct parts; the age of the canons, from 708 to 965, and the age of the Benedictines, beginning in 965. In fact, the early eleventh-century *Miracula* is only the earliest of several texts that show that twelve canons served the sanctuary from 708 until the later twelfth century, when Robert de Torigny successfully petitioned the pope that their number be reduced to three.[49] Other texts, including the abbey necrologies, show that a Benedictine community had existed at the Mont since at least 868, when Abbot Conwoion of Redon died.[50] In other words, there were two distinct communities at Mont-Saint-Michel; one a college of canons established by the bishop of Avranches in 708, the other a monastery of Benedictine monks established between *c.* 820 and 860 by a founder or founders whose identity had been forgotten within two or three generations. By 965 the canons and monks had co-existed in the service of St Michael at Mont-Saint-Michel for over a century.

For most of that time there had been no active bishop in Avranches, a fact of some significance because it made the abbey the premier ecclesiastical institution of the diocese, free from the episcopal jurisdiction that was normal. The restoration of the Norman bishoprics in 989 therefore had the potential to trouble the relationship between monks and canons. The problem emerged, apparently for the first time, in the early eleventh century, when the canons and monks quarrelled briefly but acrimoniously over the

49 Delisle, *Torigni*, ii, no. XLII, pp. 312–113.

50 Remembered on 5 January in the abbey Necrology, MS Avranches 214, part II, p. 109.

relics of St Aubert, which were eventually translated to the abbey church. The canons wanted to retain control of the relics of their founder, but the monks now formed the more important community and were equally determined to control the saintly relics essential to monastic prestige. (Even so, St Aubert had still not been adopted as their founder and nor had a liturgy yet been developed for his only feast, the Translation of 16 June, at the time the first abbey sacramentary, now New York, Pierpont Morgan ms 614, was written, *c.* 1060.)[51] This obscure but important incident, mentioned in the *Miracula*,[52] occurred in the time of Abbot Hildebert I (1009–17), during the episcopate of Norgod (989–1022), the first restored bishop of Avranches. Tensions between abbot and bishop rapidly escalated in this period, as evidenced by the surviving text of an accommodation between Abbot Ranulf (c. 1058 – *c.* 1083/5) and Bishop John of Avranches, dated 1061 (**Appendix ii.5**), which both confirms the uninterrupted place of St Aubert's canons as guardians of his relics in service to St Michael at the Mont, and also exposes as fraudulent a claim to exemption from episcopal jurisdiction, interpolated into an otherwise authentic charter of Richard II (no. **2**) sometime between 1028 and *c.* 1058.[53] The charter, which can be dated from witnesses to *c.* 1022, has been thought to have been one of a group given at Fécamp in 1025, shortly before Richard's abdication, but in fact it is more closely associated with nos. **4** and **31**, both of which belong to *c.* 1015, and no. **3**, which was given around 1022.[54] Lemarignier assigned the interpolation of this charter to the same period as the fabrication of a bull of Pope John XIII, to which the interpolation refers. Lemarignier's suggestions require radical revision.

The text of the forged bull was inserted into an equally (though less obviously) spurious diploma of King Lothar in the *Introductio* compilation. Two mid-eleventh copies of the conflated text survived until 1944 and were used in the *Recueil des actes de Lothaire et de Louis V* by Halphen and Lot.[55] They accepted the diploma as broadly authentic[56] and were the first to suggest that the forging of the bull belonged to the period *c.* 1058 when, they hypothesized, the monks were trying to coerce William II into permitting

[51] Henri Tardif, 'La Liturgie de la messe au Mont Saint-Michel aux XIe, XII et XIII siècles', *Mill. mon.* i, 353–377 esp. p. 368.

[52] Beaurepaire, pp. 435–442.

[53] J. F. Lemarignier, *Etude sur les privilèges d'exemption et de juridiction ecclésiastique des abbayes normandes depuis les origines jusqu'en 1140*, Paris 1937, pp. 156–160.

[54] *Ibid.*, pp. 264–66.

[55] *Recueil des actes de Lothaire et de Louis V, rois de France (954–987)*, ed. Louis Halphen and Ferdinand Lot, Paris 1908, no. 24. There is no evidence of the two acts existing independently. The text of the annals and of *Introductio* both indicate that their authors only knew the conflated version in which the texts were written onto the same parchment.

[56] The diplomatic is apparently sound. I shall suggest elsewhere authentic models on which the monks might have based this diploma.

them to elect their own abbot, after a string of abusive appointments by the Norman rulers. The principal plank in this hypothesis is the extraordinary *Perpendant igitur* passage which contains a lament for the recently dead Abbot Ralph whose successor had yet to be appointed. The text offers a devastating gloss on the principal provision of the bull concerning the monks's right to elect their abbot by asserting that St Michael has not permitted the bodies of any of the intruded abbots to rest at the Mont (i.e. Thierry, who died at Jumièges, Suppo, who had returned to Fruttaria, and even the lamented Ralph, who died whilst returning from a pilgrimage). However, the interpolation of a false exemption from episcopal jurisdiction into a charter of Richard II concerned a quite-separate issue. Here, the bull was falsely credited with conferring exemption from episcopal jurisdiction. No mention was made of the Lothar diploma, which was merely designed as the vehicle by which to present the forged bull. In fact, as we shall see, the forgeries were produced about twenty years earlier than the date suggested by Lemarignier and were unrelated to the interpolation of Richard's charter.

Both forgeries satisfied the monks, but modern historians should take heed of significant anomalies not just in the self-evidently forged bull, but also in the alleged diploma. The monks were unaware that no papal bulls were issued for monasteries in Normandy during the tenth century,[57] or that a request for a royal diploma confirming the restoration or reformation of a monastery should have come from the *senior* of the region, in this case the *dux Francorum*. Hugh Capet.[58] The diploma did not even name Hugh, who himself became king in 987 and whose descendants graced the throne of France at the time it was forged.[59] The forger assigned the whole confection a date in early February 966 when John XIII was a prisoner in Rome and when Richard of Normandy was still at war with Theobald of Chartres, who had the support of King Lothar.[60] Examination of royal diplomata of this period

57 See Tabuteau, *Transfers of Property in Eleventh-Century Norman Law* (1988), pp. 193–4.

58 A point made to me by Hubert Guillotel, who was the first to condemn the Lothar diploma as a forgery; see H. Guillotel, 'Les temps des rois VIIIe – Xe siècle', in A. Chédeville and H. Guillotel, *La Bretagne des saints et des rois Ve – Xe siècle*, Ouest-France 1984, 336–7.

59 The only authentic charter of a Norman ruler dating before Hugh Capet became king in 987 is Fauroux, 3, in which Richard I restored Berneval to Saint-Denis, *cum assensu senioris mei Hugonis Francorum principis*. The act is dated in the fourteenth year of King Lothar and attested by the same seigneur, *Hugo Francorum ducis*. See K. F. Werner, 'Quelques observations au sujet des débuts du "duché" de Normandie', in *Droit privé et institutions régionales. Etudes historiques offertes à Jean Yver*, note 4, pp. 692–3.

60 Determined from the dating clause of the copies used by Halphen and Lot; the abbey annals and the Cartulary assigned the combined diploma and bull to 965. Although in the *Recueil* Lot rejected the redating he had earlier suggested for the Lothar diploma, his argument for the date of the peace of Gisors in mid 966

further shows that a confirmation of this type would always have named the monastery's abbot in the body of the act. Moreover, almost all tenth-century papal bulls relating to monasteries were solicited by abbots, who were always named even in the handful of exceptions. In this case there is no mention whatever of Mainard I in the diploma, and he occurs merely in the dating clause of the forged bull. Another feature of tenth-century acts for restored or reformed monasteries missing here is a confirmation, general or specific, of the monastery's landed endowment. We must not be misled by the otherwise authentic diplomatic. The Lothar diploma contains significant anachronisms, demonstrating the remoteness from a purported mid-tenth century context that can only be attributed to a forger. The diploma was never cited in any subsequent authentic document. For the cartularist, it provided an otherwise lacking royal act, but its true, and indeed, sole relevance to the overriding purpose of the cartularist, as to its eleventh-century creator's, was as the vehicle which carried the forged bull confirming the monk's right to elect their abbot.

The earliest extant Mont source to mention Richard I of Normandy is a set of annals written soon after 1035 which state Richard II's co-operation in the rebuilding of the abbey with Abbot Hildebert II (1017–23).[61] The only mention of Richard I simply noted his death in 996. The fullest entry in the sparse and brief text of the annals (**Appendix i.1a**), under 965, concerns the bull of John XIII and the diploma of Lothar that confirmed the right of the monks to elect their abbot. The failure to mention Richard I and his alleged reform here is damning: the first three entries in the annals are indubitably taken from Dudo's work.[62] The last two entries concern the appointment of Abbot Suppo in 1033 and the death of Robert I of Normandy in 1035. The annals clearly antedate the withdrawal of Suppo in 1048. Their failure to mention the assassination in 1040 of Count Alan of Brittany, a major benefactor of the abbey in the time of Abbot Almod (1027–32) (nos. **17**, **23**), probably means that the annals were indeed written shortly after the entry for

remains convincing; Lot, *Les derniers carolingiens*, App. VIII.

61 The annals stop in 1035 and were copied in the mid-eleventh century into BL Royal A XXIII. Cf. a slightly later version printed in Delisle, *Torigny*, ii, pp. 235–6. Despite the text of the annals, it seems clear that Richard II's patronage of building work is most likely to have been in the time of Hildebert I (1009–17). Hildebert was Richard's choice to succeed Mainard II when he was dismissed in 1009, and the earliest authentic charters of the Norman ducal family belong to the period of his abbacy. The *Miracula* stories of the rediscovery of the lost relics of St Aubert strongly suggest major building works in his time, doubtless a consequence both of the catastrophic fire that had occurred under Mainard II and Hildebert's own programme of recovering and enhancing the abbey's patrimony.

62 Dudo's *De moribus* contains only four dates, all of them in the annals 872, 912, 943, and 996, the death of Richard I. The text was certainly well-known to the monks. Berlin Deutsche Staatsbibliothek, MS 1854, one of the most important surviving manuscripts of Dudo's work was copied at Mont-Saint-Michel *c.* 1060.

1035. That means that the forged bull and diploma existed by that time. These two forgeries are later than the original, uninterpolated version of Richard II'S charter (no. **2**), which dates to *c.* 1022–25.[63] The most obvious reason for their existence concerns the monks's election of one of their number, Almod, in succession to Abbot Thierry in 1027. The forgeries were aimed not at William II, but at his father, Robert I (who in fact removed Almod and replaced him in 1033 with Suppo). The interpolation of Richard II's charter (no. **2**), on the other hand, was concerned with episcopal jurisdiction; the target of the interpolation was the bishop of Avranches, rather than the Norman ruler. This question arises in the Cartulary solely through the interpolated act, which was the only version of it available to the cartularist of 1149.

We can confidently conclude, therefore, that the forgery of bull and diploma was occasioned by the election of Abbot Almod in 1027, and that the interpolation of a false claim to episcopal exemption occurred some time later, shortly before the accommodation between Abbot Ranulf and Bishop John of 1061 acknowledged the true situation.

The elaboration of the reformation myth subsequently enshrined in the *Introductio* began around 1027, with the forging of bull and diploma. At the date of the Annals, 1035, it was still clearly acknowleged that genuine Norman influence at the Mont began with Richard II. By 1086, when the *Introductio* compiler was working, the reformation myth had at least started to take root. It was an unquestioned certainty by the time the cartularist worked, in 1149–50. The process left one other trace visible in the Cartulary. The oldest surviving charter text to be preserved by the monks (no. **32**) is the grant of vines at Le Mortier in the Touraine by Abbot Maiol of Cluny (d. 994), dating probably to 982 or 983.[64] The charter, which was solicited by Mainard I (d. 991) of the Mont, is stated to have been the first record of the grant. A later confirmation of *c.* 1096/9 by Fulk IV of Anjou (**Appendix i.3**, authentic version of no. **62**) shows that the Mont retained the property and established a small vineyard there.[65] The land granted belonged to the ancient

[63] This is where I diverge from the dating suggested to me by Professor Bouet, who sees the forged bull as a production of *c.* 1058, closely associated with the *Perpendant igitur* passage.

[64] The charter's date in the forty-first year – *anno xli* – of King Lothar (954–86) is clearly erroneous. It should be read as *anno xii*, the twelfth year, which, significantly, yields the date 966. The date has occasioned some difficulty. Cf. Dubois, 'Dépendances', *Mill. mon.* i, 640–1. The use of an 'l' form as a long 'i' occurs elsewhere in the cartulary, normally within personal names such as Haimo (see no. **44**). See K. S. B. Keats-Rohan, 'Une charte de l'abbé Mayeul de Cluny et la Réforme de l'abbaye de Mont-Saint-Michel', in *La Normandie autour de l'an mil, ed. J.-P. Chaline* (Société de l'histoire de Normandie, 2000).

[65] Olivier Guillot, *Le comte d'Anjou et son entourage*, t. 2, <C 26>, p. 307, and C 417, pp. 259–60.

and prestigious monastery of Marmoutier at Tours. Marmoutier is one of the abbeys known to have been reformed by Cluny, although of all the reforms initiated by Maiol it was the least enduring. There is no doubt that the Mont copy in the Cartulary is dated in the twelfth year of King Lothar, i.e. 966, but that date is undoubtedly a falsification. Hugh Capet, a close friend of St Maiol and an active patron of the Cluniac reform movement, certainly acted as lay abbot of Marmoutier in 969.[66] In all other respects, the charter is an authentic product of Cluny under Abbot Maiol. Especially striking is the notarial phrase *Data per manum Randuini sacerdotis*, a standard feature of Cluniac charters which is foreign to Mont charters. Randuin also occurs as scribe of a charter of December 978.[67] It is a natural assumption that Maiol is acting in this charter as abbot of both Cluny and Marmoutier, in which case the charter presumably postdates the Cluniac reform of 982, when twelve monks from Cluny were established there under Abbot Maiol, and predates the death of Lothar on 2 March 986.[68] This charter is important for revealing the identities of some of those monks. The witness-list is predominantly if not entirely composed of Cluniac monks, four of whom are well-evidenced in other charters of Cluny at dates between March 966 and 982 (see below, pp. 232–3).

Solicited by the abbot of an established Benedictine house from a prestigious monastery recently reformed by Maiol of Cluny – arguably the greatest reformer of the day and a personal friend of Hugh Capet, patron of the Cluniac reform movement and, after July 987, king of France – the charter is a set-piece of the tenth-century reform movement. The stipulation that the grant was valid so long as regular Benedictinism was observed at the Mont was conventional in gifts from one monastery to another, so its appearance here is of considerable importance.[69] The fact that this charter was granted by one of the acknowledged giants of the reform movement when at the height of his power and influence is invaluable testimony to the esteem in which Mainard and his monks were held. A world away from the great upheaval portrayed by the *Introductio*, in this charter Mainard and his monks extend support and encouragement to the future saint Maiol and the Cluniacs who have undertaken the restoration of Marmoutier. Unlike anything written at Mont-Saint-Michel or in other Norman monasteries, it provides authentic evidence as to the stature of Mainard I as a spiritual leader. Ironically, Mainard could successfully have petitioned the grant of a bull from a pope, but there is no evidence that he did.

66 Guillot, *Les comtes d'Anjou*, i, note 183, p. 174.

67 *Recueil des chartes de l'abbaye de Cluny*, ed. A. Bernard et A. Bruel, 6 vols., Paris, 1876–93, vol. 2, no. 1455.

68 *Gallia Christiana*, xiv, c. 20.

69 The condition of Benedictine observance is common in intra-monastic gifts such as this, though the phenomenon is still poorly understood, according to Dubois, 'Dépendances et prieurés', *Mill. mon.*, i, p. 640–1.

c. Purpose

When Boinet first discussed the Cartulary in 1909 he remarked that the 'cartulary properly speaking begins on folio 17'.[70] By this he meant that part of the cartulary which records the texts of the abbey's charters. But he failed completely to understand that the prefatory, pseudo-historical, material contained in the *Historia* was essential to the Cartulary because it announces the programme and the purpose of the cartularist. The *Revelatio* emphasises the celestial origins of both the abbey and its patron, Archangel Michael. Neither can submit to a terrestrial authority. These points are subsequently emphasized in the four drawings each of which, as Nortier pointed out, show members of the Norman ducal family in positions firmly subordinate to the Mont's celestial masters. The *Introductio* emphasizes that the community is Benedictine, hence subject to the Rule of St Benedict, which provides in its sixty-fourth chapter that an abbot should be elected by the community he is to rule. With the forgery of the bull of John XIII, St Michael's monks dotted the 'i' on their their determination to defend the Benedictine right of abbatial election, which they had spelled out in the unlikely name of Richard I of Normandy. The Cartulary is concerned with the abbey's archives as evidence of its rights and the organization of its properties, and with its benefactors. But the specific purpose of the abbey community in creating the cartulary was to defend its right to elect its own abbot, a clear reference to the election of Abbot Geoffrey in 1149 and the attendant problems.[71]

The famous drawings in the Cartulary continue to be controversial since art historians are unable to agree on the meaning of all four pictures. Consensus has been reached on three of them. The frontispiece relates the vision of St Aubert, based upon a passage interpolated into *Revelatio* in the early eleventh century (pp. 14–15, above) (fol. 4v). The drawing on fol. 19v illustrates the contention of *Introductio monachorum* that the right of abbatial election was confirmed to the monks in 965/6 by Pope John XIII, King Lothar and Richard I of Normandy. The three-quarter page drawing on fol. 23v is assumed to represent the donation of Gunnor, mother of Richard II. Such a subject is in marked contrast to the two previous drawings, but Gunnor's grant was undoubtedly important as the first genuine grant by the Norman rulers to the abbey and the first of an important series of further grants by the dukes and their vassals. The subject of the fourth picture, on fol. 25v remains obscure. Various interpretations have been suggested, none of them convincing. It was loosely assumed that the picture, which shows a central crowned figure as actor in four distinct episodes arranged on two levels, concerned the donation of Robert I of Normandy, whose charter

70 A. Boinet, 'L'illustration du cartulaire du Mont-Saint-Michel', *Bibliothèque de l'ecole de Chartes* t. lxx, 1909, 335–4, 337.

71 Several names corresponding with the founders and benefactors recorded in the Cartulary are found in the Necrology and Martyrology-Necrology of the abbey, found in MS Avranches, 214.

precedes the drawing. The fact that the central actor is crowned, and is therefore a king, shows that he cannot be Robert. The drawing relates a series of events in some detail, but there is nothing to relate it to a specific text in the Cartulary. A recent interpretation by Ursula Nilgen has suggested that the figure is Edward the Confessor, who granted St Michael's Mount in Cornwall before he mounted the English throne.[72] This is equally unconvincing. The charter is short on detail and was eclipsed in abbey records of St Michael's Mount by the more important donations made by Robert, count of Mortain. A much more convincing candidate is William I of England, son of Robert I and half-brother of Robert of Mortain. There are several acts by William in the cartulary (nos. **6**, **7**, **8**), given both before and after he became king of England. A charter of Robert of Mortain, assented to by King William, his wife and sons (no. **11**), alleges that he carried the banner of St Michael at the battle for England in 1066. William had previously allowed the monks the free choice of one of their own, Ranulf, as abbot. Subsequently Ranulf supported William's new enterprise by supplying him with several senior monks of the abbey as heads of English monasteries.[73]

It was clear to me from very early on that the cartulary cannot have been commissioned by Robert of Torigny. It seemed likely that the commissioning abbot could have been Bernard of Bec, whose tireless work restoring the abbey's fortunes could well have accommodated a project such as the cartulary. Bernard not only restored the abbey's temporal possessions, but also enhanced the terrestrial appeal of its spiritual possessions. It is he who is credited with the mounting in gold and silver of the skull of St Aubert and it was certainly he who instituted the practice of having lay benefactors make their grants *per brachium Sancti Auberti*, a phrase which occurs for the first time in charters of his abbacy.[74] If his successor Geoffrey was his close associate, perhaps the monk Geoffrey L'Eveque, then that could explain why work on the cartulary continued even after Bernard's death, which certainly occurred before the cartulary was finally abandoned. One of several indications of his death is the unmistakable phrase *Bernardus venerabilis memorie abbas*.[75] Dom Jean Huynes, a Maurist monk of the abbey who wrote

72 Ursula Nilgen, 'Le Cartulaire du Mont-Saint-Michel et la miniature anglaise', in *Manuscrits et enluminures dans le monde normand (Xe–XVe siècles)*, ed. P. Bouet and M. Dosdat, Caen 1999, pp. 29–49, esp. pp. 40–41.

73 Four monks from the Mont became abbots in England: the prior Rivallon became abbot of Hyde, the treasurer and scribe Scolland, abbot of St Augustine's, Canterbury, Serlo, a former canon of Avranches, abbot of Gloucester, and William d'Agon, abbot of Cerne. Ms Avranches 213, fol. 178r (printed *PL* 202, col. 1326B).

74 Cf. François Bougard, 'La relique au procès: autour des miracles de Saint-Columban', in *Le règlement des conflits au Moyen Âge. Actes du XXXXIe congrès de la SHMESP (Angers, 2000)*, Paris, 2001, 35–66.

75 No. 78, fol. 85–6; also no. 83, fol. 89v: contigit autem in tempore Bernardi abbatis,

its history in 1640, described Avranches 210 as: 'a book written in the time of Abbot Bernard'.[76] The intellectual circumstances of Bernard's abbatiate, combined with the crisis of 1138, very probably produced the background to the idea of a cartulary. Nonetheless, it is Abbot Geoffrey, an otherwise entirely shadowy figure whom even the monks largely forgot to remember, who most clearly emerges as the cartulary's probable originator.

Geoffrey's election by his monks provoked a clash with ducal authority, which demanded a high fiscal price that the monks were willing to pay. To emphasize this legitimacy of electoral right, Abbot Geoffrey sought and obtained the first genuine papal bull ever granted to the abbey. The circumstances were fortuitous. Bernard was appointed to the abbacy by Henry I (who had removed his three predecessors at the monks' request) but he was probably committed to the defence of Chapter 64 of the Rule. The speed with which his monks, who certainly held him in high regard, elected his successor strongly suggests that he had encouraged them to proceed to a swift Benedictine election after his death. The mid-twelfth century papacy was committed to the support of Benedictine privileges against lay abuse. In Eugenius III the monks found a true champion, albeit one who took grave risks with the abbey's future prosperity in challenging Henry of Normandy. In his bull for Mont-Saint-Michel (**Appendix ii.11**), Eugenius explicitly acknowleges Geoffrey as abbot. Citing from Chapter 64 of the Rule of St Benedict, he orders that when Geoffrey dies his successor: 'should be appointed whom the whole community, or the wisest part of it, chooses in the fear of God'.[77] Geoffrey's reign was brief, lasting only eighteen months. But given the haste of execution – of which one indication is the duplication of two of the acts – and its unfinished state, the Cartulary could easily have

---

and no. 98, fol. 100v, florebat eo tempore in hac ecclesia Bernardus abbas vir sapientissimus et disertissimus et nimie eloquentie.

[76] Huynes, *Histoire générale*, ii, 232. Boinet, note on p. 33, wrote: 'Pertz (Archiv, t. viii, p. 381) pensait que le cartulaire avait été composé entre 1150 et 1154, c'est-à-dire sous l'abbatiat de Bernard le Vénérable (1131–1154), mais cette opinion ne semble pas acceptable'.

[77] *...obeunte vero te nunc ejusdem loci abbate vel tuorum quolibet successorum nullus in predicta ecclesia qualibet surreptionis astutia seu violentia preponatur nisi quem fratres communi consensu vel pars fratrum consilii sanioris secundum dei timorem et beati Benedicti regulam previderint eligendum*; occurs as: *ut hic constitiatur, quem sibi omnis concors congregatiosecundum timorem dei, siue etiam pars quamuis parua congregationis, saniore consilio, elegerit* in a copy of the Rule of St Benedict, cap. 24, in Bib. mun. Avranches 214, part ii, p. 65. The Bull of Eugenius III, dated 15 December 1150, was edited from a vidimus of Jehan d'Anneville, lieutenant général du bailli du Cotentin, dated 28 December 1523, in *Cartulaire du Jersey. Recueil de documents concernant l'histoire de l'ile conservés aux archives de la Manche. Edition Société Jersiaise* (vol. 23), Jersey 1918–20, no. 9, 13–15, and J. Ramackers, *Papsturkunden in Frankreich* 2te Band, *Normandie*, Göttingen 1937, no. 60, 135–7. The abbey's possessions are listed without reference to diocese.

been produced during Geoffrey's abbatiate. It is inconceivable that, had the work been completed, the bull of Eugenius III would not have been included. That it was abandoned before the bull was copied suggests that the reason for the abandonment was Abbot Geoffrey's death a mere fortnight after Eugenius issued the bull, perhaps before a copy of it reached the abbey. Geoffrey's is the forgotten abbatiate of Mont-Saint-Michel. It is not unlikely that the achievements of his brief administration were simply the continuation of a programme already set in motion by his predecessor Abbot Bernard. Even so, the issue of abbatial election burned in Geoffrey's time as never before and it was he who successfully sought the pope's intervention for the first time in the abbey's history. It is surely time now to restore to Abbot Geoffrey the honour of having commissioned one of the most important manuscripts to survive from medieval France.

III. ASSESSING THE CARTULARY IN THE CONTEXT OF OTHER MONTOIS MATERIAL

Further understanding of Avranches 210 as codex and as cartulary can come from examining its text in relation to other archival material produced at Mont-Saint-Michel. I have already emphasised the importance of treating the Cartulary text as a single unique written work, which must not therefore be submitted to any form of editorial correction. Because a cartulary is in fact a unitary compilation, composed of a number of smaller texts deliberately arranged to form the whole, it is important to compare the individual texts with the texts of surviving originals in order better to understand the nature and purpose of the Cartulary. As is well-known, the better part of the abbey's archive was at Saint-Lô on the fateful night in June 1944 when Allied bombing destroyed it. Only a handful of originals survive in scattered collections. To this can be added a handful of facsimiles that were published before 1944, as well as a few copies of the originals made by scholars such as Dom Denys Briant, Lechaudé d'Anisy and, in the twentieth century, Gaston de Beausse and Geneviève Beauchesne.[78] Of the 115 acts in the cartulary, three membranes or fragments thereof survive from eleventh-century Normandy, containing a total of four Norman ducal acts; none of these are genuine originals in our modern sense. Two of them, one an interpolated act of Robert I, are written on the same membrane. One part of a chirograph of 1121–4 survives in the British Library in London, and a Norman charter of 1131–42 survives in the Bibliothèque Nationale in Paris. A single charter, given by a Norman benefactor in 1054, survives as an original at Saint-Lô. To

[78] Dom Briant's work, now B. N. fr. 22325, is discussed below. Lechaudé d'Anisy's copies are now in B. N. lat. 10072, Beausse's in Arch. dépt. de Calvados, F5276, and Beauchesne's in Arch. dépt. de La Manche, 6 J 70. Beauchesne's interests were confined to Breton charters; see Geneviève Beauchesne, *Les possessions en Bretagne aux XIe et XIIe siècles des abbayes bénédictines de Touraine, d'Anjou et de Normandie*, Position des thèses ... de l'Ecole des Chartes, 1935, pp. 5–13.

this meagre total can be added the facsimile publication of an additional 6 items, and the post-medieval copying from the abbey's charters of a further 34 items, making a total of 47 items out of the 115 in the cartulary, of which 4 items were copied from eleventh-century pseudo-originals.[79] Whilst not an impressive total, the range thoughout the chronological and geographical reach of the Cartulary provides a more than adequate means of comparison between the charters themselves and the cartularist's account of them. Examination reveals only minor divergences, arising out of changing orthographical conventions and simple haste on the part of the scribe. The cartularist clearly set out faithfully to record his originals.[80] The programme announced in the initial *Historia*, the abbey's claim to its spiritual privileges, was followed by an authentic record of its archives, arranged, albeit loosely, around individual priories and their founders and benefactors. A constant theme is lay usurpation and the attempts by the abbots to recover such losses. Bernard figures prominently as an abbot who recovered land, but the emphasis of such items is always upon the use of the arm of Saint Aubert in the ceremony of restitution rather than upon the restitution itself.

The Cartulary is not a complete record of the abbey's archives at the time it was undertaken, in 1149–50. It is unlikely ever to have been intended to be a complete record, but at least one omission must have been due to force of circumstance rather than deliberate choice. Since the work begins with a forged papal bull confirming the right of the monks to elect their abbot, the cartularist would certainly have wanted to include the authentic bull of Eugenius III confirming the same privilege in the words of St Benedict himself. Whatever else might be said of the quasi-legendary *Historia* that prefaces the Cartulary, it was at least in part a manifestation of the community's genuine interest in its history, which can be traced throughout the whole period of its existence. The earliest annals of the abbey were written *c.* 1035 (**Appendix i.1a**) One of several later annals is thought to have been written by a monk under Abbot Bernard, though it continues after the abbot's death up to 1154.[81] The *Historia* was also a reflection of the community's enduring commitment to the Benedictine rights of election. A quire in Avranches 211 contains Annals of Mont-Saint-Michel which were written first in the early twelfth century and later continued down to 1292. One of the entries memorably betrays the *idée fixe* of the community: *Eodem anno Rannulfus abbas et monachus huius loci pie memorie [obiit]. Huic successit*

79 For the surviving originals and facsimiles see Alexander, *Illumination*, 41–2.

80 On the copying of texts into cartularies see Alexandre Bruel, 'Note sur la transcription des actes privés dans les cartulaires antérieurement au XIIe siècle', *Bibliothèque de l'Ecole des chartes* 36 (1875), 445–6; Guyotjeannin et al., *Diplomatique médiévale*, pp. 278–85.

81 Hourlier, 'Les sources écrites', *Mill. mon.* i, 267ff, describes the Annals for 506–1154, published in *Torigni*, ii, 230–35, from a fifteenth-century ms, Avranches 213, as: 'élaborées sans doute au Mont sous Bernard du Bec'.

Rogerius Cadomensis non electione monachorum sed vi terrene potestatis (fol. 75v).[82] Within a few years of the death of Abbot Bernard a monk of the Mont, William de Saint-Pair, wrote a three-part verse history in Norman French of the abbey, of which parts one and two were based upon the *Revelatio* and *Introductio*. This verse history, the *Roman du Mont-Saint-Michel*, requires brief consideration for the light it can shed upon the Cartulary itself.[83]

William de Saint-Pair (*de Sancto Paterno*) first occurs in a Mont document of 1155. His last dated attestation was in 1172. In the prologue to his *Roman du Mont-Saint-Michel* he described himself as a young man working under Robert de Torigny, perhaps indicating that the work belonged to a period early in Robert's abbacy when the memory of the events that led to the undertaking and abrupt abandonment of the cartulary were still fresh.[84] The avowed aim of the work, according to the Prologue (vv. 9–17), is to make accessible to a lay audience the salient facts about the monastery. A particularly striking feature of the *Roman* is a lengthy passage occurring in the so-called *Liber secundus* (vv. 2189–2355). Here William discusses at length the abbey's charter of privileges granted by Richard I of Normandy and confirmed by King Lothar and Pope John XIII. Richard is said to have had two further copies made (2204–6). Quotations are made from all three charters, all of which are said to have been 'presented on the altar' (2325–8). William repeatedly stresses that the monks have the absolute right to elect their own abbot. The passage ends (2328–55) with a warning that St Michael has always ensured that any abbot appointed by authorities external to the Abbey (*de main laie*, 2333) has been forced to resign and has been lucky to escape with his life. The fact that William could write this in the time of Robert de Torigny – elected by the monks with the approval of Henry of Normandy – probably indicates that the community as a whole backed the fight for the Benedictine right of election in 1149/50, though the warning about alien abbots might be a jibe at those monks who had broken ranks to support Robert Hardy in 1152. It recalls the *Perpendant igitur* passage in the *Introductio* in which an eleventh-century author rails against alien abbots as

82 Delisle, *Torigni*, ii, p. 222.

83 *Li romanz del Munt Saint-Michiel par Guillaume de Saint-Pair*, ed. Francisque-Michel, Caen 1856 (*Mémoires de la Société des Antiquaires de Normandie*, t. xx), includes an *étude sur l'auteur par* M. Eugène de Beaurepaire; also edited by Paul Redlich, *Le Roman du Mont Saint-Michel*, Marburg 1894, and by Graham Birrell in an unpublished doctoral thesis, Aberdeen 1978. On the text see G. Birrell, Romania 100, 1978, 260–70; R. Herval, 'Un moine jongleur au Mont Saint-Michel: Guillaume de Saint-pair', *Mill. mon.* ii, 383–96. I am greatly indebted to Professor Ian Short in this discussion of William's Roman. References to the text given below are to Redlich's edition.

84 *Guillelme a non de Seint Paier / Cen vei escrit en cest quaier / El tens Robeirt de Torignie*, vv 17–19.

ravening wolves, *lupos rapaces*, whose bodies St Michael had not permitted to rest at Mont-Saint-Michel. William's remarks contained a kernel of truth. Seven of the eleven abbots of the Mont between 1028 and 1152 were ducal appointments. Only one of them, Bernard of Bec, died, still in office, in his bed at the abbey. According to William (2346–7), even the allegedly lamented Abbot Ralph had died on pilgrimage in the Holy Land whilst under suspicion of simony.[85]

The most important of the two surviving manuscripts of the *Roman* was certainly produced at the Mont and was still there in the fifteenth century.[86] A third manuscript, now lost, was also produced at the Mont and seen there in 1739 by Montfaucon.[87] Clearly, as the Prologue claimed, the *Roman* was produced for the benefit of lay persons, specifically those who came to the abbey as pilgrims and for whom the Latin texts of the *Revelatio* and *Introductio* were closed books. William also included material added to the *Miracula* section of the *Introductio* during the twelfth century (all *Miracula* material was omitted in the Cartulary version), and a text by Baldric de Bourgeuil, archbishop of Dol, *De scuto et gladio*.[88] The *Roman* highlights the fact that texts produced in monasteries by monks had very specific and restricted audiences in mind. The pilgrims who heard or read the *Roman* may well have taken its message away with them, but the primary purpose of the work for the monks was to enable them to communicate with their pilgrims and perhaps also with the lay congregations of their priories. Souvenir or guide books continued to be produced at the Mont: one such was written by the sixteenth-century prior Sebastien Ernault whose name was written on folio 4r of Avranches 210, which obviously was one of his sources.[89] The Cartulary, on the other hand, was a production of and for the community of monks. Evidently designed as a beautiful book and beginning with a lectionary for the Feast of the Dedication of St Michael's Basilica on 16

85 Apart from Almodus, Ranulf de Bayeux, Geoffrey and Richard de Musca, all the abbots from 1028 were appointed by the rulers of Normandy. Most had troubled careers. Cf. the eleventh-century abbots Thierry and Suppo, and, from the twelfth century, Roger I (resigned 1106), Roger II (deposed by Henry I in 1123) and Richard de Méré (deposed *c.* 1128). Dom Jean Laporte, 'Les séries abbatiale et priorale du Mont Saint-michel', *Mill. mon.* i, 267–81.

86 BL MS Add. 10289, discussed by Tony Hunt in an article in *Medioevo Romanzo* 13, 1988, 25–37. The other is BL MS Add. 26876. Redlich's edition is based on both manuscripts, Michel's only on Add. 10289, which is lacunary.

87 *Roman*, ed. Redlich, p. viii.

88 Cf. Hourlier, 'Les sources écrites', 122. Texts of the *Miracula* and parts of the *Historia* are found in the first part of Bib. mun. Avranches 211, fol. 1–66.

89 Huynes, *Histoire*, ii, 232. Cf. Dom Laporte, 'L'épée et le Bouclier dits de "Saint-Michel"', *Mill. mon.* ii, 397–410. Nortier, 'La bibliothèque', p. 152–3, says that Sebastian is the only monk interested in books to have left some imprint of himself. In MS Avranches 130 he noted that he had received the habit from Jean de Lamps on Christmas Eve 1518.

October (the *Revelatio*), the ceremonial function of the Cartulary both as artefact and as a collection of texts seems evident. Surely this was an altar-book, designed for use by the monks in their abbey church. As such the cartulary belongs to a group of eleventh- and twelfth-century, as well as later, manuscripts produced for ceremonial use by monastic communities. While each is unique, all draw from a common pool of characteristics relating to their histories, their saints or founders, their royal and papal privileges. In essence their function is memorialization. They may also contain overtly liturgical texts such as the Gospels. A particularly fine parallel is afforded by the Sherborne Cartulary, a late twelfth-century English manuscript which contains the four Gospels each adorned with a beautiful illuminated portrait of its Evangelist. The earliest quires contain historical texts relating to the abbey and its English past, written in Anglo-Saxon. In addition to royal and papal confirmations, it also contains a copy of the abbey's entries in Domesday Book.[90] In terms of both was was accomplished and what was intended in the matter of illustration, the Cartulary eclipses both known French examples of illustrated cartularies of about this period, the cartularies of Vierzon and Marchiennes.[91] In its historiographical self-awareness and

90 BL MS Add. 46487, discussed by Francis Wormald, 'The Sherborne "Cartulary"', in *Fritz Saxl Memorial Essays*, ed. D. J. Gordon, London 1955. One may mention also the celebrated mid-twelfth century *Liber Landavensis*, Aberystwyth, NLW., Gwysaney I, discussed by John Davies in *Anglo-Norman Studies* XXI (1999), and by E. D. Jones, 'The book of Llandaf', *National Library of Wales Journal* iv (1945–6), 123–57, and D. Haws, ib. (1987), the superb thirteenth-century Chertsey Cartulary, BL MS Cotton Vit. A 13, and a thirteenth-century illustrated history of Crowland Abbey, BL MS Harley Y 6. BL MS Cotton Nero D vii is a late-fourteenth century *Catalogus Benefactorum* for St Albans, with painted portraits of the benefactors. There are important observations by P. Stirnemann, 'L'illustration du cartulaire de Saint-Martin-du-Canigou', in *Les cartulaires. Actes de la table ronde* (Paris, décembre 1991), ed. O. Guyotjeannin, L. Morelle et M. Parisse, Paris, Ecole des Chartes, 1993. I know of no comparable example of the same period to have survived from Normandy. In terms of the quality of materials and execution, possible French parallels from the first half of the twelfth century are furnished by the *Livre Noir* of Saint-Florent de Saumur and the Cartulary of Saint-Quentin de Beauvais (BN MSS. lat. nov. acq. 1930 and 1921), neither of which is illustrated. I owe to Graham Loud the following references to two striking examples from Italy. The Chartulary of St Sophia, Benevento, Cod. Vat. Lat. 4939, also known as the *Chronicon Sanctæ Sophiæ*, written in 1119, has been discussed by J.-M. Martin, 'Quelques réflexions en vue de l'édition du Chronicon Sanctae Sophiae', Bulletino dell'istituto storico italiano per il medio evo xvix, 1993, 301–17; cf. G. Loud, 'A Lombard abbey in a Norman world: St Sophia, Benevento, 1050–1200', ANS xix, 1997, 273–306; the *Chronicon Vulturnense*, a 'cartulaire-chronique' completed *c.* 1120, has been edited by V. Federici (3 vols, *Fonti per la storia d'Italia*, 1924–38), and discussed by H. Hoffmann in *Deutsches Archiv für Erforschung des Mittelalters* xix, 1966.

91 *Le Cartulaire de Vierzon*, ed. G. Devailly, Paris 1965; A. de Loisne, 'Les miniatures

importance it stands comparison with a much larger work, the cartulary of Cluny, which has been described as: 'caractéristique d'une époque (XIe siècle) ou le cartulaire est aussi un produit de "scriptorium" et une pièce maítresse de l'historiographie monastique'.[92]

If Avranches 210 is now the only surviving cartulary of the abbey, it was not the only one that was produced. The later cartulary known as *Major cartular[ium] albus* has been lost since the eighteenth century, but it had been seen by several scholars who made copies of part of its contents, including Dom Denys Briant, historian of Brittany whose work survives in MS fr. 22325 of the Bibliothèque Nationale. This manuscript is priceless for its report of the state of the abbey's archives at that time. In a section headed *Cartulaire du Mont Saint-Michel*, Briant begins with a description of the *Livre Blanc* (described simply as *Le cartulaire*) which he dates to the fifteenth century, the latest items in it belonging to the year 1413. 'Before the muniments – *titres originaux* – copied in the cartulary there are several chapters of historical material which can also be read in a compilation of the monastery's history written in the same century, as well as in an older cartulary, perhaps of the thirteenth or fourteenth century. After a long eulogy of the early Norman rulers, there follow charters of King Lothar, Pope John, Duke Richard ... ' etc.[93] He goes on to say that the early ducal items were followed by a bull of Alexander III of January 1179, which appears to have been the most detailed and comprehensive confirmation of its possessions that the abbey ever received from a pope.[94]

---

du cartulaire de Marchiennes', *Bulletin archéologique du Comité des Travaux historiques et scientifiques*, 1903, pp. 476–489, pl. XXXVIII–XLII.

92 Guyotjeannin, *Diplomatique médiévale*, p. 279. See Dominique Iogna-Prat, 'La confection des cartulaires et l'historiographie de Cluny', in *Les Cartulaires*, ed. Guyotjeannin *et al.*

93 BN fr. 22325, p. 695: 'Extrait de cartulaire du Mont Saint-Michel. Le cartulaire est ecrit dans le 15e siecle. Il y a des actes de 1413. Avant les titres originaux qui y sont copies, il y a quelques chapitres d'histoire qui se lisent encore dans une compilation d'histoire du monastère ecrite dans le meme siècle. Et meme dans un autre plus ancien cartulaire comme du 13e ou 14e siecle. Apres un grand eloge de La Normandie et les Normans [*in the margin: 'ibi de Angelus, Campania ... Calabris a Normannis possessis* (marque que l'auteur n'est past fort ancien)'] il rapporte que St Aubert ev. d'Avranches au temps du Roy Childebert (etc.) [there follows extensive citations from the *Introductio*, with a comment on the origin of some of it in Dudo de Saint-Quentin] ... (p. 696): 'suivent les chartes du Roy Lothaire, du Pape Jean et du Duc Richard pour Saint-Paterne et pour Versun, puis du Duc Robert.'. He then cites a charter of Richard's wife Gunnor and follows this with extracts from bulls of popes Alexander III and Adrian IV.

94 The bull of Alexander III survives as a damaged original in BN lat. 9215, no. 60 (Mont Saint-Michel no. 4). Edited from a *vidimus* of Jehan d'Anneville, 28 December 1523, in *Cartulaire de Jersey*, no. 11, p. 19–22. There is also an excellent edition in Delisle, *Torigni*, ii, 313–21.

There are several points of interest in this account. First it is clear that the now lost cartulary commissioned by Abbot Pierre Le Roy – the *Livre Blanc* – had essentially the same format as the abbey's earliest cartulary, Avranches 210. Both began with the so-called official history, the *Revelatio, Introductio monachorum* and related texts. Where in Avranches 210 the forged and interpolated papal, royal and ducal confirmations relating to the tenth-century stand in the place of authentic material, Le Roy's cartulary was able to follow copies of these confections with genuine papal, royal and ducal confirmations. The founders and benefactors material found in Avranches 210 was also in the *Livre Blanc.* Although the purpose of the *Livre Blanc*, according to remarks in a fifteenth-century *Gesta* of the abbot later elaborated by Dom Huynes, was to preserve a complete copy of the charter archive as it then stood, its model was undoubtedly Avranches 210, with its rather different purpose.[95]

An earlier cartulary, 'perhaps of the thirteenth or fourteenth century' had also been mentioned. Briant goes on to describe this older cartulary, in a passage headed *Ex antiquiori cartulario*, noting that before the cartulary proper several acts occur. From the extracts he then gives of these acts it is clear beyond all doubt that he is describing acts of the fourteenth and the thirteenth century copied on folia 2 and 3 respectively of Avranches 210. This is reconfirmed by the subsequent description of the *Revelatio*, and of the note on fol. 113r referring to *anno quo Robertus abbas vocatus est.*[96]

A third item was mentioned besides the two cartularies, namely a fifteenth-century compilation of historical material relating to the abbey. This manuscript can also be identified and is extant as MS Avranches 211. Avranches 211 is a manuscript almost as remarkable and as fascinating as Avranches 210, but the two are quite different. It has been described in detail by Léopold Delisle in his appendix to Torigny's chronicle.[97] Known as *Chronicon majus Sancti Michaelis de Monte*, it is a compilation of six separate

95 Huynes, i, 192: '... le grand desordre que estoit dans le chastrier, il se resolut luy mesme de feuilleter tous les papiers et de les mettre d'ordre... Et afin que tous les originaux depuis la fondation de ce monastere jusques à son temps demeurassent toujours sains et entiers il les fit tous transcrire dans un gros livre de parchemin qu'on nomme *livre blanc*'. He notes *ibid.* that: 'les bulles et lestres sont en ce monastere et au cartulaire B [i.e. the *Livre Blanc*], fol. 15, 17 (*bis*), 132, 317, 20, 30'.

96 *Ib.*, p. 697: '*Ex antiquiori cartulario.* Avant le cartulaire meme y est ecrit ce qui suit: *Anno domini 1372. In festo translationis B. Nicolai venerunt Anglici apud Tumbam Helene causa inibi morandi... Cooperunt itaque Dani superficiem terre sicut locuste*' [= first lines of fol. 1 verso – quoted in note 16 above – and 3 verso of Avranches 210, where capital 'c' of cooperunt is missing]; then, p. 699: '*Anno domini 1251 mense Maii die Martis* [= fol. 3 recto of Avranches 210]... (*ib.*): commencement dudit cartulaire. Incipit revelatio ecc. S. Michaelis in monte...'; (p. 703): 'ad finem supradicti cartularii AD 1155 ... anno quo Robertus abbas vocatus est' [= Avranches 210, fol. 112v].

97 *Torigni*, ii, 209–214.

parts bound together in the seventeenth century. The third part, folia 78–83, is a *Gesta* of Abbot Pierre Le Roy, who assembled the material for histories of the Mont found in MSS Avranches 212, 213, 214 and the first part of 211.[98] The sixth part of Avranches 211 is the earliest surviving copy of the ninth-century *Revelatio*, which is here arranged as a lectionary of seven lessons for the feast of the dedication of St Michael's basilica on 16 October. The script is in a late-tenth-century hand that carefully imitates a much earlier exemplar. All subsequent versions of the *Revelatio* derive from this copy, including Avranches 210, which contains a modification of the text made after the discovery of the skull of St Aubert, around 1010/14 (see above, in section II.b).[99]

The fourth part of Avranches 211 is a two-part compilation dating respectively to 1308 and 1326. The first part, on folia 84 to 113, is a register of mainly thirteenth and fourteenth century acts relating to the abbey. The second part, from folio 113 verso to folio 155, contains an inventory of the abbey's archives. Although there are some misplacements, the arrangement of the inventory is very methodical, suggesting that Pierre Le Roy's task in restructuring the abbey's archives after 1384 was not exactly Herculean. It begins with ducal, royal and papal confirmations, including the 1150 bull of Eugenius III, and then presents each charter according to the priory to which it relates. This material can be compared to the surviving Cartulary, and to the contents of the lost *cartulari[um] albus* or *Livre Blanc* as described by the eighteenth-century scholars who copied extracts from both the lost cartulary and the abbey's charter deeds. Such reports can also be supplemented from the works of the Maurist historians of the early seventeenth century, Jean Huynes and Thomas Le Roy. Comparison shows that the charters copied into the Cartulary were common to all three manuscripts. Avranches 210 emerges very much as a book of founders and benefactors, as well as a thematic enterprise concerned with abbatial elections. The format of Abbot Le Roy's *Livre Blanc* continued the blend of programmatic defence of spiritual privileges, embedded in quasi-historical texts, with the copying of charters of founders, benefactors and others. Interestingly, according to the copies made by Gaston de Beausse and deposited in the archives at Caen in 1929, there were copies of material from the *Livre Blanc* in the *Série* H of the *Archives départementales de la Manche* at Saint-Lô until 1944. One was a 'modern copy' of a charter of 1066 given by Gerbert de Poterel (no. 70) made from *Livre Blanc*, folio 176r (*ex libro albo pagina 176 recto*). Another was a copy of a charter by Niel the priest of Sainte-Columbe (no. 43) which Beausse

98 Published as an appendix to Reulos, 'L'organisation et l'administration', *Mill. mon.* i, 191–209.

99 Dom Hourlier, 'Les sources écrites', 120–128. The scribe has been identified as the monk Heriward, who was active *c.* 995 to 1015: J. J. G. Alexander, 'A Romanesque copy from Mont Saint-Michel of an initial in the Corbie psalter', *Mill. mon.* ii, p. 241 note 10.

made from 'une feuille en parch[emin d'un] cart[ulaire du] xve s.' i.e. a leaf detached from the fifteenth-century cartulary, which measured 21.9cm in height and 14cm in width.[100]

There is fragmentary evidence from the second half of the twelfth century for an attempt to go beyond Avranches 210 – probably its base text – in strengthening the part of the *Introductio* that deals with the right of Benedictines to elect their abbot, i.e. the forged acts of Lothar and John XIII. This is revealed in some very pointed additions, taken from the writings of Gregory the Great, to the *Perpendant igitur* passage that follows the forged bull of John XIII (below, **Appendix i.1b**).[101] Whether there was a larger purpose to this work is now unknown. It survives only as part of a quire bound with a Pontifical, itself produced at the Mont, probably at a similar date in the second half of the twelfth century.[102] The binding together was probably done at the Mont before the manuscript went to Saint-Victor in Paris at an unknown date after *c.* 1220, since between *c.* 1200 and 1220 another hand copied onto blank pages in this quire the text of a remarkable agreement made in 1061 between Bishop John of Avranches (d. 1077) and Abbot Ranulf (**Appendix ii.3**).[103]

From all these different types of evidence it is clear that the abbey took great care to preserve and maintain its archives from at least the mid-eleventh century onward. The community of the 'City of Books' was much less successful in preserving intact its collection of manuscript codices, which starting haemorrhaging long before the seventeenth century. What remained of the abbey's manuscript collection was sent at the time of the French Revolution to the library at Avranches. By an irony too appalling to dwell upon, it was to be the manuscript collection that would survive until our time and not the carefully cherished charter collection. The charters were not, however, obliterated completely in 1944 in that most of them had been copied more than once, both by monks into manuscripts of Mont-Saint-Michel and by scholars whose copies are now in archives such as the Bibliothèque Nationale.[104] In fact, one could – and no doubt someone should – publish a weighty *cartulaire factice* for Mont-Saint-Michel. The *chartrier* of the abbey to the early fifteenth century is probably quite fully preserved in extant Mont manuscripts, especially Avranches 210 and 211. The survival also of several copies of the *Historia* and the *Miracula* means that is unlikely that much if any of the contents of the lost *Livre Blanc* is wholly inextant. A sizeable amount of charter and other material survives for later

100 Archives départementales de Calvados, F 5276. The charters are items 70 and 43 in the Cartulary (fos 81, 65). Cf. Fauroux, no. 132.

101 See F. Combaluzier, 'Le Pontifical dit d'Avranches', *Mill. mon.*, i, pp. 396–7.

102 On this manuscript, now Paris, B. N. lat. 14832, see F. Columbaluzier, 'Le Pontifical dit d'Avranches', *Mill. mon.* i, 383–398.

103 Cf. Lemarignier, *Etudes sur les privilèges*, 158–60.

104 Cf. Hourlier, cited note 98 above.

periods in a more scattered fashion within Mont manuscripts and the various copies of post-mediaeval scholars. So long as manuscripts Avranches 210 to 215 survive, the carefully recorded, indeed, cultivated, history of the abbey will survive for exploitation by historians. Avranches 210 and 211 are especially precious; Avranches 210 partly because of what it can tell us about the most controversial period of the abbey's history, the tenth-century. But these manuscripts can only be used once they are understood as artefacts and as texts. Overdue since the fifteenth century, that process has now begun for Avranches 210.

IV. THE CARTULARY TEXT

The cartulary covers a period, from 982 to 1150, of just under two hundred years. Almost half of it relates to a period before 1100. The material relating to the period *c.* 990 to *c.* 1040 is especially important, because it is the sole coherent body of documentation for the border regions of Brittany, Normandy and Maine to survive from that time, and one of the few means we have for controlling the account of Norman history produced by Dudo de Saint-Quentin. The charters for the period 982–1100 yield a sort of *Almanach de Gotha* for north-west France (see further the Notes on Persons below). Nonetheless, not all those who occur in the text are well-known, or even otherwise known, and some of these lesser figures can offer interesting if oblique insights into their time. Walter de Mont-Saint-Jean in Maine, for example, whose grant of vines at Sillé-le-Guillaume (no. **37**) was probably made in Abbot Bernard's time (1131–49), was known as *Diues*, 'the Rich'. He made a pilgrimage to Rome in the company of Martin *feneratorem meum fidelem*. Falling ill at Le Mans on his return, Walter became a monk of the abbey. He was so ill at the time of his gift that Martin had to place the gift on the altar for him. The word *fenerator* has the meaning 'usurer', but probably here indicates a financier with whom Walter the Rich was in business.

The Cartulary falls into three principal sections. The first deals with its foundation history (no. **1**), the second presents the important charters of endowment and benefaction that effectively founded most of its principal priories, and the third presents a series of charters of restitution, representing challenges by their heirs to the grants of the principal early benefactors. The second and third groups overlap, but most of the foundation material occurs in nos. **2** to **65**. The major period in the development of the abbey's patrimony is covered by these charters, some of which reveal attempts at recovering parts of an original endowment lost at the beginning of the tenth century (nos. **2**, **26**, **47**). Important acquisitions were made of the church and castle of Pontorson in 1158 and 1162, Mont-Dol in 1158, and a sizeable estate in Guernsey in 1176. Subsequent grants consolidated rather than extended the monastery's endowment.[105] The considerable importance of this second group

[105] Dubois, 'Dépendances', pp. 648–50.

of charters is implicit rather than explicit in the Cartulary. There are no specific references to individual priories, or to any of the benefactors as founders of a priory, in any of the titles assigned to each text, nor any other formal indications of organization, such as the use of running titles, but there was a deliberate attempt to separate acts relating to different priories by the use of blank lines between items. This system was abandoned on fol. 67r, after the Saint-Berthevin charter (no. **45**), but reappears after no. **69** on fol. 81r.

The over-arching theme concerns the monks's claim to the Benedictine right to elect their abbot. Absent from the third section, its place is taken there by the new cult of St Aubert initiated by Abbot Bernard, who made swearing oaths *per brachium Sancti Auberti* an integral part of the ceremony of restitution of abbey property.[106] A nice symmetry is being observed here. The restitutions were made by the descendants of the principal founders and benefactors of the second section, many of whom swore to respect the restitutions on the relic (arm) of Saint Aubert, whose foundation of the community was related in the first section. The towering contribution of Bernard as restorer of the abbey's fortunes is perhaps the most striking aspect of the second half of the Cartulary. It is in his charters that we notice the emergence of a small group of laymen associated with abbey administration, normally as provosts.

There is a clear emphasis throughout on the role of the abbot in protecting the abbey's endowments. Several of the early foundation grants were made at the behest of abbots Mainard II, Hildebert I and Almodus (nos. **17**, **23**, **26**, **30**, **35**, **47**). William the Conqueror acted at the behest of Abbots Ranulf and Roger (nos. **6**, **67**). Exceptionally, Abbot Suppo is in one charter accused of an illegal alienation (no. **6**). Ranulf de Bayeux and Bernard de Bec were especially important in the maintenance of the abbey's endowments. The role of the abbot may have been accentuated in view of the abbey's vulnerability as an outpost of a marcher region constantly subject to warfare. War is a constant theme of the charters, both in referring to depredations due to war and in the preparations made by the abbey and its military tenants.[107]

Mont-Saint-Michel was the only premier abbey of the dioceses that later formed Normandy, or of Brittany, whose monks were not driven into exile by the Norse raids of the late ninth and early tenth centuries.[108] Nevertheless,

[106] The relic was the saint's right-arm, chased in silver, *dexteram argenteam* (nos. 83, 87). See nos. 75, 78, 83–4, 86–88, 97, 113, 114, 116; Appendix ii.10). The date range suggests that the practice was instituted sometime around 1135. The phrase is found in an accord dated 1155 in the abbacy of Robert of Torigny but referring to a restitution in the time of Abbot Bernard (Delisle, *Torigni*, ii, 261–2).

[107] See especially nos. 21, 24, 26, 45, 54, 83, 90; Appendix ii.9).

[108] Lucien Musset, *Les Invasions* (Paris, 1965), pp. 221, 242; Jean Renaud, *Les Vikings en Normandie* (Rennes, 1989), p. 80 and p. 70, where he notes the absence of colonization by the Vikings in the Avranchin. Hubert Guillotel, 'L'exode du clergé breton devant les invasions scandinaves', *Mémoires de la Société d'histoire et*

those were not easy times and the community lost control of some of its mainland property (eg. no. **26**), and hence must have suffered considerable loss of revenue. Several sources external to the Cartulary, including the necrologies, show that a major period of revival and spiritual renewal began at the abbey under Mainard I, perhaps as early as the 940s, certainly in the 950s.[109] By the 990s there is clear evidence in the products of the monks's scriptorium also of intellectual and artistic renewal. More settled political conditions also led to an economic revival, as shown in the efforts of abbots Mainard I (d. 991), Mainard II (991–1009) and Hildebert I (1009–17) to rebuild the landed wealth of the abbey, both by seeking restitution of previously owned property and churches and in solliciting fresh grants. Several items in the Cartulary reflect this drive. All the earliest restitutions and grants were of land in the Touraine, Brittany and Maine (nos. **22**, **26**, **27**, **28**, **30**, **32**). There were no similar restitutions or grants of property in what was then Normandy until *c.* 1015 (nos. **2**, **3**, **4**, **31**), when charters were granted by Richard II of Normandy, his mother Gunnor and his half-brother Robert, count of Avranches. The charter of Ivo fitz Fulcoin (no. **26**) is especially interesting for its explicit statement that Ivo is restoring property granted by his ancestors but lost to the monks during the Norse invasions, i.e. at some time during the later ninth or early tenth century. The property lay at the confines of the Avranchin and Maine. It was to become the priory of Villarenton or L'Abbayette and as such the focus for many future grants in the same region.

About the same time parts of two churches were sold to Hildebert I by Guy, who held in right of his wife Rainburgis (no. **47** and no. **30**). These churches at *Centrannis* may have been at Saint-Berthevin-la-Tannière, in the same region as Villarenton (the identification is far from certain: see Notes on Persons under nos. **30** and **47**). These were probably two of a number of churches which should have been served by the monks but which had fallen into lay hands and been absorbed into lay patrimonies. The Gregorian reform of the eleventh century inspired many lay families holding churches voluntarily to restore them to monasteries, a process still visible in the twelfth century (nos. **38**, **39** and **41**).[110] The early abbots had considerable success in attracting grants from Conan I of Brittany and his son Geoffrey I, though Alan III, a major benefactor of the 1030s, complained of the abbots's

---

d'archéologie de Bretagne lix, 1982, 301–316.

109 K. S. B. Keats-Rohan, 'Francs, scandinaves ou normands? Aperçus sur les premiers moines des monastères normands', forthcoming in *Les Fondations scandinaves et les débuts du duché de Normandie: Colloque de Cerisy-la-Salle, septembre 2002*, ed. Pierre Bauduin and Claude Lorren.

110 See Hubert Guillotel, 'Combour: proto-histoire d'une seigneurie', in *Family Trees*, ed. Keats-Rohan, pp. 269–298. The problem continued into the time of Robert of Torigny: see A. Dufief, 'Vie monastique au Mont pendant le XIIe siècle', *Mill. mon.* i, pp. 113–116.

negligence in respect of part of his father Geoffrey's grant (no. **23**). Equally spectacular was a series of grants from Hugh III, count of Maine, and a number of his senior vassals. This included the grant of the monastery of Saint-Victeur at Le Mans (no. **25**), which became an important priory of the abbey. Property was also acquired in areas more remote from the abbey, at Créans in the Loire valley (no. **36**, around 1110), Tours (no. **32**, 982), Gohory in the Chartrain (1081, no. **34**) and Rouen (1088, no. **69**). These holdings were important to an abbey that was a major European centre of pilgrimage. From the mid-eleventh century onward, the abbey also began to acquire property in the Channel Islands and, especially after the Norman Conquest of 1066, in England (nos. **7**, **9**, **10**, **11**, **12**, **79**, **88**, **108**).

The monks of Mont-Saint-Michel did not hesitate to interpolate or forge documents in order to protect what was important to them. Such actions were almost routine in medieval monasteries, but the monks of Mont-Saint-Michel were strikingly reticent when it came to their property. They cannot be shown to have deliberately forged a document with the intention of establishing their claim to certain property, although they did interpolate precision about property into authentic confirmation charters (eg. no. **5**), and there is no surviving authentic version of the charter by which Conan I of Brittany made the grant that established the priory of Villamée (**Appendix ii.1**). The location of the abbey made it peculiarly vulnerable to the endless viscisitudes of the relations between Brittany, Normandy, England and France. It suffered greatly during the struggle between the Angevin and Blésois heirs of Henry I after 1135 (nos. **83**, **Appendix i.5**). The latest forgery in the Cartulary is probably no. **62**, an alleged act of Fulk IV of Anjou of 1090 confirming abbey holdings in Anjou and the Touraine and protecting them against any forfeiture incurred in Normandy. Olivier Guillot has shown that this is an interpolated version of a genuine act, absent in the Cartulary but printed here in **Appendix i.3**; he suggests that the interpolation is explicable only as fear of reprisals by a count of Anjou holding power in Normandy, a situation that arose first in 1144. The context for incurring such a forfeiture is completely obscure in the document. It is difficult to advance concern about the effects of the civil war as the context since the abbey had already suffered for its support of the Angevins, enduring the attack by partisans of Stephen of Blois in 1138 related by Orderic Vitalis. The context may be vague because the fear is of a present danger pregnant with as yet unknown future consequences. When Abbot Bernard died on 8 May 1149, Geoffrey Le Bel of Anjou was duke of Normandy, but early in 1150 he invested his son Henry with the duchy. The struggle over the successor to Abbot Geoffrey is known to have incurred the wrath of Duke Henry. It is possible that no. **62** was forged during the abbacy of Geoffrey, who was himself elected by his monks and not with the approval of the Norman duke. The monks had felt sufficiently exposed to seek from Eugenius III a bull confirming all their property and their right as Benedictines to elect their abbot. The minting of this forgery and the supplication of the bull are likely to be intimately linked to the composition of the cartulary at the same date.

Some 59 of the texts begin with an invocation of the Trinity, *In nomine Patri et Filii et Spiritus Sancti. Amen*. Although just under half the items begin with this *invocatio*, it is frequent enough justifiably to be regarded as characteristic of Mont charters. Many of the charters have a preamble or *arenga*. One of these, a lengthy statement beginning: *Antecessorum nostrorum institutionibus sancitum decretumque est quatinus si...*, occurs nine times.[111] The word *antecessor* specifically related to a forebear occurs in 22 charters.[112] An extract from the Gospel of Mark (xii, 42), *uidue suffecit quadrans*, is among a handful of such quotations to turn up regularly in the preamble.[113] Notifications occur in 32 charters with the phrase *notum sit*, several of them among the *In nomine* charters, which span the entire chronological range of the cartulary.[114] Most of the charters have an anathema clause, in 21 of which the traitor Judas is mentioned and in 11, Dathan and Abiron.[115] 11 charters refer to the fear of hell (*gehenna*).[116] There are 23 references to the devil and 12 to damnation. Less than half the charters are dated. Dating is normally in the form of a year of the Incarnation, often fortified with references to regnal and other years. 17 such items are further dated by indiction, frequently incorrectly.[117] In 16 charters the donor or his close kinsman becomes a monk of the abbey.[118] We should expect most of the 72 charters given in the period 966–1100 to have been written at the abbey, although the charter of Maiol (no. **32**) was a Cluniac product of Marmoutier, and the charter of Conan (**App. ii.1**) was first written at Rennes. The same is likely also for the 46 twelfth-century charters, 29 of them belonging to the period of Bernard's abbacy, i.e. 1131–1149, and most of them concerning restitutions of abbey property.

As the scribe hurtled towards the untimely conclusion of his work there are perhaps signs of haste in the fact that two of the three final items, nos. **117** and **119**, lack validation and attestation clauses. The scribe was careful throughout to copy the whole of his exemplars including the witness lists. While the omission of such clauses is not uncommon in cartulary copies, it is very rare in the Cartulary of Mont-Saint-Michel. Although the balance of the surviving text is such that it seems unlikely that it was ever intended to be much longer than it is, the Cartulary was undeniably abandoned incomplete.

111 Nos. 2, 4, 9, 27, 31, 34, 39, 53, 60.

112 Nos. 49, 51, 55–6, 63, 68–9, 71–2, 75, 77, 82–3, 87–91, 95, 97, 107, 114.

113 Nos. 2, 3, 5, 22, 31, 34, 60.

114 Nos.16, 18, 29, 48, 51, 55–6, 58, 62, 64–6, 69–70, 73, 77, 79, 82, 88–9, 91, 93, 96–9, 101, 105, 109, 111, 112, 117.

115 Nos. 2–3, 17, 21–4, 28, 34, 42–4, 49, 53, 64–5, 74, 80, 86, 88–9, 101, 107.

116 Nos. 19, 20, 29, 39, 43, 53, 73, 79, 87–9.

117 Nos. 9, 11, 16–17, 19, 23, 39–10, 43, 50–1, 61, 66, 71, 82, 102.

118 Nos. 9, 33, 43, 61, 70, 75, 83, 88, 92, 93, 93, 98, 110, 111, 113, 117.

The principal evidence is the the large blank space place, spreading over more than page, on fol. 48–49r, that was clearly intended to contain one or more texts that were never copied. Given that the monks and post-medieval scholars made so many copies of Mont charters, it is not entirely idle speculation to wonder what texts the cartularist might have included if the work had been completed. Many charters which might have been included relate directly to charters that are found in the Cartulary. Their omission might therefore be explained quite simply as superfluous to the streamlined design of the work. A number of such texts have been gathered together in the Appendix below.

Speculation about what might have been intended for the Cartulary must ultimately focus on the large gap left on folia 48 and 49, for which the surrounding texts provide a context. The first step is to determine how the different charters were viewed by the monks. The single most important surviving evidence for the abbey's view of its muniments is contained in manuscript Avranches 211, folia 113 verso to 135 verso, an inventory, dating to 1326, of muniments arranged by priory. The inventory begins with a list of *Priuilegia*, including papal, royal and ducal confirmation charters. On folio 115 there begins a series of lists describing deeds held *in armariolo* of each priory. None of the lists contains a full description of any item it includes, but the name of the person who issued the charter, often accompanied by a date, is usually given. For the earlier charters, of the period before around 1200, the description is normally impersonal and often terse. Individual acts are described as *cyrographum*, *carta* or *littera*. Very rarely, words such as *confirmatio* or *donatio* are used instead. One or two are described as *copia*. The act is introduced by one of the three principal terms and followed by a place-name. The order is not chronological, nor are the acts arranged according to their description. It becomes clear, however, that the most important acts of any priory are those described as *cyrographum*, followed by those called *carta*. Most of the *cyrographa* can be identified from the Cartulary texts by the place-name in their description in the inventory, which will match an element in the title with which most of the cartulary texts were provided. *Cyrographum de Vedobris*, for example, on folio 117v of Avranches 211, refers to the cartulary text entitled *Carta de Vedobris*, a formal act of Hugh III, count of Maine, granting the land of Voivres to the abbey (no. **35**). The *cyrographa* of Avranches 211 clearly match the principal charters of benefaction in Avranches 210, that is, the charters which bestowed churches that then or later became a priory of the abbey. Exceptionally, the term was also extended to other important early endowments, principally grants of vines or of fisheries, such as the grants of vines in Le Mans by Ralph *vicomte* of Le Mans (no. **28**), which became part of the endowment of Saint-Victeur au Mans when it was given to the abbey in 1040, and Conan III of Brittany's grant of vines (no. **63**). The use of the term *cyrographum* is not obviously explained at first sight. Facsimile copies of some of the acts so described show no signs of a chirograph form, in which a single parchment recording two copies of the act would have been cut apart so that later disputes about its form could be resolved by reuniting the two pieces: only the original parchments would make the required match. Almost all the acts called *cyrographum* would originally have been written by the monks on behalf of their lay benefactors, persons of the quality of Hugh III of Maine and Alan III of Brittany who might have required a copy for their own archives of acts destined for the abbey archives. In fact, it had been acceptable to use it to mean 'act', without any connotation of indenture or duality, since the eleventh century and it is soon obvious that this is the way it is used in Avranches 211. No. **6** in the Cartulary refers to a formal act by Robert I of Normandy as a chirograph.[119] It also occurs in the diploma of King Lothar. The acts described in Avranches 211 as *cartae* are of a similar period, often granted by the same benefactors, and are only less important than the *cyrographa* because they do not include the first grant of a church that later became a priory church, or some other gift that was regarded in some sense as a foundation grant. The Cartulary titles describe most of the *cyrographa* as *cartae*. In the third group, of charters described as *litterae*, the unifying features are that these were grants by a layman below the rank of seigneur from his inheritance. Normally the consent of his overlord is explicitly mentioned. There was sometimes a link to a previous grant by an ancestor that had been obstructed by the present grantor, but these were not simple acts of restitution or quitclaims. The charter of Abbot Maiol of Cluny (no. **32**), given in 966, stands out as an anomaly in this group among the acts relating to the priory of Créans, founded by a grant of churches *c.* 1100; it is better placed among the *cartae*. Nonetheless, the importance to the monks of the great abbot's charter, so clearly linked to the mid tenth-century Benedictine reform movement, is obvious in its inclusion early in the Cartulary text, where it has the status otherwise designated by the term *cyrographum* in the inventory.

Overall, 90 of the 119 texts in the Cartulary can be securely identified among the priory registers in Avranches 211. These include both the copies of the forged Lothar diploma containing the forged bull. These occur on fol 114r, under the heading 'Dona et confirmationes regum francorum et ducorum normannorum facta...', as: 'Confirmatio Lotharii regis francorum de Monte qui dicitur Tumba. confirmata a domino Iohanne Pape in eodem cyrographo [*paragraphum*] Item idem de eodem'. Hints that the reorganization carried out 60 years later by Abbot Pierre Le Roy would be necessary are contained in the odd misplacement. A charter of Baldwin fitz Homenes for the Breton priory of Saint-Broladre, no. **89** in the Cartulary, is

119 Cf. Michel Parisse, 'Remarques sur les chirographes et les chartes-parties antérieures à 1120 et conservées en France', *Archiv für Diplomatik* 32 (1986), 546–67.

included among the charters for Guernsey in the inventory. Hugh III of Maine's charter granting Voivres (no. **35**) was placed among the charters of Villamée in Brittany, rather than Saint-Victeur in Maine. A charter of Robert fitz William (no. **71**), son of William fitz Wimund of Avranches (no. **73**), was ascribed in the inventory to Robert II of Normandy; Conan III of Brittany's grant of the fishery of *Verreis* (no. **63**) was ascribed to Alan III; the inventorist also exceeded the authority of his text in making the Robert who granted no. **38** into one of the Roberts de Saint-Denis who granted no. **39**. A few of the charters existed in more than one recension (nos. **25**, **65**), a fact reflected in the priory registers. It is also apparent that there was more than one copy of important acts, such as the charters of the dukes of Normandy.

Forty-one of the Cartulary texts inventoried in Avranches 211 were described as *cyrographum*. Although the composition of abbey priories changed over time and was not the same in 1326 as in 1149, the relationship between the *cyrographa* of the inventory, the Cartulary foundation charters and the priories is clear. The Cartulary texts relate to the priories existing in 1149 at Saint-Meloir-des-Ondes and Saint-Broladre in Brittany, Saint-Victeur-au-Mans and L'Abbayette in Maine, Guernsey, Saint-Pair, Saint-Germain-sur-Ay, Pontorson, Genêts, Balland and Chapelle-Hamelin in western Normandy, Créans in Anjou and St Michael's Mount in England. There is a striking anomaly in the case of the priory of Gohory (Eure-et-Loir, cant. Brou), in the Chartrain. The Cartulary texts are found in more than place, but tend to be a string of minor grants, mostly entitled *de eodem*. The earliest and most important of these was initiated by a grant of Theoderic Oculis Canis and his brother Walter, to which the grant of other persons were appended (no. **34**). The form suggests that it might have been a *pancarte* written in the early twelfth century. The contents of another *pancarte* were probably scattered in the cluster formed by nos. **100–106**, as is clear from the heading of no. **100**, *Incipit hic domini sub nomine cartula summi*. The central grant was no. **102**, a charter of Ralph Oculus Canis beginning with the invocation of the Trinity. These charters were recorded together in the *Confirmatio* noted in Avranches 211. This lack of formality, compared to the charters of all other priories, is reflected in the inventory, which does not record a single *cyrographum* for Gohory, though it does mistakenly include the *cyrographum* for the later priory of Locmikael (no. **42**) among the Gohory muniments (fol. 126v).[120] A Gohory charter given by Odo de Montigny is described as *cyrographum* but is wrongly assigned to the priory of Villarenton (L'Abbayette). The grant of Theoderic does indeed occur, on fol. 126v, but simply as *Theodericus Oculus canis et Walterus [...] principales donatores de Goheri et pertinentibus.*

120 Abbé Marquis, 'Gohory, son prieuré de Saint-Michel', *Bull. de la Soc. Dunoise*, t. v (1885–7), 257–76. Cf. Le Roy, *Les curieuses recherches*, p. 135.

The Cartulary also contains several charters for the priory of Saint-Martin-de-Villamée (Ille-et-Vilaine, cant. Louvigné-du-Désert) in north-east Brittany, but the one that specifically granted the church of Villamée was not described as *cyrographum* in Avranches 211. The church was conceded by Bishop Main of Rennes and his clergy in 1050 (no. **40**), an act enregistered in Avranches 211 (fol. 117v) as one of two *littera*, the second of them being an act of Bishop Stephen of Rennes dated 30 September 1164.[121] Nonetheless, the inventory in Avranches 211 does contain a *Cyrographum de Villameirs* for the priory of Villamée. The charter in question is known from other Mont sources as a charter of Conan I of Brittany given on 28 July 990, two years before his death at the battle of Conquereuil and subsequent burial in the chapel of Saint Martin at the Mont.[122]

The charter existed in three separate recensions, all of them interpolated by the monks. It has been discussed in detail by Hubert Guillotel, who has described it as a forgery.[123]Nonetheless, the grant is fundamentally genuine. Possibly the original perished or was severely damaged in the fire of Mainard II's time;[124] the latter seems more likely since one recension preserves a detailed witness list that would have been impossible for the monks subsequently to invent (printed here in **Appendix ii.1**). This text is a charter-notification which was written in Rennes. Conan's grant of the demesnes of Villamée, Lillèle, Passillé and Villeperdue was certainly regarded by the monks as the origin of the priory of Villamée, but, surprisingly, the charter was not included in the Cartulary. Quite possibly, it was intended to have been included. The gap on folia 48 and 49 would not only have easily accommodated the first and most authentic recension of the Conan charter, it is also the right place for it to have been copied, coming after a series of Breton charters relating to the priories of Mont-Roualt, Saint-Broladre, Saint-Meloir and Treverez or Locmikael (nos. **17–24**), and immediately after a charter relating to the church of Poilley (no. **24**), which was included among the charters of the priory of Villamée in Avranches 211, where it was described as *cyrographum*. The reason for the omission of Conan I's grant is perhaps unrelated either to the haste with which the Cartulary was executed and its sudden abandonement or to doubts about the authenticity of the text. Ironically, the monks certainly 'improved' the text as it has survived in all

121 Delisle, *Torigny*, ii, pp. 271–2.

122 MS Avranches 215, fol. 165v.

123 Printed in Morice, *Histoire ecclésiastique et civile de Bretagne: Preuves* t.1 (Paris, 1742), col. 350–1; edited by H. Guillotel, 'Les actes des ducs de Bretagne (940–1148)', doctoral thesis, Paris, 1976, no. 6, 21–30, and discussed by *id.*, 'Des vicomtes d'Alet aux vicomtes de Poudouvre', *Société d'histoire et d'archéologie de l'arrondissement de Saint-Malo*, Annales 1988, 205; compare Potts, 'Normandy or Brittany', 145 and note 46.

124 Dom Le Roy, *Les curieuses recherches*, p. 97. The *Introductio* dates the fire to a time 'thirty years and more' after 966.

three recensions, but they never remedied its essential defect. In the first and most authentic recension of Conan's charter, the demesnes containing the parishes are stated to have been held from Conan by Main, nephew of the archbishop of Dol, and Rorgo fitz Gauzlin of Maine. It does not explicitly mention the church of Villamée, the essential element in a grant that was regarded as establishing (then or later) a priory, yet the basis of the priory of Villamée was the abbey's possession of the parishes of Villamée and Poilley. The grant of the church of Poilley by one Gradeloc, before 1009, is referred to in the charter of his sons Ansger and Hervé, *c.* 1027 (no. **24**), which has the status of *cyrographum*. Bishop Main of Rennes's concession of the churches of Villamée and Poilley in 1050 (no. **40**) did not end the uncertainty. The matter was still in dispute in 1070, according to Thomas Le Roy, with the churches still claimed by the diocese of Rennes. This may have been the moment when the document was reworked, as Guillotel suggested. The two later recensions were provided with a new witness list which brings together men active in the period 1032 to 1038 (discussed under Notes on Persons, **Appendix ii.1**). A further concession and recognition by Bishop Stephen I (1164) of Rennes came too late for inclusion in the Cartulary. One striking difference between the Conan charter and other 'foundation' charters in the Cartulary is that it is a notification expressed as a third person *reportage*. Almost all the charters of donation (as distinct from the restitutions) in the Cartulary were copied from the original, first-person grants of their donors. The original of this act would doubtless also have been in the first person. The principal problem with the surviving recension is its detailed but thoroughly anachronistic description of jurisdictions exercised by Conan. These have no parallel in any other text in the Cartulary, whether the fully authentic texts or the forged or interpolated texts, which makes dating the reworking of the charter extremely difficult.

Additional important evidence as to what was intended to have been in the Cartulary is provided by the bull of Eugenius III (**Appendix ii.11**). It unmistakably confirms to the abbey the church of Villamée, thereby strengthening our hypothesis further.[125] Two further items missing from the Cartulary might be indicated by Eugenius's confirmation of the vill of Saint-Clement in Jersey and the church of Le Poislay (Loir-et-Cher) in the fief of Odo Borrel, seigneur of Courtalain. The latter grant was the subject of a challenge by the donor's heir, as appears from a notification of Goislan de Lèves, bishop of Chartres from 1149 to 1155, concerning the concession by Odo Borrell and others of his grandfather and homonym's grant of Le Poislay to the Mont in the time of Bishop Ivo (1092–1115).[126] Perhaps the omission of Odo Borrell's charter and that of Conan I of Brittany was due less to the abrupt conclusion of work on the Cartulary than a reluctance to anticipate

125 *Cartulaire de Jersey*, no. 9, p. 14.

126 Copy in B.N. lat. 1530A, pp. 89–90. The charters of Odo Borrell and the bishop head the inventory list for the priory of Gohory in MS Avranches 211, fol. 126r.

the confirmation requested – and in fact granted – from the pope. It is very probable that it was intended to complete the Cartulary with copies of the three anomalous grants confirmed by Eugenius III and with a historiated copy of the papal bull itself. The symmetry and balance of design which make the Cartulary a textual masterpiece even though unfinished would have been perfected by Eugenius's bull.

Of the 119 texts in the Cartulary (two of them repeats of others), 47 can be checked against surviving originals, facsimiles or modern copies, a process that confirms the reliability of the cartulary texts, with the exception of the few early Norman acts interpolated by the monks before about 1060 (see above, pp. 18–21). Almost all the texts are charters or notifications expressed in the first person. With few exceptions (nos. **33**, **54**, **117** and **119**), all of them have witness lists, or contain a statement that the donor and other persons mentioned in the body of the text have appended their signature to the deed (cf. nos. **13–15**, **29–30**, **80**). In the handful of cases where the text is presented in the third person, witness lists are still present. In one case, no. **109**, a quitclaim to the church of Saint-Ouen in Jersey by Philip de Carteret, there is clear evidence that the text was re-written in the third person form at the abbey since the first person version has been published from an early modern copy that was formerly held at Saint-Lô.[127] There may have been more than one recension of no. **65**, a third person notification of a grant of revenues by William fitz Hugh de Sillé-le-Guillaume, but the Cartulary version is certainly defective. A better version is printed in **Appendix i.8**.

At least 91 of the 119 charter texts (including the forgeries found in the *Introductio*, no. **1**) can be identified in the inventory of abbey muniments in MS Avranches 211. Of this 91, 35 were important 'foundation' charters described in the inventory as *cyrographum*, 22 were described as *carta* and 20 as *littera*. Most of the items in the Cartulary were given a title. Sometimes the charters follow on from each other, with the second and following being titled simply *De eodem*. Of the rest, 42 have titles describing them as *carta*. Of the 119 texts, a small but significant group, including the charter of Ralph *vicomte* of Le Mans, are apparently known from the cartulary alone. Hence, although most of the Cartulary texts were copied several times and many have been printed more than once, the Cartulary is an important source of otherwise unknown texts. It is also a text of unparalleled importance in its own right. As has already been shown, examination of the whole text reveals that it had a specific purpose, that it was the product of a specific moment in time and that it was shaped by a very specific crisis in the affairs of the monastery. The whole circumstances of its commission and creation are an illuminating window into how a monastic community worked. No monastic community was divorced from the lay community of its benefactors, many of

[127] *Cartulaire de Jersey*, no. 34, 'collationné à une copie ancienne sur papier existant aux archives de la Manche'.

CONCORDANCE OF INFORMATION IN THE CARTULARY, MS AVRANCHES 210, AND THE INVENTORY, MS AVRANCHES 211

No.	Priory	Donor	211 fol.	211 type	210 Title	Status	Date
1a			114r	Confirmatio			
1b			114r	Confirmatio			
2	Saint-Pair	Richard II of Normandy	114r/120	Cyrographum	Carta quam Comes Richardus fec	interpolated	1022–6
3	Bretteville	Richard II of Normandy	133v	Carta	Carta de Verson	genuine	1017–26
4	Bretteville	Gunnor widow of Richard I	133v	Cyrographum 1/2	Carta de Britauilla et de Domn	genuine	1015
5	Guernsey	Robert I of Normandy	114r/136	Cyrographum	Carta quam fecit comes Rotbert	interpolated***	1027–35
6	Genêts	Robert/William I Normandy	127r/128	Carta/Donatio	Carta de molendino comitis	later redaction***	1061–76
7	Guernsey	William I of Normandy	136r	Copia	–	genuine***	1035–48
8	Guernsey	William I of Normandy	136v	Cyrographum	Donatio de Cruce	genuine	1037–46
9	Guernsey	William Pichenoht	135v	Carta	Carta de Perrella	genuine***	25/12/1054
10	Anglia	Edward Ætheling			–	genuine	1027–35
11	Anglia	Robert count of Mortain	137r	Cyrographum	Carta de Cornubia	forgery	*c.* 1070
12	Anglia	Robert count of Mortain	137r	Donatio et confirmatio	Item de eodem	genuine	1087–94
13	Saint-Germain	Rainald fitz John & bros	123v	Cyrographum	Carta de Fulquereuilla	genuine	1061–87
14	Saint-Germain	Ralph	123v	Carta	Carta de Heiantot	genuine	*c.* 1087–94
15	Saint-Germain	Humphrey de Cambernon			Item de eodem	genuine	*c.* 1087–94
16	Genêts	Thomas de St John & bros	128v	Carta de reconciliatione	–	cygrograph***	1121–4
17	Mont-Roualt	Alan III of Brittany	133r	Cyrographum	Carta de Monroalt et de Laua e	genuine*	5/4/1030
18	Saint-Meloir	William Rivallon of Dol			Carta de Landeguihii	genuine*	1065/6
19	Saint-Broladre	Rivallon fitz Walter	124r	Littera	Carta de ecclesiis sanctorum P	genuine*	1109
20	Saint-Broladre	William fitz Irsoi	124r	Carta	Carta de decima Sancti Broelad	genuine*	*c.* 1096
21	Saint-Broladre	Trihan fitz Brien	124r	Carta	De sancto Broeladro	genuine*	1081
22	Treverez	Guihenoc de Porhoët	125v	donatio	Carta de Porrohot et Sancto Ig	genuine*	*a.*1000
23	Saint-Meloir	Alan III of Brittany	125r	Carta	Carta de ecclesiis de Pooeleth	genuine*	1032
24	Villamée	Ansger de Pollei & bros	117v	Cyrographum	Carta de ecclesia de Pollei	genuine*	1023–7
25	St-Victeur au Mans	Rainald [de La Suze]	119r	Cyrographum	Donatio de Sancto Victurio	genuine**	March 1040
26	L'Abbayette	Ivo fitz Fulcoin of Maine	118r	Cyrographum	Carta de Villarenton	genuine**	997/1004
27	St-Victeur au Mans	Hugh III of Maine	118r	Cyrographum	De sancto Victurio	genuine**	992–1015

28	St-Victeur au Mans	Ralph vicomte du Mans	118r	Cyrographum	Carta de clauso uinearum Cenom	genuine	992–1015
29	St-Victeur au Mans	Odo of Le Mans	118r	Cyrographum	De uineis Cenomannis	genuine	1033–40
30	L'Abbayette	Hugh [de Sillé] & bros	118r	Littera	Carta de ecclesia Centrannis	genuine	1009–15
31	Genêts	Count Robert	127v	Cyrographum	De Tissiaco	genuine*	*c.* 1015
32	Créans	Maiol abbot of Cluny	119v	Littera	De uineis Turonis	genuine	966–86
33	Guernsey	Restald Nauclerus	135v	Donum	De Keteho	genuine	1027–35
34	Gohory	Brunel/Oculus canis	126v	Littera	Carta de Gohere	genuine	1081–93
35	Villamée	Hugh III of Maine	117v	Cyrographum	Carta de Vedobris	genuine**	1014
36	Créans	Josbert Guastevin	119v	Littera	Carta de Criant	genuine*	1109–16
37	St-Victeur au Mans	Walter de Mont-St-John	118r	Cyrographum	Carta de Vineis de Sille	genuine	
38	L'Abbayette	Robert [de Levaré]	118v bis	Cyrographum	Carta de Liuare	genuine	*c.* 1098–1100
39	L'Abbayette	Robert de St Denis	118r	Littera	Carta de sancto Dionisio et de	genuine	1116
40	Villamée	Main, bp Rennes	117v	Littera 1/2	De ecclesiis de Villamois et P	genuine*	1050
41	L'Abbayette	Geoffrey Rivallon	118r	Cyrographum	De Liuare	genuine*	1082–1100
42	Treverez	Hugh, bp Treguier	126v	Cyrographum	Carta de Hirglas	genuine	1086
43	Saint-Germain	Niel priest of Cotentin	123v	Carta	De Sancta Columba	genuine*	1054
44	Saint-Broladre	John Rivallon of Dol	124r	Confirmatio	Carta de Bernols	genuine*	1066–85/6
45	L'Abbayette	William de Gorron	118r	Littera	Carta de Sancto Bertuino	genuine	July 1128
46	L'Abbayette	Hugh/Hilduin de Montenay	118r	Cyrographum	Carta de Montenai	genuine	*c.* 1128
47	L'Abbayette	Guy	118r	Littera	De ecclesia Centrannis	genuine**	997–1004
48	St-Victeur au Mans	Geoffrey IV of Anjou	119r	Carta	De Sancto Victurio	genuine*	1129–35
49	Saint-Meloir	Geoffrey William Goion	125r	Littera	De Pooleth (de Sancto Melorio)	genuine*	19/8/1142
50	Chapelle-Hamelin	Hildiardis	116v	Cyrographum 1/2	De Capella Hamelini	genuine	1085–94
51		Robert de Larpenty			De Lentilleis	genuine	1099
52		Richard II of Normandy			De substitutione Hildeberti	genuine	1009
53	Saint-Meloir	Clamarhoc fitz Richer	125r	Cyrographum	Carta de Pooleth	genuine*	1093–1100
54	Saint-Meloir	Clamarhoc fitz Richer			Item de eodem	genuine	1093–1100
55		Ilger fitz Waldin			Carta de Follomuzhum	genuine	1131–49
56	Saint-Broladre	Trihan fitz Brien et al	124r	Carta	De Sancto Broeladrio	genuine*	1070–1100
57	Saint-Meloir	William Goion et al			De cymeterio Sancti Melorii	genuine	1070–1100
58	Saint-Meloir	Geoffrey Walter	125r	Cyrographum	De Sancto Melorio	genuine*	1131–49
59	Saint-Meloir	Geoffrey Chaorces	125r	Cyrographum	Item de Sancto Melorio	genuine	1131–1149
60*	Genêts	Count Robert	127v	Cyrographum	Carta de Thessiaco	genuine	*c.* 1015

61	Pontorson	Ascelin de Caugé	116v	Cyrographum	Carta de Calgeio	genuine	*c.* 1056
62	Créans	Fulk IV of Anjou	119v	Cyrographum	Carta de uineis Andegauis et T	forgery	1/12/1090
63	Saint-Meloir	Conan III of Brittany	125r	Carta	Carta de piscatoria de Vereis	genuine*	1116–40
64	L'Abbayette	Main de Albini	118r	Littera	Carta de Albinneio	genuine	*c.* 1100
65	St-Victeur au Mans	William Hugh de Sillé	119r	Littera	De Silleio	genuine*	1087
66	Villamée	Rannulf de Pollei	117v	Cyrographum	De Polleio	genuine	*c.* 1093
67	Bretteville	Robert fitz Haimo	133v	Carta	De Scai	genuine*	1086
68	Bretteville	William & Alex d'Esquay	134r	Carta	–	genuine***	1131–42
69	Ardevon	Robert II of Normandy			De feria Ardeuum	genuine***	1088
70	Genêts	Gerbert de Poterel	128r	Cyrographum	Carta de Poterel	genuine	1066
71	Genêts	Robert d'Avranches	128v	Carta	De decima de Luoth et de Seruu	genuine*	1104
72	Genêts	Robert d'Avranches			De decima de Ponz et Luoth de	genuine	1129
73	Genêts	William d'Avranches			De eodem	genuine	1066
74	Genêts	Rannulf de Camples	128r	Cyrographum	Carta de Campels	genuine	1068–85
75	Genêts	Ralph de Camples	128v	Carta	De eoderm	genuine	1143
76	Genêts	Ranulf Avenel			Carta de Sartilleio	genuine	1124–30
77	Genêts	Robert de Ducey	127v/51	Littera	Carta de Fulgereio	genuine*	1106–27
78	Genêts	William Robert de Ducey	127v/51	Carta	De eodem	genuine	1131–49
79	Guernsey	Niel of Cotentin	136r	title, as in 210	De quadam terra in Greneroi	genuine	1058–86
80	Guernsey	Hugh, bp. Avranches			–	genuine	1032–48
81	Guernsey	Rainald fitz Hugh	135v	Carta	De terra Rainaldi filii Hugoni	genuine*	*c.* 1130–49
82	Guernsey	Rainald/Philip de Cartrai	135v	Confirmatio	De Carterio	genuine*	1135
83		Abbot Bernard			–	genuine	1142–49
84	Bretteville	Osbern d'Evrecy	134v	Cyrographum	De ecclesia de Vreceio	genuine	1144
85	Saint-Pair	Ranulf de Colleville	120r	Conuentio	De terra de Colleuilla	genuine	1134
86	Saint-Pair	Baldwin Blondel			De Estolleia	genuine	1131–5
87	Ardevon?	Gelduin de Hauce			De decima de Lusmeths	genuine	1142
88	Guernsey	Richard Malmarche			De homine huic ecclesie reddit	genuine	1131–49
89	Guernsey	Baldwin fitz Homenes	135v	Carta	De Sancto Broeladrio	genuine*	1131–5
90	Saint-Pair	William Paynel	121r	Littera	Conuentio inter abbatem et Gui	genuine	1070–81
91	Saint-Meloir	Prima uxor Alani	125r	Cyrographum	De piscatoria que uocatur Gros	genuine	1142–49
92	Saint-Germain	Niel de Flameville	123v	Carta	De Flameuilla	genuine	1131–49
93	Pontorson	Richard de Boucey	116v	Carta	–	genuine*	1142–49

94	Gohory	Odo Potarius			De Gohere	genuine	1131–9
95	L'Abbayette	Odo de Montenay	118r	Cyrographum	De eodem	genuine	1139
96	Gohory	Theobald de Daniol			Item de eodem	genuine	1131–49
97	St-Victeur au Mans	Simon de Balliol	119r	Carta	Carta de Veteri Villa	genuine**	1131–49
98	Ardevon	John de Huisnes	114v	Cyrographum	De ecclesia de Husnis	genuine	1131–34
99	Ardevon	Ranulf Manducans	114v	Item de eodem	Item de eodem	genuine	*c.* 1142–49
100	Gohory	Geoffrey Godeschal		Littera	Carta de Gohere	genuine	*c.* 1100
101	Gohory	William II Goet			De eodem	genuine	*a.* 1125
102	Gohory	Ralph Oculus canis	126r	Confirmatio	De eodem	genuine	1097
103	Gohory	Ralph Oculus canis			De eodem	genuine	1099
104	Gohory	Eustachia Goet			Item de eodem	genuine	*a.* 1125
105	Gohory	Ralph Oculus canis			De eodem	genuine	*c.* 1100
106	Gohory	Odo Godeschal			Item de eodem	genuine	*c.* 1100
107	Créans	Hugh Chalibot	119v	Carta	De Criant	genuine	*a.* 1100
108	Anglia	Henry I of England	136v	Littera	De Budelel	genuine	1123
109	Guernsey	Philip de Carteret	135v	Littera	De ecclesia sancti Audoeni in	genuine	1135–49
110	Guernsey	Restald Nauclerus	135v	Donum	De Ketheho	genuine	1027–35
111	Saint-Meloir	Robert fitz Ascelin	125r	Littera	–	genuine*	1100–35
112	Bretteville	bp of Bayeux	134r	Littera	De ecclesiis que sita sunt in	genuine	
113	L'Abbayette	Ralph de Pincey	118v	Donatio	De decima de Pinceio	genuine*	1131–49
114	Saint-Broladre	Helias Boterat			De Sancto Broeladrio	genuine	1131–49
115	De perditiis huius	record of losses			De perditis huius ecclesiae	genuine	1035–*c.* 1140
116	Balland	Peter de St. Hilaire			Secunda carta de Cruce	genuine	1135–40
117		Salomon fitz Grento			–	genuine	
118	Saint-Broladre	Eudo Geoffrey de Marais			–	genuine	1066–93
119	Saint-Meloir	William Goion			–	genuine	1084–1100

*** = original or pseudo-original extant.
** = facsimile or partial facsimile exists.
* = copy or copies of the original or pseudo-original survives.
1/2 = one of two.
a. = *ante*.

whom provided the abbey's new recruits. Sometimes the respective agenda of monks and benefactors overlapped, sometimes they were complementary, but the preoccupations of the lay benefactors are of interest and importance in their own right. Additional information on some of them will be found in the Notes on Persons Occurring in the Cartulary below. The interaction between monks and benefactors is particularly interesting in the case of Mont-Saint-Michel because of its location in a marcher region, and because the cartulary spans a dramatic and formative period in the region's history.

V. EDITORIAL PRINCIPLES

Every effort has been made to remain as faithful as possible to the Cartulary text, though full capitalization for proper names and for *nomina sacra* has been introduced, and all abbreviations have been expanded in full. The scribe's orthography, punctuation and errors have been retained. The scribe's auto-corrections are noted in the text where they occur. Material that was written superscript is indicated within square brackets in the text. Nothing in the text has undergone any editorial correction or addition. Where evidence exists for an original text, and where that evidence contains variants of interest or significance, these are noted after the cartulary text to which they relate. Reference to previously-printed versions of the various charters, or to manuscript copies of them, also follow the individual texts. Also noted is the number of blank lines separating items in the scribe's system of textual division.

The following conventions have been used in the text:

italics are used for the titles of each item in the Cartulary, and for editorial comments;

square brackets indicate material written superscript in the text;

the corrections made by the scribe, *Corr[exit]*, are indicated by the *a.c.* (*ante correctionem*) reading found in brackets after the corrected word;

additions made by a later hand, *supp[leuit] man[u] rec[entior]*, ...

angle brackets enclose interpolated text;

where variant readings from an original are available these are indicated by superscript letters at the relevant point in the text;

in the Appendix // indicates the line breaks in the originals as noted by those copying them;

the abbreviations *a.* (*ante*), *p.* (*post*) and *c.* (*circa*) are used throughout.

This edition concentrates primarily on the Cartulary text, using other material as appropriate in order to establish an explicable text for the Cartulary. In general every effort has been made to limit the amount of commentary on the items in the text. Additional commentary is provided in the notes on the charters found in the Notes on Persons section. Every effort has been made to trace originals or copies of originals, but no effort has been made simply to list all manuscript copies of the charters, many of which are copies of the Cartulary or copies of copies. For the same reason, a partial modern copy of the Cartulary, B.N. nov. acq. lat. 1024, is not cited here. The same principles apply to the texts in the appendices, which are provided as comparative material to the Cartulary texts. Several have had to be printed with the anachronistic modern orthography in which the copy was made from the medieval original.

DATE CONCORDANCE FOR KEY SECULAR AND ECCLESIASTICAL FIGURES

i. Abbots of Mont-Saint-Michel

Mainard I *ante* 966–991
Mainard II 991–1009
Hildebert I 1009–1017
Hildebert II 1017–23
Theoderic (also abbot of Jumièges) 1023–1027
Almodus 1023/4–1032
Suppo *c.* 1032–1048 (d. 1061)
Ralph 1048–1056/8
Ranulf de Bayeux 1057/8–1083/5
Roger I *c.* 1088–1106
Roger II *c.* 1106–1123
Richard I de Méré 1126/7–1130
Bernard of Bec 1131–1149
Geoffrey I 1149–1151

ii. Secular Rulers

Brittany

Conan I 970–992
Geoffrey I 992–1008
Alan III 1008–1040
Conan II 1040–1066
Hoel 1066–1084
Alan IV 1084–1115/6
Conan III 1115/6–1148

Maine

Hugh III 992–*c.* 1015
Herbert I *c.* 1015–1035
Hugh IV *c.* 1035–1051
Herbert II 1051–*c.* 1062
Gersendis/Hugh V *c.* 1062–1063
Helias 1092–1110
Eremburg, wife of Fulk V of Anjou 1110–1126

Normandy
Rollo 911–925/7
William I Longsword 925/7–942
Richard I 942–996
Richard II 996–1026
Richard III 1026–27
Robert I 1027–1035
William II the Conqueror 1035–1087
Robert II 1087–1106
William II, king of England 1087–1100
Henry I, king of England 1100–1135
Stephen, king of England 1135–1154
Geoffrey IV of Anjou, duke of Normandy 1144–1150
Henry of Anjou, duke of Normandy 1150–89

Anjou
Fulk le Bon 942–960
Geoffrey Grisegonelle 960–987
Fulk Nerra 987–1040
Geoffrey Martel 1040–1060
Fulk IV le Réchin 1065–1109
Fulk V 1109–1141 (King of Jerusalem 1129–42)
Geoffrey le Bel 1141–1151

France
Louis IV 936–954
Lothar 954–986
Louis V 986–987
Hugh Capet 987–996
Robert I 996–1031
Henry I 1031–1060
Philip I 1060–1108
Louis VI 1108–1137
Louis VII 1137–1180

iii. Ecclesiastics
Algar bishop of Coutances 1132–1137
Avesgod bishop of Le Mans *c.* 1004–35
Baldric archbishop of Dol 1107–1130
Benedict bishop of Alet *c.* 1090–1110/11
Brice bishop of Nantes 1114–1140
Donoald bishop of Alet 1135–1142
Geoffrey archbishop of Rouen 1111–1128
Geoffrey bishop of Coutances 1049–1093

Gerald bishop of Evreux 988–1006
Gilbert bishop of Evreux *c.* 1014–1014
Guy bishop of Le Mans 1125–1135
Herbert bishop of Lisieux 1022–1149
Hildebert bishop of Le Mans 1096–1125, archbishop of Tours 1125–1133
Hoel bishop of Le Mans 1081–1096
Hugh archbishop of Rouen 942–989
Hugh archbishop of Rouen 1129–1164
Hugh bishop of Avranches 1028–1059/60
Hugh bishop of Coutances *c.* 989–1025
Hugh bishop of Evreux 1015–46
Hugh bishop of Lisieux 1049–1077
Hugh bishop of Sées *ante c.* 1017
Hugh bishop of Treguier occurs 1086
John III bishop of Avranches 1060–1067
John bishop of Lisieux 1107–1141
Judhael archbishop of Dol *c.* 1035–1075
Junguené archbishop of Dol 1008–*c.* 1039
Main archbishop of Dol in 990
Main bishop of Rennes *c.* 1050–1075/6
Mainard bishop of Le Mans *c.* 950–969/70
Maiol abbot of Cluny 948/64–994
Mauger archbishop of Rouen 1037–55
Maugisus bishop of Avranches 1022–1025/6
Maurilius archbishop of Rouen 1055–1067
Michael bishop of Avranches 1068–1096
Norgod bishop of Avranches 990–*c.* 1017
Odo bishop of Bayeux 1049–1097
Richard de Beaufour bishop of Avranches 1134–1139
Richard II de Subligny bishop of Avranches 1142–1153
Richard fitz Samson bishop of Bayeux 1106–1133
Robert archbishop of Rouen 989–1037
Robert bishop of Sées *c.* 1071/2–1081/2
Roger bishop of Lisieux *c.* 985–1021
Roger bishop of Salisbury 1102–1139
Rotrou, archbishop of Rouen 1164–1183
Seifrid bishop of Le Mans 969/71–*c.* 1004
Stephen I bishop of Rennes 1156–1166
Stephen II de Fougères bishop of Rennes 1168–1178
Turgis bishop of Avranches 1094–1134
Turold bishop of Bayeux 1097–1106
Warin bishop of Rennes *c.* 1030–50

CONTENTS OF THE CARTULARY

1. History (largely spurious) of the sanctuary of St Michael at Mont Tumba from 708 until 966, with appended diploma (forgery) of King Lothar and interpolated bull of John XIII (forgery).

2. Grant (interpolated) by Richard II of Normandy, 1022–26.

3. Grant by Richard II of Normandy of his allod at Verson, 1022–26.

4. Grant by Gunnor, widow of Richard I of Normandy, or her dower lands at Bretteville-sur-Odon and Domjean, 1015.

5. Charter (interpolated) of Robert I of Normandy, 1027–35.

6. Notification concerning the mill of Vains, confirmed to the abbey in 1061 by King William, 1061–76.

7. William of Normandy grants the isles of Sark and Aurigny in exchange for lands in Guernsey formerly conceded by his father Robert, 1035–48.

8. Confirmation by William of Normandy of the grant of La Croix-Avranchin by his father's knight Adelelm, 1037–54.

9. Grant of land at La Perrelle by William Pichenot, 25 December 1054.

10. Charter of Edward, later king of England, granting land in Cornwall, 1027–35.

11. Notification of a grant of Robert, count of Mortain (forgery based upon a genuine original of c. 1070).

12. Charter of Robert, count of Mortain, 1087–94.

13. Grant of land at Saint-Germain-sur-Ay by Rainald, William and Geoffrey, sons of John, c. 1061/87.

14. Charter by which Ralph grants land in his demesne at Le Bingard in the Cotentin, probably before c. 1087–94.

15. Grant of land near Le Bingard by Humphrey de Cambernon, vassal of Robert count of Mortain, c.1050–1094, probably c.1087–94.

16. Cyrograph relating the circumstances of an accord reached between Thomas de Saint-Jean and his brothers and the monks, 1121–25.

17. Charter of Alan III of Brittany, 5 April, 1030.

18. Restitution to the abbey by William fitz Rivallon of land Abbot Suppo had alienated to William's late father, 1065 or 1066

19. Rivallon fitz Walter concedes the grant made by his father and his mother of the third part of the churches of St Peter and St Broladre in Saint-Broladre, 1109.

20. Notification concerning the grant of the tithe of Saint-Broladre made by William fitz Irsoi, 1107–30.

21. Grant of land and tithes in the parish of Saint-Pierre and Saint-Broladre by Trihan fitz Brien, 1081.

22. Grant of three vills by Guethenoc, later *vicomte* of Porhoët, his wife Allarun and sons Goscelin, Maingui and Tutgual: c. 990.

23. Charter of Alan III of Brittany restoring, at the request of Abbot Almodus, the churches of Saint-Meloir and of Saints Méen and Judicaël (Cancale), in the pays d'Alet, 1032.

24. Charter of Ansger and Herve concerning the church of Poilley, 1023–7.

25. Grant by Rainald *miles* and his mother Hersende of the monastery of Saint-Victeur in the suburbs of Le Mans, March 1040.

26. Charter by which Ivo fitz Fulcoin, at the request of Abbot Mainard II restores eight vills, including *Villarenton*, or L'Abbayette, all in the commune of La Dorée, 12 October, 997–1003/4.

27. Charter of Hugh III count of Maine, 992–1015.

28. Charter of Ralph *vicomte* of Le Mans, c. 992–1000.

29. Grant of vines by Odo, citizen of Le Mans, and his wife Hersende, 1033–40.

30. Sale, at the request of Abbot Hildebert, of two parts of the church of Centrannis, by Hugh [de Sillé] and others, 1009–15.

31. Grant of an allod at Tissey by Count Robert [of Avranches], c. 1015.

32. Grant of land at Le Mortier (Indre-et-Loire, cant. Tours, comm. Saint-Symphorien) in the Touraine by Abbot Maiol of Cluny at the request of Abbot Mainard I, 21 March 982–6.

33. Grant of the isle of Guetehou (east of Guernsey) by Restald, former ship-master to Robert of Normandy, 1027–35.

34. Pancarte containing a series of three grants by the Oculus Canis and Brunel families of Châteaudun establishing the priory of Gohory, 1081, 1087, 1093.

35. Charter of Hugh III of Maine, 1014.

36. Grant of two churches, and other benefits, on the Loir at Créans by Josbert Gaustevin, 1109–16.

37. Grant of 4 arpents of vines in Sillé-le-Guillaume by Walter the Rich of Mont-Saint-Jean, 1131–49, probably 1145–9.

38. Charter by which Robert grants, from his inheritance, the churches of St Victeur at Lévaré and St Berthevin(-la-Tannière), c.1098–1100.

39. Charter of Robert de Saint-Denis confirming his father Robert's grant of the church of Saint-Denis-de-Gastines, 1116.

40. Charter of Main, bishop of Rennes, and his clergy, conceding and confirming to the abbey the churches of Villamée and Poilley, 1050.

41. Charter of Geoffrey fitz Rivallon granting the church and tithes of Levaré, c. 1082–1100.

42. Charter of Hugh de Saint-Pabual, bishop of Tréguier, granting land in his inheritance at Lokmikael in Elliant (Finistère, arr. Quimper, cant. Rosporden), 1086.

43. Niel grants the allod of Sainte-Colombe, 1054.

44. Charter of John fitz Rivallon of Dol confirming grants made by his tenants, c. 1066–85/6.

45. Notification by Guy d'Etampes, bishop of Le Mans, that Mont-Saint-Michel and Abbot Richard have recovered in his diocese the church of Saint-Berthevin (-la-Tannière) in the pays d'Ernée, 12 July and 26 July 1128.

46. Charter of Hugh alias Hiluin of Montenay, c. 1128.

47. Charter by which Guy sells to the abbey, at the request of Abbot Mainard II, two parts of the church of *Centrannis*, 12 October 997–1004.

48. Charter of Geoffrey IV Le Bel of Anjou, c. 1129–35.

49. Confirmation and restitution by Geoffrey Goion of grants made by his father William Goion at Saint-Meloir-des-Ondes, 12 January 1120–19 August 1142.

50. Charter of Hildiardis granting, *inter alia*, the church of Saint-Martin de La Chapelle-Hamelin, 1085–94.

51. Charter by Robert de Lapenty granting the tithes of Lentillé, 1099.

52. Act by which Richard II of Normandy removes Abbot Mainard II from office on grounds of his advanced age, 1009.

53. Charter of Clamarhoc fitz Richer making grants in the region of Saint-Malo (pays d'Alet), 1093–1100.

54. Notification of a further grant made whilst he still lived by Clamarhoc fitz Richer of 60 acres at Saint-Ideuc, c. 1093–1100.

55. Notification concerning grants by Ilger son of Waldin *vicomte*, 1131–8 May 1149.

56. Grant of land and tithes and other benefits, including his rights in churches, at Saint-Broladre by Trihan fitz Brien, and others, 1070–1100.

57. Restitution of cemetery rights at Saint-Meloir-des-Ondes by William Goion, Guigan *vicarius* of Alet and others, 1070–1100.

58. Notification of a quitclaim of all rights claimed in the church of Saint-Meloir-des-Ondes by Geoffrey fitz Walter, 1135–49.

59. Notice concerning the grant made by Geoffrey Chaorces at his death, for the soul of his brother Main Pointel, to the priory of Saint-Meloir-sur-Ondes, 1131–49.

60. Repeat of no. 31 above.

61. Charter of Ascelin de Caugé, 1069–94.

62. Confirmation (spurious) of vines in Anjou and the Touraine by Fulk IV of Anjou, 1 December 1090.

63. Charter of Conan III of Brittany, 1116–24.

64. Notification of a grant of land in Chauvigné by Main de Saint-Aubin-d'Aubigné, c. 1100.

65. Notification of a grant by William fitz Hugh de Sillé, 1097.

66. Grant of three acres in Poilley by Ranulf, before 1124.

67. Robert fitz Haimo grants, from his inheritance, the church and tithes of Esquay-Notre-Dame, 1086.

68. Accord between Abbot Bernard and the brothers William and Alexander, knights from Esquay, 1131–1142.

69. Grant of a market and an annual fair, on the feast of the Nativity of the Virgin, at Ardevon by Robert II of Normandy, 1088.

70. Record of a convention between Abbot Ranulf and one Roger concerning land at Poterel, Bonneville, 1066.

71. Restoration by Robert fitz William (of Avranches) of tithes at Le Luot and Servon, 1104.

72. Notification of a grant by Robert of Avranches of tithes of land in Ponts and its vicinity at Funeçon and Caviné or Cauvigny, 1129.

73. Grant by William fitz Wimund (of Avranches) of the whole tithes of all his vavassores and himself at Le Luot, 1066.

74. Notification by Abbot Ranulf concerning a grant of land by Ranulf de Champeaux, c. 1068–85.

75. Notification of the restitution of the land of Ranulf de Champeaux by his grandson Gilbert, 1143.

76. Ranulf Avenel restores the tithes of St Evremund of Sartilly, 1128–29.

77. Robert de Ducey confirms, with the assent of Earl Hugh of Chester, the grants made his father, c. 1121–1127.

78. William son of Robert de Ducey confirms his father's grants, 1131–8 May 1149.

79. Notification that a certain Niel, from the Cotentin, conceded the land of *Plemmunt* in Guernsey previously granted by his brother Hugh, 1058–85.

80. Charter of Hugh bishop of Avranches stating that he restores to the abbey, *post mortem*, tithes in Guernsey that were granted him by Abbot Suppo on condition that he will it back to the abbey, probably c. 1032–1048.

81. Notification concerning the conversion of a mortgage of land in Guernsey to a grant by Rainald fitz Hugh, 1131–49.

82. Notification concerning the grant by Rainald de Carteret of the church of Saint-Germain de Carteret, 1125, 1135.

83. Concerning Roger, an aged priest, and his nephews, 1135–1142.

84. Notification concerning Osbern d'Evrecy, 1144.

85. Notification of a mortgage agreed between Abbot Bernard of Mont-Saint-Michel and Ranulf de Colleville, 1134.

86. Restitution, by Baldwin Blondel son of Hermer, of a grant made by his father and challenged by him of the farm of the fee of *Estolleia*, 1131–5.

87. Grant by Gelduin fitz Odo de Aucey of the tithe of *Lusmeths*, 1141.

88. Restitution of the 'land of the great mill' and the service of a man of the abbey in Guernsey by Richard fitz Robert Malmarche, 1131–8 May 1149.

89. Restitution and confirmation for Saint-Broladre (Ille-et-Vilaine, cant. Pleine-Fougères) by Baldwin fitz Homenes, 1131–42.

90. Recital of a detailed convention made at Bayeux in the presence of the queen between the abbey and William Paynel, 1070–81.

91. Grant by Prima wife of Alan, with Alan's consent, of the fishery called *Grossim*, 1142–8 May 1149.

92. Notification of a grant by Niel de Flamanville, 1131–49.

93. Grant of land in Boucey and Sacey (Manche, cant. Pontorson) by Richard fitz Richolin, 1142–8 May 1149.

94. Notification concerning a sale of meadow at Montemont to the priory of Gohory, before 1139.

95. Grant to the priory of Gohory, in the time of Prior Brien, by Odo de Montigny-le-Ganelon, 1139.

96. Charter of Theobald de Dangeau for the priory of Gohory, c. 1131–49 .

97. Notification of the restitution by Simon de Bailleul of the rights of their parishioners in Vieuvy, before 8 May 1149.

98. Notification concerning the grant of the fourth part of the church of Huisnes-sur-Mer made by John fitz Garner de Huisnes, 1131–19 August 1142.

99. Notification concerning the grant made of rights in the church of Huisnes by Ralph Manducans, 1142–49.

100. Grant By Geoffrey fitz Godeschal, with the assent of Hugh *vicomte* of Châteaudun and his wife Agnes, of a small portion of land at Montemont, c. 1100.

101. Grant to Abbot Ranulf and the monks of his colibert Rainer by William II Gouet of Montmirail, c. 1083–85.

102. Quitclaim for the priory of Gohory by Ralph Oculus Canis, who concedes the grants of his brother Walter, 1097.

103. Notification by Mangis, prior of Gohory, of a plea held before Hugh, *vicomte* de Châteaudun, concerning misappropriation of priory property by Ralph Oculus Canis, 1099.

104. Grant of tolls by Eustachia, wife of William II Goet of Montmirail, and Nivelon [de Fréteval]: probably c. 1080–85.

105. Quitclaim for the priory of Gohory by Ralph Oculus Canis with the consent of his son Warner: c. 1100.

106. Quitclaim for the priory of Gohory by Odo Godeschal, c. 1100.

107. Quitclaim and confirmation of his father-in-law Gausbert Gastevin's grants at Créans by Hugh Chalibot and his wife Ermensendis, 14 April 1109–15 January 1126.

108. Notification by Henry I of England that he has given the abbey 12 librates of land in Budleigh, Devon, in exchange for the churches of Wargrave and Cholsey, Berkshire, which he has given in free alms to Reading Abbey, 11 June 1123–16 October 1123.

109. Notification of a quitclaim by Philip de Carteret of the tithe of the church of Saint-Ouen in Jersey, 1135–May 1149.

110. Repeat of **33**.

111. Grant of the revenues of a salt-pan (*patella*) in the castelry of Dinan by Robert the steward, son of Ascelin, 1135–49.

112. Convention with the bishop of Bayeux concerning four churches in the Bessin at Bretteville, Domjean, Evrecy and Esquay: after the grant of Notre-Dame d'Esquay in 1086 (see no. **67**).

113. Notification of the grant of all the tithes and half of his land at Montdaigne by Ralph de Pincey and his son John, on the day that Ralph became a monk: 1131–49.

114. Notification of the restitution and grant by Helias Boterat and his two eldest sons of land, mills and tithes in the parish of Saint-Broladre, c. 1135–49.

115. Record of losses sustained by the abbey: i) during the time of William II of Normandy, ii) after William's death in 1087, iii) the usurpations of Hilgerius in the time of Abbots Ranulf (c. 1058–86) and Roger (1086–1106).

116. Notification of a quitclaim by Peter de Saint-Hilaire-du-Harscouet concerning abbey property in La Croix-Avranchin, 1135–40.

117. Salomon fitz Grento grants a tithe held from St Michael, c. 1080–1100.

118. Restitution by Eudo fitz Geoffrey and his mother Hebrea of land in Marais-de-Dol, 1107–30.

119. Notification by William Goion that he relinquishes all claim to a tithe belonging to Saint-Meloir, c. 1084–1100.

Appendices

i – *Material Related to the Contents of the Cartulary*

i.1 B.N. lat. 14832, fol. 178v [inserted after the perpendant paragraph in no. **1**].

i.2 B.N. lat. 5430A, pp. 107–8, version of the charter of Josbert Gastevin [cf. nos. **36**, **107**]: 1109–16.

i.3 B.N. lat. 5430A, p.100, from an 'original sans datte ny scel', charter of Fulk IV of Anjou, authentic version of no. **62**: 8 May 1082 – 1098.

i.4 Letter of Abbot Roger to Bishop Roger of Salisbury concerning an exchange of churches, granted by Henry I, between the Mont and Reading Abbey; cf. no. **108**: probably latter half of 1123.

i.5 Copy by Gaston de Beausse of a quitclaim by John son of Thomas and his brothers of the claim on a daily share in the provisions offered to St Michael earlier renounced by their uncle, following a vicious campaign against the abbey, described in no. **83**: 1142.

i.6 B.N. fr. 22357, p. 783 (cf. B.N. lat. 5430a, p. 209) another version of no. **58**: 1135–49.

i.7 Copy by G. Beauchesne, Arch. dépt. de La Manche, 6 J 70, M 11, of a grant by Trihan de Saint-Broladre and his wife and son: cf. nos. **21**, **56** and **89**: 1075.

i.8 B.N. Coll. Moreau 36, 141; another version of no. **65**, charter of William fitz Hugh de Sillé-le-Guillaume (Sarthe): 1087.

ii – *Material Omitted by the Cartulary*

ii.1 Guillotel, *Actes des ducs de Bretagne*, no. 6, redaction 1, charter-notification relating grants by Conan I of Brittany: 28 July 990.

ii.2 *Cartulaire de Saint-Victeur*, no. ii, from the original, charter of Hugh III of Maine granting three mills on the river Sarthe in the *faubourg* of Le Mans: 1000–1015.

ii.3 Charter by which Robert I of Normandy renounces all the rights claimed by his ancestors (Fauroux, 65, from a nineteenth-century copy of a twelfth-century redaction): 1027–33.

ii.4 Copy by G. de Beausse of a now-lost original in which the monks appoint Rivallon I de Dol-Combour as custodian and defender of their rights at Pontorson: 1040–65.

ii.5 B.N. lat. 14832 fol. 183v–184r, copy of a convention between Abbot Ranulf (d. 9 December 1084/5) and John, bishop of Avranches: 1061.

ii.6 Copy by G. De Beausse of (now lost) Arch. dépt. Manche H 15173, Abbot Ranulf makes a series of conventions: 1058–83/5.

ii.7 Copy by G. de Beausse of a lost original once in Arch. dépt. Manche, of grants made by William de Tracy: 1110.

ii.8 Arch. dépt. de La Manche, 6 J 70, M1, copy, by Geneviève Beauchesne, of a now lost original charter given by Hugh fitz Ranulf for the Mont's priory of Saint-Broladre: 1096–1139.

ii. 9 B.N. lat. 5430a, p. 270–1: memorandum concerning the chamberlain Roger who joined the abbey's enemies after the death of Henry I: after 1138.

11.10 Copy by G. de Beausse of a now lost original charter by which Peter fitz Desirée granted, on becoming a monk, all his inheritance in Guernsey: 1131–49.

ii.11 *Cartulaire de Jersey* no. 9, pp. 13–15, printed from the now lost original. Bull of Eugenius III confirming to the abbey, at the request of Abbot Geoffrey, its possessions and taking it under the protection of St Peter: 15 December 1150.

THE CARTULARY OF THE ABBEY OF MONT-SAINT-MICHEL

1

Version of the 'official History' of the abbey of Mont Saint Michel, starting with the early ninth-century *Reuelatio*, a lectionary for the feast of the Dedication of the Church of St Michael on 16 October, relating the foundation of the sanctuary of St Michael in the time of Childebert by Bishop Autbert of Avranches (Manches), who instituted twelve canons there, with an account of the saint's early miracles; a second text, commonly known as *Introductio monachorum*, compiled *c.* 1080–90, follows, with a pseudo-historical account of the subsequent restoration and refoundation of the sanctuary as a Benedictine monastery in 966 by Richard I of Normandy, with appended bull of Pope John XIII (forgery) and diploma of Lothar king of the West Franks (forgery).

[fol. 5r] INCIPIT REVELATIO AECCLESIĘ SANCTI MIÇHAELIS ARCHANGELI: IN MONTE QUI DICITVR TUMBA: IN OCCIDVIS PARTIBVS:· SUB CHILDEBERTO REGE FRANCORVM ET AVTBERTO EPISCOPO

POSTQVAM GENS FRANCORVM CHRISTI GRATIA insignita longe lateque undique per prouintias superborum colla perdomuisset. Childeberto piissimo principe monarchiam tocius occidui et septemtrionis:· nec non et meridiei partes strenue gubernante. quia omnipotens Deus non solum in omnibus gentibus uerum etiam in omnibus mundi partibus quem ipse fecit. per subiectorum spirituum agmina principatur:· beatus MICHAEL archangelus unus ex septem in conspectu domini semper adsistentium. qui etiam et paradysi prepositus saluatorum animas in pacis regione collocaturus legitur:· post eam manifestationem qua se in monte Gargano ad adorandum. ac glorificandum. quomodo et qualiter [fol. 5v] uoluit sicut in scriptis habetur ostendit:· his ut comprehensum est per beatum archangelum patratis. illuminatis Christi gratia cunctis gentibus in orientalibus Romanie partibus:· accipe quibus sese indiciis manifestare idem princeps beatissimus uoluerit presulem occidentalium populorum. ut qui quondam benedicto in patriarchis populo Israhelitico defensionis attribuerat opem:· ipse custos existeret ac preuius uocatis filiis per adoptionem. Namque legitur in uisione Danielis prophetae:· dicente eidem archangelo. Nemo est adiutor meus in omnibus iis:· nisi MICHAEL angelus princeps uester.[1] Princeps inquit uester:· populi uidelicet Iudeorum. Christo

[1] Daniel, x, 21.

uero domino in propria ueniente. atque a suis non recepto quin pocius prodito:· ipso ad patrem remeante dum aboletur obseruatio priscę legis. constabilitur annuntiationis euangelicę admirabile sacramentum:· dum exeunte per omnem terram sono apostolorum. cerimonie transferuntur sacrorum. per ministeria angelorum. *Quod beatus* MICHAEL *archangelus:· Christianorum rector dicatus esse asseritur.* Aiunt etenim historiae ecclesiastice:· quod post passionem et ascensionem Domini ad caelos. post diu expectatam Israhelitarum penitudinem. cum appropinquaret. tempus desolationis quod saluator sacro uenturum pre[fol. 6r]nuntiauerat eloquio cum fletu humanitatis:· ecclesia apud Ierosolimam monitu diuinitatis. per cunctum orbem gentibus euangelizatura diffunditur. Cunque congregatus undique ex omnibus locis populus. paschalis festiuitatis prestolaretur diem:· sacerdotibus solitas excubias obseruantibus uoces subitas uigiles audiunt dicentes. Migremeus ex iis sedibus. Voces uero subite per angelos emisse. que enuntiauerunt beatorum spirituum demigrationem:· angelicum ministerium insinuarunt ad ecclesiam gentium transferendum. Ex quibus patenter insinuatur:· quod beatus MICHAEL archangelus ministerium quod exercuerat in Dei quondam populo. idem sortitus sit apud gentium electionem. Hęc ita esse deuotio credit fidelium:· propter ostensionem signorum. Notum enim se fieri uoluit mortalibus etatis nostre temporibus:· quo se humanum genus in electorum spirituum societatem cognosceret deuocatum. Denique aduertendum est:· quo mysterio locum mortalibus preuiderit in partibus occiduis. ubi ex omni orbe confluit ueneranter angelicum deprecatura subsidium. religiosa multitudo fidelium. *De Situ loci*

Hic igitur locus:· tumba uocitatur ab incolis. Qui in morem tumuli quasi ab arenis emergens:· in altum in spatio ducentorum cubitorum porrigitur. Oceano undique cinctus locus. angustum admirabilis insulę prebet spatium:· inter ostia situs. [fol. 6v] ubi immergunt se mari flumina Segia necnon et Senuna:· prebens quoque habitantibus hinc inde non breue nimium spatium. Longitudine uero ac latitudine a radice qua prominet:· non multum distat ut conicitur ab eo opere quo saluatum immo seruatum est humani generis incrementum. Qui ab Abrincatensi urbe sex distans milibus:· occasum prospectans. Abrincatensem pagum dirimit a Brittannia. Nulla ibi exerceri ualet actio mundialis. Iis solis congruus extat locus. qui Christum sedulo uenerari disponunt:· et hos suscipit. quos ad ęthera ardens uirtutum amor euehit. Copia tantum piscium ibidem repperitur:· quę plerunque fluminum marisque infusione congeritur. Procul uero cernentibus:· nil fore aliud quam spatiosa quedam. immo speciosa turris uidetur. Sed et mare recessu suo deuotis populis bis in die desideratum iter prebet:· beati petentibus limina archangeli MICHAELIS. Prefatus locus sicut a ueracibus cognoscere potuimus narratoribus opacissima claudebatur silua. longe ab oceani ut estimatur estu milibus distans sex:· abtissima prebens latibula ferarum. Et quia [*corr.*] secretiora cęli per contemplationis subtilitatem rimari uolentibus gratissima esse solent remotiora heremi loca: inibi olim inhabitasse comperimus monachos. [fol. 7r] ubi etiam nunc duę extant ecclesie. priscorum manu constructe. Nam ipsi monachi ibidem domini seruientes. dispensatione cuncta regentis Dei sustentabantur: presbitero quodam de uilla quae dicitur nunc Asteriacus. taliter eis ferente auxilium. Vt enim illis sine quo humana non potest exigi uita deerat uictus: fumo signifero discurrente altaque cęli petente. onerabat asellum dapibus dilectione uera farcitis: sicque duce inuisibili preuio per loca ibat inuia ac redibat. ferens Domini iussa. illisque necessaria. Sed quia hic locus nutu Dei futuro parabatur miraculo. sanctique sui archangeli uenerationi: mare quod longe distabat paulatim assurgens. omnem silue illius magnitudinem uirtute complanauit sua. et in arenę suę formam cuncta redegit: prebens iter populo terrae. ut enarrent mirabilia Dei. Iam uero ad illud ueniendum est: qualiter idem princeps beatorum spirituum. angelica reuelatione dedicauerit predictum locum. *Quomodo angelica reuelatione. signorumque ostensione: sacer locus construi ceptus est.*

Quodam tempore cum religiosissimus et Deo amabilis prefate urbis antistes AUTBERTUS nomine sopori sese dedisset: admonitus est angelica reuelatione. ut in iam dicti summitate loci construeret in honore archangeli aedem: ut cuius celebrabatur ueneranda comme[fol. 7v]moratio in Gargani monte: non minori tripudio celebraretur in pelago. At sacerdos dum reuoluit illud apostoli. probate spiritus sancti si ex Deo sunt: iterata admonitus est uisione quo perficeret quod iubebatur. Et quia spiritus prophetarum non semper est prophetis subiectus: distulit adhuc presul constructionem. sed adhibuit intercessionem: quatinus super istiusmodi negotio domini Ihesu Christi simulque beatisssimi archangeli agnoscere ualeret deliberationem. Contigit per idem tempus: ut taurum cuiusdam quem furtim quidam instinctu prauitatis subtraxerat. in eiusdem deponeret saxi cacumen: ut dum is qui amiserat iuuencum repperiendi amitteret spem. turpe latrunculus lucrum efficeret ex eodem. Interea tercia admonitione uenerandus episcopus pulsatur austerius. apparente in eiusdem presulis capite usque in hodiernum diem in testimonio foramine:[1] ut qui non adquieuerat bis admonitus. locum adiret celerius: a quo tamen se sciret egrediendum nullatenus priusquam perficeret quod fuerat iussus. Ad cuius fidei confirmationem monstratur etiam ibidem usque in presens petra quasi digito hominis inscripta: super quam memoratus episcopus resedit. quoat usque opus ad finem adduxit. Percunctanti igitur episcopo qui edificationi congruus posset uideri locus. angelica in hunc modum est responsione dictatum: ut loco eo ędificaretur ędes. quo inerat taurus abscondite religatus. Cunque de loci requireret ampli[fol. 8r]tudine uel quantitate: eisdem cognouit responsis. edificationi eum debere statuere modum. quem uideret iuuencum in circuitu pedibus protriuisse. Post hęc quoque iussum est: ut suo prereptus dominio. restitueretur taurus. Venerabilis

1 *apparente ... foramine*, the phrase added after the rediscovery of the skull of St Aubert, sometime between 1010–14 (see Introduction, above, pp. 14–15).

uir domini AUTBERTUS de angelica uisione iam tercio sibi data factus certissimus. cum ymnis et laudibus predictum locum ingressus. exercere imperatum opus aggressus est:· congregataque rusticorum maxima multitudine locum purgauit. atque in spatium complanauit. In cuius medio duae preminebant rupes:· quas operantium multorum mouere non poterant manus. nec a suo diuellere statu. Qui cum diu hererent. nec omnino quid facerent haberent:· nocte insecuta uisio apparuit cuidam homini nomine BAINO. in uilla quę dicitur Itius:· qui duodecim filiis ampliatus. magnum inter suos tenebat dignitatis locum. Hic ergo per uisum monitus ut cum laborantibus et ipse labori insisteret. festinus ad locum cum filiis uenit:· impleturus quod fuerat iussus. Qui cum peruenisset:· quod humana non poterat uirtus. mirum in modum tam facile molem tante magnitudinis remouit:· ut nullum pondus inibi esse uideretur. At omnes in commune collaudantes Deum sanctumque archangelum MICHAELEM:· cepto attentius insistebant operi. *De extructione sacre basilice.* Dum uir domini AVTBERTVS de magnitudine construende basilicę adhuc dubius cogitaret:· nocte media sicuti quondam [fol. 8v] Gedeoni in signum uictorię. ros iacuit supra uerticem montis. Vbi autem fundamenta locanda erant:· siccitas fuit. Dictumque est episcopo. Vade:· et sicut signatum uideris fundamenta iace. Qui statim omnipotenti Deo gratias agens. sanctique implorans angeli MICHAELIS auxilium:· exurgens letus. opus aggressus est. Extruxit itaque uir domini AVTBERTVS fabricam. non culmine subtilitatis celsam. sed in modum cripte rotundam. centum ut estimatur hominem capacem:· illius in monte Gargani uolens exęquare formam. in monte prerupti silicis angelico apparatu facta terrigenis ad laudem et gloriam Dei habitatione:· manifeste docens semper in celestibus diuini muneris opem esse poscendam. altaque contemplationis intuitu penitrare theris astra:· non terrenis limosisque paludibus rotantia hominum ponere corda. Quod cum non post multum tempus esset opem ferente Deo edificatum:· beato uiro Dei AVTBERTO episcopo manente anxio. proinde quia cernebat sibi deesse sancti archangeli pignora. beatus MICHAEL eundem sacerdotem admonuit. uti fratres celerrime usque ad locum quo memoria uenerabiliter colitur sanctissimi archangeli dirigeret in Gargano:· et eam quam se patrocinante referrent benedictionem. cum summa exciperet gratulatione. *Qualiter a Gargano:· sacra sint pignora deportata.* Interea:· missi nuntii adeunt locum. Qui benignissime ab abbate loci illius sus[fol. 9r]cepti. uestibusque mutatis ac tanti fastigatione itineris sulleuati:· cuncta quę sue contigerant regioni. simul ad quod uenerant pandunt. Quae uerba cum ipsius abba loci suo retulisset antistiti:· uberrimas laudes omnipotenti Deo uterque retulit. qui prolapsis nature fragilitate terrigenis asistentium sibi ministrorum dignatur prebere suffragium. Hinc cum qua decebat ueneratione sumptis a loco pignoribus quo beatus archangelus sui memoriam fidelibus commendauerat. partem scilicet rubei pallioli quod ipse memoratus archangelus in monte Gargano supra altare quod ipse construxerat posuit. et partem marmoris supra quod stetit. cuius ibidem usque nunc in eodem loco superextant uestigia. iam dictis fratribus usque ad sacrum locum referenda patrocinia contradidit:· conditione interposita. uidelicet ut quos una angelice reuelationis sociauerat causa. una quoque ętternaliter necteret caritatis connexio. Summi interea nuntii repedantes:· post multa itineris spatia ad locum quo digressi fuerant ipso die quo fabrica completa est in monte iam dicto in occiduis partibus. quasi nouum ingressi sunt orbem:· quem primum ueprium densitate reliquerant plenum. Quo dum propinquant:· incunctanter sacerdos domini AVTBERTVS occurrens cum multis laudibus. cum canticis spiritualibus. in sacrum montem angelica mortalibus deuehit profutura presidia. Dici non [fol. 9v] potest. quanto in aduentu ut ita dicam angelico circumiacentes prouintiae gauise sunt gaudio:· quippe quę sibi uidebant diuinitus superni auxilii tribui donum in hoc quod beatum MICHAELEM archangelum celestis miliciae principem merebantur obtinere signiferum:· cognoscentes etiam signa et mirabilia quę Dominus per ministrum suum operatur mortalibus. ita ut per huius itineris spatia duodedim ceci illuminati pluresque diuersis infirmitatibus acti pristine redditi sint sanitati:· et quod iis addendum est. mulier quedam orbata luminibus de uilla que dictitur Asteriacus. dum prosequitur preciosissima munera summi archangeli. mox ut [at]tigit planitiem harenamque maris. diuinitus factum recepit uisum:· admirans se subito de tenebris in lucem mutatam. Sed et usque hodie:· per summum ministrum suum. hec eadem Dominus cotidie ad laudem et gloriam nominis sui in eodem loco operari non desinit. *De dedicatione sacri templi:· ac diuini cultus adhibito apparatu.* Igitur eo die qui est .xvii. kal. nouembris. ueneranda completa templi dedicatione:· uir domini AUTBERTUS post quam omnia sagaciter sub ordine disposuit officia quoque seruientium clericorum constituit deputans hos inibi sub numero consistere duodecim:· qui legitimis obseruationibus perpetualiter in beatissimi MICHAELIS archangeli persisterent famulatu. quamuis non eiusdem numeri in eodem loco a successoribus [fol. 10r] beati uiri sint clerici constituti. Simul etiam de episcopio suo eidem loco seruientibus uillas contradidit:· uidelicet iam dictam uillam ITIVM. et Genitium.

De optenta aqua:· per angelicam demonstrationem

Interea idem presul cuncta peruidens congruo patrata o[r]dine:· hoc unum quod poterat ualde uideri difficile a sancto censuit expetendum archangelo. aquę scilicet elementum:· sine quo constare nequit uita mortalium. Super hęc domini Ihesu Cristi simulque sancti archangeli dum expetit cum grege commisso auxilium. ut qui quondam produxerat sitienti populo de petra poculum. ipse a suis seruis amouere dignaretur aquę penuriam:· tandem angelica ostensione locum didicit. ubi in prerupto silice dum concauum foramen exciditur. mirum in modum aquarum mox abundantia repperitur. quae possit habitantibus competentem prebere usum. Eadem uero aqua profluens. quod sit haustu salubris:· multis est ostensum modis. Celerem nanque febricitantibus fert opem:· quotiens desiderium prouenerit sumendi.[1]

1 End of the 9th-century *Revelatio*.

PROVINTIA LUGDVNENSIS SECVNDA[1] quę nunc dicitur Normannia. non inmerito asseritur precipua ceterarum quas infra se continet Gallia: ut pote quę non solum esse sufficiens [fol. 10v] sibi rerum omnium affluentissima copia. uerum etiam circumiectis prouintiis non minima probatur conferre subsidia. Namque aeris salubritate. opime telluris ubertate. uinearum fertilitate. siluarum delectabilitate. nemorum fructiferarumque arborum apricitate. hortorum salubriumque herbarum amoenitate. metallorum quorumque congerie. siluestrium domesticarumque bestiarum multiplicitate. auium cuiusque generis multitudine. piscium marinorum dulciumque aquarum copiosa effusione. nauium cunctarumque mercium assiduitate. clarissimarum urbium dignitate. nobilium coenobiorum numerositate. illustrium uirorum animosissimorumque militum populositate: ut testimonio sunt Cenomannicus pagus. Anglica regna. Campania. Apulia. Calabria. Sicilia. aliaque plura ab eis armis adquisita diuerso tempore: cunctis ad postremum commodis humane uite. omni sue uicinitati noscitur longe pręstare. Hęc maxima sui parte ab occidente scilicet orientem uersus per totum septemtrionalem circulum occeano cingitur. ab oriente Epta. a meridie Sarta. ab occasu Coysnum fluminibus. oceanoque disterminatur. Et cum omnibus ut dictum est uite emolumentis ceteras precellat. uniuerso tamen occidenti in hoc longe superemicat: quod infra se in monte qui dicitur Tumba beati MICHAELIS continet patrocinia. Ibidem nempe haberi patrocinia eiusdem celestis milicię principis. concursus pene tocius testatur orbis: quo innumerabilibus choruscauit. nostraque adhuc [fol. 11r] ętate choruscat miraculis. angelice tantum sublimitati congruis. Ex quibus aliqua quorumdam nostrorum bone uoluntatis fratrum compulsi precibus. nullo fastu sed amore sancti ipsius. memoriae mandare studuimus: pro ut uel ipsi nostra ętate uidimus. uel a nostris maioribus subnixe auctoritatis uiris audiuimus.

IGITUR tempore gloriose recordationis Childeberti Francorum regis: beatus AVTBERTVS presul tunc temporis Abrincensis. iussus est ab angelo ecclesiam construere in cacumine montis in honore sancti MICHAELIS: ut cuius memoria uenerabatur in Gargano a fidelibus populis. eius etiam ibi patrocinium excoleret plebs occidentalis climatis. Venerabilis ergo episcopus huic angelice uisioni minus existens credulus. dum sibi iussa implere differt etiam secundo ammonitus: tertia apparitione angeli pulsatur austerius: sicque demum cum hymnis et laudibus predictum locum ingressus. quantocius aggressus est implere quod fuerat iussus. Ad huius autem austere pulsationis testimonium. in capite eiusdem sancti hodieque apparet foramen haud exiguum: quod diligenter oculis adtrectatum nullum cauterii siue iaculi. manifeste uero diuine uirtutis prebet inditium. Et licet ad hanc partem quosdam minoris ut sic dictum sit fidei incredulos uideamus: nos tamen quod

[1] Composed at different times in the 11th century, the text from this point is known as *Introductio monachorum*. It is separated from *Revelatio* by a two-line gap into which the capital *P* of *PROVINCIA* projects.

angelico testimonio roboratum esse scimus ut suo tempore liquebit insequentibus et credimus. et uerum esse profitemur. Vir itaque domini AUTBERTUS ut iussus fuerat ęcclesiam in predicto [fol. 11v] loco construxit. delatisque sacris a Gargano monte reliquis eam decenter dedicans insigniuit:· atque inibi ad Deo seruiendum duodecim clericis constitutis. cunctisque necessariis largiter attributis:· ad propriam sedem gaudens remeauit. Hoc ergo ordine . per. ccc^tos^. et eo amplius annos idem monasterium feruntur tenuisse clerici:· a tempore uidelicet incliti regis Childeberti usque ad tempus Lotharii. Quo regnante:· precellentissimus dux Normannorum Richardus filius Guillelmi. eiectis eodem loco canonicis censura iusti iudicii:· diuino instinctu ibidem monachos substituit. Quomodo autem per tantum tempus isdem floruerit locus. uel quibus quantisque choruscauerit uirtutibus incognitum habemus:· numquam tamen illic defuisse uirtutum insignia a maioribus percepimus. quorum relatu duo quedam mira quę cognouimus suo tempore. narrąbimus. Quia uero egregii principis Richardi mentionem fecimus. non incongruum narrationi immo plurimum suppetere uidetur. ut quo de sanguine cretus. quis quantusue fuerit breuiter intimemus:· et sic quomodo monachili ordine eundem locum insignierit narratione continuata. ad ceptum opus redeamus. *De aduentu Rollonis in Frantia. et qualiter sacrum baptisma consequutus. a saeculo migrauerit.*

ANNO IGITUR DOMINICĘ INCARNATIONIS .dccc.^{mo} lxx.^{mo} vi.^{to} inclite nobilitatis Rollo cum ingenti Dacorum [fol. 12r] iuuentute nauigio per Sequanam appulsus est Rodomo:· atque a ciuibus ipsius urbis exceptus in pace continua. Inde irruptione creberrima huc illucque discurrens depopulando cuncta. et grauissimis cladibus atque preliis sicut in scriptis habetur pertriuit francigenas:· ad postremum cunctis habitatoribus timore resolutis. igni ferroque deseuiendo libere circumcirca. Frantiam pene pessumdedit:· per plura annorum spatia. Tandem autem deuictus precibus Franconis Rotomagensis archiepiscopi. cum Francis eorumque rege KAROLO pacem fecit:· ipsiusque dono terram quam deuastauerat suscipiens. eius fidelitati se commisit:· atque ab eodem Francone archiepiscopo baptizatus. cunctos similiter sui exercitus in fide sanctae trinitatis ui. precibusque baptizati fecit. Inde per quinquennium quod superuixit. cultum Christiane religionis toto mentis adnisu excoluit:· ęcclesias destructas a paganis per totam sue ditionis terram restaurauit. monasterio sancti Michaelis terram ample possessionis quinto die sui baptismatis dedit:· leges iustissimas suis condidit. Brittones rebelles armis sibi subiugauit. atque de eorum cibariis se suosque habundantissime pauit. De hinc coram cunctis optimatibus suis dedit Guillelmo ex Popa nobili Francigena suo filio totam terram sui iuris:· sicque in senectute bona plenus dierum hominem exiuit:· ac sepultus est honorifice Rotomagi in ecclesia beate MARIAE perpetue uirginis.

De Willelmo Rollonis Filio

[12v] Rollone ergo defuncto:· cuncti eius optimates fideliter se conmiserunt supra dicto Guillelmo ipsius filio. qui tanto patri dignus heres

substitutus:· Deo et omnibus se amabilem prebuit hominibus. Hic ut pauca de multis eius memoremus gestis. Brittones sua naturali infidelitate rebellantes sibi armis uiriliter subiugauit. Alannum auctorem huius rebellionis transmare effugauit. Riulfum cum multitudine innumerabili imminentem sibi cum .ccc.tis tantum prelio fudit. Ludouicum regem paterno regno restituit. eundemque suis eum deicere regno molientibus Vesegum usque deducens Henricum trans Renanum regem illi inextricabili federe deuinxit. aliaque plurima strenue egit:· ut legitur in libro qui de eius proprie inscribitur gestis.[1] Inde labilem terreni principatus contempnens honorem. quod etiam superstite patre cupierat habitum suscipere disposuit monachilem:· conuocansque conspicuum optimatum suorum agmen. Richardum filium suum de quo sermo agitur. illorum assensu sibi constituit heredem. Nec multo post ab Arnulfo Flandrensi ad colloquium mutuum euocatus. ipsiusque fraude dolo peremptus:· eternae beatitudinis aulam ut credimus perpetuo intrauit uicturus. Cuius corpus cum ingenti luctu Rodomo delatum:· atque in ecclesia beate MARIę semper uirginis decentissime est tumulatum.

De Richardo Eiusdem Willelmo Filio

[13r] Anno ergo ab incarnatione domini .dcccc.mo xl.o iiii.o Willelmo Normannorum duce prescripto ordine humanis rebus exempto:· cuncti sui optimates subdiderunt se fideliter eius filio Richardo:· tenerrime adhuc etatis puero. uice cordis manus dando. Pudet autem omnino memorare. quot quibusue fraudibus eum Ludouicus rex iniuste disposuit perdere. uel quotiens aggregatis exercitibus plurimis consilio Arnulfi aggressus est eum suosque delere:· aut etiam quotiens Lotharius rex ad colloquium eum euocans molitus sit interimere. siue quomodo Tetboldi Carnotensis suasu terram ipsius sibi temptauerit uendicare. quę omnia iusto iudicio Dei prosequente. illis nequaquam cesserunt impune. Namque Normanni Hairoldo accito Danorum rege cum robore ipsius gentis. captum bello Ludouicum regem custodie manciparunt. bis nouem comitibus ample opinionis eodem bello peremptis:· qui priusquam sue redderetur potestati. eidem puero sacramenti interpositione auctorauit quicquid Rollo suus auus susceperat dono Karoli regis:· seque deinceps fidelissimum tutorem illi et contra omnes inimicos defensorem itidem datis sacramentis spopondit. Sequenti deinceps tempore Lothario rege prelibatis preiudiciis compellente. isdem Richardus egregie forme Ephebus. mixta animositate Normannica cum Dacigena feritate. indicibus cladibus [13v] inimicos suos protriuit circumquaque eorumque terras pessumdedit pene:· per quinquennium continuum Vulcano Marteque seuiente. Sic tandem furore satiato. adung[u]em cum Lothario rege suisque ceteris inimicis diu oratam fecit pacem. eorumque amicitiarum suscipiens conexionem:· firmissimam cunctis sue ditionis contulit quietem. Danorum autem alios sacro baptismate lauatos ad sua remisit maximis muneribus ditatos:· alios uero quos immobiles uidit in paganismo. citra mare emisit bello pulsare Mauros:· ne in aliquo

[1] Dudo, *Moribus*, *Liber Tertius*, ed. J. Lair, pp. 182–200.

officerent Francię regno. Optabili ergo potitus prosperitate: omni reliquo quoad uixit tempore. Deo in omnibus satagebat placere: et ad celestis uite gloriam toto mentis desiderio anhelare. Monachorum clericorumque semper curam gessit ex animo. quos feruentes uidebat in suo ordine summopere honorando. quos uero desides ac tepidos: in melius mutari compellendo. Æcclesiarum alias a fundamentis edificauit: alias a suo statu deiectas predictis malis. in multo ampliore quam prius fuerant statu propriis rebus reparauit. Vnde ut superius prelibatum est paucis: in monasterio sancti MICHAELIS quod est situm in monte Tumba in confinio pagi Abrincensis: monachos sub theorice uite palestra domino militaturos aggregauit. Gaudebat etenim plurimum: intra terminos sui iuris tante auctoritatis haberi locum. Cernens autem potentiores quosque res ipsius ęcclesię canonicorum nomine sibi [fol. 14r] uendicare. ad seruitium uero sancti quosdam abiectissime uilitatis clericulos quasi m[*corr.*]ercenarios annuatim conducere: hoc inhibuit laudabili seueritate. illos tantum decernens canonicos ibi esse. qui Deo legitime deseruire uellent assidue. Quos dum post modum comperisset omnino dissolute uiuere seruitiumque Dei penitus neglegere: ad se eos conuocatos sepissime. ut regularis uite modum susciperent minis blandiciisque satagebat ammonere. Illi uero nichil eius ammonitione mutati in melius: solis comesationibus. uenationibus ceterisque intenti erant uoluptatibus. E contra ille frequentius iterans identidem ammonitionem: nullam eis immittere ualuit morum emendationem. Accito itaque uenerabili Hugone archiepiscopo. simulque fratre suo comite Radulfo singularis magnanimitatis ac prudentię uiro: cum his habuit consilium eiectis clericis ibidem substituere monachos. Hoc acceptabilissimum Deo fore eorum addi[s]cens responsione. iussit eos summo silentio hoc tegere: donec perquisitis idoneis monachis eos illuc deduceret sicut et fecit oportune. Clerici autem animaduersa aduersum se eiusdem principis indignatione: quid uel quantum potuit quisque eorum ex rebus ipsius ęcclesię studuerunt loco emittere. sibique fidelibus aliorsum committere. satius ducentes si sic res urgeret loco cedere: quam sub regularis uitae norma ibi degere.

Qualiter ibidem sint monachi constituti

[14v] FAMOSVS interea Normannorum princeps Richardus: quod ex eodem loco facere disposuerat. haud quaquam procrastinare uoluit diucius. Missis itaque e latere suo strenue nobilitatis uiris: Romane sedis antistiti rem ex ordine. simulque suam super hoc deliberationem insinuauit. Qui benigne hanc suscipiens legationem: apostolica auctoritate adiudicauit religiosi principis debere impleri intentionem. Regressis ergo nuntiis cum licentia apostolice sedi presidentis: isdem princeps aggregatis undecumque idoneis in sancta religione monachis. Abrincis quasi alia tractaturus uenit: iubens monachos se euestigio subsequi. Confestimque de suis unum optimatem ad iam dictum sancti MICHAELIS direxit montem: mandans clericis ut aut sacri monachatus ordinem susciperent. aut a loco exirent. Qui cum uenisset. atque

clauibus reliquiarum ornamentorumque loci a custodibus receptis principis mandatum retulisset: pari obstinatione monachilem ordinem refutantes. iuxta quod premeditauerant ut predictum est loco cedentes. ut cuique uisum est diuersas abierunt in partes. Duo tantum ex eis Durandus uidelicet atque Berneherius dicuntur remansisse: quorum alter eiusdem sancti amore. alter uero scilicet Berneherius corporis detentus est infirmitate. Is ergo ostensa sua infirmitate: orabat ut in suo prefato cubiculo quod erat continguum basilice. quoat uiueret sineretur habitare. Hoc tamen non [fol. 15r] religionis optentu: sed maliuola mente ut corpus sancti AUTBERTI quod ibidem absconderat clanculo furaretur. extorquere nitebatur. Quod isdem legatus omnino cepit denegare: dicens substituendis monachis id molestissimum fore. ipsamque cellulam non infirmis sed ipsius ęcclesię custodibus delegatam fuisse. E contrario ille paucorum saltem expetebat indutias dierum: quasi in quibus perquireret locum habilem sibi adhabitandum. Cumque ille responderet. certissime tribuendam sibi domum quamcumque alias placuisset: ad postremum ipsius diei sequentisque noctis spatium sibi dari instabat procaciter. iurans quod non ante nisi ui cogeretur inde emigraret. Tanta eius quibus res commissa erat pertesi importunitate. simulque reputantes ut sese ueritas habebat eum aliquid ibi abscondisse. quod nocturno silentio moliretur auferre: efferri eum fecerunt inde et in quadam domo poni quae sita erat in eiusdem montis latere. cuncta necessaria illi iubentes tribui habundantissime. His ita gestis: isdem optimas quibusdam suorum ad loci custodiam derelictis. retrogradum iter arripuit: Richardo duci quid egerit nuntiauit. Qui [*corr. ex* quid] e uestigio cum episcopis. abbatibus. ceterisque optimatibus suis ad sepe dictum montem accessit. ac sacram ędem ingressus cum laudibus et hymnis monachos ibidem constituit: domnumque Mainardum abbatem eis prefecit. uirum [fol. 15v] conspicue nobilitatis totiusque sanctitatis. Qui quandiu in reliquum uitali fruitus est aura. paterna seueritate. maternaque affectione ibi constitutis regularia disposuit iura: simulque iuxta preceptum sancti Benedicti assumens sibi curam nuntiandi operis Dei. custodiamque sacre edis: predictum cubiculum Berneherii tam sibi quam fratribus quibus idem officium specialiter commisit ad repausandum delegit. haberi autem quicquam super laquear ipsum nulla suspicio erat. quod nec muribus esse. peruium uidebatur ullo foramine uel exiguo. Mansit ergo incognitum idem corpus beati AVTBERTI .xxx.[ta] et eo amplius annis. usque ad tempus domni Mainardi secundi abbatis quando facto diuinitus miraculo delatum est ab eodem abbate in ecclesiam beati MICHAELIS. ut suo tempore in sequentibus liquebit.

RICHARDVS uero dux menia congrua monachis de suo ibi edificari fecit. altariaque monasterii tabulis aureis et argenteis mirabilis precii decorauit: calices aureos cum crucibus et candelabris incredibilis ponderis addidit. ecclesias. uillas. cunctaque necessaria monachis pro eorum uoto concessit: sicque gaudens a loco discessit. Iam dictus uero abbas sui[que] monachi [*corr. ex* sui monachis] pie tractantes predictum Durandum. ipsius monasterii eum constituerunt capellanum:· et quicquid sui iuris extra maiorem ęcclesiam fuerat benigne sibi reddiderunt. Eodem modo Berne[fol. 16r]herio predicto fecerunt. sua uidelicet restituendo et cuncta uictui necessaria dapsiliter amministrando. Cui licet tantam exibuerint humanitatem. in nullo potuerunt emollire eius animi ferocitatem. quo non post longum tempus supra scripta passione defuncto:· quicquid possederat concesserunt idem monachi supra dicto eius nepoti Fulcholdo. Qui effectus eis fidelissimus. multiplici gaudio eos postmodum exhilarauit [*corr. ex* -arant]:· referendo qualiter ipse suusque auunculus furtiue transtulerint sancti AUTBERTI corpus:·.

RICHARDVS preterea dux cuius studium diuinis cultibus potissimum inuigilabat:· ad idem sancti MICHAELIS monasterium sepe ueniens. maioribus exeniis priora accumulabat:· et magis ac magis in melius prouehi locum conspitiens. ingenti cordis leticia exultabat. Et ne quid minus esset. loco ipsi unde agitur sermo:· tale priuilegium contulit communi optimatum suorum consilio. ut ibidem nullus nisi loci eius monachus. abbatis fungeretur nomine uel officio:· nec alius nisi is quem secundum regulam Sancti Benedicti concors elegisset monachorum congregatio. Quod si necesse foret ibidem prefici monachum alterius congregationis. non a balio eum eligi censuit quam ab eiusdem loci monachis:· hoc obseruato omnimodis ne id omnino fieret. si inter eos huic ordini aptus possit reperiri:· uel extremus congre[fol. 16v]gationis. Huius itaque priuilegii super altare ipsius sancti MICHAELIS posuit concessiuum donum. sibi retinens tantum potestatem tribuendi fratri electo pastoralem baculum. Recogitans uero ne forte ut sese habet proteruitas presumptionis humane. aliquis in posterum uel hęc priuilegia loco auferrre. uel etiam inde monachos moliretur eicere:· a Lothario Francorum rege auctorizari fecit regalis cyrografi preceptione. ut in omni successura progenie isdem locus cum predictis priuilegiis monachili insigniretur ordine. Deinde consilio et hortatu predicti regis. idem cyrografum regię preceptionis domno IOHANNI pape qui Octauiano successerat misit:· orans ut hęc sancita ab eis roborare dignaretur. scripto apostolice auctoritatis. Qui eorum pie assentiens peticioni:· pari consensu Romani concilii subscribendo supra scripta firmauit. cunctosque potioris dignitatis qui eidem generali concilio preerant manibus propriis confirmare fecit:· terribiliter intorquens in illos sententiam excommunicationis. quicumque uel predicta priuilegia auferre monachis. uel eos a loco eicere temptauerit. Vtriusque igitur et regis scilicet et domni predicti apostolici sacrum. sepe dictus dux Richardus super aram sancti MICHAELIS ad perhenne posuit testimonium:· diligenter illud seruari percipiens in posterum. ad noticiam sequentium. E quibus ne uideremur talia commentari a nobis. preceptum ipsius domni papae [fol. 17r] IOHANNIS his subindere libuit:· aduersus eos qui non ut pastores per hostium. sed ut fures et latrones aliunde se ingesserunt. uel ingerere querunt eidem sancti MICHAELIS ouili.

Sacrum.[1] *Domni pape Iohannis. Super priuilegium coenobii montis sancti Michaelis.*

NOVERIT CVNCTORVM noticia fidelium. quod ego IOHANNES pii conditoris clementia sancte Romane sedis existens indignus papa. gloriosi Francorum regis LOTHARII. nec non et sanctae Rotomagensis ęcclesię archipresulis HUGONIS. atque RICHARDI Normannorum marchissi. summisso pulsatus rogatu. pro Monte Sancti MICHAELIS uidelicet in maris pelago sito. quem ipsi acti amore superi regis in melius restaurarant monachorum inibi aggregantes normam. preceptoque regali firmauerant:· quod et ipse hoc facere non differrem. Quorum assentiens benigne peticioni:· astruo et corroboro. quo finetenus in eo quo nunc pollet permaneat monachili ordine:· ipsique monachi de suis sibi adhibeant pastorem. Siquis autem id molitus fuerit contraire:· ex auctoritate patris. et filii. et spiritus sancti. sancteque Dei genitricis. ac sancti MICHAELIS. sanctorumque canonum. perpetue sit addictus maledictioni. [fol. 17v] nisi resipuerit. Nostraque stipulatio inconuulsa permaneat. Actumque est hoc:· tempore Mainardi eiusdem montis abbatis.

HAEC igitur iam dictus rex Lotharius sacro scripto Luduni confirmauit. xii. anno regni sui. qui fuit nongentesimus sexagesimus quintus dominice incarnationis:· quo etiam anno similiter auctorata sunt Romę ut dictum est. ab eodem papa. in sinodo generali.

PERPENDANT igitur contemptores huius interminationis:· quante subiaceant sententie excommunicationis. Et quidem beato Petro principi apostolorum:· Christus ligandi soluendique presulatum. clauesque simul tradidit regni celorum. Romane autem sedis antistes:· ipsius apostolici uicarius. potestatisque potissimum noscitur heres. Hoc suo tempore sancte memorię predictus Iohannes extitit:· ad id promotus Dei tociusque electione populi. Si ergo decretum beati Petri apostoli est ratum:· consequenter et Iohannis apostolici [*corr. ex* apostoli] est ratum. Sed nemo uel demens:· ratum esse Petri decretum denegat. Nemo igitur sane mentis:· dissimile fore Iohannis repugnat. Aut igitur isti concedentes beato Petro suisque successoribus collatam a Christo potestatem. transgredi timebunt tante excommunicationis auctoritatem:· aut flocipendentes cum diabolo suisque consimilibus prescripte maledictionis sibi adquirent perpetuitatem. Hoc etiam memoratu non excesserit:· quod [fol. 18r] sanctus MICHAEL prouisor loci. nullius horum corporis tumulatione ipsum maculari permiserit:· licet iam quosdam non abbates sed lupos rapaces potentia secularis ibi quasi persepem precipitauerit. Constat enim nullum extraneorum idem cenobium sibi preripuisse. quem non constiterit nec sine dedecore amisisse. nulla hoc monachorum machinatione:· sed Dei sancteque auctoritatis agente ultione. Huius autem noxam offensionis fons misericordiae famulo tuo Radulfo abbati indųlgere digneris:· cuius nos obitu absentiaque tristes. heu in salicibus in medio Babilonis nostra

1 Sacrum ... fatebitur, B.N. lat. 14832 fols. 177v–178r. After *fatebitur* B.N. lat. 14832 adds material not in the cartulary but printed in the appendix below.

suspendere organa dedisti.[1] Nemo itaque hęc legens despiciat:· nemo uel subirascendo se palam notabilem faciat. Nam si irascitur:· de alio forte prolatum. de se dictum fatebitur.

[7 blank lines]

SIGNVM GLORIOSISSIMI LOTHARII REGIS [fol. 18v] IN NOMINE SANCTE ET INDIVIDVE TRINITATIS LOTHARIVS GRATIA DEI REX

Si ea quae predecessores nostri diuina dignatione illuminati. et piis ammonitionibus seruorum Dei instigati. pro utilitatibus ecclesiarum et necessitatibus seruorum Dei supplendis statuere decreuerunt nostris confirmamus edictis. regiam exercemus consuetudi[*corr. ex* a]nem:· et hoc nobis ad presentem uitam felicius peragendam. et ad futuram capessendam profuturum. proculdubio confidimus. Iccirco notum sit omnibus fidelibus nostris presentibus scilicet atque futuris. quendam esse locum montem sancti MICHAELIS dictum. situm in maris pelago. quem modernis diebus amore ductus regis eterni Richardus Normannorum marchisus cum auctoritate domni Iohannes sancte Romane sedis pape restaurauit in melius. aggregans monachorum cetum diuinarum legum sanctionibus iugiter inherentium. Pro cuius perpetuo roboramine atque stabilitate domni prefati pape. nec non memorati marchisi. atque Hugonis sancte Rotomagensis ęcclesię archiepiscopi. ad cuius diocesim pertinet iam dictus locus:· nostras deuenit ad au[fol. 19r]res peticio. id ipsum nostro perpetuo manendum roborare fulcimine. Quorum rato decreto nostra excellentia hilaris reddita. ac eorum uoluntati aurem accommodantes:· ueluti postulauerant [*corr. ex* -uerunt] fieri adiudicauimus. Vnde regali auctoritate et indulgentia. per hoc preceptum nostre confirmationis stabili iure eundem locum in eodem quo nunc pollet ordine uidelicet monachili permanere concedimus omni tempore eui:· precipientes regia potestate. ut nemo successorum nostrorum regum. neque quislibet eiusdem regni marchisus. neque qui in sancta Rotomagensi ecclesia presul per subuenientia tempora successerit. quod nostro roboratum est inuiolabili decreto infringere audeat. quatinus inibi Deo seruientes ac diuini seruitii cultores libere Deo seruiant:· et pro nobis ac tocius regni nobis a Deo collati conseruatione exorare queant. Et hoc preceptum quod ob amorem omnipotentis Dei et remedium animę nostrae. roborauimus. ut firmiorem obtineat uigorem. manus nostrę conscriptione subter firmauimus:· et de anulo nostro sigillari iussimus. [fol. 19v is an illustration]

Printed: E. de Beaurepaire, in Th. Le Roy, *Les Curieuses Recherches* (1878), i, 407–35; *Gallia Christiana*, xi, Inst. col. 106. There are numerous manuscript copies of these texts, especially the *Revelatio*. A full list will be found in the editions currently being prepared by Pierre Bouet.

The diploma of Lothar was printed in *Recueil des actes de Lothaire et de Louis V, rois de France (954–987)*, ed. Louis Halphen and Ferdinand Lot, Paris 1908, no. 24.

[1] Psalm 136(/7), i.

For a critique of the history of St. Autbert see M. Lelegard, 'Saint Aubert', in *Mill. mon. MSM*, i, 29–52; Dom Jacques Hourlier, 'Sources anciennes de l'histoire montoise', *ib.* 121–132.

2

Grant (interpolated) by Richard II of Normandy of the abbey of Saint-Pair in the Cotentin, with appurtenances in an area limited in the east by the public road to Coutances, in the north by the river Venlée, in the west by the sea and the isle of Chausey and in the south by the stream named Thar; the church of Chanteloup, with interests at Bricqueville, Flamanville and Lengronne; the moiety of Hérenguerville and land at Vesly; also in the *pagus* of Coutances, La Colombe, and the land of Abbot Hildebert's father Bernard at Rouilly, a hamlet of Cérences; in the *pagus* of Bayeux, the domain of Verson with its dependent churches and the moiety of Mondrainville; he confirms his mother's gift of dower land at Bretteville-sur-Odon (no. **4** below), and restores grants by his grandfather William Longsword of demesnes and churches in the Avranchin that had later been usurped by Count Robert (see no. **31**) at Moidrey, Charcey, Marigny, Curey, Forge, Soligny, Dameigné, Macey, Les Challiers, *Peleton*, Cormeray, all in the modern canton of Pontorson, Vergoncey (cant. Saint-James), Meigné (cant. Ducey), and the vill of Saint-Jean-le-Thomas (cant. Sartilly), with vines, mill and pasture, and the vill of Le Mesnil-Ranger (now Le Mesnil-Adelé, cant. Juvigny) in the vale of the castelry of Mortain; he cedes his right to the tolls from itinerant merchants and the right of appointment of clergy to the church of Saint-Pierre, on the flanks of the Mont; the act concludes with an interpolation, made *c.* 1058/60, in which Richard is made to confirm the privileges granted by Richard I and Pope John XIII that were forged by the monks of Mont-Saint-Michel *c.* 1027/30: dated from the episcopacy of Maugis at Avrances, 1022–1026.

[fol. 20r] *Carta quam Comes Richardus fecit Sancto Michaeli ante obitum suum Fiscanno*

IN NOMINE. SANCTE. ET INDIVIDVE. TRINITATIS. PATRIS. ET FILII. ET SPIRITVS SANCTI. AMEN. Antecessorum nostrorum institutionibus sancitum decretumque est quatinus si quis suarum facultatum quiddam loco sanctorum alicui uite superne accensus amore perhenniter possidendum tradere uoluerit:· sollempne exinde idonearum personarum plurimis astipulationibus fulcitum. ut id inconuulsum permaneat testamentum faciat. Referentibus enim quam plurimis sancte Dei ęcclesie doctoribus. diuinum esse preceptum didici:· ut illic nostri recondantur thesauri. ubi omnis aberit furum formido. omnisque tinearum demolitio. Esseque quoddam peccatorum purgatorium elemosinam. et quod Deus in largiendo munificos exposcit:· qui se in retribuendo preparat munificentissimum. Detur igitur Deo:· non nostrum sed suum.[1] Quid enim

[1] Cf. Mark xii, 17; Matthew xxii, 21.

aliud nos habere [fol. 20v] putamus. quam quod ab eo accepimus? Tribuatur frigidę aquę calix. ut eterna recipiatur merces. Tanti ualere regnum audimus Dei: quantum habemus. Suffecit uidue: quadrans.[1] Profuit et Zacheo bonorum dimidium distributio.[2] Que denique ad id quod finitur. ad id quod non finitur comparatio? Scilicet pro terrenis cęlestia. pro perituris mereri perpetua? His et aliis diuine auctoritatis incitatus hortamentis. ego Richardus gratia Dei dux et princeps Normannorum penas inferni cupiens effugere. et paradysi gaudia desiderans habere post mortem corporis: loco sancti archangeli MICHAELIS sito in monte qui dicitur Tumba. fratribusque ibidem Deo monastice famulantibus. trado abbatiam sancti Paterni sitam in pago Constantino cum terris cultis et incultis. cum ecclesiis et molendinis. cum pratis et siluis. quę terminatur ab oriente uia puplica tendente Constantias: A septemtrione: riuulo nomine Venleia: A meridie fluuiolo nomine Tarn: Ab occasu: mare occeano cum insula quę dicitur Calsoi: Do etiam uillam quę dicitur Chantelou cum ecclesia et molendino. cum siluis et omnibus apendiciis. terram quoque Grimbaldi quę sita est in Briqueuilla. et in Flamencuilla. et in Lengrona. et medietatem Erengartuille. terram etiam Durandi quę est intra termi[fol. 21r]nos uille quę nuncupatur Verlei. et terram Petri monachi quę est in insula Gersoi. Columbam iterum sitam in eodem supra nominato pago. cum ecclesia et molendino. et cum siluis. Terram etiam Bernardi patris domni Heldeberti abbatis quę est in territorio uille quę nominatur Rotoloi. cum molendino et pratis. Trado etiam donatione perpetua quandam uillam sitam in pago Baiocasino nomine Versum cum omni terra quę ad eam pertinet culta et inculta. cum ecclesiis et molendinis omnibus et siluulis. Medietatemque uillę Mondretuillę. quae huic adiacet terre. Confirmo insuper donationem matris meę de Britauilla. quam de suo dotalitio. loco superius dicto obtulit. pro patris mei suaque salute. ac mea. meorumque fratrum. Villulas quoque quas auus meus Willelmus in pago Abrincantino sancto MICHAELI tradidit. sed Robertus comes postea ui abstulit reddo. quę his uocitantur nominibus. Maldrei. Carcei. Marrinnei. Curei. Forges. Solinnei. Dummannei. Macei. Scallei. Peleton. dimidium Cromeret. Verguncei. Mannei. Sancti Iohannis iterum uillam prope litus maris sitam. cum ecclesia et uineis. et molendino. et pratis. et uillam in ualle castelli Moretoin quę dicitur Maisnilranger: do. Teleonumque tocius abbatie. et de mercatoribus uenientibus et pertranseuntibus; Monasterium etiam Sancti Petri [fol. 21v] apostolorum principis situm in latere montis ipsius tribuo. ea lege ut abbas uel monachi ibidem pro mea meorumque filiorum salute clericos constituant. quos uoluerint. Si quem autem ex illis sordide aut neglegenter res sanctae Dei ęcclesię tractare perspexerint. potestatem habebunt diuinum officium ei interdicendi: et nisi correxerit. eo deposito alium in illius locum subrogandi. <Omnes ad postremum consuetudines ipsius uille tam ad me quam ad

[1] Mark xii, 42.

[2] Luke xix, 8.

Abrincatensem episcopum pertinentes: sicut sanctę memorie pater meus Richardus auctoritate Romani pape constituit perpetualiter possidendas tribuo: ea ratione. ut in omni successura generatione abbas uel monachi ipsius Montis omnes leges omnesque forisfacturas clericorum ac laicorum. uirorum ac mulierum eiusdem burgi. absque calumpnia cuiusquam nostrorum successorum. seu predicte sedis episcoporum possideant: et queque corrigenda fuerint corrigant. Qui si in aliquo a rectitudinis tramite quod quidem absit deuiauerint. curamue animarum incolarum loci neglexerint: iam dicte sedis episcopus. siue Deum timentes uicini in noticiam hoc deferre curent[*corr.*] principis qui illis temporibus Normannorum dux fuerit. ad quem deinceps pertineat corrigere ea. consilio Rotomagiensis archiepiscopi. ceterorumque optimatum prouintiae. Porro de ordinatione abbatum uel monachorum siue clericorum loci hoc de[fol. 22r]cernimus: ut iuxta quod a supra dicto meo genitore sancitum est generali assensu Romani concilii. monachi sepefati monasterii ordinandos sibi eligant: et ut sibi placuerit a quolibet episcopo sue uicinitatis. aut in illius sede. aut in suo monasterio ordinari faciant. > Hęc omnia prenotata Deo sanctoque archangelo MICHAELI in eius predicti Montis monasterio placuit tradere: pro meę redemptione anime . pro mei quoque patris uel matris et uxoris filiorumque meorum Richardi et aliorum salute quorum uoluntate consensuque id ago. sub testimonio Christi tociusque ęcclesię. eo tenore. ea lege. ut absque calumpnatione seu contradictione omnium succedentium. siue parentum seu quorumcumque aliorum. prefatus locus et habitantes in eo habeat. teneat. possideat. Quod si aliquis diabolice prauitatis telo iaculatus qualicumque modo his calumpniationis uim inferre presumpserit: ipse consentientesque sibi tocius excommunicationis atque maledictionis cum Iuda traditore et Dathan et Abiron. perhennibus perhenniter irretiatur uinculis. Vt autem huius donationis auctoritas [*corr. ex* -tatis] uerius credatur. et diligentius per omnia conseruetur. firmiusque futuris teneatur temporibus: manu propria subter firmare curaui. fideliumque meorum nomina quorum consensu id egi subscribi imperaui:

Signum + Richardi. comitis. [secundus. filii magni Richardi qui et uetus dicitur]. Signum + Richardi [tertius] filii eius. [fol. 22v] Signum + Rotberti filii eius. Ego Mangisus sancte Abrincatensis ęcclesię episcopus: hanc donationis cartulam manu propria uoluntariae confirmo. + Rotbertus archiepiscopus. Hugo episcopus Baiocacensis. Robertus episcopus Constantie. Hugo episcopus Ebroicensis. Herbertus episcopus Luxouiensis. Niellus uicecomes. Tursten uicecomes. Alueredus uicecomes. Walterius uicecomes. Richardus. uicecomes. Guimundus. uicecomes. Hubertus. Osbernus. frater comitisse. Hunfredus. frater eius. Roscelinus. Normannus. Silueron. Bernardus filius eius. Osbernus. filius Arfast. Rannulfus frater eius. Hugo clericus. et multi alii.

Printed: Fauroux, 49, from the cartulary. The original of this act, which must date between 1022 and 1026 is lost. As Fauroux notes, Dom Leroy made a copy from the original in the Archives du Mont in the seventeenth century in B. N. fr. 18950, p. 8. However, this 'original' contained the passage printed here between brackets which was certainly an interpolation added *c.* 1058–60. On the interpolation see J.-F. Lemarignier, *Etude sur les privilèges d'exemption et de jurisdiction ecclésiastique des abbayes normandes depuis les origines jusqu'en 1140* (Paris, 1937), p. 29 and note 10, pp. 156–61, 252–4, and especially pp. 264–6. Lemarignier thought that this charter, interpolation apart, could belong to a group of charters given at Fécamp in August 1025, printed as Fauroux, 34–36, though only further analysis could determine this. In fact, Fauroux, 53 is likely to have been a fourth member of the group, of which the Mont-Saint-Michel charter did not form part. The formulae in the Mont charter are directly comparable to nos. **4** and **31** in the Cartulary, charters of Gunnor and of Count Robert, the substance of which is referred to in this charter. The opening of the *arenga* is the same in both no. **2** and no. **4**, and similar to that in no. **31**; the same quotations from the Gospels occur in all three, which also have very similar comminatory and corroboration clauses. (The opening *arenga* and the gospel citations all reappear in the opening of the Gohory pancarte, no. **34**). There are also strong textual echoes in no. **3**, in which Richard grants the allod of Verson mentioned in no. **2**. The charter heading indicates that the charter was given late in Richard's reign, before his death at Fécamp in August 1027, but does not mean that the charter was given at Fécamp. Given the intimate relationship between this charter and nos. **4** and **31**, and Richard's important rôle as patron of the Mont, it is most likely that the charter arose out of a visit of Richard to Mont-Saint-Michel, perhaps soon after the installation of Bishop Maugis in 1022, and soon after the grant made in no. **3**.

3

Grant by Richard II of Normandy of his allod at Verson, in the Bessin, for the redemption of the souls of himself, his parents, his wife and his children; attested by Richard's second wife Papia and by Bishop Maugis: 1022–1026.

Carta de Verson

IN NOMINE SANCTE ET INDIVIDVE TRINITATIS PATRIS [ET FILII] ET SPIRITVS SANCTI. Inter cetera bene agende uite opera non minima. laude predicatur [elemosina] sicut ait saluator noster. date elemosinam:' et omnia mundabuntur uobis. Et alio loco. Sicut aqua extinguit ignem:' ita elemosina extinguit peccatum. Redemptio enim anime uiri:' diuitie eius. Salutare quippe opus ualde nobis est. si ea quae conditor noster nobis misericorditer tribuit:' ei reddamus. Quae namque coemptio felicior potest esse. quam dare obolum et recipere caelum? Dare peritura. et recipere aeterna? Dare terrena. et assequi cęlestia? Venale siquidem regnum celorum dicitur. Ad quod [fol. 23r] emendum. unicuique sufficit proprius census:' cum bona uoluntate. Viduae suffecit quadrans:' Bonorum dimidium:' Zacheo. Iusto:' frigide aque calix. Quid plura? Tantum credimus ualere regnum celorum:' quantum quisque habet. His et aliis diuine auctoritatis incitatus hortamentis. ego Richardus gratia Dei dux et princeps Normannorum:' penas inferni cupiens effugere. et paradysi gaudia desiderans habere post corporis mortem:' loco sancti MICHAELIS sito in monte qui dicitur Tumba. fratribusque ibidem Deo monastice seruientibus:' trado quandam

uillam mei proprii Alodi. sitam in pago Baiocasino nomine Versun. cum omni terra quę ad eam pertinet culta et inculta. et omnibus molendinis. cum pratis. et siluulis. Hoc autem facio pro redemptione anime mee. patris mei matrisque mee et uxoris. meorum quoque filiorum. Quod si aliquis huius donationis testamentum. quod ego hodie constituo pro salute mea. aliquando uiolare presumpserit:· perpetua maledictione dampnetur cum Iuda traditore domini. et cum omnibus fidem dominis suis non seruantibus. Vt autem huius donationis auctoritas uerius credatur. et futuris temporibus per omnia firmius conseruetur:· manu propria subter firmare curaui. Signum. Richardi magni comitis. Signum Richardi filii eius. [fol. 23v] Signum Rotberti filii eius. Signum Willelmi. Signum Gonnor matris comitis. Signum Papię uxoris comitis. Signum Rotberti archiepiscopi. Signum Hugonis Baiocacensis episcopi. Signum Hugonis Ebroiacensis episcopi. Signum Mangisi Abrincatensis episcopi.
[Illustration]

Printed: Fauroux, 47, from the cartulary: original lost. V. Hunger, *Verson*, p. 3 no. 3, printed a facsimile of the original *vidimus* by Philip VI, December 1334, which was destroyed in the Archives de la Manche in 1944. Printed in *Cartulaire de Jersey*, no. 3, pp. 5–8, from the *vidimus*.

4

Grant by Gunnor widow of Richard I of Normandy, for the salvation of her husband, her sons, including Richard II and Archbishop Robert, and herself, of the allods of Bretteville-sur-Odon (Calvados, cant. Caen) and Domjean (Manche, cant. Tesssy-sur-Vire), part of the extensive dower settled on her by her husband: the occurrence together as witnesses of Hugh bishop of Bayeux and Robert Uspac abbot of Jumièges fixes the date as 1015, the year in which Uspac died and Hugh became bishop.

[fol. 24r] *Carta de Britauilla. et de Donno Iohanne*

IN NOMINE SANCTE ET INDIVIDVE TRINTITATIS PATRIS ET FILII ET SPIRITVS SANCTI. Antecessorum nostrorum institutionibus sancitum decretumque est quatinus si quis suarum facultatum quiddam loco sanctorum alicui. [*corr. ras*] uite superne accensus amore perhenniter possidendum tradere uoluerit:· sollempne exinde idonearum personarum plurimis astipulationibus fulcitum ut id inconuulsum permaneat testamentum faciat. Quodcirca ego Gonnor esse tam presentibus quam absentibus omnibus utique sub christianitatis titulo degentibus notum uolo. quod meorum inmensitatem criminum metuens uiteque celestis gaudium desiderans:· duo aloda Brittauillam uidelicet et Donnum Iohannem quę michi meus sanctę recordationis uir Richardus comes. cum plurimis in dotalicium dedit loco beati MICHAELIS fratribusque ibidem regulariter Deo seruientibus pro anime ipsius dicti uiri precipue remedio. deinde pro meę animę et corporis. filiorumque meorum Richardi comitis. archiepiscopique Rotberti et aliorum salute. quorum uoluntate.

consensu. donationeque id ago: perpetualiter possidenda trado et tribuo. Referentibus et enim quam plurimis ecclesiasticis doctoribus. dinoui diuinum esse. preceptum ut illic nostri recondantur thesauri. ubi omnis aberit furum formido: omnisque tinearum demolitio. Esseque [fol. 24v] quoddam peccatorum purgatorium elemosinam. Et quod Deus in largiendo munificos exposcit. qui se in retribuendo preparat munificentissimum. Detur igitur Deo: non nostrum sed suum. Quid enim habere putamus. quam quod ab eo accepimus? Tribuatur frigide aque calix. ut eterna recipiatur merces. Tanti ualere regnum audiuimus Dei: quantum habemus: suffecit uidue. quadrans: profuit et Zacheo: bonorum dimidium. Quę denique ad id quod finitur. ad id quod non finitur comparatio? pro terrenis scilicet celestia. pro perituris mereri perpetua? His igitur et aliis multimodis salutiferis incitata documentis. predicta aloda loco prelibato confero sub Christi tociusque aecclesiae testimonio. cum terris cultis et incultis. cum ecclesiis. cum molendinis. cum pratis. et cum omnibus omnino appendiciis. atque cum reditibus et consuetudinibus cunctis. quas [*corr. ex* quos] in predictis uillis usque ad diem istam habui. eo tenore. ea lege. ut absque calumpniatione seu contradictione omnium succedentium siue parentum siue quorumque aliorum. prefatus locus et habitantes in eo habeat. teneat. possideat. Quod si aliquis diabolice prauitatis telo iaculatus. huic donationi calumpniationis alicuius uim inferre presumpserit: tocius excommunicationis atque maledictionis perhennibus perhenniter irretiatur uinculis. Vt autem huius donationis auctoritas uerius credatur et diligentius per omnia conseruetur firmiusque futuris teneatur temporibus: [fol. 25r] manibus filiorum meorum comitis quidem archiepiscopi subter firmandam corroborandamque tradidi. + Rotberti archiepiscopi. + Maalgerii + Roberti. + Hugonis Constanciensis episcopi. + Hugonis Baiocacensis episcopi. + Hugonis Sais episcopi. + Rogeri. episcopi. + Norgoti episcopi. + Heldeberti abbatis. + Willelmi abbatis. + Vspac abbatis. + Willelmi laici. + Rotberti comitis. + Godefredi. + Willelmi. + Radulfi. + Tursteni . + Tescelini uicecomitis. + Herluini. + Anschetil. uicecomitis. + Willelmi filii Tursteni. + Hugonis laici. + Gerardi. + Osmundi clerici. + Gaufredi. + Arfast. + Nielli. + Guimundi. + Anschitilli. + Milonis. + Rainaldi. + Odonis. + Rannulfi. [*within a monogram* Richardus comes] [9 blank lines, folio 25v is an illustration]

Printed: Fauroux, 17, from the cartulary, and Hunger, *Histoire de Verson* (1908), pièces just., p. 1, no. 1: original lost.

5

Charter (interpolated) of Robert I of Normandy by which, for the salvation of himself, his parents and his brothers and sisters, he renounces the rights on the abbey claimed by his forebears; he also concedes the moiety of the isle of Guernsey and its revenues, reserving the other moiety which is held by his *fidelis* Niel, vicomte of the Cotentin; the domain of Saint-Jean-le-Thomas, the forest of Bevais and rights pertaining to Saint-James-de-Beuvron, in the county of Avranches; five mills in the domain of Verson on the Odon, in the county of Bayeux; passages interpolated later concede also interests at Tissy, Dragey and elsewhere which were among those usurped by Count Robert of Avranches (no. **31** below); the monks are to hold free from all obligations and interference by officers of the state, as if the benefice was part of the dominical fisc: 1027–35.

[fol. 26r] *Carta quam fecit comes Rotbertus Sancto Michaeli de omnibus que dedit ei postquam consulatum suscepit*

IN NOMINE SANCTE ET INDIVIDVE TRINITATIS PATRIS ET FILII ET SPIRITVS SANCTI <AMEN>

Ego Rotbertus comes filius magni Richardi. gratia Dei dux. et princeps Normannorum: reddo sancto MICHAELI altare suum cum toto monasterio. quod predecessores mei sibi hactenus uindicauerant. Reddo autem illud tali conditione: ut quecumque a fidelibus populis ibi Deo et sancto MICHAELI fuerint oblata. monachi ibidem Deo seruientes omnino habeant. teneant. et possideant. in loci utilitate: nec ulterius ueniat in custodia clericorum aut laicorum. nisi abbatis et monachorum. Et hoc facio pro remedio animarum parentum meorum. patris et matris. fratrum et sororum: et mea. Concedo etiam de rebus quas ad proprios usus iure hereditario possidebam. et in usus seruorum Dei in eodem loco sancti MICHAELIS archangeli seruientium sollempniter transfundo. id est medietatem insule quae dicitur Greneroy ad integrum. et ex altera medietate quam quidam fidelis noster nomine Nigellus in beneficio tenet omnes consuetudines quas in meos usus retinebam. [fol. 26v] hoc est melagium.[a] et omnia quecumque ex ipso beneficio meis usibus proueniunt. Concedo denique in comitatu Abrincatensi uillam quę dicitur Sancti Iohannis. sitam supra mare. cum omnibus ad eam pertinentibus. <uidelicet Drageium cum ecclesia et Poterel. et Tisseium. et Tisseel. et Goolt. et Obreium. et Landam. et Belleuillam cum cęteris omnibus.> Siluam quoque quę dicitur Biuia cum siluulis quibusdam aspicientibus ad eam. <scilicet Crapout et Neiron.> In eodem siquidem comitatu dono. et in perpetuum donatum esse uolo in burgo quod appellatur Beurona[b] quicquid in eo mei iuris erat. cum. viii.^{to} molendinis. et teloneo. et <cum> omnibus consuetudinibus ad totum ipsum burgum pertinentibus in omni parte. <cum omnibus terris quę in circuitu sunt.> Addo quoque molendinos quinque et ęcclesiam in comitatu Baiocacensi in uilla quę dicitur Verson super fluuium qui dicitur Oldum[c] ut habeant iure perpetuo. Hęc omnia pro animę meę remedio et genitorum meorum. nec non etiam fratrum et sororum transfundo libens. et concedo in usus cotidianos seruorum Dei. qui die noctuque peruigiles diuinis obsequiis uel nostris adsunt temporibus. uel futuri sunt in prenominato sancti archangeli MICHAELIS cenobio: ut his temporaliter sustentati. quietam et tranquillam Dei miseratione. et nostra heredum quoque nostrorum tuitione agant uitam: et ne aliorsum ullis unquam temporibus [fol.

27r] querentes uictus subsidia ab assiduitate diuinorum obsequiorum seiungantur: uolo ut hęc iure perpetuo teneant. possideant. habeant. absque ulla reclamatione. et publicorum ministrorum inquietudine. sicut res ad fiscum dominicum pertinentes. Precor autem eorum qui michi in hoc quem propicia diuinitate teneo successerint honore animos. ut sicut suę auctoritatis inconuulsa quę locis sanctis pro suarum remediis animarum constituent obtabunt precepta. ita hoc nostre deuotionis preceptum inconuulsum et incontaminatum obseruent: ne quod michi spe firmissima per Dei gratiam profuturum credo ad animę meae salutem. uiolatorum temeritati quod absit. proueniat ad dampnationem. Si quis autem aliquando postposita hac peticione instinctu diaboli commotus hoc decretum uiolare. uel aliorsum uertere presumserit: in diem magni iudicii Deo et sancto MICHAELI rationem reddere cogatur. Et ut hoc inconuulsum permaneat. et omnibus seculis notum: manu propria subter firmo. fidelium quoque nostrorum testimoniis firmandum trado. + Roberti archiepiscopi. Signum Herberti episcopi. Signum Hugonis episcopi. Signum Hugonis Ebroicacensis episcopi. Signum +. Ego Rotbertus princeps Normannorum gratia Dei dux. hanc donationem manu propria corroboraui. et meis fidelibus corroborandum tradidi. Signum Rogerii filii Hugonis. Signum Rotberti pincerne. Signum Nielli uicecomitis. [fol. 27v] Signum Nielli filii eius. Signum Goiffredi. Farsels uicecomitis. Signum Aymonis uicecomitis. Signum Hugonis uicecomitis. Signum Rogerii filii Radulfi. Signum Turstingi uicecomitis.

Printed: Fauroux, 73, from a facsimile of the original, destroyed in 1944, in Arch. dépt. de la Manche, H, fonds du Mont-Saint-Michel; Hunger, *Histoire de Verson* (1908), pièces just., p. 5, no. 5, accompanied by a photograph of the original; *Cartulaire de Jersey*, no. 114, from a *vidimus* of 1270; Lechaudé d'Anisy, *Arrondissement de Caen*, p. 111, no. 4, following the Cartulary. In a gap between the end of the act and the subscriptions to it a contemporary scribe inserted an original charter of Robert's son William II (no. 7). The twelfth-century interpolations in the cartulary are given in brackets above. These have the character almost of glosses and were probably associated with the composition of the Cartulary. Other variants from the original were: [a] melaium [b] Beuerona [c] uocatur Oldon. The original adds further witnesses: Gozilini uicecomitis, Rodulfi uicecomitis, Turoldi constabili. Compare Fauroux, 65 (**Appendix ii.3**), a shorter version of the same act and one which certainly belongs to the time of Abbot Almod (1027/8–1032).

Calendared in Round, *Calendar of Documents in France*, no. 705, from the original.

6

Notification concerning the mill of Vains (Manche, cant. Avranches), confirmed to the abbey in 1061 by William II of Normandy, earlier granted by Robert I but subsequently alienated to Ranulf *monetarius* by Abbot Suppo after Robert's death at Nicaea in July 1035; Abbot Ranulf subsequently redeemed the mill from Ranulf's son Waleran and his kindred, and gave 33 pounds of Le Mans to William II for his confirmation of the mill to the abbey in perpetuity; fifteen years later, Abbot Ranulf sought the judgement of William, now king of England, against a claim by John son of Richard on the mill; the king appointed Bishop Geoffrey of Coutances to hear the case and finally gave judgement for the abbey: *c.* 1061–76.

Carta de molendino comitis

IN NOMINE SANCTE ET INDIVIDVE TRINITATIS PATRIS ET FILLI ET SPIRITVS SANCTI AMEN. Antiquorum sollers prouidentia. approbabili more instituit. super quasque possessiones ecclesiarum cartarum adhiberi testimonia: quibus uiriliter opprimatur quotiens emerserit calumpniatorum peruicax insolentia. Ea ergo intentione commodum duximus noticie posterorum tradere: qualiter deuenerit in dominio monachorum sancti MICHAELIS molendinum <comitis>. de quo Iohannes filius Richardi conatus est eidem sancto archangelo calumpniam struere: et qualiter eadem calumpnatio oppressa sit iusto iudicio optimatum patrię breuiter· annectere. Igitur gloriose recordationis Rotbertus dux Normannorum qui abbatiam montis sancti MICHAELIS amplis fundorum reditibus nobilissime dilatauit. prefatum molendinum quod in proprio iure tenebat aliaque quam plurima eidem loco sollempni largitione condonauit: et ne quisquam sequentum[a] auderet adimere quicquam ex iis iuri sancti MICHAELIS cum terribili [fol. 28r] anathemate cyrographum fieri imperauit. digestumque. manu sua roborauit. Qui postquam in reditu Ierosolimitano apud Niceam hominem exiens ęternę uite ut credimus sullimatus est solio. Suppo abbas ipsius loci contra ius fasque idem molendinum dedit Rannulfo monetario. monachis id contradicentibus unanimi consilio. Post modum autem iam domni Rannulfi abbatis temporibus. idem molendinum Gualerannus filius Rannulfi optinuit ceteris suę parentele multipliciter deficientibus. a quo prefatus domnus abbas Rannulfus non minimo pretio illud redemit pluribus adhibitis testibus: etiam gloriosissimo seniore nostro Guillelmo tunc quidem Normannorum principe. deinceps quoque Anglorum rege id annuente scriptoque confirmante coram suis fidelibus. ut liquet ipsius uerbis insequentibus quę ex alia huic membranule annexa sunt propriis caracteribus.

Ego Willemus gratia Dei tocius Normannie comes. rogatus multis modis ab abbate Rannulfo monasterii beati archangeli MICHAELIS quod est in monte qui Tumba antiquitus nuncupatur. concessi eidem loco molendinum in uilla[b] quę Veim uocatur perpetuo possidendum: largiente michi eodem abbate sua spontanea uoluntate ob memoriale sempiternum triginta tres libras Cenomannensium. Et ut hęc mea donatio inconuulsa in posterum successionibus maneat perpetim;[c] subter manu propria sig[fol. 28v]num uiuifice crucis imprimere curaui. Signum gloriosissimi Normannorum ducis Guillelmi. +. Testes autem affuerunt. Iohannes presul Abrincensis. +. Hugo presul Luxouiensis. + Rotbertus [Bertram] .+. Richardus uicecomes. +. Radulfus cubicularius .+. Radulfus filius eius. et alii quam plurimi.

Hinc iam post quindecim plus minusue annorum intersticia. prefato serenissimo rege Willelmo indepto ac nobiliter gubernante Anglici regni fastigia. supradictus Iohannes ad calumpniandum idem molendinum insperate prosiliit sui consimilium animatus insania:˙ et quasi precepto eiusdem incliti regis ipso penitus ignorante saisiuit illud non premissa iuste probationis audientia. Sepefato uero domno Rannulfo abbate haud eneruiter obsistente. et tale preiuditium sancto MICHAELI ac sibi illatum esse regi suggerente:˙ tandem in regali curia locus datus est disceptandi utrinque numerositate optimatum patrię assidente. E quibus domnus Gaufredus Constantiarum presul est delegatus regali auctoritate discussor et iudex huius disceptationis. pariterque Rannulfus uicecomes. Niellus filius Nielli. Rotbertus de Vezpunt. aliique quam plures iudices amplę opinionis:˙ qui diligenter et ad unguem disquirentes originem contentionis. legali iudicio diffinierunt idem molendinum debere sancto MICHAELI suisque monachis manere in perpetuitate omnis [fol. 29r] successionis. Hanc diffinitionem uictoriosissimus rex Guillelmus approbans et confirmans regali suffragio. iussit hęc mandari scripture testimonio:˙ idque ad perhenne monimentum per uerba sequentia roborauit affixo signo proprio. Ego Guillelmus gratia Dei rex Anglorum ac princeps Normannorum. per hoc signum sancte crucis confirmo decretum meorum optimatum supra scriptorum:˙ ut molendinum comitis quod abbas Rannulfus me fauente a Gualeranno redemit perpetuo sit iuris sancti MICHAELIS ad uictum suorum monachorum. nec habeat potestatem quisquam meorum successorum seu eiusdem montis abbatum uel monachorum hoc a me meisque sancitum immutare qualibet occasione. aut quantalibet numerositate preciorum. Signum uictoriosissimi regis Guillelmi. +. Signum nobilissime Mathildis regine .+. [8 blank lines to foot of fol. 29r; 12 blank lines to middle of fol. 29v]

Printed: Bates, *RRAN*, no. 213, and (down to *Hinc iam*) Fauroux, 148. Fauroux shows that there were three redactions of this act, the first two were charters and the third was written in the form of a notification after 1066. The Cartulary text is a copy of the third redaction. All three copies have perished. Fauroux's text reconstructs the third redaction from photographs surviving at Saint-Lô of three-quarters of the document. The Cartulary gives the following variants from the reconstructed third recension: [a] sequentium [b] uillam [c] perpetuum

Also partially printed from the Cartulary in L. Delisle, *Histoire de Saint-Sauveur-le-Vicomte*, pièce justificative. no. 36, p. 40, and by Lechaudé d'Anisy in *Grand rôles des Echiquiers de Normandie*, in *Mémoires de la Société des antiquaires de Normandie*, t. 15, Paris, 1845, p. 196. Copies or partial copies of the first two redactions occur in B. N. Lat. 5430a, p. 243, Le Roy's *Histoire*, B. N. fr. 18950, fol. 15r, and Lechaudé d'Anisy, B. N.lat. 10072, fol. 150r. Round, *Calendar of Documents in France*, nos. 711-712.

The charter is discussed in Emily Tabuteau, *Transfers of Property in Eleventh-Century Norman Law* (1988), pp. 29–30.

7

William II of Normandy concedes the isles of Sark and Aurigny in exchange for lands in Guernsey formerly granted by his father Robert, which he now restores to Ranulf fitz Ansquetil: 1035–1042.

[fol. 29v] EGO GVILLEMVS COMES Normannorum filius Rotberti comitis. concedo sancto MICHAELI suisque semper seruientibus quasdam nostras insulas Serc. et Aurrene.[a] propter medietatem Grenere.[b] quam pater meus Rotbertus eis ob suam animam dederat. quam ego Rannulfo filio Anschitilli reddidi. Ego Guillelmus princeps Normannorum et Dei gratia dux. hanc donationem manu propria corroboraui: Isti sunt [fol. 30r] testes donationis Guillelmi filii Rotberti comitis. Hugo episcopus Abrincensis. Willelmus filius Guillelmi. Niellus iuuenis. Hatuuardus[c] rex. Hunfredus Namo. Guillelmus filius Ranoldi.[d] Rogerius filius Hunfredi. Ioffredus.[e] uicecomes. Hugo filius Huberti. Hunfredus paruus. [8 blank lines]

Printed: Fauroux, 111, from a facsimile of the original, which was written onto the same parchment as no. 5 above; the facsimile was published in V. Hunger, *Histoire de Verson*. p. 7.

Calendared in Round, *Calendar of Documents in France*, no. 706, from the original.

[a] Arenon [b] Greneroy [c] Haduaiardus [d] Rainoldi [e] Losfredus

Also printed in Delisle, *Saint-Sauveur*, pièces just. no. 17, p. 19; *Cartulaire de Jersey*, no. 115, from the Cartulary.

8

Confirmation by William II of Normandy of the grant of La Croix-Avranchin (Manche, cant. Saint-James), situated between Saint-James (formerly Beuvron) and Mont-Saint-Michel, and its dependencies (Villiers-le-Pré, Ballant, Saint-Georges, and three carrucates in the island of Jersey) by his father's knight Adelelm, who attests the act with his wife Beatrice and son Robert: 1037–46.

Donatio de Cruce

PREDESTINATIONE omnipotentis Dei patris et filii et spiritus sancti a quo omne datum optimum est et omne donum perfectum. cuius omnis terra et plenitudo eius. orbis terrarum et qui habitant in eo. qui etiam matrem ecclesiam ita dignatus est in terris exaltare. ut per eam promereatur fidelis populus ad cęlestem [fol. 30v] patriam hanelare: accidit quod Rotbertus nobilissimus Normannorum dux piissimi Richardi principis filius. uicum Crucis qui situs est inter Biuronem et Montem Sancti MICHAELIS. dedit in beneficium cuidam militum suorum nomine Adelelmo. Qui catholicus Dei aspiratione compunctus. predicto principe mundanis rebus adempto. apud eis filium uenerandi patris heredum dignissimum deuotissime postulauit: ut pro religione diuina tam ad anime sue quam ad parentum suorum redemptionem. et maxime abbate Suppone de rebus ęcclesię promerente: beneficium quod tenebat sanctissimo Michaeli archangelo sibi liceret contradere. uidelicet predictam Crucis uillam atque talia eius menbra Vilers. Baleent. Sanctum Georgium. terram trium carrucarum in insula Gersoi cum omnibus quę ad hec pertinent:' theloneo scilicet et toto terrarum usu fructuario. Hanc igitur condonationem religiosus princeps et fieri permisit:' et de sua parte fieri in perpetuum archangelo concessit. Eo quidem tenore. ut quicumque aliquatenus huic statuto presumpserit contraire:' Dei omnipotentis atque omnium sanctorum excommunicetur auctoritate. Huius itaque cartule firmantium subscribuntur nomina testium . +. Ego Willelmus Dei gratia Normannorum dux et princeps. hanc donationis cartulam propria manu corroboraui:' et meis episcopis ac primatibus corroborandam tradidi. + . Signum Adelelmi militis huius [fol. 31r] donationis largitor et auctor. Signum Beatricis uxoris eius .+ Signum Rotberti filii eius. N. Ego Hugo Abrincacensis episcopus manu propria firmo .+. Signum Malgeri archiepiscopi. +. Signum Hugonis Ebrocacensis episcopi. + . Signum Hugonis Luxouiensis episcopi. +. Signum Nielli uicecomitis. +. Signum Guillelmi filii Guillelmi comitis. +. Signum Rotberti pincerne. +. Signum Richardi uicecomitis. +. Signum Guillelmi fratris eius. Signum Haimonis uicecomitis. +. Signum Radulfi. +. Signum fratris eius Hernisi. +. Signum Gaufredi uicecomitis. +. Signum Gisleberti Crispini. +. Signum fratris eius Guillelmi. Signum Hugonis uicecomitis. +. Signum Turstinci filii. Rainaldi. +. Signum Guillelmi fratris eius. +. Signum Turstinci uicecomitis. +. Signum Hugonis filii Huberti. Signum Hugonis Paisfolet. +. Signum Turstinci Gazel. +. Signum Guidonis filii Rainaldi comitis. +. Signum Richardi filii Turstinci. +. Signum Rotbertis fratris eius. +. Signum Rannulfus filii Ascelini.

[7 blank lines]

Printed: Fauroux, 110, from the cartulary: *Cartulaire de Jersey*, no. 151, from the cartulary; original lost. A *vidimus* of Philip VI, now Arch. nat. JJ 66, fl. 660r, contains a copy of the original. The witness list contains an internal contradiction in that Hugh of Evreux died in 1046 and Hugh of Lisieux did not become bishop until 1049. Fauroux used the dates of Mauger's episcopacy at Rouen (1037–55) and Hugh's at Evreux (1015–46) to establish a date of 1037–47.

9

Charter by William Pichenoht granting land at Perrelle (Guernsey, par. Saint-Sauveur) on taking the habit at Mont-Saint-Michel; the act was confirmed by William II of Normandy on Christmas Day in Rouen cathedral in the presence of Archbishop Malger and Bishop Hugh of Avranches: 25 December, 1054.

[fol. 31v] *Carta de Perrella*

IN NOMINE SANCTE ET INDIVIDVE TRINITATIS. PATRIS ET FILII ET SPIRITVS SANCTI. Antecessorum nostrorum constitutis atque decretis uere compertum habemus. ut quicumque Christi fidelium bonorum cupidus celestium quiddam suarum facultatum cuilibet loco sanctorum pro anime sue remedio donauerit: exinde litterale testamentum nobilium personarum corroborationibus assignatum faciat. quatinus ab omni contradictione uel calumpnia malorum ipsa donatio firma et intemerata atque integra futuris temporibus permaneat. Qua propter ego Guillelmus Pichenoht cunctiş Christianis tam presentibus quam futuris notum esse uolo. quod meorum pro magnitudine peccatorum perpetuas metuens inferni penas. et celestis regni desiderio accensus: pro salute anime meę et parentum meorum. monachilem habitum in ecclesia Sancti MICHAELIS de Periculo Maris accipio. et pro animabus antecessorum meorum do sancto MICHAELI et suis monachis PERRELLAM et omnia quę Perrelle appendent. Hanc donationem concessit Guillelmus[a] egregius comes Normannie Rotberti comitis filius. atque propria manu firmauit in die natalis Domini ante altare sanctę MARIAE metropolitane Rotomagensis ęcclesię. uidentibus et audientibus Malgerio[b] archiepiscopo Rotomagensi. Hugone episcopo Abrincatensi. Rogerio de Bello Monte. Rogerio de Montgulmerio. Richardo uicecomite. Et ex hominibus sancti MICHAELIS: Hilgerio de Ardeuone. et Thescelino [fol. 32r] fratre eius. Rainaldo de Grande Villa. Radulfo de Sancto Iohanne{;} Fecit etiam Guillelmus comes a predictis episcopis ante altare sancte Marię excommunicationem[c] fieri super omnes illos qui molirentur hoc donum uiolare. uel qui uellent monachis sancti MICHAELIS aliquid de dono isto tollere. uel facere molestiam rebus sancti MICHAELIS pro isto dono.

Guillelmi + comitis. Anno ab incarnatione domini .M°.L°. iiii°. Indictione septima. facta est hęc donatio. Malgerii + archiepiscopi. Hugonis + episcopi Abrincatensis. + Rogerii de Bello Monte. + Rogerii de Mongulmerio. +. Richardi uicecomitis. +. Hilgerii de Ardeuone. + Thescelini fratris eius. + Rainaldi de Grandeuilla . +. Radulfi de Sancto Iohanne. [7 blank lines]

Printed: Fauroux, 133; *Cartulaire de Jersey*, no. 116. The original survives in Arch. dépt. de la Manche, H, fonds du Mont-Saint-Michel; a facsimile was published in V. Galbraith and P. Chaplais, *Facsimiles of Norman and Anglo-Norman Charters*, Oxford, 1962, pl. XLII. [a] Willelmus [b] Maalgerii [c] cummunicationem

Copied from the original by Lechaudé d'Anisy in B. N. lat. 10072, no. 14.

10

Charter of Edward Ætheling, later king of England, granting St Michael's Mount and the whole of Winniaton Hundred in Cornwall, and the port of (Old) Romney in Kent to the abbey: 1027–35.

[fol. 32v] IN NOMINE SANCTE ET INDIVIDVE TRINITATIS. Ego EDVVARDUS Dei gratia rex Anglorum. dare uolens pretium redemptionis animę meę. uel parentum meorum. sub consensu et testimonio bonorum uirorum. tradidi sancto MICHAELI archangelo in usum fratrum Deo seruientium in eodem loco. sanctum MICHAELEM qui est iuxta mare. cum omnibus appendiciis. uillis scilicet. castellis. agris. et ceteris attinentibus. Addidi etiam totam terram de

Vennesire. cum oppidis. uillis. agris. pratis. terris cultis et incultis. et cum horum reditibus. Adiunxi quoque datis addere portum qui uocatur Ruminella. cum omnibus quę ad eum pertinent:· hoc est molendinis. et piscatoriis. et cum omni territorio illius culto et inculto. et eorum reditibus. Si quis autem his donis conatus fuerit ponere calumpniam. anathema factus. iram Dei incurrat perpetuam. Vtque nostre donationis auctoritas uerius firmiusque teneatur in posterum. manu mea firmando subter scripsi:· quod et plures fecere testium. Signum regis EDVVARDI. +. Signum Roberti comitis. +. Signum Rabel. Signum Rotberti archiepiscopi Rotomomagensis. +. Signum Hereberti. Luxouiensis episcopi. +. Signum Rotberti episcopi Constanciensis. +. Signum Vmfredi. +. Nielli uicecomitis. +. Anschtilli. +. Signum Radulfi. +. Signum Choschet. +. Signum Turstini. +.

Printed: Fauroux, 76, from the cartulary: original lost. Copy in lat. 10072, no. 6, from the cartulary.

Reprinted and discussed by S. Keynes, 'The Æthelings in Normandy', *Anglo-Norman Studies* xiii (1991), 190–4, who shows that the charter is genuine, despite its apparent improbabilities, and suggests identifications for the places mentioned as Winniaton hundred and the port of (Old) Romney in Kent.

11

Charter notifying the grant of St Michael's Mount, Cornwall, and appendages, to Mont-Saint-Michel by Robert, count of Mortain, who, after the birth of his son, further grants three acres of land in the Meneage, Traboe and Lesneage in St Keverne, Tregevis and Carvallack, with the assent of his half-brother William I of England and of Leofric bishop of Exeter: dated 1085 in numerals, but 1076 by dating-clauses. Based on a genuine grant of *c.* 1070, the Cartulary version is a forgery probably produced in the twelfth century, around the time that Abbot Bernard founded the priory of St Michael's Mount in 1135.

Carta de Cornubia

[fol. 33r] IN NOMINE SANCTE ET INDIVIDVE TRINITATIS PATRIS ET FILII ET SPIRITVS SANCTI AMEN. Ego Rotbertus Dei gratia Moritonii comes igne diuini amoris succensus. notifico omnibus sancte ecclesie matris nostre filiis habens in bello sancti Michaelis uexillum quoniam pro anime meę salute atque meę coniugis seu pro salute. prosperitate. incolumitate Guillelmi gloriosissimi regis atque pro adipiscendo uitae ętернę premio. do et concedo montem sancti MICHAELIS de Cornubia. Deo et monachis ecclesie Sancti MICHAELIS de Periculo Maris seruientibus cum dimidia terre hidia. ita solutam et quietam ac liberam ut ego tenebam ab omnibus consuetudinibus. querelis. et placitis. et constituo eciam ut ipsi monachi concedente domino meo rege ibidem mercatum die quinte ferię habeant. Postea autem ut certissime comperi. beati MICHAELIS meritis monachorumque mereri suffragiis michi a Deo ex propria coniuge mea filio concesso. auxi donum ipsi beato milicię celestis principi. dedi et dono in

Amanech tres acras terrę. Trauelaboth uidelicet. Lismanaoch. Trequauers. Carmailoc. annuente piissimo domino mei Guillelmo rege cum Malthide regina atque nobilibus illorum filiis. Rotberto comite. Guillelmo Rufo. Henrico adhuc puero. ita quietam ac liberam de omnibus placitis. querelis. atque forifactis. ut de nulla re regie iusticię monachi res [fol. 33v]pondebunt nisi de solo homicidio. Hanc autem donationem feci ego Rotbertus comes Moretonii. quam concesserunt gloriosus rex anglorum Willelmus atque regina et filii eorum sub testimonio istorum. Signum Willelmi regis. Signum Regine Mathildis. + . Signum Rotberti comitis .+. Signum Willelmi Rufi filii regis. +. Signum Henrici pueri. +. Signum Rotberti comitis Moretonii. +. Signum Mathildis comitisse. +. Signum Willelmi filii eorum . +. Signum Willelmi filii Osberni.[1] + Signum Rogeri de Montegomeri. +. Signum Tosteni uicecomitis. +. Signum Guarini. +. Signum Turulfi. +. Firmata atque roborata est hęc carta anno m^{o}. $\cdot$l^{mo}xxxv^{ta}. ab incarnatione domini. Indictione .xiiii. Concurrente .iii. Luna. viii. apud Peneuesel Signum Liurici Essecestrie episcopi. +. Ego quidem Liuricus Dei dono Essecestrię episcopus. iussione et exhortatione domini nostri reuerentissimi Gregorii pape. regisque nostri et regine. omniumque optimatum tocius regni Anglię exhortatus. ut ecclesiam beati archangeli MICHAELIS de Cornubia utpote quę officio et ministerio angelico creditur atque comprobatur consecrari ac sanctificari:· quatinus eam ab omni episcopali iure. potestate. seu subiectione liberarem atque exuerem. quod et facere tocius cleri nostri consensu et hortatu non distuli. Libero igitur eam et exuo ab omni episcopali dominatione. subiectione. inquietudine. et omnibus illis qui illam ecclesiam suis cum beneficiis et elemosinis expecierint et uisitauerint:· terciam partem penitentiarum condonamus. [fol. 34r] Et ut hoc inconuulsum et immobile et eciam inuiolabile finetenus permaneat:· ex auctoritate patris et filii et spiritus sancti omnibus nostris successoribus interdicimus. ne aliquid contra hoc decretum usurpare presumant.

For the date and a full discussion of the status of this charter see D. Bates ed. *Regesta Regum Anglo-Normannorum, William I*, no. 213, which also identifies the Cornish places mentioned. Cf. the discussion by P. Hull, 'The foundation of Saint Michael's Mount, Corwall, a priory of the abbey of Mont-Saint-Michel', in *Mill. mon.*, i, 703–24.

Printed: P. L. Hull, ed., *The Cartulary of St Michael's Mount*, no. 1; Bates, *RRAN*, no. 213, pp. 669–70; *Mon. Ang.*, vi^{3}, 987.

The copy from the archives of the abbey in B. N. fr. 22325, pp. 723–4, omits *ipsi beato milicie ... Carmailoc*, and everything after *Signum Turulfi*. Another copy, B. N. lat. 10072, no. 15, from the archives of Saint-Lô, has an asterisk at *hec carta* and comments: 'cette dernière partie est notée dans le cartulaire, mais elle ne se trouve pas dans la charte'.

12

Charter of Robert count of Mortain and his wife Countess Almodis for St Michael's Mount, Cornwall, granting land in Ludgvan belonging to Richard fitz Turold, and the land Bloic used to hold in Truthwall, for the soul of

William I and his son William, for his own defunct wife Matilda, his living wife Almodis and their children; Robert, his son by Almodis, concedes the grant, as does William, his son by Matilda, to whom the land would revert should Robert die without an heir of Almodis. In Domesday Book the hide of Blohin the Breton at Truthwall in Ludgvan was described as having been taken from St Michael by Robert of Mortain, who, in this charter, was in effect selling it back to the monks since they are said to have paid 60 pounds in the money of Caen for it; the land mentioned in fact never returned to the monks but remained in the hands of the heirs of Richard fitz Turold and Blohin: in the time of Abbot Roger and William II of England and before Robert's death in 1094, 1087–1094.

Item de eodem

EGO Rotbertus comes Moretoniensis et Almodis comitissa mea uxor damus Deo. et sancto MICHAELI. et monachis:· Ludahanum manerium Richardi Turulfi filii.[1] quod est iuxta Montem. Et damus illi illud quod Bloicus habebat in Treiuhalo manerio.[2] et ferias ambas de Monte. Istud dat comes Deo et sancto MICHAELI pro anima Willelmi Anglorum regis. et pro anima Willelmi regis eius filii. et pro suimet anima. et pro anima mulieris suę defuncte Mathildis. et pro uiuenti Almodi. et pro pueris eorum. Caritatem istam concessit Rotbertus filius comitis Moretonii ille quem de Almodi comitissa habuit. et Willelmus eius alter filius concessit ita si de Almodi supradicta non remaneret heres. et ad istum Willelmum reueniret terra:· quod concederet. Istius caritatis istiusque conuentionis existunt testes a parte comitis. Rannulfus Auenel. et Rotbertus Guauterides. et Rotbertus Giroldi filius. et Herueus Auenel. et Ricardus dapifer. Et ex parte sancti Michaelis:· Albertus monachus. et Rainfredus de Sai. monachus. et Ilgerius prepositus. et Rogerius de Ardeuone. et Guido de Monte. De conuentione ista et caritate fecit Rogerius abbas. et monachi caritatem comiti. lx^{ta}. librarum [fol. 34v] Cenomannensium. Hoc factum fuit uiuente Rotberto comite Normannię. et Willelmo rege Anglorum regis Willelmi filio.

Printed: P. L. Hull, ed., *The Cartulary of St Michael's Mount*, p. 62. Discussed by Hull, in *Mill. mon. MSM*, i, 720; B. Golding, 'Robert of Mortain', *Anglo-Norman Studies* xiii, p. 143.

13

Grant of land and the church in *Fulquereuilla* (now comm. Saint-Germain-sur-Ay, cant. Lessay, dépt. Manche), with salt-pans and a fishery on the river Ay, by Rainald, William and Godfrey for the salvation of their parents; a moiety of the land had originally been given by their father John shortly

[1] *Domesday Cornwall*, 5.3;27, Richard fitz Turold holds Ludgvan from the count.

[2] *DB Cornwall*, 5.25;5, Blohin Brito holds Truthwall (*Treuthal*) from the count, who had taken it from St Michael's Church; *id.* 4.1 St Michael's Church holds Truthwall.

before his death; their mother Eva survived her husband by a few days, during which she granted a sixth part of the land for her salvation: perhaps about 1061–87.

Carta de Fulquereuilla

IN NOMINE PATRIS ET FILII ET SPIRITVS SANCTI. VT sa[o *a.c*]cra testatur pagina. ueras appetere necesse erit diuitias. si ueri culmen cupimus honoris pertingere. Non enim terrena. sed celestis diuites efficit lucratio. Nostram itaque illic condere conuenit substantiam. ubi nec erugine. nec contaminetur tinea. Felix denique conmertium. pro perituris perpetua. pro terrenis adquirere celestia. Huiusmodi igitur aliisque quam plurimis diuine auctoritatis hortamentis admoniti ego scilicet Rainoldus. fratresque mei Willemus. et Godefredus. notum esse uolumus tam presentibus quam futuris. uiuentibus denique et nascituris. quoniam uille Fulqueri cuius medietatem pater noster sancte memorię Iohannes adhuc uiuens pro salute animę suę sancto MICHAELI donauerat. mater quoque nostra Eua postmodum per aliquos dies superstes sextam similiter eiusdem uille partem predicto archangelo pro remedio anime sue tradiderat. ipsius siquidem uille reliquas patres quę post eorum obitum paterno hereditario ad nos deuenerant iam dicto loco sancti Michaelis fratribusque ibi Deo seruientibus sollempni donatione pro salute patris [fol. 35r] nostri anime matrisque nostre concedimus. tradimus. donamus. pro nobis etiam ipsis: quatinus ipse sanctus MICHAEL nostra in hoc seculo in Dei seruitio reddat corpora perseuerabilia. animasque post funera ad regna perducat celestia. Donamus quidem cum terris cultis et incultis. et cum salinis. et cum omnibus iam dicte uillę appenditiis. cum suis etiam certis notisque terminis. cum ecclesia. ea ratione ut habeat. teneat. possideatque ipsius sancti locus archangeli. fratresque ibi Deo seruientes. sine omnium succedentium parentum nostrorum seu quorumque contradictione et calumpniatione. Quod si aliquis diabolica fraude instigatus hoc testamentum contaminare uoluerit. perpetuali maledictione dampnetur. Preterea eadem donatione piscaturam quandam in fluuio sitam nomine Hunua donamus perpetualiter habendam predicto loco. Vt autem huius donationis testamentum firmius ueratiusque futuris temporibus per omnia conseruetur: manibus propriis subter firmauimus. [4 blank lines]

14

Charter granting his allod at *Heiantot* (probably Le Bingard, comm. Saint-Sauveur-Landelin, cant. Muneville-le-Bingard, Manche) in the Cotentin by Ralph, his wife Asa and son Nigel; the grant includes all land cultivated and uncultivated, rents and dues pertaining to the allod: undated, but probably before *c.* 1087–94.

Carta de Heiantot[1]

1 A later hand writes in the margin: *pro prioratu Sancti Germani le Bingard unito abbatie, cum charta sequenti.*

[fol. 35v] IN NOMINE PATRIS ET FILII ET SPIRITVS SANCTI. Ego Radulfus notum esse omnibus tam presentibus quam futuris uolo. quoniam peccatorum meorum magnitudinem nimium timens. uitamque ęternam michi et omnibus parentibus meis adquirere ualde desiderans. dedimus et tradidimus ego scilicet et uxor mea nomine Asa filiusque meus Niellus sancto MICHAELI et fratribus ibi Deo sanctoque MICHAELI seruientibus pro nostrorum remissione peccatorum quoddam alodum. uillam uidelicet Heiantot sitam in Constantino pago. cum consensu omnium meorum parentum. Tradidimus quippe eam integerrime cum terris cultis et incultis. et cum omnibus censibus et debitis qui exinde exeunt:· hęc omnia scilicet quę ad ipsum alodum pertinent. eo tenore eaque ratione. ut habeant. teneant. possideant sine contradictione omnium meorum parentum. siue quorumcumque successorum. Quod si aliquis meorum successorum stimulatus diabolo donationem istam calumpniari uoluerit. ex parte Dei omnipotentis et omnium sanctorum excommunicetur. Vt autem donatio ista inuiolata futuris temporibus perseueret:· manibus propriis subter firmauimus. Signum Radulfi [+]. Signum Asę [+]. Signum Nielli .+.

15

Grant of land near the abbey's holdings at *Heiantot* (Le Bingard, comm. Saint-Sauveur-Landelin) by Humphrey de Cambernon (Manche, comm. cant. Coutances), vassal of Robert count of Mortain, whose assent he has sought and who subscribes the act: *c.* 1050–1094, probably *c.* 1087–94.

Item de eodem

EGO Vnfredus miles de Campo Bernulfi. do sancti MICHAELI fratribusque in monte Tumba Deo seruientibus quandam terram mei iuris in Con[fol. 36r]tantino pago sitam. quam dirimit uia publica ab eorum possessione quae dicitur Heiantot. perpetim possidendam:· acceptis ab abate [*sic*] .xl. solidis. in mea redemptione. ita ut monachi Deo sanctoque MICHAELI seruientes ipsam terram teneant. atque absque ulla parentum meorum calumpnia in euum possideant. Si quis autem huic donationi calumpniam per succedentia tempora inferre presumpserit:· perpetua maledictione multetur. Vt uero hęc donatio stabilis permaneret:· assensum domini mei Rotberti comitis quesiui. qui annuens subscribit.

[6 blank lines]

16

Chirograph concerning the destruction and depredation of abbey property in the seigneuries of Saint-Pair (Manche, cant. Granville) and Genêts (Manche, cant. Sartilly), and the forests of Neirun (now lost, Manche, cant. Sartilly, comm. Champeaux), Crapault (Manche, cant. Sartilly, comm. Carolles) and Bevais (now lost, Manche, cant. Sartilly), by Thomas de Saint-Jean-le-Thomas when building his castle at Saint-Jean-le-Thomas, and the subsequent restoration and restitution by Thomas and his brothers in a detailed accord with Abbot Roger II, whose knights they are, approved and confirmed by the bishop of Avranches and Henry I of England; some of the depradations mentioned here occur also in no. **115**: dated 1121 with discordant dating-clauses, though the act contains confirmation clauses added in the time of Abbot Richard de Méré (1124–31): 1121–25.

NOTVM SIT TAM PRESENTIBVS quam futuris quod Thomas de Sancto Iohanne incepto castello suo apud Sanctum Iohannem cepit nemora de Nerum. et de Crapalt omnino in edificatio[fol. 36v]ne sui castelli dissipare et destruere quod et opere compleuit. Deinde insatiabili cupiditate succensus transiit ad nemus Biuie. et simili modo cepit deuastare et terras plurimorum uauasorum in honore Sancti Paterni et in honore Genecii preocupare et inuadere. Hoc siquidem audientes monachi ęcclesiae beati archangeli MICHAELIS. toto uoto cordium ad Deum conuersi sunt ut Deus oculos sue misericordie super ecclesiam sui sanctissimi archangeli reduceret: et de tam iniusto malefactore uelocem uindictam citissime capere non desineret. Instituerunt etiam clamorem piissimum celebrare nullo intermisso die coram altare sancti MICHAELIS dum missa cantabatur ante sacratissimum et uerissimum corpus domini nostri Ihesu Christi. cantantes cum lacrimis miserere mei Deus. et clamantes Kyrieleison: ne iniusticia iusticiae. et falsitas ueritati preualeret. Hoc autem Thomas audito exhorruit. et festinus uelut furibundus ad Montem Sancti Michaelis cum fratribus Iohanne uidelicet et Rogerio. e[a] maximo agmine comitum uenit: interrogans et perquirens qua de causa super se et suos fratres monachi clamorem Deo faciebant. At monachi nichil percunctantes neque metuentes dixerunt. pro eo quod nemora illorum dissipauerat et terras ecclesie iniuste inuaserat. Ille uero consilio fratrum suorum et procerum qui cum eo erant pedibus abbatis donni Rogerii de Gemmetico et monachorum prostratus cum omni comitatu suorum [fol. 37r] petens misericorditer. ut sui atque fratrum suorum misereri dignarentur: et cum eis iusta consideratione amicorum ecclesie se suosque fratres reconciliari et pacificari permitterent. Abbas equidem ut pote uir misericordie cum consilio monachorum interrogans quo pacto et qua conditione ipse et fratres eius ecclesiae uellent reconciliari. quoniam nullo modo illos absoluerent neque clamorem intermitterent. nisi res et possessiones quas preocupauerant iniuste omnino relinquerent. At Thomas respondens dixit. Concedo domine. ut omnia dominia ecclesie in pace et cum amore dimittam. sed tantummodo illorum hominum seruitium michi fratribusque meis concedite. qui carnis propinquitate nobis coniunguntur excepta Montis custodia. et de hominibus illorum habeatis moltam. theloneum. taillas. auxilia. et cetera seruitia quę iuste maiori domino debentur. Solummodo michi seruitia militum concedantur. et ego seruicia uobis faciam: et cetera cuncta uobis remaneant. Nominatim autem et determinate supplex cum fratribus meis deposco. ut harum terrarum seruitia michi concedatis. In honore Sancti Paterni uolo ut michi concedatis terram Rainaldi coqui. eo tenore quod si heres eius me requisierit:· sine mora et contradictione illi reddam retento illius proprio seruitio. Radulfus Malregart terram suam dum Appuliam iuit. cuidam nepoti uestro nomine Radulfo de Port propter duodecim marchas argenti inuade[fol. 37v]moniauit. et nunc amicis nostris inter nos colloquentibus ad tantum conuenimus:· quod accepit a me duodecim libras Cenomannensium pro terra. tali pacto atque tenore[b] quod dum filius Radulfi Malregardi illius etatis fuerit qua terram tenere et regere potuerit. fide mea fratrumque meorum legaliter et fimiter assecuro quod nulla ui nec aliquo machinamento nequitie nec nos nec aliquis heredum nostrorum terram illam retinebat. sed sine dilatione et contradictione redditis nobis duodecim supra dictis libris siue heredibus nostris. finetenus terram illi restituemus:· et ut fidelius indubitanter nobis credatur nostrique sequaces hęc audiant et teneant. iuro atque contestor fratresque mei mecum sponte nostra super sacrosancta euangelia:· quod hęc et a nobis et a nostris heredibus tenebuntur. Terram Rogerii de Grandeuilla hactenus in custodia mea habui. quia armiger meus erat. sed nunc miles factus in presentia uestri et horum omnium tam monachorum quam laicorum reddo eam sibi. quoniam ueraciter scio quod abbatibus huius ecclesie sicut alii barones abbatie seruire debet. et pro hoc humillime imploro. ut seruitium Rotberti filii Iuonis michi concedatis retentis uobis omnium suorum hominum consuetudinibus. Guillelmus de Pomeria et Stephanus de Tabula submiserunt se ut perfidi Rogerio fratre meo:· cui consulo et laudo ut pro illorum seruitio uobis hominum faciat. et sit huius ecclesie homo. tali pacto et condictione ut uauassores illorum ubicumque necesse [fol. 38r] fuerit uobiscum et[c] monachis uestris eant. et deserant manticas et pannos monachorum. et reddant uobis decimas. moltam. telonea. auxilia. quia nolumus minuere debita et consuetudines huius sancte ęcclesię:· cuius beneficio et nutrimento educati et procreati sumus. Tunc Rogerius exsurgens:· abbati hominium fecit. iurauitque super sacrosancta euangelia fidelitatem ęcclesię. et quod in nullo consuetudines et debita monachorum inuaderet:· neque terras illorum presumptuose sibi usurparet. In honore Genecii apud Poterel inuadimoniaui ego/Thomas terram Gathonis. tali conditione quod si abbas uel monachi michi uel alicui heredum meorum quattuor libras Cenomannensium reddere uoluerint:· in pace illam habeant. Niellus presbiter uineam suam michi propter unam marcham argenti habiens Ierusalem inuadimoniauit. tali pacto ut si monachi huius ęcclesię a me uel ab aliquo heredum suorum eam redimere uoluerint in pace habeant.[d] et dum in manu mea uel heredum meorum fuerit precipio cum sacramento ut terragium plenissimme et legaliter reddatur. Et de illa et de aliis uineis rusticorum quę meę manui subiacent:· hoc idem concedo et precipio. ne umquam uinum moueatur:· donec terragium ad thorcular sancti MICHAELIS deferatur. Theloneum de Dunis quod iniuste michi usurpaueram uobis reddo. et si aliquid inde forisfeci:· peto ut michi indulgeatur. Terram Rainaldi de

Monasterio uobis reddo. quoniam didici quod a quodam perfido [fol. 38v] persuasum est michi ut eam reciperem. Similiter terram Garenberti quę super uillam Genicii est uobis finetenus restituo. quoniam uerissime cognoui quod Robertus filius Haymonis cum ad monachatum uenit:' illam pro anime sue salute huic ęcclesię dedit. Terram Theboldi liberi quam Hugo de Inferno de me tenet rogo ut michi concedatis. quia decem solidos Cenomannensium habeo de illo. quos amittere nolo. Quedam prata quę sunt sub uineis de Brium quę idem Hugo sub meo patrocinio iniuste ponit uobis relinquo. quoniam certissime scio quod de dominio sancti MICHAELIS existunt.

Rursum Thomas quadam altera die cum episcopo Abrincatensi et fratribus et multis aliis baronibus ad Montem uenit. abbatemque et monachos adiens:' ut hominium illius benigno amore susciperent. Quod et factum est. Deinde dixit. Confiteor domini quod .xx[ti]. solidos Cenomannensium. consuete reddere debeo. ad nundines[e] de Monte Martini omni anno pro terra Lamberti aurifabri. et pro terra Rainaldi filii Serlonis. huic ęcclesię. Si autem uestre prouidentie placeret ut hos michi .xx[ti]. solidos alternaretis:' et patrem meum atque matrem meam meque ac fratres meos in beneficio huius sacratissime ęcclesię reciperetis. in uestra uoluntate sine ullo clamore cuiuslibet hereditatis. neque mei neque meorum successorum nemus uestrum quod omnino destruitur ad horam et ad tempus fidelissime custodirem. et terram do-Blelli[f] quę michi reddit .viii[to]. quartaria frumenti. [fol. 39r] uobis uariando concederem. et omne frumentum quod in circuitu nemoris est sicut consuete sit. et de hominbus qui circa nemus morantur. et de landis si unquam lacrate[g] fuerint. et de molendino Haię ad horreum uestrum eat. Cui ab has monachique respondentes dixerunt. Quoniam ut ait dominus filii huius seculi prudentiores filiis lucis sunt:' si non crederemus nos uestris fallacibus et fraudulentis uerbis decipi. uos in primis consortes et cum participes beneficiorum huius ęcclesię efficeremus:' et deinde .xx[ti]. solidos. ut petitis alternaremus. et in morte et in uita uobis benigo amore hęc omnia concederemus. Tunc Thomas exsurgens fratresque sui cum eo coram episcopo et omni conuentu monachorum de manibus abbatis cum textu euangelii susceperunt beneficia monachorum. et eis osculatis;[h] hęc omnia se conseruanda firmiter statuerunt. Quin etiam terram nemoris omnino quietam clamauit. et dixit. quod nullus heredum meorum neque fratrum meorum nullomodo illam repetat. Hoc testamentum factum est in capitulo sancti MICHAELIS tempore Rogerii abbatis. et postea quam Thomas de captione rediit de Gorram ante piissimum et glorissimum regem Henricum apud Argenteium abbate Richardo hanc ecclesiam tenente istis coram rege presentibus. Gaufrido archipresule Rothomagensi. Iohanne Luxouiensi. Richardo Baiocensi. Signum Rotberto + dapifero de Haia. [Signum +] Guillelmi de Tancardeuilla. [Signum +] Guillelmi pincerna de [fol. 39v] Albinneio. [Signum +] Guillelmo Britone cum multis aliis. Post hęc autem[i] reuersus est Thomas cum fratribus suis ad Montem Sancti MICHAELIS et hoc quidem in capitulum eiusdem ęcclesię reiterando corroborauit et confirmauit istis presentibus uidentibus et audientibus. Signum Turgiso presule Abrincensis ęcclesię. +. [Signum +] Richardo abbate. [Signum +] Thoma. [Signum +] Iohanne fratre eius. et [Signum +] Rogerio. [Signum +] Rotberto de Abrincis. [Signum +] Gisleberto de Abrincis. [Signum +] Otoele de Sulligneio. [Signum +] Radulfo de Vehim. [Signum +] Hugone de Hulmo. [Signum +] Radulfo de Brai. [Signum +] Iohanne de Monte. [Signum +] Gauterio filio Hingandi. [Signum +] Hugone Talemascha. [Signum +] Philippo de Sancto Petro. et Alanno[j] fratre eius. aliisque multis. HOC AVTEM FACTVM EST ANNO M°. C°. XX°.I°. INDICTIONE XI[MA]. CONCVRRENTE .VI[TO]. REGNANTE PIISIMO REGE HENRICO.

[9 blank lines]

Original: One half of the chirograph survives as B.M. Add. Chart. 66980 . Copied in B.N. fr. 22325, p. 701–3.

The original, endorsed *cirographum Thome de Sancto Iohanne*, reads: [a] et (*corr. ex* a) [b] thenore [c] et cum [d] habeat [e] nundinas [f] doblelli [g] lucrate [h] ? euangelia *add.* (the parchment is damaged here, but contained one or two words not in the cartulary) [i] autem denuo [j] Alammo

B. N. lat. 10072, no. 112, copied the Cartulary, noting: 'La presente copie est conforme à son original en parchemin ... presenté par le R[d]. P. dom François Corit, pro. en garde de cet abbaye 1719'.

Printed, with full discussion, in Jacques Boussard, 'Thomas de Saint-Jean-le-Thomas et l'abbaye du Mont-Saint-Michel (début du XIIe siècle), in *Droit privé et institutions régionales. Etudes historiques offertes à Jean Yver*, 87–93.

Calendared: *RRAN* ii, 1422, where the suggested date is 1124. Discussed by André Dufief, 'La vie monastique...', in *Mill. mon. MSM*, i, 89.

17

Charter of Alan III of Brittany making grants, at the request of the abbot, of various demesnes, including land at Mont-Roualt (Ille-et-Vilaine, cant. Pleine-Fougères), the vill and marsh of *Bohel* on the river Couesnon, and the vill and mill of 'the land of Lavas' (cant. Pleine-Fougères), also on the Couesnon, which had been held by his vassal Guy before he became a monk of the abbey; he also confirms the grants of his father Geoffrey, including the church of Saint-Meloir and the demesne of Lande-de-Qui (in Meillac, cant. Combourg, Ille-et-Vilaine), the demesne of Cancale (Ille-et-Vilaine) and a neigbouring port (Porpican); attested by his mother Hadvisa and his brother Eudo: the date and dating-clauses accord: 5 April, 1030.

[fol. 40r] *Carta de Monroalt et de Lava. et de Cancauena*

IN DEI SVMMI NOMINE. EGO ALANVS. Britannorum Dei gratia comes. omnibus catholicae fidei cultoribus. tam presentibus quam etiam futuris precipueque nostris successoribus notum fieri uolo: hanc conscriptionem mea uel matris meę Adhugisis adhuc uiuentis preceptione. necnon et procerum nostrorum consensu esse factam atque firmatam. Petiit itaque nostram excellentiam abbas et monachi de loco qui dicitur Mons Sancti MICHAELIS. qui est satis proximus nostre regioni. situs intra Abrincatensem pagum:˙ quatinus terras quas meus pater Gaufredus comes Deo et sancto MICHAELI pro salute sue anime et pro filiorum suorum incolumitate intra Britanniam donauerat. nostro etiam munere adaugere atque ampliare deberemus. Beneplacitum igitur diuine pietati esse credens. ecclesias eius sancto nomini dicatas pie honorare. et seruis Dei necessaria contribuere. et pro hoc me ab eo eternam animę retributionem conse[i *a.c.*]cuturum sperans:˙ predictorum seruorum Dei peticioni libens assensum prebui. Deliberans ergo inueni aliquid intra terminos regni nobis a Deo commissi:˙ quod et eidem loco sanctissimi archangeli satis uicinum. et pro sua [fol. 40v] oportunitate satisfactioni uoluntatis seruorum Dei uideatur accommodum. Peccatorum itaque meorum indulgentiam apud Deum obtinere cupiens:˙ pro salute et remedio meae animae. et patris mei Gaufredi. ac matris meae Adhugisis adhuc uiuentis. uel fratris mei Eudon. filiorum etiam si quos michi Deus donore dignatus fuerit:˙ pro diuturna quoque nostrorum corporum sanitate. nec non et pro continua regni nobis a Deo commissi conuersatione:˙ Deo et sanctissimo MICHAELI archangelo. quasdam mei iuris terras uoluntarie in eodem loco contradidi. et ex eis donum super altare sancti MICHAELIS quadam uice ibidem adueniens posui. Vtque hoc factum omnimodis stabile. et inconuulsum omni sequenti teneatur tempore:˙ ad testimonium ueritatis hoc fieri scriptum cum subscriptione plurimorum nostrorum fidelium mandaui. Eo uero tenore hoc fieri precepi:˙ ut monachi in eodem loco Deo et sancto archangelo famulatum exhibentes. in suis orationibus apud Deum nostri continuam memoriam habeant:˙ et eundem summum archangelum intercessorem pro peccatis meis habere merear. Terre uero ipse supradicte. quas Deo et sancto archangelo donare disposui. non in uno loco sunt posite:˙ et ideo non uno nomine appellate. Prima enim ex eis est posita super fluuium qui uocatur Coisnun:˙ et nominatur ipsa terra uilla Bohel. Hanc uillam cum omni maresco quod ad eam pertinet:˙ Deo et sancto MICHA[fol. 41r]ELI in perpetuum possidendam trado. Item aliam uillam quę uocatur terra de Lauas:˙ cum uno molendino quod ad eam pertinet. Quam terram Wido quidam meus homo de me ante in alodum tenuit:˙ et postea monachus factus est in eodem Monte Sancti MICHAELIS. Hanc terram cum toto molendino sicut dixi:˙ similiter sicut uillam Bohel sancto MICHAELI trado. Aliam quoque uillam quę iuxta supradictam terram est posita. quodam medio fluuiolo intercurrente. quę uocatur Monsrohalt cum dimidio molendino quod ad eam pertinet:˙ eodem modo sicut et alias dono. Preter istas uero terras quas ego exproprio dono Deo et sancto MICHAELI propter supradictam rationem contrado:˙ alias quoque terras quas pater meus Gaufredus comes pro salute suę animę et filiorum suorum incolumitate sancto MICHAELI dederat:˙ sicut ille dedit sic et ego concedo. confirmo. et corroboro. ut in perpetuum ab eisdem sicut dixi pro patris mei ac mea elemosina possideantur. Est autem in regione Britannię quę uocatur Poohæleth una uilla quę uocatur Cancauena. cum uno portu qui illi adiacet. Sed et quedam ęcclesia quę dicitur Semmeler. Item alia uilla in alio loco. quę uocatur Landeguedhoi. cum tota terra quę ad eam pertinet. Hoc dedit pater meus Gaufredus comes in elemosinam suam sancto MICHAELI:· et ego post eum [eam *a.c.*] approbo et confirmo. Et omnibus his quę uel ego ex mea propria parte in meam elemo[fol. 41v]sinam:· uel pater meus ex sua parte in suam elemosinam dedimus. omnes consuetudines uel red[d]itus qui de terris Britannie secundum morem patrię exire possunt. teste Deo ex hoc nunc et usque in seculum Deo et sancto MICHAELI famulantibus ex integro fideliter concedimus. de omnibus terris uidelicet quas supra nominauimus. Si quis uero de omnibus his quecumque ego uel pater meus sicut supra scriptum habetur Deo et sancto MICHAELI eisdemque deseruientibus perpetualiter obtinenda. in nostram elemosinam pro salute et remedio animarum nostrarum fideliter tradimus. per aliquod ingenium siue per aliquam artem aliquid diminuerit uel decreuerit. siue absque uoluntate eorum quibus ego ea trado aliquid retinere temptauerit. seu etiam quicumque de omnibus his aliquid per uim abstulerit. siue quocumque modo sancto MICHAELI sibique famulantibus contrarius esse conatus fuerit:· sit ille ex auctoritate patris. et filii. et spiritus sancti. ab omni Christianorum consortio uel communione alienatus et separatus. atque anathematizatus. omniumque sanctorum aeterna maledictione dampnatus. et de hoc cum sancto MICHAELE archangelo in iudicio ante Deum contendere habeat. Sit quoque illi portio dampnationis in igne ęterno. cum Pilato et Caipha. atque Iuda traditore Domini:· nisi de hoc ad emendationem per penitentiam et satisfactionem uenerit. Hoc autem nostrae [fol. 42r] preceptionis scriptum ut perpetuam et inuiolabilem obtineat omni tempore firmitatem:· manu propria illud subter firmaui. et primorum nostrorum fidelium subscriptione similiter illud roborari et signari feci. Signum Alani comitis. Signum Adhuhis comitisse matris eiusdem comitis. Signum Eudonis fratris comitis. Signum Gingonei Dolensis archiepiscopi. Signum Bodici Namnetensis comitis. Nomina testium. Cario. Willelmus filius Heruei. Herueus de Acignei. Rainaldus Monte Premer. Alui filius Bernardi uicecomitis. Willelmus frater Bernardi. Bernardus filius Alui. Nemenoi filius Nemenoi. Gestin filius Terint. Gernogon presbiter. ACTA VEL FIRMATA EST HVIVS CARTAE CONSCRIPTIO ANNO AB INCARNATIONE DOMINI NOSTRI IHESV CHRISTI. M°. XXX. INDICTIONE .XIII. IN OCTAVIS PASCHE. IN EODEM MONTE SANCTI MICHAELIS QVANDO MISSA SOLLEMPNITER CELEBRABATVR.

[3 blank lines]

Printed: H. Guillotel, *Les Actes des Ducs de Bretagne (944–1148)* (Thèse pour le Doctorat en Droit, Juillet, 1973, Paris), no. 18, pp. 66–73. Other copies omit the witnesses from Cario to Rainald [de] Monte-Premer, but add *Roiantelina filia Riuuall, Hugonis filius eius, Gauffredi filii eius, Gisleberti filii Geu.*

Amongst several copies there are two in B.N. lat. 17723, of which the first, on fol. 165–7, was copied from the lost *Liber Albus*; the second, on fol. 329–30, contains variants from an original redaction of the charter, on to which was copied no. **18** below (cf. nos. **5** and **7**).

18

Restitution to the abbey by William fitz Rivallon, with the assent of his mother Eremburg and his brothers John and Gelduin, of the land at Lande-de-Qui (in Meillac, cant. Combourg, Ille-et-Vilaine) that Abbot Suppo had given from the abbey's lands to William's father Rivallon; Rivallon had previously settled a claim on the land by R. fitz Ascelin by payment of 100 shillings in the money of Le Mans: enacted at the castle of Dol eleven days after Rivallon's death, attested by Conan II of Brittany and Archbishop Juhel of Dol, in 1065 or 1066.

[fol. 42r] *Carta de Landeguihii.*

Notum sit omnibus presentis atque futuri aeui hominibus. quod ego Guillelmus filius Riuallonis una cum consensu matris meae Heremburgis fratrumque meorum Iohannis atque Gelduini. reddo sancto MICHAELI suisque monachis terram quę dicitur Landeguihu quam dono abbatis Supponis. pater meus possederat hactenus: tali conditione ut absque cuiusquam calumpnia ab ipsis monachis possi[fol. 42v]deatur. ipsique monachi pro eiusdem patris mei. aliorumque meorum parentum animabus. Deum exorent enixius. Ipsam terram. calumpniabatur. R. filius Ascelini. quam calumpniam pater meus omnino ademit: datis centum Cenomannensium solidis. Ad confirmationem autem istius donationis. manu mea signum crucis impressi. meisque fratribus atque amicis eodem modo facere suasi. Signum eiusdem Guillelmi. Signum Iohannis fratris eius. Signum Gelduini fratris eius. Signum Heremburgis matris eorum. Signum Maini filii Tehen. Signum Guillelmi filii Vrsoen. Signum Galterii filii Riculfi. Signum Hatonis fratris Flotaldi. Signum Ademi filii Harscut. Signum Galterii filii Aimonis. Signum Riuallonis filii Gurgar. Acta est hęc conscriptio carte. xi die post obitum Riualloni. in castro Dolensi. in domo eiusdem Riuallonis coram filiis eius.[a]
[blank line]

Printed: *Cartulaire de l'Abbayette*, no. 5 (from the cartulary).

B. N. lat. 17723, fol. 168, copies one of the original redactions, which was written at the foot of the parchment containing the act of Alan III (no. 17 above) and which was endorsed *Carta de Monte Roaldi et de Landeui et de Cancaure*: adds at [a] Riuuallono priore. Guillelmo priore. The names of two further witnesses, which seem to have been written on the left of the text in two lines placed at a 90° angle, were also present in the original, which read: *signum Conani comitis, Signum Juhaeli archiepiscopi.*

B. N. fr. 22325 (p. 681) and 22357 (pp. 763–4) appear to have copied an eleventh- or twelfth-century copy of this charter, which, according to fr. 22357, was written on the same parchment as a copy of no. 19 below.

19

Rivallon fitz Walter concedes the grant made by his father, Walter fitz Lingulf, and his mother of the third part of the churches of St Peter and St Broladre in Saint-Broladre (Ille-et-Vilaine, cant. Pleine-Fougères), with the assent of the priest Hervé who had claimed that the portion was in his inheritance: 1109.

Carta de ecclesiis sanctorum Petri et Broeladri

IN NOMINE SANCTAE ET INDIVIDVAE TRINITATIS. AMEN.

Ego Riuallonus Galterii filius a nonnullis catholicis uiris frequenter audiui. omnes illos perpetuis fore subiciendos tormentis:· qui ex rebus propriis aliquid domino Deo pro stola immortalitatis induenda negligunt elargiri. uel qui surripiunt ecclesiis siue sanctis quibuslibet locis:· quę concessa sunt a [*in ras.*] predecessoribus ob consequen[fol. 43r]dam gloriam ęternę iocunditatis. Volens itaque gehenne perpetue flammas et labores omnimodis euitare. celique gaudia sine defectu obtinendo considerare:· dono et concedo omni deinceps calumpnia deposita illud donum quod pater meus Galterius filius Lingulfi.[a] et mater mea. pro animę sue saluatione Deo sanctoque MICHAELI archangelo eius[b] monachis ad Dei seruicium in monte qui Tumba ab incolis nuncupatur constitutis. deuote intentionis proposito in perpetuum contulerunt:· terciam uidelicet partem ecclesiarum sancti Petri. sanctique Broaladri. concedente Herueo presbitero qui in prefatis ecclesiis hereditario iure portionem clamare solitus fuerat. Sed ut huius doni concessionem libentius facerem. et firmius ego et mei heredes finetenus tenerent:· abbas et monachis datis michi pro hac confirmatione .xxx.[ta] solidis:· me et meam uxorem. meosque filios ac filias. omnesque meos parentes:· fecerunt eorum fraternitatis participes. Facta est[c] huius donationis renouatio. anno dominice incarnationis .m°. centesimo nono. Secunda indictione. Istius res datores. concessores. et testes cum eorum signis:· pagina sequens ostendit. Qui ergo[d] hoc donum quod ego Riuallonus renouaui infregerit.[e] nisi resipiscat. anathema sit.

[2 lines blank]

B.M. lat. 10072, fol. 29, no. 23, copies an original formerly at Saint-Lô. [a] Ingulfi filius [b] eiusque [c] est autem [d] uero [e] infringerit

Copies by G. Beauchesne, Arch. dépt. de La Manche, 6 J 70, M 10, from an original formerly at Saint-Lô. She records a blank after *mater mea*, and four crosses for signatories whose names were left blank. Also, B.N. fr. 22357, p. 764; B.N. fr. 22325, p. 720, omitting *Istius res..ostendit*; described as 'Copie faite de ce temps-là apparement pour servir d'original'. Defective copy in fr. 22325, p. 682.

20

Notification concerning the grant of the tithe of Saint-Broladre made by William fitz Irsoi, who held it from the archbishop of Dol, before he went to Jerusalem; his brother Hervé, to whose patrimony it also pertained, took it back from the monks, for which he was excommunicate for a long time; Hervé finally conceded the grant on his death-bed, on the advice of Archbishop Baldric of Dol, appointing his nephew and heir Hugh to ensure that the grant was made; after his death, the archbishop and Hugh met with the monks in the Chapter, where the monks agreed to Hervé's wish to be remembered with a trental and a yearly anniversary for some years thereafter:

in the archiepiscopacy of Baldric of Dol, 1107–30; Dom Huynes, in B.N.fr. 18947, fol. 145r, dates this to 1109.

[fol. 43v] *Carta De Decima Sancti Broeladri*

CERTA REI GESTE RECORDATIO. Guillelmus Irsoii filius. Heruei autem frater. iturus Ierusalem quandam decimam de Sancto Broeladro quam[a] tenebat de Dolensi archiepiscopo. Sancto MICHAELI et monachis de Monte dedit. Herueus uero frater suus qui ei ad patrimonium suum heres surrexit. decimam illam monachis abstulit:· pro quo sacrilegio diu excommunicatus fuit. Tandem Dei respectu misericorditer flagellatus est:· et ad mortem usque infirmatus est. Vocauit autem ad se Baldricum Dolensem archiepiscopum. cuius monitu et concessu decimam illam reddidit:· et cum beniuolentia et rogatu Hugonis nepotis sui qui ei erat successurus et successit illud totum fecit. Conuenerunt autem in Sancti Michaelis capitulo post mortem Heruei archiepiscopus prelibatus et Hugo. et causa ista retractata. et beneficio[b] quod a monachis postulauerat memorato. uidelicet tricennale unum. et per quotquot annos anniuersarium suum:· rem istam taliter scribi mandauerunt. et scriptam cartulam manibus suis confirmauerunt. Testibus his. Signum Baldrici archiepiscopi. Signum [+] Hugonis filii Rannulfi. Signum Gilduini Dolensis ducis. Signum Gilduini filii Haymonis. Signum Guidonis filii Rannulfi. Signum Girardi filii Ernaudi. Signum Briendi.[c] Signum Willelmus [*sic*] pin[fol. 44r]cerne. Signum Eudonis Gofredi filii. Signum Eudonis Gobio. Signum Garuueni Guillelmi filii. Signum Alueredi de Trahan. Signum Gofredi archidiaconi. Signum Guillelmi decani. Signum Stephani canonici. Signum Gofredi Gingonei filii. Signum Heruei dapiferi. Signum Eudonis Baderonis filii.

Copied from the original in B. N. fr. 22357, p. 763. [a] quia [b] benedicto [c] Giraldi filii Ernaudi de Briendi. In B.N. fr. 22325 the copyist remarks, p. 679, of the names after *Briendi*: 'Les noms qui suivent sont d'une autre écriture beaucoup moins ancienne que la precedente'. In fr. 22327 these names are placed in a group under the first set of names, which are in a list. Also copied in B. N. lat. 5430A, pp. 57–8, preceded by a charter of Hugo fitz Rannulf, printed below in **App. ii.6**. Copied from the Cartulary by G. Beauchesne, Arch. dépt. de La Manche, 6 J 70, M 8.

21

Grant of land and tithes in the parish of Saint-Pierre and Saint-Broladre (Ille-et-Vilaine, cant. Pleine-Fougères), the tithe of the mill and a vineyard, and the rents due to the church by Trihan fitz Brien, with the consent of his wife Adelina and son Geoffrey, on condition that he be given food and wine when he visits the abbey for prayer; if he should remain on the Mont in time of war, he would receive the same daily portion of food and wine as a monk; should he or his heir wish to become monks, they would be made monks; cf. no. **56**; the land granted is identified by name in another version, dated 1075, given in **Appendix i.7** below, which provides a link with no. **89**: 1081.

De sancto Broeladro

IN NOMINE SANCTAE ET INDIVIDVE TRINITATIS PATRIS ET FILII ET SPIRITVS SANCTI. Ego Trihan Brientii filius do sancto MICHAELI et monachis ei seruientibus concedente uxore mea Adelina et Gaufrido filio meo duodecim acras terrae. et unam ad faciendum ortum. et quicquid habeo decimarum in parrochia Sancti Petri et Sancti Broeladri. et decimam molendini mei et uirgulti. et quicquid habeo in eisdem ęcclesiis de redditu qui ad ecclesiam pertinet. Hoc totum dono sancto MICHAELI pro salute animę meae et antecessorum meorum et successorum. tali condicione quod quando perrexero ad sanctum MICHAELEM causa orationum habebo caritatem sancti MICHAELIS de pane et uino. Et si per guerram mansero apud Montem quamdiu ibi fuero habebo cotidie de pane et potu quantum unus monachus. et si forte uoluero effici monachus aliquando. cum parte possessionis meae in omni re mobili et censu. facient me monachi monachum. et heredem meum simi[fol. 44v]liter. Quod si quis heredum meorum hanc donationem calumpniari aut auferre aut etiam minuere uoluerit: cum Iuda traditore Domini in perpetuum sit dampnatus. et gehenne igni traditus. amen. Huius rei sunt testes Guillelmus Trossel. Homenes. Gaufredus Hosa. Euenus Roillei. Guillelmus Bordon. Actum est hoc anno ab incarnatione domini millesimo. lxxx°. primo. Tempore Rannulfi eiusdem loci abbatis. Signum Trihani. +. Signum filii eius. +. Signum uxoris sue. +.

[13 lines blank]

Copy from the original in B. N. fr. 22325, p. 719. Copy of uncertain provenance in fr. 22325, p. 682

22

Grant of three vills, including Kerbéquet and the modern 'lieu-dit' Saint-Iger, and the moiety of a mill in the *uicaria* of Ménéac (Morbihan, arr. Ploërmel, cant. la Trinité-Porhoët), and one vill, Quénogé, in the *uicaria* of Mohon (Morbihan, arr. Ploërmel, cant. la Trinité-Porhoët) by Guethenoc, later *vicomte* of Porhoët, his wife Allarun and sons Goscelin, Maingui and Tutgual: probably 992, after the death of Conan I of Brittany.

[fol. 45r] *Carta de Porrohot. ę Sancto Igaro*[1]

IN NOMINE SANCTE ET INDIVIDVE TRINITATIS PATRIS ET FILII ET SPIRITVS SANCTI.

Inter cetera bene agende uite opera. non minima laude predicatur elemosina. Peccatorum enim eme[*corr. ex* u]ndationem. diuina pagina testatur esse elemosinam. Date inquiens elemosinam. et omnia mundabuntur uobis. Flammarum etenim sicut est aqua extinctio. sic et peccaminum elemosina. Denique redemptio animę uiri: diuitie eius. Salutare quippe creditur esse opus. sique nobis misericorditer indulget conditor ei reddamus. si de his quę uel moriendo amittimus. uel quae nos uiuentes deserunt: celeste mercemur introitum. Quę namque felicior ualet esse coemptio. quam dare obolum. et recipere celum? Dare peritura. et recipere aeterna? Dare terrena. et assequi

[1] A later hand added: 'De S. Iquier en Meneac'.

cęlestia? Venale siquidem regnum celorum dicitur. Ad hoc igitur emendum: cuicumque proprius cum bona uoluntate census sufficit. Vidue suffecit quadrans. Dimidium bonorum: Zacheo. Iusto: frigide aquę calix. Quid plura? Tanti ualere regnum cęlorum credimus: quantum quisque habet. His et quam plurimis igitur Christiane institutionis ego Guestenoc[a] incitatus hortamentis. nosse uolo tam presentes quam absentes. quod criminum [fol. 45v] meorum ualde multitudinem metuens. uiteque perpetue gaudium post mortem adipisci desiderans. de patrimonio meo loco sancti MICHAELIS fratribus ibi Deo monastice seruientibus quattuor uillas sitas harum tres in uicaria nuncupata Meiniac.[b] quarum hęc sunt uocabula. Tretgkented.[c] et Kaibesgel.[d] et Ros. quarta in uicaria Mothon. hęc est Kainotker. et medietatem unius molendini in uicaria ubi site sunt tres predicte uille perpetualiter possidendas donatione sollempni tradidi ea lege. eoque tenore ut absque contradictione omnium meorum successorum predictus locus eas teneat. habeat. possideat. cum omnibus ipsis uillis appendiciis. et cum omni debito preter decimas. quę pertinent ad sancti Petri ecclesias. Quod si aliquis huius donationis testamentum quod et ego et uxor mea Allarun et filii mei. Goiscelinus. Mainchi.[e] et Tutgual hodie pro salute nostra constituimus diabolice prauitatis telo iaculatus contaminare uoluerit. perhenni maledictione cum Dathan et Abiron infernalibus perhenniter cruciandus tradatur ignibus. Vt autem eiusdem donationis auctoritas uerius credatur. diligentiusque per omnia conseruetur. firmius denique futuris teneatur temporibus: manu propria subter firmauimus. Signum Guestenoc.[f] Signum Allaron. Signum Goiscelinus. Signum Mainchi. Signum Tutgual. Signum Kenuuarchoc.[g] Signum Breselumarchoc.[h] Signum Boio. Signum Ogerius. [fol. 46r] Signum Gausbertus Abba. Signum Bergalt. Signum Petrus. Signum Omnes. Signum Inisan.[i] Signum. Iudichel. Signum Mainchant.[j] Signum Bilionu.[k] Signum Idgun.[l] Signum Nomenoi.

[5 lines blank]

The copy in fr. 22357 (pp. 677–8) is a 'copie par *vidimus* de l'original sain et entier par le bailly de Costentin la ditte copie dattée du 2e de may l'an 1366'; it begins 'Ego Guihenocus'and presents the witnesses in a different order. Partial copy in B.N. fr. 22325, pp. 769–70. [a] Guihenocus [b] Miniac [c] Tregentel [d] Herbischel [e] Maingi [f] Guethenoci [g] Kermerhoc [h] Breselmarhoc [i] Enisiant [j] Moankaut [k] Bilio [l] Idguin

See Hubert Guillotel, 'De la vicomté de Rennes à la vicomté du Porhoët', *Mémoires de la Société d'Histoire et d'Archéologie de Bretagne*, t. lxxiii, 1995, pp. 8–9.

23

Charter of Alan III of Brittany restoring, for the souls of his parents, his brother Eudo and himself, at the request of Abbot Almodus, the churches of Saint-Meloir and of Saints Méen and Judicaël (Cancale), in the pays d'Alet, previously granted by his father Geoffrey but subsequently lost by the mismanagement of the abbot's predecessors, with the proviso that should any of the abbot's successors seek to alienate the churches and associated gifts of land at Cancale (Ille-et-Vilaine) and a neighbouring port (Porpican) from the abbey, the whole should revert back to Alan or his successor: (interpolated) 1032.

Carta de Ecclesiis de Pooeleth

IN NOMINE SANCTE ET INDIVIDVE TRINITATIS PATRIS ET FILII ET SPIRITVS SANCTI AMEN. Diuine scripture incitatus hortamentis quae nos precipit terrenis mercari celestia. perituris mansura mutari:· testante domino date inquiens elemosinam et omnia munda erunt uobis:· Ego Alannus gratia Dei comes et dux Britannice gentis. notum esse uolo cunctis presentibus atque futuris quod adierit me Almodus abba Montis Sancti MICHAELIS necnon et monachi ipsius loci obsecrantes benignitatem nostram quatinus pro remedio anime nostre patrisque ac matris meę fratris quoque mei Eudonis ęcclesias duas sitas in territorio quod uocatur Pooleth scilicet Semmeler[a] atque Semmeuuen[b] Iudichel quas pater meus Gaufridus comes ac ma[fol. 46v]ter mea Hadeuuis olim pro salute animarum suarum ipsi sancto loco tradiderant:· sed ob incuriam antecessorum abbatum uel monachorum a loco penitus segregate fuerant:· restituerem. Terram quoque prope litus maris sitam quę dicitur Chancaure. et portum qui nominatur Porpican. Quorum peticionibus annuens. dignum duxi satisfacere uoluntati eorum. reddens eis ęcclesias superius nominatas. et quicquid ab ecclesiis recipitur. <uidelicet decimas et omnino oblationum primitias. absque cuiuspiam contradictione cuiuscunque dignitatis uel ordinis sit;[c]> ea uidelicet ratione. ut ipsi monachi eas omni tempore ad proprios usus retineant. Et ne quis abbatum per succedentia tempora aliter commutari audeat:· prohibemus. Quod si fecerit. aut in nostra redigantur potestate:· aut triginta libras michi persoluat. Si quis autem huic nostrę redditioni calumpniam inferre conatus fuerit damnationem ęterne mortis accipiat. excommunicationique cum maledictis subiaceat. sitque pars eius cum Dathan et Abiran:· et cum Iuda traditore Domini. Vt autem hoc per labentia tempora custodiatur firmiusque teneatur:· propria manu subter firmare curauimus. fidelium quoque meorum nomina sub quorum presentia hęc acta sunt:· annotari iussimus. Signum Alanni comitis. + Signum Hadeuuis comitissæ +. Signum Heudo comes. Signum Gingonei archiepiscopi. Signum Warini episcopi Reddonensis. Signum [fol. 47r] Trischan abbatis. Signum Budici comitis. Signum Gotselini uicecomitis. Signum Riuallonis. Signum Trischan filii eius. Signum Radulfi cantoris. Signum Ratfredi clerici. Signum Gorenton. Signum Adselini. Signum Otberti. Signum Aldronis. Signum Radulfi Angli. Signum Gaufredi filii Hugonis. Acta uel firmata est huius carte conscriptio:· anno ab incarnatione domini nostri Ihesu Christi . m°. xxx°. ii°. Indictione xv.[d] Concurrente vi. Epacte .vi. Regnante Henrico. Rotberti regis filio. anno primo. [3 blank lines]

B. N. fr 22357 (pp. 782–3) is a copy of the original. The cartulary version of the indiction is correct. [a] sancti meler [b] sancti meuuen [c] *deest* [d] xii
Printed: Guillotel, *Actes des ducs de Bretagne*, no. 22, pp. 85–8.

24

Charter of Ansger and Herve relating how their father mortagaged the church of Poilley (Ille-et-Vilaine, cant. Louvigné-du-Désert) to the abbey in the time of Abbot Mainard (II) but subsequently granted it to the abbey in return for the supply of horses to him and his sons by the abbey in time of war; because the abbey failed to supply the horses, the church reverted to the brothers, who now regrant it to the abbey and Abbot Thierry (1023–7) in return for the promise of asylum there in time of war, persuading their other brother William to accept the agreement, which was confirmed by the signature of Alan III of Brittany, his vassals and their own, and their children: 1023–7.

Carta de Ecclesia de Pollei

IN NOMINE SANCTAE ET INDIVIDVE TRINITATIS PATRIS ET FILII ET SPIRITVS SANCTI. Ego Ansgerius et Herueus frater meus:· commendauimus facere istam cartam. Aperta causa est satis. quod pater noster Gradelocus. unam ecclesiam dedit sancto MICHAELI de uilla quę dicitur Pollei tempore Mainardi abbatis in uadimonium;[a] propter quattuor libras denariorum. Postea ductus amore Dei et sancti MICHAELIS uenit in locum illum. et dedit eandem ecclesiam sancto MICHAELI in proprium alodum pro remedio animę suę:· retentis quattuor libris denariorum quas prius acceperat. Sed et mater nostra:· pro eadem causa unum uesti[fol. 47v]mentum ualde bonum habuit de pallio. ea uidelicet ratione. ut quocienscunque eueniret patrem nostrum uel nos ire in prelium:· a monachis sancti MICHAELIS duos equos prestitos haberemus:· deinde sanos redderemus. Quod si tanta necessitas eueniret. ut aliter fieri non posset:· omnis locus sancti MICHAELIS nobis esset ad refugium. Qua auctoritate eandem ecclesiam semper tenuerunt et patris nostri tempore:· et nostra ętate. donec deficiente ab eis conuentione de caballis quia grauis erat. eandem ecclesiam recepimus. Nunc autem prouidentes utilitatem anime patris nostri et nostrarum animarum:· reddimus eam sancto MICHAELI tempore Theoderici abbatis. laxata conuentione de caballis:· et acceptis octo libris denariorum in testimonium. Et si necessitas Werre nobis euenerit:· habeamus refugium ad sanctum MICHAELEM. Et quia Guillelmus frater noster clamorem facit in ista causa:· donamus omnem fidutiam quia conparticipem eum fecerimus de ceteris bonis patris nostri. de quibus expers est:· dabimus ei pro isto clamore aliorsum iustam partem uicissitudinis. Nec sit in perpetuum ex omni progenie nostra:· qui iam amplius in ipsa ecclesia clamorem faciat. sed sit sancti MICHAELIS in ęternum:· sicut supradictum est. Et ut hoc stabile permaneat in sempiternum. confirmandum tradimus auctoritati domini nostri ALANNI comitis. et uasallorum eius et nostre. et infantum nostrorum. Si quis autem hoc aliquando uiolare presumpserit:· [fol. 48r] maledictione et excommunicatione perpetua dampnetur cum Iuda traditore Domini et cum Achitofel periuro:· et cum omnibus inimicis Dei. Signum Alanni comitis. +.

[a] in uadimonium: et hoc in uadium **D**

B. N. fr. 22357 (p. 757) copies the original, noting: 'L'acte est original et est dans une mesme liasse avec les deux suivants' (i.e. the charters of Bishop Maino, no. 40. below, and of Bishop Stephen of Rennes).

Printed: Morice, *Preuves*, col. 350–51; Guillotel, *Actes des ducs de Bretagne* no. 17, 63–5, adding (from B. N. fr. 22327 and other copies of the original) after Alan's the signatures of *Eudonis fratris eius, Warini episcopi, Gingonei archiepiscopi.*

[rest of fol. 48r, all of fol. 48v, and 11 lines of fol. 49r, blank]

25

Grant by Rainald *miles* and his mother Hersende of the monastery of Saint-Victeur in the suburbs of Le Mans, with its *bourg* and appurtenant lands and revenues, all on the right bank of the Sarthe, facing the south of Le Mans, and other gifts including eight arpents of vines at Baugé (comm. Le Mans), revenues held in benefice from Saint-Gervais, land to the value of a carrucate at *Mansum Nouum*, all the vill of *Fraxinus*, the vines at *Montrond* of the cleric Durand, who attests the charter; the grant had been the wish of his father Drogo who died before it could be made; the abbot and monks have full discretion over the direction of the monastery: enacted at Mont-Saint-Michel, in the presence of Abbot Suppo, March, 1040.

[fol. 49r] *Donatio de Sancto Victurio*

IN NOMINE DOMINI AMEN. Ego Rainaldus miles cum matre mea Hersende notum esse uolumus omnibus sancte Dei ęcclesię fidelibus. quoniam Drogo pater meus dum uiueret monasterio sancti MICHAELIS archangeli destinauit donandum monasterium sancti Victurii quod est situm in suburbio Cenomannice urbis. ad supplementum uictus seruorum Dei ibi degentium. Quod quia preueniente morte complere non potuit. ego Rainaldus et prenominata mater mea pro remedio animę eius et [fol. 49v] nostrarum animarum redemptione. concedimus sicut ipse pater meus disposuit presente uenerabili abbate ipsius loci Suppone. sancto MICHAELI archangelo prenominatum sancti Victurii monasterium cum rebus subter notatis:· id est burgum quod est circa ipsum monasterium cis Sartam flumen cum omnibus consuetudinibus quę ad nos pertinent. et decimas uini et panis et omnium rerum quę pertinent ad ipsum locum. et octo arpentos uinearum in Monte Balgeio. et censum quem de iure sancti Geruasii in beneficio tenemus. et ad mansum nouum terram quantum sufficit ad unam carrucam[a]. et totam terram de uilla quę dicitur Fraxinus. et prata quę sunt[b] ad riuum Aldonis. et in Sarta fluuio exclusam de Marciaco. Concedimus quoque terram et uineas quas fidelis noster Durandus clericus in Monte Rotundo tenet de nobis:· ex eius consensu. Hęc omnia concedimus sancto MICHAELI archangelo. ad supplementum uictus monachorum sibi seruientium. et in perpetuum concessa esse uolumus. pro remedio anime prenominati patris mei. et nostrarum animarum. ut habeant. teneant. et possideant iure[c] perpetuo. absque ulla calumpnia. et ipsum monasterium sicut placuerit abbati et monachis disponant et ordinent. et quicquid eis placuerit ex ipso faciant. Vt

autem hęc nostre donationis carta in perpetuum firma et stabilis permaneat. manibus nostris eam subter firmauimus. et fidelibus nostris firmandam tradidimus. [fol. 50r] Actum monasterio sancti Michaelis publice. Signum Rainaldi qui hanc donationem fecit. + Signum Grodulfi qui testis est. + Signum Gosberti. +. Signum Goscelini. + Signum Goffredi. +. Signum Hersendis femine quę hanc donationem fecit. +. Signum Arnaldi. +. Signum Durandi clerici. +. Data mense martio. Regnante Henrico rege anno. xiii.[d]
[1 blank line]

Printed: Broussillon, *Cartulaire de Saint-Victeur*, noted the existence of three mid-eleventh-century recensions of this act, of which he published a facsimile of the shortest. The cartulary text is closest to the recension published as *Cart.S.Victeur*, no. 7, with the following variants: [a] ad duas carrucas [b] pratos qui sunt [c] in [d] Hilduinus cancellarius scripsit *add.* This was the original version, as shown by A. Dubois, 'Dépendances et prieurés du Mont Saint-Michel', *Mill. mon.* i, 658. The version printed as *Cart. S. Victeur*, no. 6, which was copied in lat. 1540a, p. 130–1, omits 'data mense martio' and adds after [d] *Avisgaudo pontifice ecc. B. Juliani Cenoman. presidente qui hoc elemosine donum salutifere crucis munimine subsignauit. S. Auesgaudi episcopi. Huberti clerici. Raginaldi capellani. Hugonis Brecci.* The death of Avesgaud at Verdun on 27 October 1039 shows that the witness-list in this version, produced at the Mont, was interpolated (Dubois, *ibid.*). See also R. Latouche, *Histoire du comté du Maine*, app. vi, pp. 132–4; Jacques Dubois, 'Les moines dans la société du moyen âge (950–1350)', *Histoire monastique en France au XIIe siècle* (London, 1982), 10–33. Another recension was printed in *Gallia Christ.* XI, Inst. 106–7.

26

Charter by which Ivo fitz Fulcoin, at the request of Abbot Mainard II restores eight vills (*Villarenton*, or L'Abbayette, now La Bayette, Chante-Pie, Valandré, Montgulfon in La Piffetière, all in the commune of La Dorée, cant. Gorron, dépt. Mayenne, Laserie, Villechardon, La Lortière and Le bas or Le haut Genêt, hamlets in the commune of Landivy, Mayenne) granted by his ancestors to the abbey but subsequently lost during the Norman invasions, all of them located at the point (comm. La Dorée, Mayenne) where the *pagi* of Maine and Avranches meet; he acts with the assent of his maternal uncles Bishop Seifrid and William, his sisters Billehendis and Eremburg, and his kinsmen William the cleric, Robert, Suhard and William the layman: enacted at Fresnay-sur-Sarthe, 12 October, 997–1003/4.

Carta de Villarenton[1]

IN NOMINE SANCTE ET INDIVIDVE TRINITATIS PATRIS ET SPIRITVS SANCTI. Predecessorum patrum[a] decretum traditumque est. ut si quis suarum quiddam facultatum cuilibet sanctorum loco sue pro remedio anime donauerit. seu quolibet cumque modo tradiderit. ut perpetualiter ab omnium succedentium calumpniatione inconculsa incontaminataque ipsa donatio seu traditio perseueret: exinde auctoritatis testamentum sollempniter faciat. Quocirca ego

[1] in abbatiola [L'Abbayette] *add. man. rec.*

IVO notum uolo esse omnibus tam presentibus quam futuris. quod monachi sancti Michaelis Mainardus uidelicet abba ceterique fratres sub eo degentes me adeuntes.[b] postulauerunt ut terram quam mei antecessores pro suarum salute animarum iam olim loco eiusdem sancti Michaelis donauerant. sed irruente Normannorum infestatione locus ipse per multorum curricula annorum [fol. 50v] amiserat. eidem loco fratribusque ibi Deo sanctoque archangelo seruientibus. pro meorum parentum[c] animabus nec non etiam pro meorum remissione peccaminum redderem. Quorum peticionibus pulsatus multociens.[d] adquieui tandem:· compensans quam felix foret commertium pro terrenis celestia. pro temporalibus mercari permansura. quid etiam diuina suadeat sententia. quę nos amicos facere precipit de iniquitatis mammona:· ut[e] nos in eterna recipiant tabernacula. et quoniam sicut ignis aqua. sic elemosina extinguitur peccatum:· atque illic nostros recondere thesauros. ubi eos neque erugo neque tinea deteret. Huiuscemodi igitur et aliis ortamentis submotus meorum reminiscendo peccaminum. nimiumque pertimescendo mortis perpetue exitium. gaudiique celestis tota auiditate mentis concupiscendo contubernium. reddidi predicto loco atque fratribus ibi semper Deo sanctoque Michaeli seruientibus cum consensu et uoluntate meorum parentum duarum uidelicet sororum mearum Billehendis atque Eremburgis. nec non duorum auunculorum Seinfredi episcopi et Guillelmi. atque cognatorum Guillelmi clerici. Rotberti. Sutsardi. rursusque Guillelmi laici. predictam terram. uillas scilicet. viii^{to}. nuncupatas his uocabulis:· Villarenton:[f] Cantapia: Valandrein:[g] Lacerins: Montgulfon: Cardun: Larcellosa: Genei: sitas in territorio Cenomannico in confinio Abrincatensis regionis. Reddidi quippe et tradidi eis pro salute animae [fol. 51r] meae atque patris mei Fulcoini. et matris mee Rothais. et omnium meorum parentum perpetualiter possidendas. cum terris cultis et incultis. cum siluis. cum aquis. et cum omnibus ipsis predictis uillis appendiciis. ea lege atque tenore. ut habeant. teneant. possideantque eas omni tempore:· absque omnium parentum meorum seu quoruncumque calumpniatione et contradictione successorum. Quod si quis huiuscemodi testamentum diabolice prauitatis stimulatus aculeis effringere atque contaminare uoluerit. Dei omnipotentis uirtute et sancti[h] MICHAELIS cui iniuriam facere presumpserit. atque omnium sanctorum anathematizetur perhenniter. Vt autem huius nostre redditionis auctoritas uerius credatur et dilgentius conseruetur per omnia. firmiusque futuris temporibus teneatur:· manu propria subter firmauimus. Actum castro Fraternensi .iiii. idus Octobris regnante Rotberto rege Francorum. Ego Iuo firmaui. +. Gosbertus signauit. +. Herueus signauit. +. Willelmus. signauit .+. Walterius signauit .+. Goscelmus signauit +. Tescelinus signauit. + Walterius signauit +. Lanbertus. signauit .+. Tescelinus signauit .+. Goscelinus. Signauit .+.
[3 blank lines]

Printed: B. de Broussillon, *Cartulaire de L'Abbayette*, no. 1, with a facsimile of part of the original, now destroyed.

Reprinted with full discussion in K. S. B. Keats-Rohan, 'Two Studies in North-French Prosopography: 1', *Journal of Medieval History*, 30 (1994), 1–25. The full, three-column witness list of this charter is one of the most valuable clues to its importance. The cartulary reproduces only the first column. The missing witnesses were (2nd col.) Siginfredus episcopus, Guarnerius, Hingelbertus, Harman, Erchengerius, Hugolinus Mori, Framengerius, Hugolinus, Vuillelmus clericus, Gerardus, Ingelrammus, Rotbertus, (3rd col.) Hugonis comitis, Radulfi uicecomitis, Isaac, Droco, Harduini, Haimonis, Mainardi, Vuillelmi, Hodonis tesaurarii, Huberti, Huberti clerici, Haimelini;, Hugolini.

The following variants are taken from the partial facsimile of the original published in *Cart. de L'Abbayette*: [a] patrum auctoritate [b] adientes [c] meorum parentum] eorum [d] multoties [e] qui [f] Villa Arunton [g] Val Andrein [h] sanctique

27

Grant, for the souls of his father and mother, of four arpents of vines, two at Montfort, a small hill to the west of Le Mans, one at *Montcuch*, and one at Saint-Vincent, a suburb of Le Mans, by Hugh III count of Maine, in return for daily prayers in perpetuity for his salvation: 992–1015.

[fol. 51v] *De Sancto Victurio*

IN NOMINE SANCTE ET INDIVIDVE TRINITATIS. Antecessorum nostrorum constitutis atque decretis uere compertum habemus. ut quicumque Christi fidelium bonorum cupidus celestium quiddam suarum facultatum cuilibet loco sanctorum uel donauerit pro animae remedio uel uendiderit:· exinde litterale testamentum nobilium personarum corroborationibus assignatum faciat. quatinus ab omni contradictione uel calumpniatione malorum ipsa donatio uel uenditio firma et intemerata atque integra futuris permaneat temporibus. Qua propter ego Hugo comes Cenomannensium cunctis Christianis tam presentibus quam absentibus notum esse uolo. quod meorum pro magnitudine peccatorum perpetuas metuens inferni penas. et celestis regni desiderio accensus:· pro salute anime mee meorumque parentum patris uidelicet et matris. beati archangeli Michaelis loco ibique fratribus Deo regulariter tam seruientibus quam seruituris. quattuor uinee aripennos quorum duo sunt in Montefort. tercius uero in Monte Cuch. quartus autem inter duas uias ad Sanctum Vincentium. sine ulla contradictione uel parentum uel meorum successorum perpetuo habendos tradidi et possidendos:· eo tenore quatinus pro remedio anime mee et uiui. et uiuituri. perpetualiter cotidianis Deum [fol. 52r] precibus deprecentur. Nam plurimis diuinarum scripturarum relationibus animabus[a] purgamentum peccatorumque remissionem:· elemosinarum largitionem rerumque mortalium distributionem penitus credo. Vnde michi thesauros illic thesaurizare tota mente desudo:· ubi quicquid sanctorum ecclesiis Christique famulis diuino erogatur amore redditur centuplicatum. De cetero si quis diabolica stimulatus inuidia his testamenti litterulis impedimentum quesierit.[b] mearumque erogationibus elemosinarum uim aliquomodo inferre presumpserit:· hic aeterna dampnatus maledictione.

tormentis apud inferos subiaceat imis. Quod ut uerius firmiusque futuris permaneat temporibus: manu propria subter firmare studuimus. Signum Hugonis comitis .+. Signum Guillelmi iuuenis. + . Signum Goslini. + . Signum Huberti. + . Signum Guatselini. + . Signum Alberici. + . Signum Elinalaii.[c] + . Signum Hugonis Dublelli. +. Signum Hugonis Normanni. + . Signum Garnerius clericus. + . Signum Ingelardus clericus. + . Signum Rotselinus. clericus. +.[d]
[1 line blank]

Printed: *Cartulaire de Saint-Victeur du Mans*, no. 2, with partial facsimile of the original. B.N. lat. 10072 no. 3 is a copy of the whole original. There is a *copie figurée* in lat. 1540a, pp. 134–5. Variants in the original are: [a] animarum [b] quaesierit [c] Elinalai (Elinali *ap.* lat. 10072) [d] Hubertus clericus Constantinus clericus *add.*

28

Ralph *vicomte* of Le Mans, his wife Godehild and son Ralph, when on a pilgrimage to the Mont, grant, for the salvation of their souls and those of their progeny living, dead and yet to be born, a vineyard next to a place called Vieuxpont in a suburb of Le Mans; to ensure the validity of his gift, he has his charter confirmed and authorized by Hugh III of Maine: *c.* 992–1000.

Carta de Clauso Vinearum Cenomannis

IN NOMINE DEI Rodulfus gratia Christi summi regis omnipotentis Cenomannis uicecomes. Quicumque res omnium fidelium matris sanctę Dei ęcclesiae augere conatur. bona sibi est uoluntas et optimi operis [fol. 52v] cultus. Quod ego Rodulfus gratia Dei Cenomannensis uicecomes uigili animo pertractans et sollicita mente requirens. cepi memor esse meae salutis. necnon et meae bone coniugis Godehelt. et cuncte meae progeniei. Ergo nouerit omnium fidelium multitudo. quoniam dum nuper montem sancti Michaelis causa orationis cum coniuge predicta et filio nomine Rodulfo petierim. optuli et dedi sancto Michaeli et omnibus inibi Deo seruientibus tam presentibus quam futuris clausum uinearum pro salute animae meae et meae coniugis nomine Godehelt et filii Rodulfi. et cuncte progeniei tam uiuorum quam defunctorum nec non et futurorum. Est autem predictus clausus uinearum iuxta ciuitatem in suburbio. in loco qui dicitur Vetus Pons. Sed et ut donatio quam de hac re sancto MICHAELI supra eius altare feci firma in perpetuum haberetur: cartam manu firmatam exinde fieri iussi. et eam firmandam domino meo comiti Hugoni optuli. et firmare bono animo feci. ut iure perpetuo firma permaneat. nullusque mei successor eam calumpniari presumat. et quicumque presumpserit. cum Iuda Christi domini proditore. et Anna et Caipha dampnationem accipiat. Signum Hugonis comitis. .+. Signum Radulfi uicecomitis +. Signum Godehelt uxoris eius. +.
[1 line blank]

Printed: *Cartulaire de Saint-Victeur*, no. 1, from the cartulary, which Broussillon states is the only known copy of this act.

29

Notification of a grant of five arpents of vines made by Odo, citizen of Le Mans, and his wife Hersende, when on a visit to the abbey; in return for the monks' prayers they grant a third of their vines whilst they both live; after one of them dies, the monks will have half of the vines; when both have died, all the vines will pass to the monks: enacted at Mont-Saint-Michel in the presence of Abbot Suppo: 1033–40.

[fol. 53r] *De uineis Cenomannis*

NOTVM SIT OMNIBVS VERAM SANCTĘ TRINITATIS fidem colentibus. Odonem quendam uirum Cenomannensem cum propria uxore quondam sancti MICHAELIS adisse limina. ac fratribus eiusdem sancte ęcclesię sedule Deo famulantibus quandam obtulisse donationem. Deliberatione namque habita. quinque uinearum aripenna presente Suppone eiusdem loci abbate cum ceteris monachis. predicte ęcclesiae iam dictus uir cum uxore propria pro suorum peccaminum solutione ac spirituum requię. mente deuota contulit. Hoc quoque decreuit ea fieri conditione. ut fratrum ibidem famulantium Deo in orationibus utrique facti participes. quandiu aduiuerent terciam partem suarum omnium uinearum. sancti Michaelis monachis per unumquemque mitterent annum. Dum autem eorum alter uite presentis sortitus occasum fuerit. qui superstes extiterit. iuxta sponsionem suam predictis fratribus totius uini medietatem committet. At uero postquam uterque defunctus fuerit. in ius sancti Michaelis ad usus fratrum eidem archangelo seruientium omnes prefate uineae sorte pariter cedent. Hanc igitur donationem predictus uir ODO scilicet cum uxore sua Hersendi nomine. super aram sancti archangeli scriptam deposuit. ipsius loci abbate [fol. 53v] Suppone presente cum ceteris monachis. eamque manu sua per hoc. + crucis signum firmauit. Hanc igitur oblationem sancto huic loco deuote traditam si quis subtrahendo aliquatenus uiolare presumpserit: a celesti patria seclusus. et a sanctorum omnium collegio perpetim segregatus. diabolo eiusque sociis commissus. in perpetuis gehenne mittatur ignibus. ubi per infinita tempora crutietur. Amen.
[3 blank lines]

Copy in B.N. lat. 5430A, p. 135–6

Printed: *Cartulaire de l'Abbayette*, no. 4, and *Cart. Saint-Victeur*, no. 5, from the cartulary.

30

Sale, at the request of Abbot Hildebert, of two parts of the church of *Centrannis*, by Hugh [de Sillé], his wife Regina, sons Hugh and William, and his brothers Gauslin and Heribran; he had at first refused but had finally agreed, with the assent of Hugh III count of Maine and on the advice of his own men, in return for an annual rent of eight pence, payable on the Feast of St Denis; cf. no. 47: 1009–1015.

Carta de ecclesia Centrannis

IN NOMINE PATRIS ET FILII ET SPIRITVS SANCTI
Ego Hugo nosse uolo tam presentes quam absentes. tam uiuentes quam uicturos. quod monachi sancti Michaelis abba scilicet Heldebertus et ceteri sibi commissi ad me uenientes. pecierunt ut duas partes ęcclesiae quę Centrannis uocatur eis uenderem. Quod primum aliquandiu renuens. tandem eorum postulationi adquiescens. per mei domini Hugonis assensum et per meorum fidelium consilium. uxoris quippe meae Regine nomine. et filiorum Hugonis atque Willelmi. fratrumque meorum Gauslini et Heribranni. predictas ęcclesiae partes [fol. 54r] duas eisdem monachis uendidi. eo tenore ut eas teneat. habeat. possideat locus sancti Michaelis perpetualiter sine ullius contradictione. soluant autem annis singulis ad festiuitatem sancti Dionisii octo denarios in censu. Quod si aliquis meorum successorum exinde aliquam eis iniuriam uel calumpniam inferre presumpserit. perpetua dampnetur maledictione. Vt autem huius uenditionis auctoritas uerius et perfectius futuris temporibus conseruetur. manu propria subter eam firmaui.
[3 lines blank]

Printed: *Cartulaire de l'Abbayette*, no. 3 (from the cartulary).

31

Grant of an allod at Tissey by Count Robert, for the salvation of his deceased wife Bilihild, his living wife Ascelina and his sons William, Robert and Richard, with whose consent he is acting; the act is subscribed by Richard II of Normandy, Robert, archbishop of Rouen, and Gunnor, their mother: *c.* 1015. Reappears as no. 60 below.

De Tissiaco

IN NOMINE SANCTAE ET INDIVIDVE[a] TRINITATIS PATRIS ET FILII ET SPIRITVS SANCTI. AMEN. Institutionibus antecessorum nostrorum procul dubio sancitum ac decretum esse scimus:ʼ ut si quis sacro baptismate renatus quiddam suarum facultatum perhenniter possidendum. uite celestis afflatus nectare tradere loco sancti alicuius uoluerit. firmissimum exinde fulcitumque plurimis conuenientium auctoritatibus personarum testamentum faciat. quatinus id inconculsum permaneat. ac denegari penitus non queat. Igitur ego Rotbertus comes [fol. 54v] notum esse tam a presentibus quam ab absentibus omnibus Christianitatis titulum ferentibus uolo. quod meorum inmensitatem criminum timens. et celestis uite gaudium habere cupiens. quoddam alodum scilicet Tesiacum loco beati Michaelis monachisque ibi regulariter Deo seruientibus pro animae meae salute. ac deinceps pro remedio anime uxoris meae Billeheldis[c] defuncte. et pro uiuentis Asceline. filiorumque meorum Guillelmi et Roberti. atque Richardi. quorum uoluntate. consensuque id ago. perpetualiter possidendum trado. Dinoui etenim quam plurimis referentibus sancte Christianitatis doctoribus esse quoddam peccatorum purgamentum largitionem[d] elemosinarum. et diuino monitu. illic thesauri[e] recondendi. ubi nec furis astutia inerit. nec tinearum esura incoabit. Nam quod Deo in

largiendo elemosinam tribuitur. centuplicatum in celis reconpensabitur. Legitur etenim regnum Dei tantum ualere. quantum cuique est posse. Valuit siquidem uiduę quadrans. et Petro rete et nauis. profuit et Zacheo dimidium bonorum. Nichil itaque est id quod finitur ad id quod fine non clauditur.[f] His igitur et aliis salutiferis incitamentis ammonitus. predictum alodum loco pr̨edicto tribuo sub tocius ęcclesiae testimonio cum terris cultis et incultis. cum pratis et omnibus appenditiis. eo tenore ut absque calumpnio seu contradictione successorum parentum meorum habitantes in prefato loco habeant. teneant. possideant. Et [fol. 55r] si quis stimulatus iaculo diabolice calliditatis huic dono calumpnium inferre presumpserit. tocius ęcclesię excommunicationibus perhenniter detineatur. Vt autem hęc datio uerius credatur et firmius diligentiusque futuris teneatur temporibus. manibus Richardi comitis. atque Roberti archiepiscopi. et eorum matris Gonnor. et uxoris meae Ascelinę. filiorum meorum Willelmi. Roberti. Richardique ac militum meorum subter firmandam corroborandamque tradidi. Signum Norgoti episcopi. +. Signum Geraldi. + . Signum. Radulfi.[g] +. Signum Eremberti. + . Signum Petri. + . Signum Nielli . + Signum Drogonis. +.
[3 lines blank]

Printed: Fauroux, no. 16; the original was destroyed in 1944, but an edition of it was published by Delisle, *Saint-Sauveur*, pièces just. p. 1, no. 1. Additional witnesses are given in another copy of the charter later in the cartulary; see no. 60 below. Variants from the original as published by Delisle and Fauroux: [a] indiuisibilis [b] actoritatibus [c] Bileeldis [d] largitio [e] thetauri [f] claditur [g] Rodulfus

32

Grant by Abbot Maiol, with the consent of the monks of Cluny and of Marmoutier, of land at Le Mortier (Indre-et-Loire, cant. Tours, comm. Saint-Symphorien) in the Touraine at the request of Abbot Mainard and the monks of St Michael; the monks may hold and possess the land for as long as they live according to the Rule of St Benedict, and render each year on the Feast of St Martin a rent of twelve pence each year to Leutbald and his son Dacfred: the date in the forty-first year of King Lothar – *anno xli* – is clearly erroneous. It was clearly intended at the Mont that the date should be read as *anno xii*, the twelfth year, i.e. 966. The use of an 'l' form for a long 'i' occurs elsewhere in the cartulary, normally within personal names such as Haimo; see below no. 44; however, the charter belongs to the period of Cluniac reform at Marmoutier, hence, 21 March 982–6.

De uineis Turonis

IN NOMINE SVMMI SALVATORIS DEI. Ego quidem frater Maiolus abbas una cum consensu fratrum Cluniensium. nec non et fratrum Maioris Monasterii. feci traditionem de terra quę sita est in pago Turonico in uilla Morter propter deprecationem domni Mainardi abbatis. nec non et fratrum sancti MICHAELIS ibidem Deo seruientium in tali tenore. ut quam diu ipsi monachi secundum

regulam sancti Benedicti regulariter uixerint. teneant. et possideant. et omni anno incensum duodecim de[fol. 55v]narios reddant ad festiuitatem sancti Martini Leutbaldo et Dacfredo filio suo. Terminatur uero ipsa terra de duabus partibus terrę sancti Martini. et de aliis partibus uie publice. Est autem prima donatio ista quod fecit domnus Maiolus abbas una cum consensu fratrum suorum ad locum sancti MICHAELIS et ad monachos ibidem Deo seruientes. Signum Maioli abbatis. +. Signum Viuiani leuite. + Signum Hunibaldi sacerdotis. + signum Otmari. sacerdotis. +. Signum Achedei sacerdotis .+. Signum Rainoni sacerdotis. + Signum Azonis sacerdotis. + . Signum Otgerii sacerdotis. + Signum Leutbaldi et filii sui Dacfredi qui consenserunt. Data per manum Randuini sacerdotis in mense Marciis die .xxi. regnante Lothario rege anno xli.
[1 line blank]

Printed: from the Cartulary: K. S. B. Keats-Rohan, 'Une charter de l'abbé Mayeul de Cluny et la Réforme du Mont Saint-Michel', *Société de l'Histoire de Normandie*, 2000.

33

Grant, on fulfilling a long-standing desire to become a monk, of the isle of Guetehou (east of Guernsey) by Restald, former ship-master to Robert of Normandy, who gave the isle to him; after his death, the isle will pass in heritance to the monks on condition that Restald is remembered in perpetuity as a member of the community: 1027–35. This charter is repeated later in the cartulary (no. **110** below).

De Keteho

Ego Restaldus nauclerus quondam Roberti Normannie comitis. diuina inspiratione permotus: monachilem habitum diu ualdeque desideratum tandem suscepi. Quod factum iam dictus princeps piissimus Robertus gratanter accipiens. quandam paruam insulam quę uulgo Keitehuml uocatur perpetuo michi possidendam contradidit. Hanc autem insulam cum omnibus quę adquisita sunt a me in ea aut possidentur: post mortem meam do sancto Michaeli et fratribus sibi [fol. 56r] seruientibus iure hereditario possidendam. ea uidelicet conditione. ut factus particeps omnium elemosinarum ac benefitiorum quę ipsi faciunt. ascribi et annumerari sim dignus eorum frater atque socius in perhenni seculo.
[3 lines blank]

Printed: from the Cartulary, in *Cartulaire de Jersey*, no. 148, pp. 226–7.

34

Pancarte containing a series of three grants by the Oculus Canis and Brunel families of Châteaudun establishing the priory of Gohory (Eure-et-Loir, cant. Brou). Theoderic Oculus Canis and his brother Walter made extensive grants in Gohory, including moieties of the chapel and of certain tithes, other moieties being granted by Gerard Brunel and his sons Helgod, Ralph, Hugh and Adam; enacted at Braye in the house of Bernard de Brou, in the presence of Geoffrey fitz Godescal, lord of the fee in which the land lay, 1081. Walter Oculus Canis, wishing to go to Spain, grants the moiety of tithes in Gohory which had been retained at the time of the initial grant, at Châteaudun in the house of Geoffrey fitz Godeschal and in the presence of *vicomte* Hugh of Châteaudun, Walter's brother Theoderic and Ralph, and their brothers-in-law Hugh de Roche and William de Melleville; the grant was received by the monk Ranulf, who had the charter drawn up at Mont-Saint-Michel, 1087. On Christmas Day 1093 Walter Oculus Canis confirmed the grants by writing his cross on the charter and placing it on the altar of St Michael at the Mont, in the presence of Abbot Roger, the prior Matthew, subprior Martin and the cantor Main; 1081, 1087, 1093.

Carta de Gohere

IN NOMINE SANCTE ET INDIVIDVE TRINITATIS PATRIS ET FILII ET SPIRITVS SANCTI. Anno ab incarnatione domini millesimo [lxxx] .i°. hęc carta facta est. Antecessorum nostrorum institutionibus sancitum decretumque est ut qui suarum facultatum quiddam loco sanctorum alicui uite superne accensus amore perhenniter possidendum tradere uoluerit: sollempne exinde idonearum personarum plurimis astipulationibus fulcitum testamentum. ut id inconuulsum permaneat faciat. Referentibus enim quam plurimis sanctae Dei ęcclesiae doctoribus diuinum esse preceptum didici. ut illic nostri recondantur thesauri: ubi omnis aberit furum formido. omnisque tinearum [fol. 56v] demolitio. esseque quoddam peccatorum purgatorium elemosinam. et quod Deus in largiendo munificos exposcit: qui se in retribuendo preparat munificentissimum. Detur igitur Deo: non nostrum sed suum. Quid enim habere putamus. quam quod ab eo accepimus? Tribuatur frigide aquae calix: ut eterna recipiatur merces. Tanti ualere regnum audimus Dei : quantum habemus. Suffecit uiduę quadrans. Profuit et Zacheo: bonorum suorum dimidii distributio. Quę denique ad id quod finitur. id quod non finitur comparatio? Scilicet pro terrenis celestia. propituris mereri perpetua. His et aliis diuine auctoritatis incitati hortamentis ego Teodericus Oculus Canis et Gauterius similiter Oculus Canis uocatus frater meus. penas inferni cupientes effugere. et paradysi gaudia desiderantes habere post mortem corporis: damus sancto Michaeli de periculo maris et monachis in eodem loco Deo seruientibus quendam locum qui Goheri uocatur in Dunensi pago. capellę scilicet medietatem. et quicquid iuris ęcclesię in ea nostrum est. Concedimus eis etiam uiginti aripenna terre cum quadraginta hospitibus. et decimam eorumdem aripennorum medietatem uidelicet. Concedimus quoque eis terram unius carruce cum nostra parte decime. et terragii medietatem totius terrę nostre adiacentis. et pertinentis ad prefatum locum.

Et ego [fol. 57r] Gerardus Brunel do sancto Michaeli et suis monachis aliam partem eiusdem capelle et aliam partem decime aripennorum et carruce monachorum. Et ego Helgotus Brunel concedo. Et ego Radulfus Brunel concedo. Et ego Hugo Brunel concedo. Et ego Adam Brunel concedo. Hęc igitur damus pro remedio animarum nostrarum ac parentum et amicorum nostrorum. et ut simus participes totius beneficii monachorum sancti Michaelis sicut unus eorum. Quod si aliquis diabolice prauitatis telo iaculatus qualicumque modo huic donationi calumpniationis uim inferre presumpserit:· ipse consentientesque sibi totius excommunicationis atque maledictionis cum Iuda traditore et Dathan et Abiron. perhenniter irretiantur uinculis. amen. Hęc itaque donatio facta fuit in castrum Braio in domum Bernardi de Buslo. uidente et audiente Gaufrido Godescalli filio. cuius beneficio et admonitione istud totum factum fuit. Ipse eciam hoc concessit et Ada coniunx eius. et Hugo filius eius. Huius donationis sunt testes qui adfuerunt presentes. Bernardus de Buslo. Hosmundus de Malo Consilio. et Garnerius frater eius. Gaufridus Guarin. Rainaldus del Castel. Hugo de Arreis. Raherius faber. Girardus filius eius. Hermandus Boccharius. Gauterius filius eius. Durandus Grinnun. Anschetillus clericus. Rannulfus monachus suscepit istud donum. Rainaldus decanus testis est huius dona[fol. 57v]tionis. et ipse fuit inde per omnia procurator et adiutor. *Item.*

Anno ab incarnatione domini millesimo octogesimo septimo. Gauterius Oculus Canis uolens ire in Hispaniam. dedit sancto Michaeli medietatem decime de Goheri quam scilicet retinuerat quando primum donum dedit. et quicquid iuris ęcclesię habebat in Montemont siue in illis locis qui pertinent ad capellam de Goheri. Hoc donum tunc temporis fecit:· ut sanctus Michael qui est princeps celestis militie et dux populi Dei eum sanum duceret et incolumen reduceret. Facta est itaque hęc donatio apud Castrum Dunum in domo Gaufridi filii Godescalli presente Hugone uicecomite et concedente donationem omnium rerum quę dantur sancto Michaeli in Goheri. et presente Teoderico Oculus Canis. et Radulfo Oculus Canis qui hoc donum concesserunt. Hugo quoque de Rupe sororius eorum. et Gaufridus Rufus sororius eorum presentes adfuerunt. et Guillelmus de Melesuilla. et Gerricus famulus Gauterii de Dumo. et Garnerius famulus monachorum. et Anschetillus clericus. Hoc donum suscepit Rannulfus monachus:· et hanc cartam fieri fecit in monte sancti Michaelis. *Item*

Anno ab incarnatione domini millesimo nonagesimo tercio. perrexit Gauterius Oculus Canis ad Montem et interfuit ibi in die [fol. 58v] natalis Domini. et ut firma omni tempore hęc carta teneatur per hoc signum sancte crucis subscriptum eam confirmari uoluit:· et super altare sancti Michaelis posuit. et manu sua subscripsit. Signum Gauterii qui uocatus est Oculus Canis. +. Actum est hoc in presentia donni Rogeri abbatis. et Mathie prioris. et Martini subprioris et Maini cantoris et Guillelmi de Boilon. et Garnerii iuuenis. et aliorum multorum monachorum. Isti laici fuerunt presentes. Tescelinus .+ Robertus prepositus. + Guillelmus Calcebuef. +. Si quis igitur huic donationi calumpniam ingesserit. sit a bonis anathema. sit cum malis maranatha:· per omnia seculorum secula Amen. [1 line blank]

The copy (of a copy) found in BN lat. 5430A, pp. 84–5, was alleged to have been made from an unsealed original, probably therefore a pancarte. The copy is poor and collation yields no significant variants. Thomas Le Roy, *Les Curieuses recherches*, p. 135, noted: 'Les lettres de donation sont dans les archives de ce Mont, ainssy qu'un viel manuscript assure; je ne les ay toutefois sceu trouver. Je sçauray plus au vray tout ce qui est ausdites archives lorsque je travailleray à la transcription (aidant Dieu) que je prétend générallement faire des tiltres du monastère'; he later added: 'Je les ay veues depuis'. Cf. Abbé Marquis, 'Gohory, son prieuré de Saint-Michel', *Bull. de la Soc. Dunoise*, t. v (1885–7), 257–76.

35

Charter of Hugh III of Maine relating how he was visited several times by Abbot Hildebert and asked to grant or sell land that was near property already acquired by the abbey; after consultation with his men, Hugh agreed to give land at Voivres-lès-le-Mans (Sarthe, cant. La Suze), going personally with his men to lay the gift on the altar of St Michael: subsequently confirmed at Le Mans, 1014.

Carta de Vedobris

IN NOMINE PATRIS ET FILII ET SPIRITVS SANCTI. AMEN. Ego Hugo Cenomannensis comes hoc scriptum ad perpetuum testimonium fieri iussi:· et confirmatione proprie subscriptionis roboraui. Notum ergo tam presentibus quam etiam nos secuturis fidelibus esse uolumus. qua de causa id fieri statuimus. Adiit sepe nostram presentiam Heldebertus abbas montis sancti Michaelis archangeli de periculo maris et aliqui sub eo degentes monachi. petentes ut in uicino earum [fol. 58v] rerum quas in pago Cenomannico tam a nobis quam eciam ab aliis possident. aliquam bene utilem terram uel pretio quanto dignum esset eis uenderem:· uel sancto Michaeli pro remedio anime mee perhenniter[a] possidendam donarem. Propterea uero id tanto tempore[b] flagitabant. quatinus inde haberent unde tam ipsi quam etiam eorum equi alerentur quando aliqui eorum mitterentur ad supra dictas res preuidendas:· quia quicquid ex earundem rerum redditibus capiebant. pene totum ineundo redeundoque dispendebant. Nostrorum itaque fidelium in hac causa usus consilio. atque instinctu pulsatus diuino:· potius elemosine fructum salutemque anime ęternam quam transitorium pecunie[c] propter hoc a Deo uolui percipere.[d] quandamque nostri iuris terram quę Vedobris dicitur:· Deo et sancto Michaeli disposui donare. Videbatur autem ipsa terra satis nobis utilis et per necessaria. sed iccirco terrena et transitoria gratanter Deo dare debemus. ut ab eo celestia et ęterna recipere mereamur. Quadam igitur uice ad predictum sancti archangeli locum ueniens:· memorato abbate cum suis monachis et quibusdam nostris fidelibus coram positis. donum de predicta terra per unum cultellum super altare sancti Michaelis posui. Tradidi itaque illi loco deinceps perpetualiter absque aliqua calumpnia libere possidendam supra memoratam terram quę dicitur Vedobris. sicut eam saltus undique circuncludit. cum [fol. 59r] omnibus quę in ea sunt id est ecclesia. molendino. pratis. uiuariis:· ea ratione ut ipsi monachi pro nostra salute et pro tocius regni nostri conseruatione semper proprias orationes ante Deum et sanctum Michaelem faciant. Si quis uero huic nostro dono contradictor et uiolator[e] esse presumpserit. ante Deum in tremendo iuditio cum sancto Michaele de hac re contendere habeat. et si non emendauerit eternam dampnationem cum diabolo recipiat. Vt ergo hoc donum inconuulsum futuris temporibus conseruetur: hoc scriptum ad testimonium fieri iussum nostra subscriptione firmaui. nostrorumque fidelium nominibus signari feci. Signum Hugonis comitis. +. Signum Roscelini uicecomitis. + . Signum Auesgaudi episcopi. + . Signum Hamelini de Leido Castello. + . Signum Huberti clerici. + . Signum Haimonis. + . de Medano. Signum Rainaldi capellani. + . Signum Herberti fratris comitis. + . Signum Hugonis brecci. + Signum Droci filii Milonis. + . Signum Odilarii drudi. + .

Firmata Cenomannis anno ab incarnatione domini .m°. x°iiii°.

[5 lines blank]

Printed: *Cartulaire de Saint-Victeur*, no. 4, with a facsimile of the now lost original. [a] perenniter [b] tanto tempore] tantopere [c] pecunie] pecunie questum [d] recipere [e] uiolantor

The original spells the archangel's name *Micahael* throughout.

Copied from the original in BN lat. 10072, no. 4. The charter is listed in Latouche, *Histoire du Maine*, Catalogue d'Actes, p. 140.

36

Grant of two churches, and other benefits, on the Loir at Créans (Sarthe, cant. La Flèche, comm. Clermont-Créans) by Josbert Gaustevin, for the souls of his parents Gauslin and Hadvisa, with the assent of his lord Archembald (de Braye-sur-Maulne, Indre-et-Loire, cant. Château-la-Vallière), who subscribes the act with his wife Isabel: 1109–16.

[fol. 59v] *Carta de Criant*

Ego Iosbertus Guasteuin Guaslini filius[a] Dei benignissimi amore instigatus. concedo Deo et sancto Michaeli in monte qui dicitur Tumba. duas ȩcclesias de CRIANT super flumen Ledum. et terram ad unam carrucam. et tres arpenz de prato in dominio. et uicariam eiusdem loci et domum unam. et medietarium similiter in dominio et quiete. Ceterum de aliis reditibus id est decimis. et altaris omnibus consuetudinibus medietatem. et unam piscatoriam dimidiam. insuper et de omnibus aliis medietarium exitibus quȩ in eodem haberi possunt loco. medietatem tantum monachis sancti Michaeli tribuo. exceptis quȩ supra dixi dedisse me in dominio. De silua autem alnorum quȩ in eodem loco est similiter modis omnibus medietatem concedo. Hȩc igitur omnia quȩ supra dicta sunt assensu domini mei Erchembaldi Deo et beato Michaeli celestis militiae principi atque suis monachis. pro remedio anime patris mei Guaslini atque matris meȩ Haduisȩ concedo possidenda perpetuo. et ut si Deus michi inspirare dignatus fuerit ut ad monachum uelim ordinem peruenire: quod ipsi monachi libenti animo suscipient me. Vt autem hȩc mea donatio inconuulsa

permaneat. per cuncta succedentia tempora: nomina eorum qui mecum fuerunt cum hęc donaui hic subter imprimenda cum suis sancte crucis signis curaui. [fol. 60r] Signum Iosberti. +. Signum Erchembaldus dominus suus. + . Signum Isabel uxor Erchembaldi. +. Signum Girardus de Labarbedh. +. Signum Harduini. +. Signum Pagani filii Erchembaldi. +.
[1 line blank]

[a] Iohannes Gasteuin Gastini filius in lat. 5430A p.102; on p. 107 a charter of 'Iosbertus cognomento Gasteuin' is copied from a copy of an unsealed original; see **Appendix i.2** below.

Printed: Guilloreau, *Chartes de Créans*, no. III.

37

Grant of 4 arpents of vines in Sillé-le-Guillaume (Sarthe) by Walter the Rich of Mont-Saint-Jean (Sarthe, cant. Saint-Georges-le-Gaultier); the gift is placed upon the altar by his financier Martin, since Walter is confined to bed with a mortal illnes after his return from a pilgrimage to Rome: the grant is recorded in the bull of Adrian IV in a manner suggesting that the grant was recent, hence that is belongs to Bernard's abbacy: 1131–49, probably 1145–9.

Carta de Vineis de Sille

IN NOMINE SANCTĘ ET INDIVIDVE TRINITATIS PATRIS ET FILII ET SPIRITVS SANCTI AMEN. Ego Guaterius de Monte Sancti Iohannis qui et Diues uocitor. superni conditoris respectu compunctus. ob innumerabiles criminum meorum actus limina apostolorum Petri et Pauli Rome adire uolui. quod et Deo iuuante compleui. Sed cum regrederer. apud Cheremalam incidi inegritudine ualida. Et cum ualde affligerer. et iamiamque ad extrema me propinquari uiderem. ab amicis admoneor. ut de meo iure Deo ac sancto Michaeli archangelo in monte qui Tumba uocatur ac suis monachis pro saluatione mee anime aliquid largirer. Denique perscrutatis omnibus meis rebus nil tam de omni meo iustum repperi. quam quasdam meas uineas quas apud Sillei propria manu ac sumptu edificaueram. Has igitur perpetim sancto Michaeli possidendas absque cuiusquam qualibet iusta calumpnia trado. et hic heu miser lecto decubans. per Martinum feneratorem meum fidelem [fol. 60v] donationem hanc super altare eiusdem archangeli ponendam trado. Continentur he uinee de quattuor arpentis. Signum Guaterii. +. Signum Martini. +.
[2 lines blank]

Printed: *Cartulaire de Saint-Victeur*, no. 21, is a transcript of the cartulary containing a number of errors.

38

Charter by which Robert grants, from his inheritance, the churches of St Victeur at Lévaré (Mayenne, cant. Gorron) and St Berthevin(-la-Tannière), with the assent of Hugh de Mayenne; his gift is made on the death of previous holders who had sold the church to the abbey with the consent of Geoffrey de Mayenne (fl. 1050–1098); he also gives two carrucates of land, and cedes the moiety of all his remaining possessions to St Michael, reserving to himself alone the service of his knights, anyone of whom may make his own gift to the abbey, but will not be compelled to do so; Hugh of Mayenne assents to his grant; the confirmation of Bishop Hildebert of Le Mans is appended: *c.* 1098–1100.

Carta de Liuare

IN NOMINE SANCTE ET INDIVIDVE TRINITATIS QUĘ VVLT omnes homines saluos fieri. et ad agnitionem ueritatis uenire:ʼ ego Rotbertus, inspirante superna clementia saluti anime mee consulens, offero Deo sanctoque archangelo Michaeli et sibi famulantibus de mea hereditate duas ecclesias sitas in territorio Medani castri, uidelicet ecclesiam Sancti Victurii et Sancti Bertuini cum omnibus rebus quas iuri ęcclesię certum est pertinere, quas monachi sancti Archangeli quondam consensu Gaufredi Medani castri ducis. a possessoribus qui tunc eas sibi ue[*corr. ex* i]ndicarant acceperunt. Ego uero ipsis decedentibus fauente Hugone supra dicti Gaufredi fratre, easdem sancto Michaeli et sibi famulantibus restitui. Preterea ex meo hereditario iure famulantibus eidem archangelo contrado duarum carrucarum terram. suo dominio perpetuo possidendam. sine ulla ab hinc mea dominatione. Ex omnibus uero rebus quę michi supersunt scilicet terris. siluis. aquis. et ceteris [fol. 61r] quecunque. in talibus possidentur. quicquid adquisitum fuerit uel ut apertius dicam quicquid exinde lucri exierit:ʼ medietatem michi. et aliam sancto Michaeli concedo. Excipio tantum modo meorum militum seruitium. quod michi soli retineo:ʼ hoc etiam insuper addens. quod si aliquis ex eisdem militibus ex sua terra aliquid tradere ipsis monachis pro remedio animae sue uoluerit:ʼ sine ulla mea contradictione efficere poterit. Quin eciam hoc adiungo:ʼ quia nulli meo homini exceptis militibus:ʼ ullam uim faciam. preter commune consilium eorumdem monachorum. Hęc autem si quis instigante diabolo euellere conatus fuerit. ęterni ignis flammas sustineat. Et ut omnia supra dicta inconuulsa permaneant:ʼ manu sua Hugo dux Medani castri firmare non renuit. Deuotis fidelium beneficiis assensum non denegare et diuini muneris est et consuetudinis seruorum Dei. Vnde et ego Hildebertus sanctę Cenomannensis ęcclesię indignus episcopus prefati Rotberti beneficio assensum prestiti. saluoque nostrę matris ęcclesię iure prefatam corroboraui largitionem. Ne quis igitur prescriptam donationem uel iminuere uel adnullare presumat omnimodis prohibemus. eos anathematis iaculo confodientes quicumque in irritum quod absit prefatum deducere temptauerint beneficium. Ne quis autem dubitet prefatam a nobis prodisse confirmationem. manu propria subscripsimus:ʼ nostroque signauimus sigillo. Signum Hugonis ducis.+. [fol. 61v] Et egomet subter firmaui. Signum Rotberti datoris huius doni. +. Testibus his idoneis adhibitis. qui subter inscripti sunt. Signum Burcardi filii Rotberti. +. Signum Guarini fratris eius. +. Signum Rotberti filii Pauonis. +. Signum Fulcuini. +. Signum Stabilis. +. Signum Guillelmi filii Gaufredi. +.

Signum Radulfi. +. Signum Laurentii. +. Signum Gauterii. +. Signum Rainaldi clerici. + . Signum Fulcuini. +.

[3 lines blank]

Printed: *Cartulaire de l'Abbayette*, no. 8, from the Cartulary.

39

Charter by which Robert de Saint-Denis confirms his father Robert's grant of the church of Saint-Denis-de-Gastines (Mayenne, cant. Ernée), its tithes and other revenues, which had belonged in ancient times to the monks but had been lost to them no little time ago and had become part of the inheritance of Robert's family; the younger Robert adds the grant of a tithe called the tithe of *Prigmanei*, in return for which the monks give him a palfrey and six pounds in the money of Le Mans; Robert places his grant on the altar in the presence of Prior Rannulf; he undertakes to have the grant ratified by his lord Hamelin de Mayenne: 1116.

Carta de sancto Dionisio. et de decima de Prigmanei

IN NOMINE PATRIS ET FILII. ET SPIRITVS SANCTI:· SANCTE ET INDIVIDVE TRINITATIS. **Ab** antecessoribus nostrum statutum et sancitum est. ut si quis sancte ęcclesię et ei seruientibus aliquid iure hereditario possidendum de rebus suis aut possessionibus pro salute anime sue dederit. ipsam donationem coram Deo et testibus idoneis faciat. et autenticis scriptis confirmet. ut ipsa donatio firmius omni tempore in posterum teneatur. possideatur. et ueracior ab omnibus futuris credatur. Vnde ego Rotbertus miles de Sancto Dionisio. pro salute anime mee et patris mei parentumque meorum tam illorum qui precesserunt. quam illorum qui uiuunt et futuri sunt concedo. confirmo illam [fol. 62r] donationem quam fecit pater meus Rotbertus sancto Michaeli et suis monachis de ęcclesia sancti Dionisii scilicet in decimis et in aliis redditibus quę ad ecclesiam pertinent. quę uidelicet ipse iure hereditario possederat. Quas uidelicet res sciendum est quod antiquitus sanctus Michael et ei seruientes possederant et habuerant. sed malignorum culpa aliquanto tempore perdiderant. Reddidit itaque pater meus quod ei per patrimonium de eisdem rebus acciderat sancto Michaeli et ei seruientibus sicut dictum est:· et inde donationem coram testibus super altare sancti Michaelis fideliter optulit. Eandem igitur donationem concedens et confirmans. dono quoque sancto Michaeli et suis monachis pro salute anime mee quandam decimam quę uocatur decima de Prigmanei ut eam in perpetuum habeant et possideant. Accepi tamen inde ab eisdem monachis sub caritatis nomine sex libras denariorum Cenomannensium et unum palefridum. Hanc itaque donationem siue concessum manu mea ego Rotbertus per unum cultellum super altare sancti MICHAELIS posui. presentibus monachis Rannulfo priore. Petro Cosme qui tunc temporis ipsas res et eandem obedientiam custodiebat et possidebat. Rotberto Walcher et pluribus aliis. Presente etiam Guarmundo clerico. et Gaufredo milite de sancto Dionisio. et Euueno ac Odone famulis eiusdem ęcclesię. Hanc quoque donationem promisi me facturum concedere ab Ha[fol. 62v]melino de Meduana domino meo:' et ab omnibus de quibus opus fuerit habere concessum. Si quis igitur inuidia diaboli accensus ex his quę sancto Michaeli et ei seruientibus concedo. dono. in posterum aliquomodo aliquid abstulerit siue calumpniauerit. aut eis ad possidendum nocuerit:' sit ei pars cum Iuda traditore Domini. et in perpetuum gehennalibus penis crucietur. Et ut hec donatio firmius teneatur. ac ueratius credatur:' manu propria eam signo sancte crucis confirmo. Acta anno dominice incarnationis .M°.C°. xvi. Indictione .ix. Signum Iuhelis fratris Hamelini. Meduani. +. Signum Rotberti. +.

[3 lines blank]

Printed: *Cartulaire de l'Abbayette*, no. 9, from the Cartulary.

40

Charter of Main, bishop of Rennes, and his clergy, conceding and confirming to the abbey the churches of Villamée and Poilley (Ille-et-Vilaine, cant. Louvigny-le-Désert) belonging to the cathedral church of Saint-Pierre de Rennes, for which convention he receives a bay horse from the monk Hernald; Bishop Main and all the canons of Rennes, as well as all previous and future bishops of Rennes, are to be received into confraternity at the Mont; the act is attested by Main II, seigneur de Fougères, his wife and their suckling son Juhel (given pennies by the monk Hernald to stop his crying), and many of their vassals, as well as Robert I de Vitré, whose name is preceded by that of two men whom he held as prisoners: 1050.

De ecclesiis de Villamois et Poillei

IN NOMINE IESV CHRISTI **Ego Mainus** Redonensis episcopus. in meo pontificatu concessi cum consensu cleri mei duas ęcclesias cum parroechiis suis monachis sancti archangeli MICHAELIS:' scilicet aecclesiam de Villamois. et ecclesiam de Poillei:' ita ut eas iure hereditario absque alicuius contradictione in perpetuum possideant. sicuti actenus eas mater ęcclesia episcopatus sancti Petri Redonensis ciuitatis possedit. Hanc con[fol. 63r]uentionem quidam monachus nomine Hernaldus. sed et supra dicti monachi a me redemerunt pretio .xx[ti]. solidorum Cenomannensium. atque unius equi badii bene ambulatorii. coram testibus uidentibus et audientibus:' qui subter scripto diligenter adnotati sunt. Pro qua re. tam michi quam omnibus canonicis sancti Petri sed et cunctis predecessoribus meis atque subsequentibus episcopis. largiti sunt participationem benefactorum suorum. atque socios asciuerunt in orationibus et elemosinis:' necnon in omnibus bonis actionibus in sempiternum Amen. Si quis autem hanc conuentionem irritam fecerit. a Deo se dampnandum nouerit:' et nostro mucrone taliter se iugulari atque confodiri lugebit. Ex auctoritate omnipotentis Dei. patris. et filii. et spiritus sancti. et sanctę Marię perpetue uirginis. sancti quoque archangeli Michaelis. necnon et sancti Petri apostolorum principis. sed et omnium sanctorum Dei:' interdicimus ne

quisquam hoc testamentum faciat irritum. Quod si fecerit ;· perpetuo sit maledictus atque insolubiliter excommunicatus. Amen. Amen. Fiat. Fiat. Actum hoc anno dominice incarnatione. M°.L°. Indictione .iii[a]. Hi re geste;· testes affuerunt Mainus de castro Felicense [Signum eius]. Adelaidis uxor eius [Signum eius]. Iuthalis [Signum eius] puer filius eorum;· qui uagiens adductus inter amplexus matris. ab Hernaldo monacho duodecim denariis pacificatus quieuit. Hugo [signum eius] filius ipsius Adelaidis. Item Hugo [signum eius] frater Gaufredi qui erat in boiis.[a] Rotscelinus filius Rotberti [signum eius] [fol. 63v] de Marcilei;· qui erat in uinculis. Rotbertus de Vitrei. [signum eius] Herbertus filius Ansgerii [signum eius]. Raganarius. [signum eius] Item alii. Ansgerius uicarius [signum eius]. Guillelmus [signum eius] frater eius. Yvo bastardus [signum eius]. Hamelinus de Castelario [signum eius]. Herueus filius Albergie [signum eius]. Berengerius filius Iohannis [signum eius]. Hermengotus filius Duiseth [signum eius].
[2 lines blank]

Printed: from the cartulary: K. S. B. Keats-Rohan, 'Crime et châtiment à la manière du XIe siècle? Note sur une charte bretonne en faveur du Mont Saint-Michel', *Mémoires de la Société d'Histoire et d'Archéologie de Bretagne*, t. lxxiii (1995), 25–30; Morice, *Preuves*, col. 359.

[a] boul B. N., fr. 22357, bonis B. N., fr. 22325, bous *sic* Beauchesne

B. N. fr. 22357 (p. 758) copies the original, as probably did B. N. fr. 22325, pp. 674–5. The reading of the original was either uncertain at this point or the various copyists were unable to recognize the word. There is no doubt that the cartulary reading (from *boiae*, *-arum*) is the correct one. Geneviève de Beauchesne's copy of a now lost original (Arch. dépt. de la Manche 6 J 70, M20) noted that the date was added in a different hand, which also wrote the *signa*. The two hands were contemporary: 'date rejouté mais d'une écriture qui peut être de la même époque'. The witness names were in the hand of the text.

41

Charter of Geoffrey fitz Rivallon granting the church and all the tithes and other revenues of Levaré, (Mayenne, cant. Gorron), and land that can be cleared to yield two carrucates for exploitation, and for the building of dwellings for three rural burgesses; he also gives pannage in all his woods; he has entered into confraternity with the monks on the understanding that he will eventually be buried at the Mont; all his personal property is given to the monks should he die before his wife, and conversely: *c.* 1082–1100.

De Liuare

EGO Gaufredus Riuallonis filius. cupiens sancti archangeli Michaelis iuuari meritis et intercessionibus;· sibi ac suis monachis perpetuo in monte qui Tumba nuncupatur Christo famulantibus ex michi a Deo contraditis facultatibus do ecclesiam de LIVARE[a] cum tota decima. omnibusque suis aliis redd[*corr. ex* red]itibus qui mei iuris fore noscuntur. et terram ad duo aratra eam sufficienter excolentia. Addo tres soli areas ad trium burgensium domos

faciendas: qui sancti Michaelis cum eorum consuetudinibus sint. Concedo etiam pascua omnium siluarum mearum ad solummodo proprios eorumdem monachorum porcos alendos. absque ulla calumpnia et contradictione. Hoc autem ideo eidem beato Michaele archangelo ac sibi famulantibus concessi: quia eorum societatem tali conuentione accepi. ut consorte[b] omnium mortalium [fol. 64r] hominem[c] exiero: corpus meum huc deferatur atque ab eis sepeliatur. atque deinceps uti pro eorum fratre de me agatur. Si autem superno opifici placuerit ut ego ante uxorem moriar. omnium meam partem substantiae meę do et concedo. Quod et de uxore mea: itidem fieri uolo. Testes autem huius meę donationis extant. Radulfus. Gaufredus de Columbiers. Hamelinus. Rogerius filius Adelardi. Harduinus de Lassala [*corr. ex* -o]. Rogerius clericus. Alfred Botzart.
[3 lines blank]

Copy in B. N. lat. 10072, no. 75 and B. N. lat. 5430A, p. 146.

Printed: *Cartulaire de l'Abbayette*, no. 7, from the original, now lost: [a] Leuarei [b] cum sorte [c] hominum

42

Charter of Hugh de Saint-Pabual, bishop of Tréguier granting, for the soul of his parents and brothers, the land and tithe in his patrimony at Locmikael in Elliant (Finistère, arr. Quimper, cant. Rosporden), with the assent of his lord Count Geoffrey Boterel I and his brothers, sons of Count Eudo: 1086.

Carta de Hirglas

IN NOMINE SANCTE ET INDIVIDVE TRINITATIS PATRIS ET FILII ET SPIRITVS SANCTI AMEN. Ego gratia Dei Trigaricensis episcopus Hugo de sancto Pabutual diuina inspiratione tactus. pro salute anime mee et patris matrisque meę et fratrum meorum omniumque parentum meorum concedo Deo omnipotenti et beatissimo archangelo Michaeli celestis militie principi ad locum eius qui Mons Periculi Maris nuncupatur. et eundem locum monachis inhabitantibus et Deo sedule inibi seruientibus. eorumque per cuncta labentia tempora successoribus. montem quendam mei iuris et patrimonii perpetuo [fol. 64v] possidendum qui dicitur HYRGLAS cum omnibus appendiciis suis. et decimam meam de quadam terra quę uocatur Plegestin assensu domini mei Gaufredi comitis. et omnium fratrum eius. filiorum scilicet comitis EUDONIS. Si quis autem malignissimi hostis ueneno illectus quod absit. hanc meam donationem irritam facere uel imminuere. aboleriue quolibet modo molitus fuerit: a domino Deo patre omnipotenti et filio eius domino nostro Ihesu Christo et spiritu sancto. omniumque sanctorum et electorum sit segregatus consortio. Fiat pars eius cum omnium malorum principe diabolo. et Dathan et Abiran Achitofelque periuro. et cum Iuda proditore domini. Caypha et Pilato. Simoneque Mago. Hęc uero mea donatio ut inconuulsa perpetim atque rata consistat: subter hic sanctae ac uiuifice crucis signum mea manu inprimendum curaui. omniumque illorum quos huius rei testes adhibui. Signum Donni

Hugonis episcopi. +. Signum Gaufredi comitis. +. Signum Riualloni uicecomitis. +. Signum Stephani filii Eudonis. +. Signum Maingi filii Galterii. +. Signum Prigent filii Derian. +. Signum Osberni filii Riuallon. +. Signum Riocuh filii Brient. +. Signum Vruodi filii Miloni. +. Signum Riuualt filii Wegant. +. Signum Guihomarc filii Riualloni. Acta est hęc donatio anno ab incarnatione domini millesimo octuagesimo vi. regnante rege Philippo in Frantia. In Anglia uero: rege Guillelmo sub archiepiscopo Rothomagensi Guillelmo. et Michaele Abrincensi episcopo. et abbate eiusdem loci Rogerio feliciter.

B. N. lat. 5430a contains a partial copy of a confirmation of this act given in 1209. B. N. fr. 22325, p. 703, gives a partial copy from the cartulary.

Printed: H. Morice, *Preuves...*, ii, col. 460.

The location of this grant was identified in P. Peyron, *Recherches sur le culte de saint Michel au diocèse de Quimper et de Léon* (Rennes, 1896).

43

Niel, a priest in the service of William duke of Normandy finds himself, in the company of the duke's chaplain Stephen, at Mont-Saint-Michel; seriously infirm and solicitous for his soul, he becomes a monk of the abbey and grants the allod of Sainte-Colombe (Manche, cant. Saint-Sauveur-le-Vicomte) which he has from William of Normandy; at the request of the monks, Duke William adds his concession and subscription to the charter: 1054.

[fol. 65r] *De Sancta Columba*

IN NOMINE SANCTE ET INDIVIDVE TRINITATIS PATRIS ET FILII ET SPIRITVS SANCTI AMEN. EGO NIELLVS presbiter apud Montem Sancti Michaelis in seruitio Guillelmi Normannorum principis cum Stephano capellano ipsius degens. grauissima depressus infirmitate ac sollicitus de anime mee salute. cum consilio meorum concedo Deo sanctoque Michaeli ac suis monachis terram quę dicitur sancta Columba quam habui in alodum a Guillelmo Normannorum duce: tali conuentione ut ipsi monachi qui nunc me recipiunt in suum consortium sub monachili professione. absque ulla calumpnia meorum heredum ipsam in perpetuum terram in dominio possideant in omni successura generatione. Precor autem eundem piissimum principem ut huic meę donationi assensum prebeat. quia tam pro sue et heredum suorum quam pro meę salute anime fateor me sancto Michaeli id dare beneficium. ut apud Deum ipsum habeamus intercessorem assiduum. Quoniam igitur omnino sentio diem obitus michi imminere: precor omnes qui se fatentur me integro amore dilexisse. ut si aliquis quod absit temptauerit huic mee donationi calumpniam inferre. mei uice studeant unanimiter obsistere: ne aliquo modo hanc sancto Michaeli eiusque monachis possit auferre. Qui uero hanc inuadere presumpserit: Deo sanctoque Michaeli archangelo cogatur rationem reddere in die iudicii. atque cum [fol. 65v] Iuda traditore domini ceterisque ad sinistram constituendis. ęternis gehenne tradatur incendiis. Huius donationis testes sunt qui signum

crucis subter impresserunt. Signum Nielli. +. Signum Hugolini filii Giruardi. +. Signum Waleranni. +. Signum Osberni Pauionis. +. Signum Restaldi scutellarii. +. Signum Guarini. filii Ernaldi. +. Signum Morini pistoris. +. Ego Guillelmus Dei gratia Normannorum dux supplici peticione rogatus abba[ba]te[1] et fratribus montis sancti Michaelis plurimisque meis fidelibus concedo Deo et sancto Michaeli sibique seruientibus monachis terram quę dicitur Sancta Columba. sicut eam dedit Niellus clericus qui eam de me tenebat in alodum quem etiam ob hoc monachi secum receperunt sub habitu monachili. Consuetudines quoque et seruicia omnia quę de terra exeunt secundum morem Normannię ipsi sancto et monachis in ipsa terra perpetualiter POSSIDENDA TRADO. Si quis autem de ipsa terra uel de consuetudinibus aliquid subtrahere sancto uoluerit: ex auctoritate patris et filii et spiritus sancti perpetue sit addictus maledictioni. reddatque rationem de hoc sancto Michaeli in die iudicii. Ad corroborandam hanc donationem: manu propria, signum uiuificę crucis subpressi. Signum Guillelmi comitis Normannię. +. Signum Maurilii archiepiscopi. +. Signum Gaufredi episcopi Constantiensis. +. Signum Odonis episcopi Baiocensis. +. Signum Hugonis episcopi Abrincensis. +. Signum Nielli uicecomitis. +. Signum Guillelmi filii Osberni [fol. 66r] Signum Guillelmi de Vualuilla. +. Acta est hęc carta et firmata anno ab incarnatione domini millesimo. liiii. Indictione septima. Concurrentibus .v. Epactis nouem. Regnante Henrico Francorum rege. et Guillelmo Normannorum principe.
[2 lines blank]

Printed: Fauroux, 132; see her discussion of the date and the possibility that the name of Archbishop Maurilius is an interpolation.

Copy by G. de Beausse, Arch. Calvados F 5276, of a 'feuille parchemin cart. xv, h[auteur]. 215 x 140mm',

44

Charter of John fitz Rivallon of Dol confirming grants made by his tenants, notably Adelaide, widow of Rainfred Taon, whose son becomes a monk, Hugh Taon, and the *nepotes* of Trehan, of churches, cemetery and other rights in the bourg and parish of St Bramwalator at Bernoui (Ille-et-Vilaine, cant. Pleine-Fougères, comm. Saint-Marcan): *c.* 1066–85/6.

Carta de Bernols

IN NOMINE PATRIS ET FILII ET SPIRITVS SANCTI AMEN. Ego Iohannes filius Riualloni. actus inspiratione Dei. amoreque sancti archangeli Michaelis. nec non precatu iugi monachorum eiusdem celestium principis: annuo et confirmo atque in perpetuum ratas esse decerno. donationes quorumdam meorum fidelium quas de suis beneficiis quae a me tenebant fecerunt eidem sancto archangelo suisque monachis: donationem uidelicet quam ADELAIDIS uxor Rainfredi Taun fecit

[1] This apprently clumsy correction for *ab abbate* should be compared to no. 67, where *rogatus multociens abbabate* appears.

pro anima eiusdem sui mariti proque filio suo quem de hac causa optinuit fieri monachum in eodem monasterio sancti Michaelis: donationem etiam alterius terre quam Hugo Taun. pro sua suorumque parentum animabus pari uoto contradidit. collationem quoque. ęcclesiarum. cimiterii. ac diuersorum fundorum quae in burgo ac parroechia sancti Bramuualatoris contulerunt sepefato beato Micha[fol. 66v]eli Trihant meus fidelis nepotesque sui: perpetualiter possidenda ab ipsius monachis: in omni successione posteritatis. Quicquid itidem fidelium uotiua largitione. seu coemptione. idem fratres studuerint acquirere in tota mei iuris ditione: perpetim eos censeo et annuo possidere.[a] presentis cyrographi rata astipulatione.[b] Et quoniam participationem totius eorum benefacti Dei ipsorumque gratia habeo. cunctam[c] eorum possessionem tam in Normannia quam in Brittannia me fideliter asseruaturum sub Christi sancteque ęcclesiae testimonio spondeo. fidelissimumque me illis ac suis omnibus famulatum[d] impendere quoat uixero. Si quis autem qualicumque occasione pretestatas donationum conuentiones[e] in irritum ducere. a ditioneque monachorum sancti Michaelis quę collata sunt a me meisque presumpserit subducere: cum Iuda domini traditore ac Caypha eorum quoque complicibus eterne dampnationis sententię cogantur subiacere. et eidem beato Michaeli in futuro examine rationem reddere. Gratum quoque duxi hic subindere nomina huius rei testium. ad irrefragabile testimonium quorumque sequentium. Baderon. Halmo Roaldi filius. Halmericus. Gaufredi filius. Gaufredus Radulfi filius. Ilgerius. de Brehelo. Rannulfus Tisun. Guarinus de Maldrelo. et alii multi.

[2 lines blank]

Copied from an unsealed original in B. N. fr 22357, pp. 761–2 [a] possideri [b] rata ea stipulatione [c] de eorum gratia habeo totum [d] facultatum [e] conuentionem. The copy of the witness list in B. N. fr. 22325 (pp. 679–80) shows the same 'l's, for 'i', in Haimo, Haimericus and Maldreio as the cartulary.

45

Notification by Guy d'Etampes, bishop of Le Mans, that Mont-Saint-Michel and Abbot Richard have recovered in his diocese the church of Saint-Berthevin (-la-Tannière) in the pays d'Ernée, which had long been deserted because of troubles afflicting the region, together with the cemetery and tithes of the whole parish, and other appurtenances; in the same parish, William de Gorron granted, in the presence of the bishop at the abbey of Savigny, the chapel of his new castle at La Tannière (Mayenne, cant. Gorron), with land to build dwellings for the monks and an orchard, together with various tithes, including of his forest at Haye-Mainard; the act was confirmed, after an original gift made in the Chapter of Mont-Saint-Michel, by William, his brother Henry and the chapter of Le Mans cathedral, attested by William's wife Matilda and their children, and received also the assent and approbation of Juhel, seigneur de Mayenne, his wife Clemence and their heir Geoffrey:

Guy's confirmation is enacted first at Savigny Abbey on 12 July 1128 and then repeated at Le Mans on 26 July 1128.

[fol. 67r] *Carta de Sancto Bertuino*

IN NOMINE SANCTĘ ET INDIVIDVE TRINITATIS. Ego Guido sancte Cenomannensis ęcclesię episcopus. notum facio tam presentibus quam futuris. quod ecclesia beati archangeli Michaelis de Normannia sita in periculo maris. tempore nostro et prefate ęcclesię Richardi abbatis. recuperauit in diocesi nostra ecclesiam beati Bertuuini. in pago ERNEIE uidelicet. quę tempore longo deserta fuerat per desolationem malorum ipsius patrie: cum cimiterio. et decimis tocius parrochię. et aliis beneficiis ad ipsam pertinentibus: Capellam quoque cuiusdam castri noui quod Taonaria uocatur. in prefate ęcclesie parrochia a Guillelmo de Gorram instaurati. iam dicto Guillelmo coram me apud cenobium Sauiginiense annuente. et donante. cum terra ad faciendas domos monachorum et cum uiridario ibidem propagato. cum decima quoque census hominum prefati castelli et cum decima fori sui. et cum omni decima reditus forestę suae quę [uocatur] Haia Mainardi. et cum decima molendinorum suorum. pariterque furnorum. necnon et piscium stannorum. per augmentum gratie Dei eumdem Guillelmum inspirantis iuste adepta est. Et quemadmodum ego hoc notifico. sic Deo et beato archangelo Michaeli fratribusque Deo seruientibus in predicto loco. uidelicet in maris periculo libere omnino concedo. et bene confirmo. saluo iure Cenomannensis matris ęcclesiae. Vt autem hęc Guillelmi donatio de his quę ad eum pertinent. [fol. 67v] atque nostra simul et concessio. firma et imperpetuum inconuulsa maneat: presentem cartulam inde fieri. eamque sigilli mei impressione roborari precepi. Hoc autem factum est anno ab incarnatione domini .m°. c°. xx°. viii°. iii°. idus Iulii. apud Sauiginiense monasterium. Actum tempore donni Honorii pape. et Ildeberti Turonensis metropolitani. et Ludouici Francorum regis. Fulconis Andegauorum comitis. et Goffridi filii eius itidem Andegauorum et Cenomannensium comitis. Quod postea breui tempore in capitulo Cenomannensi confirmatum est. vii°. kalendas Augusti. supradictis personis uiuentibus. sub presentia et testimonio horum quorum nomina subinferuntur. Hugo decanus qui Paganus cognominatur. Ansgerius cantor. Guillelmus archidiaconus. Hugo archidiaconus. Gradulfus archidiaconus. Guillelmus de Ambrariis. Iuo capellanus. Albericus Galterii. Philippus Godefridi. Guillelmus de Viliaco. Hubertus Herniensis decanus. Garmundus presbyter de Sancto Dionisio. Primo autem quando Guillelmus de Gorram et Hainricus frater eius prefatam elemosinam Deo et sancto archangelo Michaeli et seruis Dei ibidem commorantibus in capitulo ipsius montis fecerunt. interfuerunt quidam laici quorum nomina et signa inferius annotata sunt. Signum Guillelmi de Gorram. +. Signum Hainrici fratris eius. +. Signum Iordani generi eius. +. Signum Gradalonis uicecomitis. et hii alii testes sunt. Rogerius ca[fol. 68r]merarius. Riuallonus Calcebos. Girardus Bona fides. Rogerius filius Marcherii. Hainricus de Monte. Rainaudus Iansellus. Rogerius de Volta. Radulfus frater eius. Rogerius de Maldreio. et Hascoctus frater eius. Signum Matridis uxoris Guillelmi. Signum filiorum eius. Signum Iuhelli. [+] Signum Clementie. [+] Signum Gaufredi. [+] Hoc autem uidit et audiuit Stephanus notarius cancellarii episcopi. Preterea autem quia decet in omnibus bonis auctoritatem esse utriusque reuerentie persone. uidelicet sacerdotis et regis. uel alicuius eorum locum obtinentis et uices agentis: necesssario iure corroborata est supra dicta donatio a IVHELLO principe Meduane. et uxore eius Clementia et filio eorum Gaufrido primogenito. his baronibus suis presentibus et huius rei testibus. nominatim. Odone capellano. Gaufredo dapifero. Mauricio de Gorram. Helluino de Montenai. Osmundo. Pisce. et multis aliis.

Printed: *Cartulaire de l'Abbayette*, no. 10, and Broussillon, *Cartulaire de Laval*, from the Cartulary.

46

Charter of Hugh alias Hiluin of Montenay (Mayenne, cant. Ernée), restoring, for the absolution of his father's soul and his own reconciliation with God and St. Michael, the gifts his father had made of a manse on which to build a house for the monks, with two gardens and an orchard, the tithes of Gevereau, Villemenu and l'Houellerie, and the tithes of the wheat from his mills: *c.* 1128.

Carta de Montenai

IN NOMINE SANCTĘ ET INDIVIDVE TRINITATIS PATRIS ET FILII ET SPIRITVS SANCTI Ego Hugo siue Hiluinus de Montenay reducens ad memoriam quia pater meus res ecclesie sancti Michaelis auferendo in uita sua. quas antecessores sui eidem loco dederant male egerit: ideoque anathematis subiacuerit uinculis: et ego ipse qui easdem res ecclesiasticas post obitum eius iniuste retinui: Monachorum absolutionem pro anima patris mei et [fol. 68v] pro reconciliatione mei erga Deum et erga sanctum Michaelem de tanta offensione quesiui. et proprium donum secundum hoc quod diuina gratia michi inspirauit predicte abbatie feci. Mansionem ad edificandam domum monachi cum hortis duobus et uiridario. et decimam de Geurel. et totam decimam de uilla Mensius. et de Loyleria. et totam illam partem quam cum monachis accipiebam reddo totam ubique liberam. et decimam frumenti de meis molendinis. Et huic dono hi testes affuerunt. Rotbertus de Sancto Dionisio. Rotbertus Rossel, et Gauterius frater eius. Donnus Garmundus clericus. Fortin de Larouresa. Aalelmus nepos eius. Radulfus filius Heruei clerici. Signum Heluini. [+] Signum Rotberti de Sancto Dionisio. [+] Signum Rotberti fratris Heluini [+]. Signum Garmundi presbiteri. [+] Signum Fortini. [+]

Printed: *Cartulaire de l'Abbayette*, no. 11, from the Cartulary.

47

Charter by which Guy sells to the abbey, at the request of Abbot Mainard II, two parts of the church of *Centrannis* which had been mortgaged to the monks by his father-in-law (*antecessor*); on the death of Guy's *antecessor*, and of his wife, to whose dower the parts of the church pertained, the parts of the church and associated benefits reverted to Guy; Guy now makes the sale with the assent of his wife Raimburgis and her sons by a previous husband (Guy's *predecessor*); the act is confirmed by Hugh III of Maine and Bishop Seifrid of Le Mans; cf. no. **30**: probably the same date as no. **26** above, 12 October 997–1004.

De ecclesia Centrannis

IN NOMINE SANCTE ET INDIVIDVE TRINITATIS Antecessorum nostrorum auctoritate constitutum adque decretum est ut si quis suarum quiddam[a] alicui sanctorum loco uel donauerit pro[b] salute anime uel uendiderit exinde litterale testamentum plurimarum personarum[c] sed ueratium receptibiliumque corroborationibus assignatum sollempniter faciat. quatinus ab omnium prauorum postmodum successorum contradictionibus intemerata inuiolabilisque ipsa seu donatio seu uenditio. perseuerabiliter permaneat. Qua propter ego Guido[d] tam[e] [fol. 69r] presentibus quam futuris omnibus quippe Christianitatis insignitis titulo notum esse uolo quod monachi sancti Michaelis abba scilicet Mainardus et alii sui subiecti me adeuntes[f] postulauerunt ut loco eiusdem sancti Michaelis duas partes ecclesie Centrannensis uenderem quas ipsi antecessore meo uiuente in uadimonio tenuerant. Sed eo mortuo cum uxore ex cuius erant dotalicio ipse due partes predicte ecclesie ceterisque beneficiis ad me redierant. Quod primo aliquantulum contradicens tandem uictus precio atque orationibus quas pro meo antecessore assidue faciunt. quas si aliter facerem ei auferrem eis consensi. Vendidi itaque eidem loco sancti angeli cum consensu mee uxoris Rainburgis et filiorum ipsius meique predecessoris Hugonis. Goslini. Heribranni ipsas duas partes predicte ecclesie scilicet quicquid ex ipsa ad meam pertinebat potestatem ipsi perpetualiter loco et omnibus fratribus ipsi loco seruientibus possidendas ut habeant et teneant et possideant sine contradictione tam presentium quam futurorum omnium siue parentum siue quorumque amicorum. Sin autem aliquis meorum successorum aliquando diabolice prauitatis stimulatus aculeo ei loco atque fratribus exinde aliquam iniuriam uel calumpniam facere presumpserit tocius excommunicationis atque anathematis irreciatur uinculis. Vt autem huius uenditionis corroboratio ueratius credatur et perfectius per omnia conseruetur firmiusque futuris temporibus teneatur ma[fol. 69v]nibus propriis ego et uxor mea et predicti filii subter firmauimus dominoque meo Hugoni[g] atque episcopo ceterisque principibus domini mei firmandam tradidimus. Signum Hugonis comitis [+] Signum Seinfredi episcopi. Signum Odonis[h] thesauri. Signum Ysaac. Signum Drogonis. Signum Radulfi uicecomitis. Signum Harduini. Signum Haimonis. Signum Mainardi.

Signum Guillelmi. Signum Huberti. Signum Huberti clerici. Signum Hamelini. Signum Hugolini.

Copy from original in B.N. lat. 5430A, pp. 254–5

Printed: *Cartulaire de l'Abbayette*, no. 2, with a facsimile of the now lost original, Archives de la Manche, Fonds de Mont-Saint-Michel. The original read: [a] quiddam facultatum [b] pro suae [c] personarum *om.* [d] Vuido [e] nostris [f] adientes [g] H. [h] Hodonis

48

Concession by Geoffrey le Bel of Anjou of the part of the moat of Le Mans contiguous with the priory of Saint-Victeur, where the monks may erect dwellings; they may have their cellar there quit of all dues, but half the income from the tenants of the dwellings is to be paid by the monks to the count; attested by Guy, bishop of Le Mans, and William Solomon, prior of Saint-Victeur: *c.* 1129–35.

De Sancto Victurio

NOTVM sit omnibus tam posteris quam presentibus quia ego Gofridus comes Andegauorum filius Fulconis regis Ierusalem dono et concedo in perpetuum habendum monachis sancti Victurii qui sunt in suburbio Cenomannis fossatum ad faciendas domos quod est prope monasterium eorum. Ita quod monachi habeant cellarium suum in predicto fossato totum quietum omni tempore et die ab omni costuma[a] et consuetudine. et de ceteris domibus habeat comes dimidium censum et dimidiam costumam[b] sic tamen quod homines respondeant monachis: et monachi comiti respondeant. Teste Guidone episcopo Cenomannensi. et Guillelmo Salomonis priore. Michaele monacho. Galuano de Camilliaco. Pipino preposito Andegauensi. Rotberto Raginaldi. Guidone filio Hugonis. et Buterio pincerna. Guillelmo cognomine Valor. et Durando Griferio. Bernardo coquo. Petro cognomine [fol. 70r] Calopino. Aufredo Ortolano.

Printed: *Cart. Saint-Victeur*, no. 17.

B.N. lat. 10072 no 28, fol. 32, copies the original: [a] cosduuma [b] cosduumam. The copy in lat. 5430a, p. 138, copies the seal on the original (Sigillum Goffredi Martelli Andegauorum comitis).

49

Confirmation and restitution by Geoffrey Goion of grants made by his father William Goion at Saint-Meloir-des-Ondes (Ille-et-Vilaine); William had later reneged on the grant, for which he had been excommunicated; the restitution is made with the counsel of Donoald, bishop of Alet, who confirms it; in return the monks lift the sentence of excommunication from Geoffrey, his father and all his ancestors, and give Geoffrey 60 pounds in the money of Le Mans, received on his behalf by Ranulf Macer: 12 January 1120–19 August 1142.

De Pooeleth [*del. et* De Sancto Melorio *subst. manu recentior*]

IN NOMINE PATRIS ET FILII ET SPIRITVS SANCTI AMEN. Quoniam omne quod presens est paulatim succedente temporum cursu uertitur in futurum:' omnibus fidelibus tam presentibus quam successuris manifestum sit. quod ego Gaufredus Guillelmi Goion filius post patris mei decessum hereditatem paternam iure tenens ac possidens. illam donationem quam pater meus sancto Michaeli archangelo celestium spirituum principi. et monachis de monte sub eius tutela et patrocinio Deo omnipotenti die noctuque eodem in loco deuote sub religionis norma inibi famulantibus concessit. et tribuit quicquid uidelicet in ecclesia sancti Melorii et in decimis seu in quibuslibet aliis rebus possidebat ut eternis peccatoribus preparatis caream[a] tormentis. et celestibus merear perfrui gaudiis. pro anime meę et patris et matris meę et omnium antecessorum meorum salute eandem donationem prefatis monachis finetenus[b] possidendam:' concedo.[c] confirmo. et corroboro. Insuper decem solidos Redonenses. quos pater meus iniuste contra preceptum sedis apostolice et tocius sanctę matris ecclesie decretum de eadem ecclesia sancti Melorii capiebat. pro quibus etiam excommunicatus fuerat:' eisdem monachis in perpetuum sine refragatione et ullius inquietatione annuo. Propter hoc autem ipsi monachi me et patrem meum et antecessores meos in capitulo ab excommunicatione absoluerunt. et insuper michi .lxª. solid. [fol. 70v] Cenom. dederunt. quos Rannulfus Macer recepit. Verumptamen ut hoc inconuulsum permaneret et ratum:' per manum et consilium Donoaldi episcopi confirmatum est. Siquis uero ex heredibus meis et parentibus successuris id[d] contraire molitus fuerit. cum Dathan. et Abiron. et Iuda traditore Domini nisi resipuerit:' sit maledictus. Et hi testes ex parte mea. Riuallonus sacerdos. Guillelmus Pontel.[e] Girardus Bona fides. Ex parte abbatis. Ilgerius prepositus. Alanus de Monte. Riuallonus prepositus. et plures alii.

B. N. fr 22357 (pp. 783–4) copies this act from an unsealed original.

[a] careant [b] *deest* [c] et *add.* [d] successoribus ad [e] Rannulfus Macer *add.*

Partial copy in B. N. fr. 22325, p. 667, and copy in B. N. lat. 5430A, p.39.

50

Grant of the church of Saint-Martin de La Chapelle-Hamelin (now comm. Hamelin, Manche, cant. Saint-James), the chapel of Raunet (in Saint-Laurent-de-Terregatte) and land at Villier, and two manses in *burgo Petri* (perhaps Le Tertre, in Hamelin) by Hildiardis, daughter and heiress of Hamelin and wife of Escirard; she also concedes grants by her tenants, notably Isembert Popell, who accompanied her to the Mont; the grant is authorized by her son Hamelin on the day that her son William becomes a monk of the abbey, in the time of Abbot Roger (1085–1106) and Bishop Michael of Avranches (1069–94): the date of 1114 does not accord with the indiction: 1085–94; Dom Huynes's *Chronica*, in B.N. fr. 18947, fol. 145r, dates this to 1093.

De Capella Hamelini

IN NOMINE. PATRIS. ET FILII. ET SPIRITVS SANCTI AMEN. Sicut patrum relatione didicimus. quorum documento atque doctrina uite honestatem. seu morum institutionem subtili atque mirifica indagatione excepimus. quibus obtemperare absque ulla refragatione ratione magistra decreuimus. utilitati sequentium prouidendo disposuerunt. quatinus dum quilibet fidelium ęcclesiae cuilibet sub elemosine commodo aliquod rerum suarum monimentum contradere obtaret: ne a suis sequacibus siue posteris qualibet occasione ullum detrimentum ingrueret. propria manu ius ecclesie collatum in elemosina: roborari constituerunt. Qua propter Ego Hildiarda uxor Escirardi cuiusdam militis do: et concedo inspirante domino Ihesu Christo sancto MICHAELI archangelo ecclesiam sancti Martini de Capella Hamelini quę mei iuris atque patrimonii esse dinoscitur. cum omni cimiterio et cum omni decima terre mee tam de capella quam de Racineio. omniumque meo[fol. 71r]rum liberorum hominum qui in mea terra decimas uidebantur habere mecum ad Montem proficiscentium. Isemberto uidelicet Popello omnibusque aliis summo cordis desiderio sancti Michaelis ecclesie omnem partem decimarum suarum donantibus atque concedentibus. Do eciam insuper duas masuras in burgo Petri. et terram Amalrici. cum omnibus hominibus et triginta quinque acras terre tam in Capella quam in Racineio. Duodecim acras in uilla Capelle. et tres ultra Ligerim fluuium. et reliquas in Racineio ad spinam de Vileirs medietariam uidelicet patris mei Hamelini quę in meo dominio manebat. Huic autem donationi consensit Hamelinus filius meus. tali tenore. quatinus donnus Rogerius abbas Cadomensis cenobii monachus. et monachi sancti Michaelis Guillelmum filium meum ad monachatum recipient. eumque in omni spiritali doctrina erudient. Siquis autem huic donationi resistere uoluerit et eam in aliquo minuerit: ex auctoritate Dei omnipotentis et omnium sanctorum Dei in perpetuum sit maledictus. Actum est hoc anno ab incarnatione domini. m^{o}. c^{o}x^{o}. iiii^{o}. indictione .x^{a}iiii^{a}. concurrente .vi^{o}. In sede Abrincensi Michaele presule: his testibus uidentibus et audientibus. Signum Hirdiardæ. Signum Hamelini. filii eius. Signum Radulfi Brito. Signum Guillemi Castelidi fratris eius. Signum Guimundi fratris Escirardi. Signum Rainaldi de Gutellis. Signum Vitalis filii Corpi. Signum Guillelmi fratris eius.

See L. R. and L. Hulmet, 'Monographie sur la paroisse de la Chapelle-Hamelin', *Revue de l'Avranchin*, Année 95, t. 54, June 1977, 149–57, for a discussion of the topography of this charter.

51

Charter by Robert de Lapenty (comm. Saint-Hilaire-du-Harcouët), recording the grant of the tithes of Lentillé (Manche, cant. Ducey, comm. Poilley) made when he, his wife Mary and son Hamelin enter confraternity with the monks. A notification appended to the witness list adds that for this the monks have given burial rights at the Mont to his wife and sons: 1099.

De Lentilleis

[fol. 71v] IN NOMINE. PATRIS. ET FILII. ET SPIRITVS SANCTI AMEN. Ego Rotbertus de Apenticio sancti Michaelis petens limina: in fraternitatem monachorum eorum concessu cum uxore mea Maria. et Hamelino meo filio intraui. Quamobrem ego pro mei et pro antecessorum meorum animabus dedi sancto Michaeli et sibi semper seruientibus decimam quam ego habeo in uilla quae dicitur Lentilleis. concedentibus uxore mea et filiis meis. Acta est hec donatio anno ab incarnatione domini .m°. nonagesimo nono. Indictione septima. Huius mee donationis: testes sunt hii. Signum ipsius Rotberti .+. Signum eius uxoris. + Signum Hamelini. + filii eius. Signum Guillelmi Teoberti. + Signum Richardi de Tuschueio .+. Signum Guillelmi filii Radulfi. +. Signum Hugonis Paruus. +. Notum sit omnibus quod monachi michi ob hoc concesserunt et uxori et filiis sepulturam in Monte.

52

Act by which Richard II of Normandy removes Abbot Mainard II from office on grounds of his advanced age; after consultation with his bishops and barons, and at the request of the monks themselves, he dismisses Mainard's request for a co-adjutor and commends their monk Hildebert, who is in the flower of youth, to the community as successor to Mainard: 1009.

De substitutione Hildeberti

IN NOMINE SVMME. ATQVE. EXIMIE TRINITATIS. Richardus Dei dispositione princeps et marchio totius Neustrie prouincie cunctis religionis christiane fidelibus. Quicquid pro sancte religionis obseruantia. atque stabilitate plebis adeo nobis delegate ordinantes fieri disponimus. aut disponendo iusticię semitam incedentes gerimus. magnam ex hoc nobis a Deo retributionem ad futuram speramus. Nam considerantes sarcinam cure episcopali debitam [fol 72r] atque clericorum conuersationem sanctam. nec non monachorum. ac sanctimonialium religiositatem nostre subditam excellentie dignitatis. magnopere studemus in his rebus disponendis. diuine uoluntati ob capacitatem nostri intellectus minime contraire uelle. Si enim pro non bene gestis tolerari nos inpunite consideramus a Deo: multo magis retribui nobis mercedem pro bene factis speramus ab ipso. Et quoniam inter multiformia presentis sancte ecclesie instituta. excellentiores pie conuersationis gradus obtinet monastice ordo religionis: dignum censui uestre intimare presentie: quia accersierit nostram almitatem contio sancti agminis cenobii magni ierarchi celorum MICHAELIS bene prouida sue salutis. exposcens sibi patrem institui de suis sicut premonstrat oportune debere fieri de[i *a.c.*]scriptio regularis. Cuius siquidem peticio quoniam senissimo patre spiritali eiusdem cenobii Mainardo nomine ad huc superstite agitur. minime debet uideri incongrua. Pastoralis etenim curam sollicitudinis quam idem memorabilis senex perficere nequid uiribus propriis: subrogati sibi laudabiliter exposcit complere adiutorio fratris. Vnde nos per consultum episcoporum ac nostrorum nobilium uirorum maximeque prememoratorum monachorum rogatu. necnon insuper preualente iam dicti senis memorabili peticione preponimus predicto cenobio uenerabilem uirum Hildebertum iuuenili euo floridum. sed acumine uiuacis ingenii preclarum morumque maturitate grauidum. [fol. 72v] Preferentes igitur uirum priuile[i *a.c.*]gio micantem dunno. omnis uenerationis cultu monasterio expetendo magnopere commendamus seruis Dei ibidem Christo famulantibus eidem obsequendum. quia et nos talem illis ut credimus:· cui merito obsequi debeat preferimus. Vt autem hęc electio rata et inconuulsa permaneat. propria manu eandem astipulari censuimus. Actum Rotomago anno ab incarnatione domini nostri Ihesu Christi m°.viiii. Indictione :· vii. Regnante Rotberto rege Francorum anno .xx°.

Printed: Fauroux, 12, who notes that an ancient pseudo-original was destroyed at Saint-Lô in 1944. Haskins (*Norman Institutions*, p. 59), gave the reference as Arch. dépt. de la Manche H 14982, which was printed in Durand and Marténe, *Thesaurus novum anecdotorum*, t. i, p. 124. It was also copied by Lechaudé d'Anisy in B. N. lat. 10072, no. 2. The seventeeth-century Maurist historian Thomas Le Roy claimed to have used the 'original', kept in the abbey archives with the classification AA f. 67 (*Les curieuses recherches*, p. 103).

53

Charter by which Clamarhoc fitz Richer grants, in the pays d'Alet (diocese of Saint-Malo), a fishery in the sea, tithes at Le Verger, with the tithes of the sons of Moyses which had been disputed between Clamarhoc and the monks, the tithes of *Faluetrels* and the tithe of Ralph son of Mainfenit, a moiety of the proceeds of the church at Saint-Coulomb (Ille-et-Vilaine, cant. Cancale), with a moiety of burial rights and of livestock, and a third part of the tithes of Saint-Ideuc (Ille-et-Vilaine, cant. Saint-Malo, comm. Paramé), with the assent of his seigneur Geoffrey fitz Oliver de Dinan: 1093–1100.

Carta de Pooleth

IN NOMINE SANCTE ET INDIVIDVE TRINITATIS. Ab antecessoribus nostris statutum atque decretum est quod quicunque Dei fidelium cupidus bonorum celestium quiddam de suis facultatibus cuilibet sancte ecclesie loco pro spe retributionis eterne dederit. exinde litterale testamentum personarum corroborationibus assignatum fiat:· quatinus ab omni contradictione uel calumpnatione malorum. ipsa donatio firma et intemerata atque integra futuris permaneat temporibus. Vnde ego Clamarhocus Richeri filius metuens penas tartareas. et memor illius admonitionis quę dicit. date elemosinam. et ecce omnia munda sunt uobis. illius quoque memor quę dicit. sicut aqua extinguit ignem. ita elemosina peccatum:· do sancto Michaeli sibique seruientibus monachis in Pooleth unam tesuram id est piscatoriam in mari pro redemptione animę meę. Conce[fol. 73r]do etiam decimam de quodam loco qui Vergied uocatur. et decimam filiorum Moysen in quibus fuerat calumpnia inter me et predictos monachos. Do quoque decimam Faluetrels. decimamque Radulfi Mainifiniti filii. et medietatem de hoc quod exit de altari Sancti Columbani. medietatemque de sepulturis eiusdem monasterii. et medietatem decime de uiuis bestiis quę pertinent ad predictum monasterium. Do etiam terram predictis monachis in eodem loco:· quantum potest una carruca arare in anno. Necnon etiam do eis terciam partem decime Sancti Idoci de hoc quodcumque pertinet ad illud monasterium. et terram ad unam carrugam in eodem loco. Si quis igitur stimulatus iaculo diabolice calliditatis. hoc donum huic loco Sancto deuote traditum subtrahendo aliquatenus uiolare presumpserit:· a celesti patria seclusus. et a sanctorum omnium collegio perpetim segregatus. cum Iuda domini pro[e *a.c.*]ditore ac Caipha diabolo eiusque sociis commissus. in perpetuis gehenne mittatur ignibus:· ubi per infinita tempora crucie[a *a.c.*]tur amen. Vt autem hoc per labentia tempora custodiatur firmiusque teneatur:· placuit michi Clamarhoco hanc cartam ponere super altare sancti Michaelis et signum meum facere. Gaufredus etiam Oliueri filius de quo predictas res teneo hoc concessit:· et signum suum in hac carta manu sua fecit. Testes etiam qui ibi adfuerunt:· signa sua fecerunt. Signum Gaufredi de Dinam. Signum Clamarhoci. Signum Wigueni militis.

Copied from the original in B. N. fr 22357 (pp. 788–9). Full copy in B. N. fr. 18949, p. 429 ff, no. 7, and B. N. lat. 5430A, pp. 217–8.

54

Notification that whilst he still lived, Clamarhoc son of Richer made a further grant of 60 acres at Saint-Ideuc (Ille-et-Vilaine, cant. Saint-Malo, comm. Paramé), which he held of William fitz Harscoit; in return for William's confirmation of the grant, he is received into confraternity and given 60 shillings in the money of Rennes; in addition, should William be captured, the monks will offer such aid as they are able, and should William's lord, the son of John fitz Rivallon of Dol. demand aid from William, the monks will assist him according to the just value of the land he has confirmed: *c.* 1093–1100.

Item de eodem

[fol. 73v] NOTIFICETVR omnibus hoc scriptum legentibus quod Clamarhocus Richeri filius dedit sancto Michaeli dum adhuc uiueret sibique seruientibus monachis sexaginta acras terre in Brittannia apud Sanctum Idocum pro salute anime sue. Quam terram tenebat de Guillelmo Harscoit filio. Qui Guillelmus hanc donationem concessi[e *a.c.*]t:· et omnes consuetudines quę ad eum pertinent sancto Michaeli dedit et immunes esse concessit. Pro qua re concesserunt eum esse participem omnium orationum et bonorum quę agunt prefati monachi:· et dederunt ei caritatiue sexaginta solidos nummorum Redonensium. Et hoc tantummodo facient ei pro recognitione terre. quod si quando captus fuerit. dabunt ei audiutorium ut opportunum erit. Et si dominus eius scilicet Iohannis de Dolo filius quesierit aliquod adiutorium per omnem suum honorem:· predicti monachi dabunt eidem Guillelmo de eodem adiutorio secundum hoc quod terra ualebit et iustum fuerit. Quod siquis huic concessui contradixerit uel calumpniauerit:· ab omnipotente Deo maledicatur. et in eterno igne per secula cuncta crucietur. Amen.

55

Notification that Ilger son of Waldin *vicomte* has confirmed his ancestors's grant of land at *Follomuzhun* (perhaps Funeçon, Manche, cant. Avranches, comm. Ponts), and, in particular the grant of land at Villaine (hamlet of Saint-Aubin-de-Terregatte, Manche) made by his father Waldin on becoming a monk; Ilger made his concession and swore to observe it on the Gospel on the altar of St Michael, in the presence of Abbot Bernard, for which he was given 10 *solidi* in the money of Le Mans: 1131–8 May 1149.

Carta de Follomuzhum

Notum sit omnibus tam modernis quam futuris. Ilgerium filium Gaudini uicecomitis concessisse ecclesie sancti Michaelis omnem terram quam antecessores sui contulerant eidem ecclesie. terram scilicet de Follomu[fol. 74r]zhum. et illam specialiter quam pater suus Gaudinus dederat quando uenit ad monachatum. terram uidelicet de Villahenne. Hanc autem concessionem suam confirmauit iure iurando super altare sancti Michaelis et super textum. in presentia donni abbatis Bernardi tociusque conuentus. Habuit uero idem Ilgerius decem solidos Cenomannensium pro hac concessione et confirmatione. Huius rei testes sunt ex parte sancti Michaelis. et eiusdem Ilgerii. Alanus filius Haimerici. Bernardus de Moysio. Gauterius de Montroalt. Ilgerius filius Amaluuini. Briendus filius Chasnelli uicecomitis. Rossellus filius Fulcherii de Sancto Georgio. Rogerius camerarius. Iohannes de Maldreio. Enardus de Monteiterio. Demorandus de Monte.

56

Grant of land and tithes and other benefits, including his rights in churches, at Saint-Broladre (Ille-et-Vilaine, cant. Dol) by Trihan fitz Brien, and others, viz. his brother Hervé, Hervé son of Mangis, whose brother Alfred becomes a monk, and Ursoen son of Gernoen and his brothers Richard and Geoffrey: 1070–1100; cf. no. **21**.

De Sancto Broeladrio

NOTVM sit omnibus tam presentibus quam futuris. quod ego Trihan. Briencii filius. dono Deo et sancto Michaeli pro remedio anime mee. patrisque mei et matris mee. atque uxoris mee. et animabus antecessorum meorum. scilicet duodecim acras terre. et omnem partem ecclesiarum cum omnibus eisdem pertinentibus et propriam Grangiam meam. et proprium ortum meum. et decimam molendini. atque uirgulti. insuperque omnem decimam meam. et hominum meorum. Et ego Vruoh Briencii filius. concedo donationem quam frater meus Trihan facit sancto Michaeli. Preterea dono Deo et sancto Michaeli omnem partem mearum decimarum. scilicet ęcclesiarum [fol. 74v] et tocius terrę meę. et duas acras terre ubi monachi elegerint. pro remedio anime mee et antecessorum meorum.

Ego Herueus Mangisi filius dono Deo et sancto Michaeli pro remedio anime mee. patrisque mei et matris mee. atque antecessorum meorum scilicet

.xii^{cim}. acras terre. et quicquid habebam in supradictis ęcclesiis. et omnem decimam tocius terre mee de sancto Broeladrio. Insuperque Alueredum fratrem meum ad monachum faciendum.

Et ego Vrsoenus Gernoeni filius. et fratres mei. Richardus et Gaufredus. eodem modo damus sancto Michaeli pro remedio patris et matris nostre. et animarum nostrarum.

Copied from a notice of the late eleventh-century in B. N. fr 22325, p. 719, perhaps the same 'original' copied by Beauchesne from the archives at Saint-Lô, endorsed: 'littere donationis Sancti Broelardii (Arch. dépt. de La Manche, 6 J 70, M2).

57

Concession of cemetery rights at Saint-Meloir-des-Ondes by William Goion, Guigan *vicarius* of Alet, Drigon the priest and his brothers, and others, who had claimed them as held in alms from the count; cf. **Appendix ii. 10**: 1070–1100.

De cymiterio Sancti Melorii

GVILLELMVS Goion. ac Guiguen uicarius Aletensium ciuitatis. Drigonque sacerdos fratresque ipsius et tenores eorum. Dei gratia et pro salute uiuorum et mortuorum concedunt sancto Michaeli cum honore sancti Melori monachisque illius loci quietam in elemosina primam illius cimiterii cordam. quam illi cum calumpnio tunc similiter in elemosina a comite clamabant. Et si comes sancto Michaeli monachisque ipsius dono enarrare uoluerit: ueniat sine monachorum clamore et quietam sicut nunc habent illis cum pace habere faciat. Huius elemosine supra dicte existunt testes uidentes et audientes. T. Rainfredus monachus. Hamon. Gauterii filii. monachus. Hamo sancti Moclouii monachus. Anschetillus ipsius ęcclesię sacerdos. T. Guillelmus qui ipsam cartam scripsit. T. Morel. T Rotbertus filius [fol. 75r] Rotaldi. T Flaaldus. T Chemarfroch Folin: T. Pinel. T. Albericus. T. Rainfredus filius Fulchardi. T. Gauterius seruitor. Testes ita concedunt proprie corporibus sanctorum ut non inpediatur nisi domus monachi ac sacerdotis ecclesie seruientibus.

58

Notification of a quitclaim, in the presence of Abbot Bernard, of all rights claimed in the church of Saint-Meloir-des-Ondes by Geoffrey fitz Walter: 1135–49.

De sancto Melorio

NOTVM sit omnibus tam presentibus quam futuris. Gaufredum Gauterii filium in capitulum sancti Michaelis in presentia donni Bernardi abbatis. omnisque conuentus uenisse. et omnia illa quę iniuste clamabat in ecclesia sancti Melorii uidelicet in decima et in aliis rebus supra dicte ecclesie pertinentibus omnibus qui ibi aderant audientibus omnino reliquisse. Hoc etiam a se ipso suisque posteris esse tenendum: iureiurando coram donno abbate omnique conuentu firmiter stabilisse. Teste Rualem Calcebou. et Guillelmo Pulcra barba. et Vitali Leenfant et Sanuuale. aliisque quam pluribus. Et ex parte sua adfuit Guiguene Alberi filius.

B. N. fr 22357 (p. 790) copies the original. See **Appendix i. 6** for another version.

59

Notice concerning the grant made by Geoffrey Chaorces at his death, for the soul of his brother Main Pointel, of one and a half diets of land in the marsh near *Pomenoet*; Main, their other brother and all other heirs, concede the grant; Main places the gift on the altar of Saint-Meloir-des-Ondes; the monk Rainald de Saint-Jean takes seisin of the property: 1131–49.

Item de Sancto Melorio

SCIANT tam presentes quam futuri Gaufredum Chaorces dedisse Deo et sancto Michaeli ad obitum suum pro remedio anime sue fratrem Main Ponitelli unam dietam terre et dimidiam in mares iuxta haium apud Pomenoet. Hoc concessit frater eius Main Pointel. et alius frater eius: et omnes alii heredes. Qui Main ipse posuit donum super altare sancti Melorii. et [fol. 75v] et [*sic*] iurauit ut hoc inuiolatum finetenus permaneret. Huius rei testes sunt Rainaldus monachus de sancto Iohanne qui saisinam suscepit. et Iohannes presbyter. et Ruellem Pointel. et Guillelmus Seiher.

60

Grant by Count Robert [of Avranches] of his allod of Tissey (Manche, cant. Sartilly, comm. Dragey), for the soul of himself and his deceased wife Billeheldis, for his living wife Ascelina and his sons William, Robert and Richard, with whose consent he is acting; confirmed by Richard II of Normandy (repeat of no. **31** above, with additional witnesses)[1]: *c.* 1015.

Carta de Thessiaco

IN NOMINE SANCTE ET INDIVIDVE TRINITATIS PATRIS ET FILII ET SPIRITVS SANCTI AMEN. Institutionibus antecessorum nostrorum procul dubio sancitum ac decretum esse scimus. ut siquis sacro baptismate renatus quiddam suarum facultatum perhenniter possidendum uite celestis afflatus nectare tradere loco sancti alicuius uoluerit. firmissimum exinde fulcitumque plurimis conuenientium auctoritatibus personarum testamentum faciat. quatinus id [idem *a.c.*] inconuulsum permaneat. ac denegari penitus non queat. Igitur ego Rotbertus comes notum esse tam presentibus quam absentibus omnibus Christianitatis titulum ferentibus uolo quod meorum inmensitatem criminum timens. et celestis uite gaudium habere cupiens. quoddam alodum scilicet Thesiacum loco beati Michaelis. monachisque ibi regulariter Deo seruientibus pro anime mee salute. ac deinceps pro remedio anime uxoris mee Billeheldis defuncte. et pro uiuentis Asceline. filiorumque meorum Guillelmi et Rotberti atque

[1] An early modern hand has noted 'alibi infra, fol. 71' at number 31 and here 'folio 50'. An older hand also notes the repetition here.

Richardi. quorum uoluntate. consensuque id ago perpetualiter possidendum trado. Dinoui etenim quam [fol. 76r] plurimis referentibus sancte Christianitatis doctoribus esse quoddam peccatorum purgamentum largitionem elemosinarum. Et diuino monitu. illic thesauri recondendi ubi nec furis astutia inerit. nec tinearum esura inchoabit. Nam quod Deo in largiendo elemosinam tribuitur. centuplicatum in celis reconpensabitur. Legitur etenim regnum Dei tantum ualere. quantum cuique est posse. Valuit siquidem uidue quadrans. et Petro rete et nauis. profuit et Zacheo dimidium bonorum. Nichil itaque est id quod finitur. ad id quod fine non clauditur. His igitur et aliis salutiferis incitamentis ammonitis. predictum alodum loco predicto tribuo. sub totius ecclesie testimonio. cum terris cultis et incultis. cum pratis et omnibus appendiciis. eo tenore ut absque calumpnio seu contradictione successorum parentum meorum habitantes in prefato loco habeant teneant possideant. Et si quis stimulatus iaculo diabolice calliditatis huic dono calumpium inferre presumpserit. tocius ecclesie excommunicationibus perhenniter detineatur. Vt autem hec datio uerius credatur. et firmius diligentiusque futuris teneatur temporibus. manibus Richardi comitis atque Rotberti archiepiscopi. et eorum matris Gonnor. et uxoris mee Asceline filiorum meorum Guillelmi. Rotberti. Richardique ac militum meorum subter firmandam. corroborandamque tradidi. + Rotbertus comes. Noriotus episcopus. Geraldus. Radulfus. Erembertus. [fol. 76v] Gauterius. Petrus. Niellus. Drogo. Hasgerius. Griphus. Garmundus. Hubertus. Gosfridus. Osmundus. Rainaldus.

Printed: Fauroux, 16; compare no. **31** above.

61

Grant by Ascelin de Caugé (cant. Pontorson) of land he had previously had to mortgage to his friend Mainer de Monte; when the time for repayment came, Ascelin found himself with no money, and a desire to become a monk; Mainer permits him to grant the land to the abbey when Abbot Ranulf accepts him as a monk; Ascelin's son Roger Lohout then also decides to take the habit, for which Ascelin makes a further gift of the church and tithes of Caugé when they are both received into the community; he then summons his sons and *nepotes* (nephews or grandsons), Warin and William Lohout, Pailart and Roger de Boilon, and has them swear on the Gospels to respect the grant: dated 1056, during the ninth indiction, not the eleventh; Bishop Michael occurs 1069–94.

Carta de Calgeio

IN NOMINE. PATRIS. ET FILII. ET SPIRITVS SANCTI AMEN:· Nouerit cunctorum noticia fidelium. quia ego Ascelinus de Calgeio necessitate nimia constrictus. quandam partem terre de Calgeio inuadimoniaui cuidam amico meo. Mainerio uidelicet de Monte. Cum uero reddendi terminus appropinquasset quod de illo susceperam:· deficiente michi pecunia. et ipso religionis habitu cupiens indui. tandem diuina inspiratione compunctus. consilio inito consensu amicorum meorum et ipse hanelans meliorare uitam meam concessi terram illam ecclesie beati archangeli Michaelis de Monte eo tenore quod abbas Rannulfus me cum ipso Mainerio data tercia parte tocius substantie mee in monachili ordine suscipiens:· iugo Christi eiusque honeri me subiciens ut diuine contemplationi uberius deseruire ualerem. Videns autem Rogerius Lohoth filius meus amore Dei et monachico ordine me sic feruentissime succendi:· renuntiauit et ipse seculo. et facti summus monachi in ecclesia sancti Michaelis. data pro ipso Rogerio filio meo ecclesia de Calgeio cum omni decima. et sex acris terrę quę ipsi ecclesie contingebant. et uno frustro prati iuxta marescam. [fol. 77r] Vt autem hęc donatio in perpetuum permaneat. conuocaui filios meos et nepotes Garinum Lohout. et Guillelmum Lohout. et Pailart. et Rogerius de Boilon. et feci illius super sacro sancta euangelia iurare. quod numquam ipsi nec quisquam illorum super hanc donationem quicquam clamarent uel in aliquo minuerent. et excommunicando insuper anathematizaui omnes sequaces meos qui huic dono meo obuiare presumpserint. Ex auctoritate autem patris et filii et spiritus sancti sint maledicti et excommunicati omnes heredes mei. et participes cum diabolo fiant qui hoc donum meum rescindere uoluerint. Actum est hoc anno ab incarnatione domini .m°. l. vi. indictione .xi. concurrente .iiii. in Abrincensi sede Michaele presule presidente. Garino et Rainaldo de Maldreio concedentibus et uidentibus. et his etiam testibus uidentibus et audientibus Galterio de Marigneio. Richolino de Boceio. Flaaldo de Demagnio. et Richardo de Cureio. et plures alii.

Thomas Le Roy reported that this charter was copied on fol. 103 of the now-lost *Livre Blanc* (*Les Curieuses recherches*, p. 124).

62

Notification (spurious) that Abbot Roger and Prior Mathias, at Angers in the presence of Count Fulk, Rainald, bishop of Angers, Geoffrey de Mayenne and Marbod, head of the cathedral school at Angers, and many other leading men of the region, determined that the land and vines and whatever else the monks possessed in the regions of Angers and Tours, should be free from seizure and from the consequences of any forfeiture incurred in Normandy; the count signs and receives 30 pounds in pennies, his son Geoffrey conceding and signing also : 1 December 1090.

Carta de uineis Andegauis et Turonis

NOTVM sit cunctis presentibus atque futuris. quod donnus abbas Rogerius de Monte sancti Michaelis. Mathiasque prior. in urbe Andegaui coram comite Fulcone. ipsiusque loci pontifice Rainaldo. et Gaufrido de Meduana. et Marbodio. multis quoque proceribus illius prouincie presentibus anno ab incarnatione domini .m°. nongen[fol. 77v]tesimo. prima die aduentus dominici disseruerunt:· ut terre et uineę. et quecunque monachi Montis sancti

Michaelis in pago Andegauensi seu Turonensi possident. innanno non capiantur: pro forisfacto quod in Normannica tellure. uel etiam altera terra factum sit. Vt autem hęc carta firma permaneat: ipse comes uiuifice crucis signum manu propria subter inpressit. et de abbate ut res firmior esset. xxx[ta]. libras denariorum habuit. Filiusque suus concessit. et signum fecit cum quibusdam aliis. et episcopo ipsius ciuitatis: qui sub anathemate graui interdixit. ne hoc scriptum aliquis preterire audeat. Signum Fulconis comitis. Signum filii eius Gaufridi. Signum Rainaldi episcopi. Signum Marbodii magistri scolarum. Signum Gaufridi de Meduana.

Forgery based on a genuine charter (copied in lat. 5430a, p. 100, printed in **Appendix i.3** below). Discussed by Olivier Guillot, *Le comte d'Anjou et son entourage*, t. 2, <C 26>, p. 307, and C 417, pp. 259–60, who ascribes the forgery to the period when Geoffrey IV of Anjou was duke of Normandy, but it was perhaps 1150: see above, pp. 38–9. This version was printed in *Gallia Christiana* t. XI, *Inst.* p. 1098.

63

Grant by Conan III of Brittany, for the soul of his father Alan IV and salvation of himself and his wife, of a fishery called *Vereis* and an island called *Trencata*, places since lost to the sea; his wife Countess [Matilda] and his sister Hadvisa attest; the grant was kept among the charters for Saint-Meloir-des-Ondes: 1116–30 October 1140, perhaps 1116–24.

Carta de piscatoria de Vereis

IN NOMINE. PATRIS. ET FILII. ET SPIRITVS SANCTI. AMEN. EGO Conanus Dei gratia Brittannie dux amore Dei et sancti Michaelis de Monte monachorumque eiusdem archangeli ductus. dono et concedo Deo. et eidem archangelo et sibi seruientibus pro salute animę meae et uxoris mee. et pro anima Alanni patris mei. et pro animabus antecessorum meorum piscatorium quę dicitur Vereis. et insulam quę dicitur Trencata. Et ut hęc donatio inconuulsa permaneat: signa[u *a.c.*] sancte crucis firma[fol. 78r]re studui. et baronibus meis firmandam tradidi. Signum Conani comitis. Signum Bricii presulis Nannetensis. Signum Symonis filii Bernardi. Signum Pagani filii Rotaldi. Signum Gaufredi de la Guircha. Signum Guillelmi dapiferi. Signum Heruei capellani. Signum Hermer. Signum Guiho famuli comitis. Signum Oliuerii de Varesna. Signum Viuiani de Martio. Hanc donationem concesserunt et confirmauerunt Mathildis comitissa. et Haduisa soror comitis Conani. Signum Comitisse. Signum Haduise.

Printed: Guillotel, *Actes*, 151, pp. 466–8, based on the Cartulary text and a copy of the original made in 1456 by Robert Pichot, now Archives départementales de Loire-Atlantique, E 86.

64

Notification of a grant of land in Chauvigné (comm. Sens-de-Bretagne, Ille-et-Vilaine) by Main de Saint-Aubin-d'Aubigné, on a visit to Mont-Saint-

Michel with his wife Adelesia and son Robert; Main attests the act on behalf of his absent son Ralph: *c.* 1100.

Carta de Albinneio

NOTVM sit omnibus ueram sancte TRINITATIS fidem colentibus. Mainnum quendam nobilem uirum de Albinnei castro cum propria uxore quondam sancti Michaelis adisse limina. ac fratribus eiusdem sancte ecclesie sedule famulantibus quandam fecisse donationem de quadem maiteria ut uulgo dicitur. quam apud quandam uillam quę Caluinnei dicitur habebat. pro salute sui uxorisque sue infantum quoque suorum ac omnium amicorum. et ut predicti fratres assidue sui in orationibus suis sint memores. Si quis huic dono calumpniam inferre presumpserit: sit maledictus cum Iuda traditore Domini. Vt autem hoc uerius credatur. ac per labentia tempora firmius teneatur: nomina eorum qui presentes adfuerunt cum signis uiuifice crucis quę fecerunt subter notata sunt. [fol. 78v] Signum Maini [+] qui donum fecit. Signum uxoris eius Adelesie [+]. Signum Rotberti filii eius. Signum Frotgerii militis. Signum Torulfi. Signum Maini de Sancto Germano. Signum Ilgerii prepositi. Signum Guarini Ernaldi filii. Signum quod fecit Mainus [+] sub persona filii sui Radulfi qui absens erat et tamen hoc donum concessit.

65

Notification of a grant by William fitz Hugh de Sillé(-le-Guillaume, Sarthe) of all the revenues in the land the monks hold of his fief; his mother Oldeburga and her other sons assent: 1087.

De Silleio

NOTVM sit omnibus uiuentibus atque uicturis Guillelmum[a] filium Hugonis de Silliaco gratia Dei atque sancti Michaelis archangeli hoc impetrante. ob[b] omnium suorum remissionem delictorum suorumque precessorum omnium atque successorum Guillelmi[c] regis Anglorum tempore. antistitisque Cenomannensis Hoelli. nec non et uicecomitis Huberti[d] atque Goffridi de Mahena ob fraternitatem et orationes sancti Michaelis suorumque seruorum monachorum necnon et honesti munera equi. omnes consuetudines suę terre de eorum dominio monachorum illis sancti Michaelis monachis proprie et tranquille concessisse. Radulfo monacho atque Andrea huius doni[e] acceptoribus cum spine uiridi ramo. Oldeburga[+] hoc idem loco suorum aliorum filiorum concedente et ad eorum opus benefacta accipiente. Testimonio Guillelmi[f] de Verniaco. et Hamelini[g] Forestarii. et Berardi de Silliaco. Gaurini[h] filii Rogerii. Radulfi [us *a.c.*] de Dolieta. Herberti[i] [fol. 79r] de Orta. Tebaldi capellani. Dro[a *a.c.*]conis de Sancto Christoforo. Fulcones.[j] Droardi. <[k*] Fulcoini de Plassiaco. Rotberti Cognardi. Radulfi filii Goscelini de de Monte Saluonerio. Fulcoini Asneht. Gauterii filii Constantini. Gauterii de Curteleriis. Multorumque aliorum suorum militum. Atque ex parte monachorum testimonio Gosfridi de Hispania. Rotberti de Sancto Medardo. Iohannis famuli eorumdem. Et quicumque hoc auferre uel conatus contradicere fuerit: cum Iuda Domini traditore. Dathan. et Abiron: in ignem perpetuum sine fine trada[e *a.c.*]tur. >

Printed: *Cartulaire de l'Abbayette*, no. 6 (from the cartulary). Lechaudé d'Anisy copied the original in lat. 10072, no. 22, fol. 28: [a] Wilgelmum [b] ab [c] Wilgelmi [d] Vberti [e] domui [f] Wilgelmi [g] Amelini [h] Warini [i] Erberti [j] Fulconis [k] 'depuis l'asterisque cette partie ne se trouve pas dans la charte originale'. [+] B.N. 5430A, copied in B.N. Coll. Moreau 36, p. 141, preserve a fuller version of the charter, printed in **Appendix i. 8**, below.

Calendared in Round, *CDF*, no. 718.

66

Grant of three acres in Poilley (Ille-et-Vilaine, cant. Louvigné-du-Désert) by Ranulf, with the consent of his brothers and the children of all of them; the monks will receive them as brothers, with food and wine, on one occasion each year when they go to pray at the abbey: before the death of Ralph I de Fougères in 1124.

De Pollei

IN NOMINE PATRIS ET FILII ET SPIRITVS SANCTI AMEN. Notum sit uniuersis fidelibus tam presentibus quam futuris quia ego Rannulfus Dei miseratione compunctus atque permotus qui quem uult indurat et cui placet miseretur. cum consensu fratrum meorum omniumque puerorum tam meorum quam illorum concedimus Deo. sanctoque Michaeli archangelo tres acras terre in parroechia quȩ Pollei dicitur. ad fontem orguentali pacto atque conuentione ut simus participes tam nos quam nostri successores omnium beneficiorum quȩ in ecclesia sancti Michaelis archangeli fient. Annuerunt eciam ipsius cenobii nobis monachi. ut si aliquando contigerit nos ad montem sancti Michaelis gratia orationum semel in anno pergere. de suis be[fol. 79v]neficiis nos ut fratres suos honorificabunt. uidelicet de pane et potu nobis caritatem mittentes. Hanc autem donationem cupimus atque uoluimus ut inconuulsa atque integra in perpetuo permaneat. ꝼloreat. omnique euo remota cuiuslibet calumpnia seu contradictione sub iure sive sancti Michaelis dominio perseuerando subsistat. Si quis uero huic donationi molitus fuerit contraire eamque irritam facere uoluerit: ex auctoritate patris. et filii. et spiritus sancti. sancteque Dei genitricis Marie. sancti quoque Michaelis archangeli atque sanctorum canonum. sit excommunicatus atque in inferno perpetue maledictioni addictus. Et ut hȩc donatio in perpetuo permaneat: coram testibus eam firmare studuimus. Signum [+] Stephani filii Iuonis. Signum Guillelmi filii sui. Signum Gar[l *a.c.*]nerii filii[-ius *a.c.*] Restenbaldi. Signum Iuonis filii Garnerii. Signum Ansgerii uicarii. Signum Guillelmi filii [-ius *a.c.*] Ansgerii.

67

Finally giving in to many requests by Abbot Roger, Robert fitz Haimo grants, from his patrimony, the church and tithes of Esquay-Notre-Dame

(Calvados, cant. Evrecy), with the tithes pertaining to the church, except the part of two vavassors over which he has no rights; he grants in addition nine acres of land, and he agrees that should any of his men living there need to raise money by mortgaging land, they will be allowed to do so, but he limits the amount of land that they might sell: 1086.

De·Scai

IN NOMINE. SANCTE. ET INDIVIDVE. TRINITATIS. PATRIS. ET FILII. ET SPIRITVS SANCTI. AMEN. Ego Rotbertus Haimonis filius rogatus multociens abbabate [*sic*] et a monachis Montis Sancti Michaelis archangeli impericulo maris siti. pro remedio anime mee nec non et parentum meorum concedo de hereditate a parentibus meis michi relicta Deo creatori meo atque eidem archangelo Michaeli ęcclesiam [fol. 80r] quandam de uilla quadam mei patrimonii quę Scai uulgo dicitur., cum decima eidem ecclesie pertinenti:· excepta quadam parte duorum scilicet uauasssorum qui non sunt mei iuris. quorum tamen excepta sola decima reditum eadem habet ecclesia. Dono eciam nouem acras terre et insuper assentio ut si quisquam meorum hominum eandem uillam incolentium necessitate aliqua coactus de terra uel possessione sua eiusdem loci abbati aliquid inuadimoniare uoluerit:· licet hoc agat. Si uero omnino uendere uoluerit:· usque ad duas acras exceptis masuris et ortolaneis terris indissimiliter annuo. Huius rei testes sunt qui signum uiuifice crucis subtus inpresserunt. Signum Rotberti Hamonis filii. Signum Folcui de Mannei. Signum Rogerii Iuelini filii. Signum Rotberti de Buris. Signum Malgerii de Buris. Signum Rogerii clerici. Signum Theoldi. Signum Parualt. Signum Adam. Signum Radulfi de Sancto Iohanne. Signum Galterii de Coldeuilla. Signum Hugonis preposi [*sic*] Genitiensis. Signum Pagani de Bricauilla. Signum Radulfi Malreguart. Acta est hec donatio anno dominice incarnationis .m°. lxxxvi. Indictione nona. anno primo cycli decennouenalis.

Copy from a copy of the now lost original in B.N. lat. 5430A, pp. 252–3. The next charter follows in the Cartulary with only a paragraph sign to mark the break.

68

Accord between Abbot Bernard and the brothers William and Alexander, knights from Esquay, concerning tithes which they and their ancestors long held unjustly; the grant is made on the altar of St Michael in the presence of Abbot Bernard and the whole convent; the brothers are given 60 *solidi* in the money of Anjou: 1131–1142.

Quoniam omne presens tempus futurum est. esse preteritum. et omnis ętas labente temporum curriculo uertitur in senium:· dignum duximus nostris posteris ea quę nostris acta sunt temporibus memorie digna fideli scripto mandare. Perpatescat igitur cunctis [fol. 80v] hoc scriptum legentibus. siue audientibus. quod duo milites fratres de uilla quę dicitur ESCAI. decimam suam quam iniuste tam ipsi quam antecessores sui diu tenuerant Deo et sancte Marie. sanctoque Michaeli de Monte dederunt. ac super altare sanctę MARIę de

Escai inspiciente parrochia hoc donum posuerunt. Postea uero ut firmius teneretur quod fecerant donum. ad Montem ambo uenientes coram donno Bernardo abbate omnique conuentu super altare sancti Michaelis idem donum posuerunt. et ab eodem abbate. lx^{ta}. solidos Andegauensium acceperunt. Vocabantur maior natu Guillelmus. iunior uero Alexander. quod scriptum propriis manibus subter firmauerunt. Signum Guillelmi. Signum Alexandri. Hi sunt qui affuerunt. Iohannes Caisnel. Briendus frater eius. Sangualo.[a] Rotbertus de Monasterio. Lucas filius Arnulfi de Stanpis. Guillelmus filius Hugonis. Donoaldus.[b] Garinus senex. Tancredus.[c] et multi alii. et hi monachi affuerunt. domnus Bernardus abbas. Petrus prior. Rannulfus camerarius. Radulfus. Alo.[d] Richardus de Musca. Rotbertus Legatus. Gaufredus Episcopus. Radulfus plen'. Guillelmus Tro. omnisque conuentus.

The original of this act is preserved in B.N. lat. 9215, no. 59. The principal divergences are orthographical: [a] sunt testes [a] Sasualo [b] Donallus [c] Tanqueredus [d] Alo *om.*

69

Grant, for the souls of himself, his parents and ancestors and of his brother Henry, of a market and an annual fair, on the feast of the Nativity of the Virgin, at Ardevon (Manche, cant. Pontorson), and land for building a dwelling in Rouen, by Robert II of Normandy: enacted in the time of Abbot Roger, 1088.

De feria [et mercato de *add. man. rec.*] *Ardeuum* [et de domo Rothomanus *add. man. rec.*]

IN NOMINE SANCTE ET INDIVIDVE TRINITATIS. Notum sit omnibus tam presentibus quam futuris. quod ego Rotbertus Dei gratia Normannorum dux. filius Guillelmi gloriossimi Anglorum regis. pro salute [fol. 81r] anime mee. atque patris mei. matrisque mee. nec non et omnium antecessorum meorum. concedo ecclesie beati Michaelis archangeli nec non et pro anima fratris mei Henrici mercaṭum perpetualiter possidendum in uilla quę uocatur ARDEVVM. et in eadem uilla feriam annalem in festiuitate Natiuitatis beate Marie semper uirginis. Et in ciuitate quę dicitur Rotomagus. terram ad domum super edificandam. Hęc autem donatio facta est anno incarnationis dominice .m°. lxxx° viii°. presidente ecclesie prefate beati Michaelis de Monte domno Rogerio abbate uenerabili atque strenuo. Signum Rotberti comitis. Signum comitis de Mellent. Signum Simonis de Chymilleio. Signum Guillelmi de Bretuil. Signum Rotberti uicecomitis. Signum Guillelmi de Tornebu. Signum Pagani de Vilers. Signum R' Paganelli. Signum Rotberti filii Anschetilli. Signum Guillelmi monachi de Archis. Signum Alberici de Tuceio. Signum R' capellani comitis. Rotberti [+]. comitis Normannie.

[1 line blank]

De feria [et mercato de *add. man. rec.*] *Ardeuum* [et de domo Rothomanus *add. man. rec.*]

Original in Paris, Bib. Nat., nouv. acq. lat. 1674, fol. 4, endorsed: 'De feria Ardevon'; it has slits for a now missing seal.

Printed, with facsimile, from the original: L. Delisle, *Charte Normande de 1088* (Paris, 1886); calendared *RRAN* i, no. 299, and Round, *CDF*, no. 717.

70

Record of a convention between Abbot Ranulf and one Roger concerning land at Poterel (Manche, cant. Sartilly, comm. Dragey). Gerbert de Poterel, driven by poverty, had given one moiety of the land to the abbey with his son Drogo, who was to become a monk. Subsequently the abbot had purchased the other moiety from Roger, who then retired to his favourite property at Herenguerville (cant. Montmartin). Roger subsequently killed the abbey's swineherd in the forest of Bevais, for which he was exiled by the duke; unable to bear his exile, he appealed to the abbot to assist his reconciliation with duke in return for his abjuration of Poterel; after a long resistance the abbot agreed and the matter was resolved in the presence of William II of Normandy: Bonneville, 1066 (? between 27 May and 16 July).

Carta de Poterel

IN NOMINE PATRIS ET FILII ET SPIRITVS SANCTI AMEN. Notum sit omnibus non solum presentibus sed et futuris quod ego Gerbertus de Poterel deprimente me pauperie Deoque inspirante requisiui uenerabilem abbatem Rannulfum ut ad monachilem ordinem Drogonem quendam meum filium reciperet. cum medietate terre mee de Poterel quam de illo in liberali [fol. 81v] seruitio tenebam. quod ipse libenter concessit. Postea predictus abbas de quodam Rogero cui medietas alterius remanserat. ipsam medietatem decem[a] libras Cenomannensium quam pluribus uidentibus et audientibus emit. Habebat etenim ipse Rogerus terram apud Herengardisuillam quam plus diligebat. ibique recessit. Abbas autem accepta terra in dominio: ad opus ecclesie fecit de illa medietariam. Post multum uero temporis isdem Rogerus instigante diabolo quadam die in nemore BIVIE porcos sancti Michaelis inueniens fraudulenter et nequiter[b] subulcum interfecit. Quod audiens abbas Rannulfus incunctanter comiti Normannie patrati sceleris clamor[em ostendit *corr.*]. Comes autem continuo ipsum Rogerum ut sue maiestatis reum a[ac *a.c*] tocius Normannie patria eliminauit. Transacto autem non minimo temporis spatio ipse Rogerus exterminium ferre non ualens per inter nuntios multociens abbatem requisiuit. mandans[c] et multum deprecans ut co[v *sscr*]n duce Normannie ei pacem reformaret sibique reconciliari permitteret: tali pacto talique tenore ut ipse coram predicto duce et omnibus proceribus eius forsiuraret[d] illam terram de Poterel quam uendiderat. quod numquam ipse uel aliquis heredum suorum in omni successione temporum aliquid amplius in illa terra clamarent uel requirerent. Diu siquidem hoc facere et eciam[e] audire refugiens. tandem stimulatus consilio monachorum. et abbatie [fol. 82r] baronum statuto die et determinato coram Guillelmo duce Normannie conuenerunt. Recordatoque ibi pacto. et ab utraque parte concesso ante ducem Normannie Guillelmum ut predictum est conuentionem confirmauerunt. Ad hanc igitur[f] conuentionem roborandam ut firma. inconuulsa. et immobilis finetenus futuris temporibus permaneat: predictus piissimus princeps signum .+.[g] manu propria sub imprimere non abnuit. Signum Guillelmi gloriosissimi principis Normannie. Signum Rotberti filii eius. Signum Guillemi filii eius. Signum Mathildis uxoris eius. Signum [+] Rotberti Sagiensis episcopi. Signum [+] Iohannis Abrincensis episcopi. Signum Rogerii de Monte-gomeri. Signum Rogerii de Bello-monte. Signum Richardi proconsulis. Signum Turgisi de Tracei.[h] Signum Gaufredi de Sai. Signum Radulfi de Sancto Iohanne. Signum Haimonis de Bacilleio. Signum Hugonis prepositi de Genecio. Signum Morini pistoris. Signum Ilgerii[i] prepositi de Ardeuone. Acta sunt hec apud Bonamuillam eo anno quo gloriosus Guillemus princeps Normannie mare transmeauit. Angliamque[j] sibi Deo comitante subiugauit: anno ab incarnatione domini .m°.lx.vi. Epacta .xxii. Concurrente.vi.

Printed: Fauroux, 232 (from the cartulary); calendared Round, *CDF*, 713.

Copy by G. de Beausse (Arch. Calvados F 4276) of a 'copie informe moderne *ex libro albo, pagina 176 recto*' formerly Arch. dépt. Manche H non classé, i.e. Beausse copied a copy of an entry in the *Liber Albus*.

[a] 10 lib. Cen. qui pluribus videntibus et audientibus cunctis habebat et eamdem ipse
[b] nequitis [c] requisitus mandatis [d] forsiueraret [e] id [f] ergo [g] crucis [h] Ticey [i] Ligerii
[j] Angliam quam

71

Restoration by Robert fitz William (of Avranches) of tithes at Le Luot (Manche, cant. La Haye-Pesnel) and Servon (Manche, cant. Pontorson) which he had unjustly taken from the monks after the death of his father; for his salvation, his father's and his ancestors's, he also abandons all other claims to abbey possessions, notably the woods at Crapault (cant. Sartilly, comm. Carolles) and Neirun (now lost in Manche, cant. Sartilly, comm. Champeaux); in return, his knight, a provost, is made a monk, and Robert receives confraternity: 1104.

de decima de Luoth. et de Seruum

IN NOMINE SANCTE ET INDIVIDVE TRINITATIS. EGO Rotbertus Guillelmi pie memorie filius. reddo et concedo sancto Michaeli et monachis de monte decimam de Luoth. et de Seruum quas instigatus [fol. 82v] diabolo et prauorum hominum consilio post mortem patris mei eis immerito auferebam. Insuper et omnem calumpniam de Neyrum. et de Crapolt. et quicquid in omnibus possessionibus sancti Michaelis calumpniabar: diuina pietate commotus. omnino dimisi. Et pro anima patris mei. et antecessorum meorum meique salute: hoc donum confirmaui per unum cultellum quem super altare sancti Michaelis propria manu posui. Monachi autem eiusdem loci pro concessione ista quam feci. dederunt cuidam militi nomine preposito me exorante habitum sancti Benedicti: cuius loricam et equum ut donatio mea inconuulsa permaneret donauerunt michi:· et fratrem et participem concesserunt me esse totius beneficii sui. anno ab incarnatione domini .m°.c°.iiii°. Indictione .xii^{a}. est conuentio ista facta:· et quorundam proprius manibus qui presentes aderant signo dominice crucis corroborata. Hanc conuentionem si quis stimulatus furia diabolica uel per se uel per alium uiolare presumpserit. sit excommunicatus ante tribunal domini nostri Ihesu Christi. nec habeat hereditatem in regno Dei. Signum Rotberti. Signum Gaufredi de Cauinne. Signum Guillelmi dapiferi. Signum Gisleberti Belle cal'. Signum Guillelmi Calcebo. Signum Assonis. Signum Guillelmi Rufi. Signum Huberti presbyteri. Signum Hugonis camb'. Signum Radulfi. Hilduini filii. Signum Berneri. Fol. Signum Hildeni.

Copy of a copy from an unsealed original in B.N. lat. 5430A, p. 248

72

Notification of a grant by Robert of Avranches, with the counsel of Bishop Turgis of Avranches and the consent of the cathedral chapter, and the assent of his wife Hadvise (de Dol) of tithes of land in Ponts, (Manche, cant. Avranches) and its vicinity at Funeçon and Caviné or Cauvigny; he also demised to the abbey the vines mortgaged by John de Monte for ten pounds in the money of Le Mans, which John's nearest kinsmen will pay to the monks: 1129.

De decima de Ponz. et Luoth. de Neirum. et de Crapolt.

[fol. 83r] IN NOMINE PATRIS ET FILII ET SPIRITVS SANCTI AMEN. Quoniam antiquorum sollers prouidentia approbabili more instituit. ut elemosine quę ecclesiis Deo inspirante a quibuslibet fidelibus largiuntur. sub testimonio cartarum roborari et confirmari deberent:· memorie future successionis committere decreuimus donum et elemosinam quam in decimis suis huic ecclesie beati archangeli Michaelis Rotbertus de Abrincis consilio episcopi Turgisi Abrincarum. et concessu tocius capituli sancti Andręe. et licentia ac uoluntate sue nobilissime coniugis nomine HADVISE. et omnium amicorum suorum pio uoto feruentique desiderio fecit. Tradidit itaque in primis omnem decimam suam de Ponz. quam in propria manu et proprio dominio hereditario iure tenuerat. et decimam trium uauassorum de Folmuchunz quam similiter iure antecessorum suorum tenebat:· et decimam cuiusdam medietarie quam apud Cauinneium possidebat. Dimisit eciam huic ecclesie uineas Iohannis de Monte quas super .x^{cem}. libras Cenomannensium in uadimonium habebat. ita ut ecclesia pacifice et quiete illas haberet. donec decem libre monachis huius ecclesie a propinquis parentibus Iohannis redderentur. Facta est autem hęc sollempnis donatio elemosine. anno .m°. c°. xx°. ix°. ab incarnatione domini. Turgiso episcopo cum concessu tocius ecclesie hoc donum roborante et confirmante. his uiden[fol. 83v]tibus et audientibus. Signum Haduise uxoris eius. Signum Guillelmo de Ponz. Signum

Guillelmo Grimalt. Rogerii[o *a.c*] de Cauinne. Peuurelli [o *a.c.*] de Montabolt. Philippi [o *a.c.*] de Musca.

73

Grant by William fitz Wimund (of Avranches) of the whole tithes of all his vavassores and himself at Le Luot (Manche, cant. La Haye-Pesnel), at the instance of Michael, bishop of Avranches, and of three canons of Avranches, friends of William, with the consent of the whole cathedral chapter; the grant is made for the salvation of his soul, his wife Matilda's, and other relatives, on condition that he will be buried at the Mont, the monks undertaking to recover his body for burial from wheresoever he shall die in Normandy: 1066.

De eodem

NOTVM sit omnibus presentibus et futuris quod ego Guillelmus Guimundi filius iure hereditario patris mei tenens et possidens totam decimam omnium uauassorum meorum de Luoht. absque contradictione cuiuslibet quod inde michi placebat faciebam. Diuturno autem tempore me sic illam tenente. tandem gratia Dei cor meum illustrante quae cuius uult miseretur. et quem uult indurat. metu ęterne gehenne cepi expauescere. et amore future glorie flagrare: consilio et exhortatione reuerentissimi presulis Michaelis Abrincatensis sedis atque corumdam canonicorum amicorum meorum. Gauslini uidelicet. Iohannis magistri scolarum. Erneisi de Verduno. atque omni capitulo sancti Andree laudante et concedente. do et concedo Deo et sancto Michaeli archangelo. eiusque monachis totam hanc decimam de Luoht. uidelicet duos manipulos omnium uauassorum meorum quos in proprio dominio retinebam pro remedio anime mee. meique patris et matris atque pro salute uxoris mee Mathildis. eo tenore atque condictione quod ubicumque michi obitus euenerit in Normannia. monachi sancti Michaelis me ad Montem deferent. [fol. 84r] et sicut fratrem suum honestissime et honorifice me sepelient. atque tumulabunt. Actum est hoc anno ab incarnatione domini. m°. lx°.vi°. residente Michaele episcopo in sede pontificali qui hoc donum confirmauit. et Rannulfo abbate in ecclesia sancti Michaelis. istis uidentibus et audientibus. Signum Guillelmi [+]. Signum Mathildis [+] uxoris eius. Signum Bertranni [+] de Verduno. Signum Gaufredi [+] de Cauinne. Signum Radulfi [+] de Sancto Iohanne. Signum Radulfi [+] de Musca.

74

Notification by Abbot Ranulf concerning a grant by Ranulf de Champeaux (Manche, cant. Sartilly) of his part of the tithe of Champeaux, with the assent of Earl Hugh [of Chester], for which he is received into fraternity and given 15 pounds in the money of Le Mans; he also grants his tithe at Bréquigny (Manche, hamlet of cant. Sartilly): *c.* 1068–85.

Carta de Campels

IN DEI NOMINE VIVIFICE TRINITATIS HONORE. Ego Rannulfus abbas sancti Michaelis archangeli ecclesie. ductus eiusdem principis Anglorum amore. fretusque fratrum consilio quibus inerat cura uere sophie. peregi hanc quę sequitur conuenientiam in perpetuo seruare uolens posterum ad noticiam. Quidam miles de uico qui dicitur Campels Rannulfus nomine adiens nos cupiensque se protegi diuino solamine. concessit Deo sanctoque Michaeli partem quam in supradicta uilla tenebat decime. id est duas garbas ex medietate ipsius uici decime. annuente comite Hugone. eo tenore ut effectus particeps nostrarum precum ac orationum. ad presens susciperet a nobis .xv. libras Cenomannensium nummorum. decimaque perpetuo foret sub nostri dominio absque calumpnia et contradictione heredum suorum. Dedit eciam nobis decimam de Bricheignei [fol. 84v] simili condictione. quicquid in porcis. in agnis. seu annonis possidere uidebatur in tota decimatione. adiciens ut si quando monachicum scema suscipere uellet. uel si nolens aliquem ex filiis eidem norme summitti uellet. annueretur eius peticioni∴ cum ipso ea quę ex suo consequi posset coniungens huic donationi. Si quis uero quod non credimus de posteris hęc transgressus contraierit cum Dathan et Abiran penis auerni se deputatum nouerit. nisi Deo et sancto Michaeli contra quos rebellis extitit. digne se humiliando satisfecerit. Hęc ut perpetuo firma sit scripto dare curaui. testibusque firmare mandaui. Signum Hugonis comitis. Signum Haimerici filii [ius *a.c*] Gaufredi. Signum Tescelini filii [-ius *a.c.*] Dauid. Signum Hugonis prepositi. Signum Morini pistoris. Signum Osberni. Escolland. Signum Rogerii Grauerenth. Signum eiusdem Rannulfi. Signum Rannulfi Farsith.

75

Notification of the restitution of the land of Ranulf de Champeaux by his grandson Gilbert de Champeaux and his son William, still a child, on the day that Gilbert's brother Ralph became a monk; the restitution was made on the altar of St Michael on the relic of St Aubert: 1143.

De eodem

Anno ab incarnatione domini .m°.c°.xl°.iii°. sub Bernardo abbate. Gislebertus de Campels et Guillelmus filius eius adhuc puer reddiderunt Deo sanctoque Michaeli et monachis eiusdem loci duas garbas decime aratri sui quam Rannulfus huius Gisleberti auus sub abbate Rannulfo sancto Michaeli cum ceteris decimis suis olim dederat. Facta est carta hęc in die qua frater eius Radulfus factus est monachus. Predictam uero decimam antecessores eius nequam ducti consilio abstulerant. quę ab eo in hac die [fol. 85r] per brachium sancti Autberti ex integro super altare sancti Michaelis est restituta. et priorum donatio confirmata. Huius rei testes∴ Richardus de Leises. Thomas de Sancto Pancratio. Garnerius presbiter. Sasualo. Vitalis Turpis infans. Signum Gisleberti [+]

76

On the day of his father's funeral, the monks ask Ranulf Avenel to restore the tithes of St Evremund of Sartilly, which he and his father had earlier granted but which he had retained for his use, and to give them the church itself; granting the request, on the advice of Robert de Ducey, he also renews his and his father's joint gift of the revenues and services due from their man Pichard in Coutances: the charter was made in the chapter-house of the abbey, during a brief vacancy in the archbishop of Rouen, 1128–29.

Carta de Sartilleio

IN NOMINE. SANCTE. ET. INDIVIDVE. TRINITATIS. PATRIS. ET. FILII. ET. SPIRITVS SANCTI. Ego Rannulfus Auenel a monachis sancti Michaelis in die sepulture patris mei deuote postulatus. ut decimam Sancti Euremundi quam pater meus predictus et ego simul dederamus sancto Michaeli quia remocior erat: ad opus meum in manu mea retinerem. et in elemosina ecclesiam de Sartilleio eis darem. cum ipsis rebus quę ad eam pertinent. Quorum postulationi quoniam digna erat: consilio Rotberti de Duxeio et aliorum amicorum meorum benigno animo annui. et ita in perpetuum hoc donum huius ęcclesię cum octo arpennis terre ad ipsam pertinentibus uolo esse confirmatum: ut a nullo successorum meorum aliquando minuatur. Preterea uero notum esse omnibus quod similiter dedimus ego et pater meus in Constantiensi uilla seruicium et censum cuiusdam hominis nomine Pichardi. et suę hereditatis successorum. His presentibus testibus sub intitulatis: facta est hęc cartula in capitulo Montis. tempore donni Honorii [fol. 85v] pape. ecclesia Rothomagense pastore orbata. Turgiso Abrincense presule annuente. Henrico glorioso rege existente principe Anglorum et Normannorum. Et hęc sunt signa eorum qui huius res interfuerunt. Signum Rannulfi [+] datoris. Signum Rotberti de Duxeio. Signum Rotberti de Romaneio. Signum Alanni filii Haimerici. Signum Rogerii camerarii. Signum Riualloni Calciabouem. Signum Trehani de Maineio. Signum Hamelini de Cortilz. Signum Hugonis prepositi Genitiensis. Signum Turgisi filii Trehani. Signum Rotberti Catti. Signum Iordani dapiferi. Signum Rannulfi.

Calendared: Round, *CDF*, 722, from the Cartulary. At the time of publication, in 1899, no original of this charter was discoverable in the archives at Saint-Lô.

77

Robert de Ducey came to the chapter-house of the abbey on the eve of the Feast of the Purification and conceded the grant of his father and other ancestors of his allod at Fougerolles (Manche, cant. Ducey), with the exception of the land that Ralph de Veim held of him; done with the assent of Earl Ranulf of Chester, *vicomte* of Avranches; it is further confirmed after his death by his widow Cecilia and his son William: *c.* 1121–1127.

Carta de Fulgereio.

IN NOMINE PATRIS. ET FILII. ET SPIRITVS SANCTI. AMEN. Notum sit omnibus presentibus et futuris. quod ego Rotbertus de Duxeio pro remedio anime mee et patris ac matris mee uigilia purificationis sancte Mariae ueni in capitulum sancti Michaelis ibique terram de Fulgereio quę alodum patris mei et antecessorum meorum fuerat ecclesie sancti archangeli Michaelis et ipsius monachis finetenus dedi et concessi. ut hanc terram teneant. habeant. et perpetuo possideant. absque omnium sequentium heredum meorum et omnium aliorum calumpnia et contradictione. Hoc autem factum est in comitis Rannulfi et baronum suorum Abrincatensium presentia. excepto Radulfi de Veim terram quam de me tenebat. Hoc donum huius terre concedo ego Guillelmus filius Rotberti post mortem patris [fol. 86r] mei cum Cecilia. Huius rei sunt testes. Rotbertus. de Duxeio. Rannulfus comes. Rotbertus Greuesac. Radulfus de Veim. Radulfus de Brei. Alueredus de Maci. Gradelonus de Taneia. Turgisus de Taneia. Guillelmus uauassor. Gislebertus filius Adam. Hamelinus filius Adam. Guillelmus de Vira. Bertrannus de Verdun. Stephanus de Eschailli. Rannulfus. et Rannulfus de Grandeuilla. Guillelmus filius Rotberti de Duxeio. Cecilia uxor Rotberti. Iudicalis presbiter. Richardus Cardonis. Alueredus de Maci. Guillelmus de Boce. Richardus Leuelatus. Rogerius. prepositus. Rogerius de Borrian. Crispinus. Rogerius de Brafer.

Copied from the original by G. de Beausse from Arch. dépt. Manche H non classé, 'orig. parch. 0^{m}.340 x 0^{m}.270. scellé, ver double queue sans repli. Le sceau manque'. In this copy all the witnesses appear in the genitive case. Calendared in Round, *CDF*, 721.

78

Notification of the confirmation of his father's grant by William fitz Robert de Ducey; William made his grant on the altar on which the relic of St Aubert was placed and he swore on the gospels that the gift should stand for perpetuity; in return Abbot Bernard made him a gift of a palfrey and gave two *solidi* to his brother: the notification postdates the death of Abbot Bernard 'of venerable memory', but the act relates to the time of his abbacy, 1131–8 May 1149.

De eodem

NOTVM ducere decreuimus tam presentibus quam futuris quatinus Guillelmus de Duxe. dedit et concessit dationem quam pater suus Rotbertus dederat Deo et ęcclesię de Monte Sancti Michaelis. scilicet terram de Fulgere liberam et quietam ab omnibus costumis. Hęc autem datio facta est ab eodem per brachium sancti AUTBERTI super altare. et iurauit ibidem super quattuor euangelium quod hoc donum inconcussum maneret in sempiternum. Vt autem hoc mente libera concederet: Bernardus uenerabilis memorie abbas unum palefridum tanto uiro dignum et fratri suo duos solidos in memoriam huius rei dedit. testibus his. Signum Guillelmi de Duxe. Signum Rotberti fratris eius. Signum [fol. 86v] Riualloni prepositi. Signum Iohannis. Bi.

Signum Thome de Leises. Signum Rotberti Taforel. Signum Rotberti de Nemore. Signum Willelmi forestarii.

79

Notification that a certain Niel, from the Cotentin, conceded, in the house of Abbot Ranulf, the land of *Plemmunt* in Guernsey previously granted by his brother Hugh; done in the presence of many laymen representing both parties in the house of Abbot Ranulf, who makes a counter-gift to Niel of ten pounds in the pennies of Rouen: 1058–85.

De quadam terra in Greneroi que dicitur Plemmunt

IN NOMINE PATRIS ET FILII ET SPIRITVS SANCTI. NOTVM SIT omnibus fidem sancte Trinitatis seruantibus. Niellum quendam de pago Constantio concessisse Deo et sancto Michaeli iure perpetuo terram unius carruce in insula Greneroi loco qui dicitur Plemmunt:· quam olim HUGO eiusdem Nielli frater dum aduiueret eodem modo dederat sancto Michaeli et fratribus [eidem] sancte ecclesie famulantibus. Deliberatione denique cum suis habita. isdem Niellus sancti Michaelis adiit limina:· atque in domni Rannulfi abbatis eiusdem loci ac monachorum cohorte multorum etiam laicorum utrarumque partium presentia. nomine elemosine pro suorum peccaminum absolutione et anime saluatione. Supradictam terram Deo et sancto Michaeli seruientibus obtulit perpetualiter possidendam. eo tenore atque conditione. ut habeant. teneant. possideantque absque omnium parentum suorum uel quorumcumque successorum contradictione. Dono eciam caritatis et confirmationis isdem abbas Rannulfus eidem Niello .x. libras Rothomagensium denariorum contribuit. quo eadem donatio et confirmatio inconuulsa stabilitate consistere possit. Hanc [fol. 87r] igitur oblationem huic sancto loco deuote traditam. si quis subtrahendo aliquatenus uiolare presumpserit. a cęlesti patria seclusus. et a sanctorum omnium collegio perpetim segregatus. diabolo eiusque sociis commissus. in perpetuis gehenne mittatur ignibus. ubi per infinita tempora crucietur. Amen. Isti sunt testes conuentionis ex parte sancti Michaelis. Ilgerius prepositus. Guillelmus. Calcebuef. Osbernus Escollant. Garnerius canonicus. Bernardus canonicus. Hugo cubicularius. Adso. Iuo. filius Restaldi. Signum Nielli [+] auctoris donationis. Testes partis illius. Signum Rotberti de Romille. Signum Serlonis. Signum Dodemani. Signum Hunfredi.

Printed: *Cartulaire de Jersey*, no. 150, pp. 228–9, from the Cartulary. Copied in B.N. lat. 5430A, pp. 269–70.

80

Charter of Hugh bishop of Avranches stating that he restores to the abbey, *post mortem*, tithes in Guernsey that were granted him for his lifetime by Abbot Suppo on condition that he will it back to the abbey: *c.* 1032–59/60, probably *c.* 1032–1048.

Nouimus fidelium moris esse. ut quicumque eorum Dei actus inspiratione. qui operatur in omnibus et uelle et perficere pro bona uoluntate. heredem sanctam Dei ecclesiam possessionum suarum uel rerum sui iuris uoluerint facere. inde testamentum componant litterale:· manus proprie signatum subscriptione. Qua propter et ego Hugo Abrincatensis ciuitatis gratia Dei episcopus. notum esse uolo tam presentibus quam futuris omnibus. quia decimam medie insule quę dicitur Greneroi. michi a domno abbate Suppone concessam dum aduixero possidere. eo tenore ac ratione. ut post excessum meum eam sancto Michaeli sibique famulantibus absque ullius successoris mei episcopi uel parentis aut heredis contradictione restituerem. Hanc [fol. 87v] inquam decimationem. et exitus ecclesiarum. terramque. unius carruce. et quicquid a predicto patre acceperam. archangelo Michaeli et monachis meis fratribus et filiis uti prefixum est. postquam terrestris domus mea huius habitationis fuerit soluta. absque ulla contradictione reddo:· quatinus edificationem habeam a Deo domum non manu factam eternam in celis. Quicunque ergo huic rei contraire siue successor seu parens aut heres noster conatus fuerit. et aliquid harum rerum sancti Michaelis quę possedi usurpare sine uoluntate monachorum uoluerit:· a me et a presentibus fidelibus omni maledictionis genere anathematizatus. et a sancta Dei ecclesia proiectus. cum Dathan. et Abiron. habeat sortem in penis infernalibus. Vt uero hoc scriptum inuiolabiliter firmiterque teneatur. manus mee subscriptione roboraui. et circunsedentibus firmandum tradidi. +.

Printed: *Cartulaire de Jersey*, no. 149, pp. 227–8, from the Cartulary.

81

Notification concerning the conversion of a mortgage of land in Guernsey to a grant by Rainald fitz Hugh when dying, with the assent of his two daughters and his son-in-law Richard, and witnessed by his confessor: dated from the witnesses, 1131–49.

De terra Rainaldi filii Hugonis

NOVERINT tam presentes quam futuri. quoniam Rainaldus filius Hugonis terram quam iure hereditario in Grenereio possidebat. monachis sancti Michaelis de Monte inuadimoniauerit pro centum solidis Cenomannensium. tali uidelicet pacto. ut si uel ipse. uel aliquis heredum suorum eosdem nummos redderet:· terram suam liberam et quietam haberet. Sed cum non post multum tempus isdem Rainaldus infirmaretur. et in gra[fol. 88r]uescente incommodo ad extrema duceretur. pro Dei amore et anime sue redemptione. eandem terram consensu uxoris sue quę presens aderat Deo et sancto Michaeli sibique famulantibus monachis concessit. et in perpetuum habendam contulit. Huius donationis presbiter qui tunc confessum eum faciebat testis fidelissimus permanet. Hoc quoque filia eius Aeles scilicet et Richardus alterius filie eius maritus pro uxore sua concesserunt. Prime donationis quam quidem Rainaldus fecerat. testes sunt hi. Iohannes presbiter. Radulfus homo eius. de Donuilla. et Rogerius homo eius. Concessionis uero quam postmodum filie eiusdem Rainaldi fecerunt testes sunt hi. Riuallo Calcebos. Hugo Testa. Sangualo. et multi alii.

Copied from original by G. de Beausse from Arch. dépt. de la Manche H non classé, 'orig. parch. sans scelleur. hauteur 0^{m}.140 x largeur 0^{m}.150', and in BN lat. 10072, no. 77. Cf. notes to no. **111** below.

Printed: *Cartulaire de Jersey*, no. 118, pp. 187–8, from the original. Calendared in Round, *CDF*, 731.

82

Notification concerning the grant by Rainald de Carteret of the church of Saint-Germain de Carteret (Manche, cant. Barneville) in 1125, in the time of Abbot Richard and Richard, bishop of Coutances, followed by an account of how the grant was challenged after his death by his son Philip, who eventually, in 1135, comes to the Mont in 1135 with his mother Lucia and brother Geoffrey, to concede the gift, with the approval and in the presence of Bishop Algar of Coutances and his chapter; he makes additional grants of the tithes of the mills, two plots of land in Jersey and one in Carteret; Abbot Bernard makes counter-gifts to him and his family: 1125, 1135.

[De carterio *supp. man. rec.*]

IN NOMINE PATRIS ET FILII ET SPIRITVS SANCTI AMEN. Notum sit omnibus sancte Dei ecclesie filiis tam prelatis quam subditis quod ego Rainaldus de Carterei[a] pro anime mee salute et antecessorum meorum obtuli Deo sanctoque Michaeli archangelo de Monte. monachisque ibidem seruientibus tempori Richardi eiusdem loci abbatis. ecclesiam beati Germani de Cartraio cum omni decima tocius parrochię. et cum terra de elemosina regis quę est sancti Germani in Gerseio. et cum decima bonorum domus meae. Actum est hoc donum anno ab incarnatione domini .m°.c°. xx°v°. Ricar[fol. 88v]do presule in Constantiensi presidente ecclesia. Defuncto autem Rainaldo qui predictum donum fecerat. Philippus eius filius quorumdam malignorum hominum consilio corruptus. donum quod eius pater fererat ipse concedere noluit sed propposse suo subtraxit. Tandem Deo inspirante ipse Philippus penituit. et ad misericordiam Dei sanctique archangeli Michaelis. donnique Bernardi abbatis atque tocius capituli eiusdem loci corde conpunctus ueniam expetiit. Quadam uero die nullo cogente orationis gratia ad Montem Sancti Michaelis cum matre sua Lucia. et fratribus suis Hunfrido et Gaufredo et quibusdam suis hominibus uenit. atque omnem donationem elemosine quam illius pater concesserat: ipse libere cum matre et fratribus suis reddidit. atque concessit. et insuper ex sua parte Philippus hęc adiunxit. decimam uidelicet molendinorum suorum. et duas plateas terre in Gerseio extra curiam suam loco congruo. et unam ad Cartraium similiter extra. loco congruo. et omnes terras elemosine sancti Germani. Pro his etenim nouis donis supradictis. et pro mala consuetudine remouenda et prorsus auferenda dedit predictus abbas Bernardus Philippo .vii. libras Rothomagensis noue monete. matrique sue unum auri

Bizanteum. et Gaufrido fratri suo unum accipitrem. et Hunfredo, quasdam ocreas. Vt autem hoc donum quod in capitulum concessit. et deinde cum matre et fratribus super sancti Michaelis altare posuit firmum et stabile [fol. 89r] et inconuulsum permaneat: istis uidentibus et audientibus nomina subter notare decreuimus. Illa uero mala consuetudo de qua superius mentionem fecimus hęc erat. quod non poterant decime collecte bladium ponere nisi in curia ipsius Philippi ubi diminuebatur. Actum est autem hoc donum et ex parte Philippi concessum presente et concedente Algaro Constantiarum episcopo coram capitulo et clero anno ab incarnatione domini .m°.c°. xxx°.v°. Indictione .xiiii[a]. Signum Algari episcopi [+]. Signum Radulfi Baiocensis decani [+]. Signum Rogeri archidiaconi [+]. Signum Osberni cantoris [+]. Signum Gisleberti archidiaconi [+]. Signum Radulfi archidiaconi [+]. Signum Philippi de Carterei. Signum Hunfredi fratris eius. Signum Gaufredi fratris eius. Signum Lucie matris eorum. Ex parte ecclesie hi adfuerunt. Prior Exaquii. Guillelmus.[b] Iohannes canonicus. Guillelmus canonicus. Simon filius Iohannis. Rotbertus Papa. Simon de Cocto Bocco. Rotbertus Hausart.[c] Rannulfus de Colleuilla. Petrus clericus de Genecio. Thomas de Leisels.[d]

Copied from the original by G. de Beausse from Arch. dépt.de la Manche H non classé, 'orig. parch. scellé ver double queue. le sceau manque. 0^{m}.255 x 0^{m}.250', and in B.N. lat. 10072, no. 113, fol. 158: [a] Philippi Cartret [b] *deest* [c] Ausart [d] Leiseus, Leiseils

Printed: *Cartulaire de Jersey*, no. 33, pp. 50–1, which was 'Collationé à l'original existant aux archives de La Manche et revêtu du sceau, mal empreint, d'Algare, évêque de Coutances.'.

Calendared, Round, *CDF*, no. 725, from the sealed original.

83

Account relating that it was the custom for laymen born in the village of Mont-Saint-Michel to be given a share in the offerings of food and other provisions made to the sanctuary of the archangel; in the time of Abbot Bernard, Roger, an aged priest, surrendered to the abbey the share he and his ancestors had held unjustly; he and his son Ruellen and William Bellebarbe, his son-in-law, place the gift on the altar; Roger makes a further grant of 25 *solidi* in the money of Le Mans, for which he is admitted to the community as a monk, with the right to become a monk if he should so wish being granted to his son; Roger's nephews, the seven sons of his brother Thomas, initially concede the gift but after the death of Henry I, in 1135, and the subsequent war in Normandy, they become enemies of the abbey and incite local opposition to the community; they remain contumacious, despite several summonses to judgement, but, at a hearing lasting several days, local and regional authorities agree to withdraw all support and refuge from the brothers: 1135–1142 (see **Appendix i.5**, an agreement reached with the brothers in 1142).

A PRICIS (*sic*) admodum temporibus in ecclesia beatissimi archangeli Michaelis de periculo maris: mos nefandus inoleuit. Quidam enim laicorum ex eadem uilla procreatorum:ʼ in altare supradicti sancti se participes fecerunt. capientes uidelicet omne genus [fol. 89v] annone tam frumenti quam leguminis. et tocius alterius generis. et dimidiam partem lanificii et linificii. et omnia genera uolatilium uiuorum et mortuorum. et preter cotidianum panem et cotidianum nummum et multa alia quę enumerare longum est:ʼ quę ibidem solent afferri. Contigit autem in tempore donni Bernardi abbatis ut quidam sacerdos grandeuus nomine Rogerus. tam senio quam infirmitate grauatus. ad quem tunc temporis hec omnia supradicta respiciebant:ʼ Dei inspiratione et amicorum suorum ammonitione. spontaneus et multis lacrimis suffusus. hęc omnia secum super altare sancti Michaelis archangeli per dexteram argenteam et per cultellum supradicti abbatis obtulit. et finetenus dereliquit. seseque cum suis antecessoribus qui hęc ipsa iniuste possederant:ʼ absolui postulauit. Hęc oblatio. immo redditio. manibus suis et manibus filii sui Ruenlenni et Guillelmi Bellebarbe generi sui cum uxore sua filia uidelicet prefati sacerdotis:ʼ super altare posita est. et omnino cunctis audientibus qui aderant concessa. Qui Rogerus continuo monachili benedictione ab eodem postulata atque ibidem accepta. professionem suam super altare posuit:ʼ monachusque effectus collegio fratrum adiunctus est acceptis ab eodem abbate .xxv. solidis Cenomannensium. quos ipse reddidit debitoribus. omnibusque indumentis ad monachatum necessariis. [fol. 90r] Filio uero eius Ruenlenno concessus est introitus monachilis cum conuerti se uoluerit. datis et ipsi .xl. solidos Cenomannensium. Nepotes uero Rogeri. filii uidelicet Thome fratris eius septem fratres qui se heredes et conparticipes huius rei confirmabant:ʼ hac occasione perdiderant. Post mortem enim karissimi domini nostri Henrici regis in abbatem dominum suum et contra tocius uille salutem nequiter compluribus huiusce mali consciis conspirationem fecerunt. Quo comperto a pluribus abbas consilio fidelium suorum eos conuenit. et super tot et tantis malis conquestus eos alloquitur. Quibus negantibus et obtestantibus:ʼ iterum fidelitatem tam sue salutis quam tocius uille iurauerunt. Qui iterum in prodicione illa uehementer grassati. hominibus alterius regionis. ad tantum facinus patrandum adheserunt. Iterum allocuti et tercio sacramentis adstricti:ʼ funditus in malitia sua perseuerauerunt. Ad ultimum congregata curia ad dies plurimos constitutos:ʼ omne iuditium subterfugerunt. et sic malicia eorum comperta:ʼ omnibus patiuit. Quo comperto liberales ipsius uille et ipsius prouincie proceres super ignominia tanta confusi:ʼ eos omnino exterminauerunt. et sacramento affirmauerunt ex tunc illos non recepturos:ʼ nec cum eis deinceps habitaturos. Huius rei testis [-es *a.c.*] est omnis conuentus eiusdem loci. Hugo prior. Godefedus. Rogerius cantores. [fol. 90v] Frogerius. Guillelmus. Carlopin. Arnulfus. Goscelinus. Ruellen Calcebou. Hugo filius Odonis. Arnulfus de Stanpis. Guillelmus Turpis Infans. Vitalis. Leeffant. et omnes alii.

84

Notification of how Osbern d'Evrecy (Calvados), on the advice of a friend, went to the Mont to restore to the abbey the church and tithes of Evrecy and the tithe of the vill called *Flavineium*, all of which were formerly granted to the monks by the lord of Normandy but had been unjustly usurped by Osbern's father and himself; he adds the grant of tithes on thirty acres he holds from the monks: he swears on the relics of St Aubert that neither he nor his heirs will make any claim on the land; his steward Ranulf later swears the oath in the presence of the whole parish of Evrecy; the year Geoffrey became duke of Normandy, 1144.

De ecclesia de Vreceio

IN NOMINE SANCTE et indiuidue trinitatis omnipotentis Dei. a quo omne datum optimum. et omne donum perfectum est. anno ab incarnatione domini .m°.c°.x°l. iiii°. Gaufredo duce ducatum Normannorum obtinente. domno Bernardo abbate ęcclesiam sancti Michaelis de Monte regente. quidam miles dictus Osbernus de Eureceio diuino ut credimus timore correptus. a quibusdam eciam amicorum suorum ammonitus Montem Sancti Michaelis adueniens. Deo et sancto Michaeli monachisque ibidem domino seruientibus prefate uille EVRECEII uidelicet ecclesiam cum omnibus quę ad eam pertinebant. et redecimam id est decimam decime tocius parroechie. quoniam decima prius monachorum erat. nec non totam decimam triginta acrarum terre quas ab abbate tenebat. et decimam cuiusdam uille quę Flauineium dicitur: sponte reddidit. Haec omnia tam ipse quam pater eius ut ipse confitebatur iniuste tenuerant: quoniam prius monachi a domino Normannorum dono acceperant. et possederant. Et ut hoc firmum seruaretur: super altare sancti Michaelis [fol. 91r] et super brachium sancti Autberti neque se neque aliquem heredum suorum aliquid in his omnibus clamaturum iurauit: et Rannulfus pincerna cum eo quod postea iurauit tota presente parroechie EVRECEII. Hi sunt testes. Guillelmus. Crassus. Ruellem Calcebouem. Guillelmus Grauerenc. de Eureceio. Rotbertus filius Garini. [de Cadomo] et Guillelmus filius Rogerii. [de Cadomo] Hugo Testa.

Calendared in Round, *CDF.*, no. 728.

85

Notification of a mortgage agreed between Abbot Bernard of Mont-Saint-Michel and Ranulf de Colleville (Manche, cant. Bréhal); Ranulf is impelled by financial difficulties to mortgage part of a mill at Chanteloup (Manche, cant. Bréhal) for 4 gold marks; later, he is obliged to raise the loan to 10 gold marks, to be repaid as a wheat render over a three-year term: 1134.

De terra Rannulfi de Colleuilla

Nouerint non solum presentes sed et futuri hoc pactum firmatum fuisse in communi capitulo: inter donnum abbatem Bernardum de Monte Sancti Michaelis et Rannulfum de Colleuilla. Vrgente siquidem prenimia necessitate supradictum Rannulfum. adiit multimodis precibus et summissis uenerabilem Bernardum abbatem ut partem cuiusdam molendini inuadimoniaret. quod habebat apud Cantalupum de quo omni anno ad mensuram nostri horrei recipiebat. xii. quartaria frumenti:· propter .iiii^or^. marchas argenti. Quod et factum est. deinde cum maiori necessitate urgeretur. rurșum requisiuit donnum abbatem ut adhuc de terra sua inuadimoniaret propter .x. marchas argenti tantum unde ad mensuram nostri horrei redderet huic ecclesie singulis annis .xxx.viii. quarteria frumenti de terra nemoris. Si uero frumentum ad reddendum defecerit:· terra in dominio remanebit. Hoc autem factum est anno ab incarna[fol. 91v]tione domini .m^o^.c^o^.xxx^o^.iiii^o^. et ab hoc usque ad tres annos. eo pacto quod si post tres annos die octauarum pasche predicta pecunia reddita non fuerit:· donnus abbas toto sequenti anno terram habebit. et hoc de anno in annum. donec pecunia supradicta reddatur:· his uidentibus et audientibus. Osbernus clericus. Gaufredus episcopus. Galterius et Rogerius canonici. Rogerius camerarius. Rotbertus prepositus. Vitalis de Beuurone. Ernaudus de Montit'. Bertrannus faber. et multi alii.

Copied by G. de Beausse from a *vidimus* of 16 June 1362 'donné sub le scel de Raven le Moyne, lieutenant du vicomte d'Avranches, Arch. dépt. Manche H'. After *et multi alii*, this continues: 'Item anno MCLVIII Robertus de Brehal et filius eius Robertus calumpniantes capellam Sancti Johannis de Colleuilla decimam feudi de Torta cauata in quo eadem capella est retinuerunt dicentes se ibi matrem ecclesiam facturos quod audientes Robertus abbas de Monte et Ansgotus decanus qui erat uicarius abbatis in Coleuilla in curia Constanciensi in presencia Ricardi episcopi querimoniam de ista inuasione imposuerunt et capellam predictam membrum esse ecclesie Colleuille ueridicis assertionibus et legitimis testibus comprobauerunt. Unde illi causa cadentes et judicio ecclesiastico excommunicati quicquid inuaserant restituerunt. Testibus Ricardus episcopus. Ricardus. Philippus. Johannes. Guillelmus archidiaconi. Guillelmus de Verdun. Robertus de Bosco. Ranulphus de Colleuilla.'.

86

Restitution, by Baldwin Blondel son of Hermer, of a grant made by his father, and challenged by Baldwin, of the farm of the fee of *Estolleia*; in return, the monks grant him confraternity and the costs of a pilgrimage to Jerusalem; the bull of Eugenius III (**Appendix ii.11**) includes *Estolleia* among the possessions of the Mont in England, where it was attached to the abbey's cell at Otterton in Devon, founded before 1086 by a grant of William the Conqueror; *Estolleia* was probably a part of Otterton manor; done in the presence of Abbot Bernard and the relic of St Aubert, on the altar of St. Michael: 1131–5.

De Estolleia

QVONIAM nouitatis tempore succedente plurima sepe traduntur obliuioni et ignorantie. tam posteritati uenture quam presenti scripto dignum duximus manifestare. quod ego Balduinus Blondel Ermeri filius totam illam firmam fedium de Estolee quam ab abbate Sancti Michaelis de Periculo Maris et a monachis tenendam a patre meo successiue clamabam. super sanctum altare beati archangeli Michaelis de periculo maris pro salute anime mee et patris mei et parentum meorum liberam et quietam omnino excepta propria hereditate mea in tempore et presentia donni Bernardi eiusdem loci uenerabilis abbatis. et monachorum. et hominum quorumdam inibi presentium assistentium dimitto. et per brachium sanctissimi Auberti [fol. 92r] episcopi et confessoris et manum meam supra [pre]dictum altare beati archangeli absque calumpnia ac successorum meorum clamatione:· iure iurando confirmo et corroboro. Hanc autem ut dixi sollempniter coram plurimis astantibus feci donationem. immo proprii domini iure redditionem:· ut preteritorum peccaminum meorum ueram perciperem remissionem. presentium ac futurorum cautelam et cognitionem. Ea propter in caritate predictus abbas cum communi tocius capituli assensu monachorum. quadraginta solidos esterllingos ad uictum et uiam in Ierosolimis perficiendam sponte dederunt. et quod maius est sui beneficii fratrem et participem in morte et in uita fecerunt. Si quis autem heredum ac nepotum meorum seu quorumlibet succedentium redditioni contraire uoluerint huic cum nequissimo Iuda traditore Domini sit perpetue addictus maledictioni nisi quam cicius salutifere. satisfactioni per confessionem penitentiam confugerit. Signum Balduini [+]. Signum Guillelmi. Pulcrabarba [+]. Signum Haimonis. Rufi [+]. Signum Guillelmi de Belueir [+]. Signum Rainaldi. de Curei [+]. Signum Ruellen Calcebos [+]. Signum Rogerii [+]. Signum Radulfi de Belueir [+]. Signum Hugo Testa [+]. Signum Sangualo [+]. Signum Briencii. Chesnel [+]. Signum Donoaldi [+]. Signum Guillelmi Calcebos [+]. Signum Gaufredi. Asini [+].P

See Dom. L. Guilloreau, *Chartes d'Otterton* (Ligugé, Vienne) 1909.

87

Grant, with the counsel and assent of Richard, bishop of Avranches, by Gelduin fitz Odo de *Hauce* (probably Aucey-la-Plaine, cant. Pontorson, Manche), of the tithe of *Lusmeths* which he and his ancestors had held contrary to church law, on condition that he be buried by the monks at the Mont after his death, and his name entered into the abbey's memorial book; should he wish to take the habit before his death, the monks will receive him with such chattels and goods as pleases him: dated by reference to the release from prison of King Stephen of England in November 1141.

De decima de Lusmeths

[fol. 92v] Nouerit tam pia fidelium religio futurorum. quam presens conuentus fratrum monachorum. quod ego Gelduinus filius Odonis de Hauce iure hereditario patris mei tenens et possidens totam decimam de terra mea de Lusmeths absque contradictione cuiuslibet. quicquid de ea michi placebat faciebam. Diuturno autem tempore me sic illam tenente. sicut et antecessores mei prius fecerant. tandem gratia Dei cor meum illustrante. quę cuius uult miseretur et quem uult indurat:· metu gehenne mortis cepi expauescere. atque amore eterne glorie flagrare. consilio et exortatione amicorum meorum. et precipue consensu uenerabilis Richardi presulis Abrincensis. et quoru[a *a.c.*]ndam canonicorum fidelium meorum do et concedo Deo. et sancto Michaeli archangelo et eius monachis ei die noctuque pie famulantibus totam decimam supradictam. uidelicet duas garbas. tam proprie mee carruge quam uauassorum meorum quas in proprio dominio meo retinebam. pro remedio et salute anime mee. patris et matris mee. atque uxoris et puerorum meorum: nec non et antecessorum meorum qui eam contra sacra matris ecclesie statuta tenuerant. Propter quod me et eos pariter in capitulo absolui feci. Hanc autem donationem in tempore donni Bernardi uenerabilis abbatis. anno quo Stephanus rex anglorum exiuit de captione. super sanctum beati archangeli [fol. 93r] Michaelis altare. mea propria manu per argenteum sancti Autberti brachium inposui. eo tenore. et conditione. quod quando hominem exiero. et dies obitus mei euenerit. supradicti monachis sancti Michaelis me ad Montem deferent. et sicut fratrem suum honestissime et honorifice me sepelient atque tumulabunt. et in Kalendario inter suos familiares propter memoriam anniuersarii mei nomen meum scribent. Si autem in uita mea monachilem habitum sancti Benedicti suscipere uoluero. quod michi concedere dignetur omnipotens Deus antequam moriar. supradicti monachi sancti archangeli Michaelis me gratanter cum honore et amore suscipient cum tali catallo et beneficio quod michi placuerit: ita tamen prout honestius potuero. Verumptamen ad confirmationem huius conuentionis presentes subtitulamus testes: quorum nomina ista sunt. Ex parte etenim monachorum. Hugo. prior. Godefredus. Rogerius. [cantores] Rannulfus [canb']. Iohannes [cogl']. Guillelmus [Calopin]. Guibertus. Rainaldus [de Sancto Iohanne]. Rogerius [iuuenis]. Mainerius [de Geneiz]. Rotbertus [Legatus]. Iohannes [de Molend']. et plures alii. Ex mea parte: Ruellen [Calcebos]. Guillelmus [Pulcrabarba]. Vitalis [Leiffant]. Haimo [Rufus]. Thomas [filius eius]. Richardus [Cardum].

88

Restitution of the 'land of the great mill' and the service of a man of the abbey in Guernsey by Richard fitz Robert Malmarche, on the advice of his uncle Robert de Grentais; the land had been usurped first by his father Robert, who had died excommunicate in possession of it, and then by Richard, who had been excommunicated several times; enacted in the presence of the prior and convent and many laymen, after which Richard prostrates himself naked before the altar to be physically chastised by the monks, before receiving absolution for himself, his relations and coadjutors: 1131–8 May 1149.

De homine huic ecclesie reddito[-io *a.c.*] *in Guernereio*

NOTUM sit omnibus tam futuris quam presentibus monachis in hoc loco degentibus. quod ego Richardus filius Rotberti Malmarche multum perhorrescens ob peccatorum meorum enormitatem [fol. 93v] ęterni incendii gehennam iniquis et sceleratis sine fine preparatam. atque gaudia celestis patrie fidelibus promissa oppido desiderans. pro redemptione et saluatione anime mee. necnon patris et matris mee. et fratris. et omnium antecessorum meorum absolutione quandam terram de molendino magno in insula uidelicet de Guernereio sancti Michaelis propriam. hominem scilicet unum cum toto tenore in terra et in uiridario uno. consilio auunculi mei Rotberti de Grentais et quorumdam amicorum meorum iuste recteque consulentium. eandem terram quam iniuste calumpniabam et tenebam pro qua eciam multociens excommunicatus et interdictus fueram:· Deo et sancto Michaeli archangelo de Monte et monachis inibi die noctuque Christo domino seruientibus. in bona pace liberam. et quietam dimitto. reddo. et concedo. Hanc tamen terram pater meus Rotbertus calumpniauerat et per multos annos excommunicatus usque ad obitum suum possedit. tandem in semet reuersus uiamque uniuerse carnis se iturum intelligens. quod male et nequiter egerat emendare festinans:· quibusdam monachis qui ibi presto aderant. prefatam terram reddidit. et hoc filio suo fratri meo concedere fecit:· et pro hoc terre tumulationem promeruit. Vt igitur tenebrosi baratri perpetuos euadere possem cruciatus. atque in celesti [fol. 94r] gloria angelicis merear adiungi ciuibus. hanc redditionem publice in conspectu tocius capituli coram multis testibus tam clericis quam laicis per brachium sancti Autberti propri[a] manu mea gratulabundus super sacratissimum altare beati archangeli Michaelis posui. deinde ante altare nudus in terram prostratus. ac uirgarum uerbere nudus disciplinatus. ab priore et monachis indulgentiam et absolutionem huius insipientie mee gratia Dei patrocinante promerui. Insuper autem patrem meum et matrem et fratrem et omnes parentes meos et omnes coadiutores meos absoluere pecii:· quod et ipsi libenter fecerunt. Denique ipsi monachi ob recordationem et memoriam futurorum. in testimonium utique uirorum:· de caritate beati archangeli michi .xv.^{cim} solidos. et Rotberto auunculo meo quinque solidos dederunt. Si quis autem heredum meorum huic donationi immo redditioni contraire uoluerit cum Dathan et Abiron quos terra uiuos absorbuit. et cum Iuda traditore Domine sit perpetue addictus maledictioni nisi citius resipuerit. Verumptamen ut hoc ratum et inconuulsum permaneat. manu mea sacro sancte crucis signo confirmare studui:· adhibitis utrobique testibus quorum ista sunt nomina. Rotbertus de Grent'. Petrus. de Verdun. Radulfus. clericus de Pontabaudo. Ex parte monachorum. Ruellen. canonicus. Guillelmus [Pulcrabarba]. [fol. 94v] Hugo. Testa. Sanuualus. et plures alii.

Printed *Cartulaire de Jersey*, no. 153, from the Cartulary.

89

Restitution and confirmation for Saint-Broladre (Ille-et-Vilaine, cant. Pleine-Fougères) by Baldwin fitz Homenes, who had long withheld the land of Torpol in Saint-Broladre, despite multiple excommunications; aware now that he is dying, he restores the land and becomes a monk, with the consent of his eldest son Warin, and his other sons and daughters: the charter was kept among those relating to Guernsey (MS Avranches 211, fol. 136v), where the monks had property at Saint-Breladre; this charter, however, undoubtedly refers to Saint-Broladre; cf. no. **21**, **App. i.7**: dated by the attestation of Prior Peter, 1131–42.

De Sancto Broeladrio

NOTVM sit omnibus tam futuris quam presentibus quod ego Balduinus filius Homenes cernens et comperiens appropinquare michi finem uite mee. cogitans et recolens quanta sint gaudia eterne glorie fidelibus omnibus repromissa. sed et nimium perhorrescens perpetui incendii tormenta tartarea. impiis et peccatoribus sine fine preparata:· tandem in memet reuersus. et malorum meorum multitudinem sedule prospiciens:· ut gehennalibus caream cruciatibus. et celestibus merear adiungi ciuibus. quamdam terram sancti Michaelis quam iniuste antea tenueram et possederam pro qua eciam multociens excommunicatus fueram:· eidem beato Michaele archangelo et monachis eiusdem loci Deo die et nocte seruientibus. eandem terram inter culturam sancti Michaelis sitam. et Torpol. pro salute anime mee. et patris. et matris mee. et omnium meorum antecessorum liberam et quietam reddo. et concedo. et hoc filiis meis. Guarino primogenito et aliis omnibus tam filiis quam filiabus concedere facio. Propter hoc autem ipsi monachi me monachum faciunt. et in suam congregationem recipiunt. sed et hoc filio meo primogenito concesserunt uel cuilibet fratrum suorum uoluerit uni soli [fol. 95r] tantummodo in beneficio et non per successionem. Si quis autem hoc contraire molitus fuerit. cum Iuda domini traditore perpetue addictus sit maledictioni. nisi resipuerit. Vt autem hoc ratum perpetuo custodiatur. ad monimentum et testimonium signo sancte crucis manu propria muniui. similiter et filii mei. Signum Balduini [+]. Signum Garini. filii sui [+]. Signum Erueillardi filii sui [+]. Signum Ernaudi filii.[a] Signum Richardi clerici. Signum Iuelli. de Maresco. Signum Pagani. Finemont.[b] Signum Radulfi. de Alnai. Signum Ansgerii.[c] filii Dauid. Signum Pines.[d] Signum Rotberti de Sancto Broeladrio. Signum Eueni. Moison. Signum Gelduini. Taum. Ex parte monachorum. Petrus prior. et totus conuentus. et Rainaudus monachus de Sancto Iohanne qui tunc erat prior de obedientia Sancti Broeladri. in cuius tempore hec acta sunt. et Donoaldus. et Rotbertus de Monasterio. Sansuualo. Briendus. Chesnel. Algarus. Tancredus. Bernerius. Pulcra Barba. Turgisus. filius Radulfi de Breeio. Lucas filius Ernulfi de Stampis. et Michael frater eius et multi alii.

Copied from the original in B. N. lat. 10072, no. 21, fol. 27, and Beauchesne, Arch. dépt. de La Manche, 6 J 70, M12: [a] S. Garini. S. Erueillardi filii mei. S. Ernaudi filii mei. [b] Ficemont [c] Ansgoti [d] Lines. [e] de Sancto Iohanne monachus [f] Algarus *om.* The charter was endorsed: *haec est carta quam Warinus filius Balduini reddidit quando Ernaudus frater eius factus est monachus.*

90

Recital of a detailed convention made at Bayeux in the presence of the queen between the abbey and William Paynel concerning the terms on which William Paynel would summon his men to defend the land the king of England gave him with his wife and the acceptance of these terms by the abbey, from whom William holds the land at Longueville-le-Val and La Lande (Manche, comm. Granville); the men are Hugh de Bricqueville-sur-Mer (Manche, cant. Bréhal) and his nephew, Robert de Chanteloup (Manche, cant. Bréhal), William Becket and the man who holds the honour of Scollant (at Yquelon, comm. Granville): 1070–81.

Conuentio inter abbatem et Guillelmum Paginellum

HAEC carta narrat conuentionem Baiocis factam coram regina inter abbatem de Monte Sancti Michaelis. et Guillelmum Paginellum. Si Willelmus Paginellus habet guerram de illa terra quam rex Anglorum dedit sibi cum femina sua. conuentio est quam Hugo de Bricauilla [fol. 95v] quadraginta diebus illi faciet de guarda uel custodia. sese septimum de caballaribus ad suum cibum. Et nepos illius Hugonis similiter faciet:· si in parage terram suam tenuerit. secundum hoc quod tenebit. Rursus si Guillelmus Paginellus illum Hugonem submonuerit. cum duobus equitibus eum in sua familia ad suum cibum habuerit. uel filium suum. si liber erit de submonitione abbatis. Nec si eum donnus abbas semper habebit:· quin Guillelmus Paginellus hoc habeat. Et ita equidem habebit in sua familia nepotem Hugonis et Rotbertum de Cantelupo. et Guillelmum Becheth. et illum qui honorem Scollant habebit. Et si uindictam uel placitum habuerit ad faciendum. homines quos tenet de sancto Michaele ita habebit:· quod insero erunt ad suas domos. Et si homines sibi deficient de his seruiciis quae hic sunt diuisa:· rectum sibi facient. ad unam mansionum quas tenet de sancto Michaele. Auxilium accipiet de terra quam tenet de sancto Michaele pro sui corporis captione. aut pro sua terra si forisfecerit eam erga regem uel abbatem. uel pro filio huius femine de qua est hereditas si captus fuerit in seruitio regis. uel abbatis. de quo est fedus. aut pro una sola filia maritanda. quam habet de hac femina. Conuentio est quoniam Guillelmus Paginellus in terra quam tenet de abbate. sta[fol. 96r]tuet unum hominem apud quem abbas mittet pro submonitionibus quas habet facere ipse abbas in terra quam Guillelmus Paginellus tenet de illo. Qui se bene submonitiones fecerit. et ille remaneat quem monuerit:· abbas suam forisfacturam unde accipiet. Quod si in illo submonitore remanet submonitio. abbati decem et octo solidos emendabit:· et abbas postea per suum legatum submonitionem suam fecerit. Conuentio est quoniam Guillelmus Paginellus uno quoque anno duodecim quercus ad suum cois accipiet in silua de Longa Villa usque ad aquam quę dicitur Ars. nec plus habet accipere nisi per abbatem fecerit. Conuentio est quoniam abbas de Monte uno quoque anno dat illi unum prouendarium de cera uel uiginti solidos. et est in cois abbatis dare. quale horum maluerit. et hoc pro releuationibus de Cantelupo. et pro pastura

de Lalande si homines de Cantelupo possunt illam de Raisneer in curia Guillelmi Paginelli de Lauidande quam Willelmus Paginellus interrogat in fedo. dum uenit in Monte Sancti Michaelis est in respectu donec coram rege. Conuentio est de septem paribus de honore quem Willelmus Paginellus tenet de abbate de Monte Sancti Michaelis: quoniam submonuerit illos in sua curia. Qui si sponte sua ambulare uoluerint: ibunt. si liberi erunt de seruicio abbatis. Si uero ire noluerint: [fol. 96v] hoc debet Guillelmus Paginellus de Raisneer in curia abbatis. per homines qui sunt de honore quem accepit cum sua uxore. qui illos uiderunt in suo seruicio per consuetudinem antecessorum suorum. Huius cause testes existunt. presul Abrincensis Michael. Episcopus Sagiensis Rotbertus. Rogerius de Montegomerii. Richardus proconsul. Rogerius de Bellomonte. Hubertus de Ria. Vnfredus de Bohon. Hubertus de Portu. Turgisus de Tracei. Alueredus Malbedenc. Gaufredus de Sai
[1 line blank].

Calendared and translated: Round, *C.D.F*, p. 255, no. 714, from the Cartulary (implying that the original had not been found in the archives at Saint-Lô in 1899). Discussed in E. Tabuteau, *Transfers of Property* (1988), pp. 56–9.

91

Grant by Prima wife of Alan, with Alan's consent, of the fishery called *Grossim*; she obtains the consent of Hugh de Barra, who had claimed the fifth part of the fishery; listed among the charters of the priory of Saint-Meloir in MS Avranches 211, fol. 125r: in the presence of Abbot Bernard, Prior Hugh and other monks, 1142–8 May 1149.

De piscatoria que uocatur Grossim

IN NOMINE PATRIS. ET FILII. ET SPIRITVS SANCTI AMEN. Notum sit omnibus tam presentibus quam futuris quod ego Prima Dei amore et sancti Michaelis accensa dedi et concessi quandam piscariam quę uocatur Grossim Deo et sancto Michaeli. concessu domini Alani sponsi mei. pro anime mee ipsiusque salute. cunctorumque antecesssorum meorum. Hoc etenim donum in presentia donni abbatis Bernardi et eiusdem loci monachorum. et quam plurimorum aliorum clericorum et laicorum super altare sancti Michaelis posui. et ut predixi finetenus concessi Hugo autem de Barra qui quintam eiusdem piscarie partem calumpniabatur, et inde duellum uadiauerat calumpniam pretermisit. et donum fir[fol. 97r]miter tenendum et inconuulse bono animo et absque contradictione concessit. Ad hanc concessionem interfuit predictus abbas Bernardus et Hugo prior. omnisque conuentus. Interfuerunt eciam alii. Petrus capellanus. Ruallen Rogeri filius. Guillelmus Pulcra barba. Ruallen Caucebof. et Guillelmus filius suus. Iohannes Chesnel. et Philippus filius suus. Richardus Becdefer. Radulfus Becdefer. Guimundus Crasboel. Escollandus filius suus. et multi alii.
[1 line blank]

92

Notification of a grant by Niel de Flamanville (Manche, cant. Les Pieux) on becoming a monk of half a mill at Flamanville, yielding 10 quarters (c. 80 bushels) of wheat per annum, with the assent of his sons Richard and William Lovel, who confirm the grant on a separate occasion: 1131–49.

De Flameuilla

QVONIAM uergente uolubili rota temporum paulatim in obliuionem cuncta labuntur. nisi aut scripto. aut fideli memorie commendata fuerint:· dignum duximus hoc scripto nostre insinuare successioni. quod Niellus de Flameuilla diuino peruentus munere. causa salutis proprie monachicum in hoc monasterio suscipiens habitum. Deo sanctoque Michaeli et sibi famulantibus monachis dimidium molendinum decem quartaria [-ii *a.c.*] frumenti singulis annis reddens. in perpetuum habendum concessit. presentibus quidem duobus quos habebat filiis:· idemque concedentibus:· ad cuius reedificationem et refectionem. precii dimidium inueniemus. Hoc autem mo[fol. 97v]lendinum est Flameuille. Sed et hoc sciendum quia post donationem ipsius Nielli. et filiorum eiusdem concessionem. quorum alter Richardus. alter dicebatur Guillelmus Louel:· maior natu Richardus scilicet iurauerit nunquam per se hoc donum irritum fieri. et si quis demonis instinctu tale quid facere presumpsisset:· in quantum posset huiusmodi uiolentiam conpesceret. Huius donationis et concessionis testes sunt hii. Turgisus de Taneia. Riuallo Calcebou. Haimo Rufus. et Thomas filius eius. Gislebertus de Canpels. Guillelmus de Bree. Hugo Testa. et multi alii. et multi monas. Signum Nielli [+]. Signum Richardi filii eius [+]. Signum Guillelmi filii eius [+]. Signum Gisleberti de Campels [+].
[2 lines blank]

93

Grant of land in Boucey and Sacey (Manche, cant. Pontorson) by Richard fitz Richolin, who, dying of infirmities acquired after his return from Jerusalem, sends the king's chaplain, Geoffrey of Pontorson, and his own priest, Bernard de Boucey, to abbot Bernard to request his admission as a monk of the abbey; the abbot sends the prior and another monk to him and they, with the consent of Richard's wife and others, make him a monk, for which Richard grants 4 acres he holds in inheritance of Michael de Sacey; his nephew Richard Cardon places the gift on the altar of the chapel of St Nicholas at Pontorson, together with a missal; Richard renews the grant in the chapter-house of the abbey, in the presence of Prior Hugh: 1142–8 May 1149.

[De Buceio et de Saceio *sup. man. rec.*]

IN NOMINE PATRIS ET FILII ET SPIRITVS SANCTI AMEN. NOTVM sit omnibus non solum presentibus sed et futuris, quod ego Richardus Richolini filius de Buceio, diuturno atque grauissimo languore confecto ut pote qui nuper ab Ierosolimis redieram. quodam tamen interuallo Deo miserante aliquantulum conualui.

uerum temporis uicissitudine redeunte:· in me denuo cepit infirmitas renouari. et intrinsecus ualde consumpsit. Et quia me ad extrema interius precognoui peruen[fol. 98r]turum. atque uiam carnis uniuerse ingressurum. gemens. flens. et tremens. misi duos uenerabiles presbiteros:· Gaufredum scilicet capellanum regis de Pontorsum. et Bernardum de Buceio sacerdotem meum. ad reuerentissimum abbatem Bernardum ecclesie sancti Michaelis de Monte:· ut amore Dei mei misereretur. rogans toto mentis conamine ac desiderio anime. ut in consortium monachorum suorum. et in habitum sancti Benedicti me susciperet. Et quoniam erat uir discretissimus nichil percunctatus transmisit ad me ecclesie sue priorem cum quodam alio fratre. ut me uisitarent:· et uice sui michi in omnibus subuenirent. Qui uenientes me disertissime et eloquentissime reppererunt colloquentem, cum consensu mee coniugis et omnium amicorum meorum concessu induerunt me monachilem habitum beati Benedicti presenti uita diutissime putantes fruiturum:· et ad ecclesiam sancti Michaelis deferre fecerunt. Pro hac igitur misericordia et hoc honore de proprio meo alodo dedi et do ecclesie beati archangeli Michaelis de Monte quattuor acras terre de meo fedo. quod de Michaele de Saceio et filiis eius hereditario iure tenebam in perpetuo per successionem meorum heredum. Hoc donum concessit Richardus Cardo nepos meus cum omnibus dominis meis atque parentibus. et a propria manu corroborauit:· ac posuit super altare primum sancti Nicholai in capella de Pontorsum cum libro missali: Istis audientibus [fol. 98v] et uidentibus. Guillelmus monachus de Terra-uuasta. Guillelmus monachus de Ardena. Radulfus de Veim. Guillelmus de Saceio. Rainaldus et Rannulfus de Grandeuilla. Guillelmus. de Archis. nepos abbatis. Deinde predictus Richardus in capitulum uenit et beneficium huius ecclesie recepit. et iterum prefatum donum super altare sancti Michaelis denuo posuit. istis astantibus et uidentibus. Hugo prior. Iohannes et Bartholomeus. filii Thome. Gerardus et Radulfus de Monasterio. et alii multi.
[1 line blank]

Copied from original by G. de Beausse, Arch. Calvados, F5276, from 'orig. parch. haut. 0^{m}.275 x larg. 0^{m}.245, non reglé' in Arch. dépt. Manche H., reading *Pons Hursonis* throughout.

94

Notification concerning a sale of meadow at Montemont (Eure-et-Loir, cant. Brou, comm. Yèvres) to the priory of Gohory (Eure-et-Loir, cant. Brou) in the time of Prior Robert de Ardevon by Odo Potarius and his family, with the assent of their lord Ingelger de Merreuil and his family, who receive counter-gifts from the prior of one penny, Ingelger himself receiving five *solidi* and confraternity: given at Odo's house in Melleray (Sarthe, cant. Montmirail): before 1139.

De Gohere

VT nobis non pigrum. sic nec sequentibus debet esse honerosum:· quod ad eorum noticiam nostrique non minus quietum. ea quae agimus:· adhibitis

testibus litteris assignamus. Tempore itaque quo donnus Rotbertus de Ardeuon prior erat Goheredi. emit isdem Rotbertus unum prati arripennum. apud Montamontem a quodam milite Odone uidelicet Potario. xxx. solidos. Concessit autem hoc uxor eius Mathildis. concesserunt et filii eius Garinus. Herbertus clericus. Hubertus Paganus. Hubertus: concesserunt etiam et filie eius. Richildis. Arenburgis: Mathildis uero uxor predicti Odonis habuit inde ob recordationem .vi. denarios. Garinus filius eius vi. den'. Herbertus ii. den'. Hubertus [fol. 99r] ii. den'. Paganus ii. den'. Testes cum ipsis. Constantinus prior de Meleriaco. Petrus clericus. Brito clericus. Paganus Martini. Adhelardus Leberti. cum monachis. Rannulfus monachus. et Turpinus eorum prefectus. Hoc autem totum factum est apud Meleriacum in domo ipsius Odonis Potarii. Concessit item hoc ipsum Ingelgerius de Merreuil: de cuius feudo pratum ipsum erat. Annuit hoc ipsum et uxor eius Ascelina. et filii eius. Galterius. Rainbaldus. Hubertus. Vnusquisque uero ex ipsis habuit inde a supradicto monacho: ob recognitionem unum denarium. Ingelgarius pater eorum quinque solidos. et societatem ecclesie eorumdem monachorum. Testes Rainbaldus monachus. Galterius Morini. Turpinus.
[1 line blank]

95

Grant to the priory of Gohory, in the time of Prior Brien, by Odo de Montigny-le-Ganelon (Eure-et-Loir, cant. Cloyes-sur-le-Loir) of land near *Pirosholdri*, for the soul of himself and his wife Agnes, and their ancestors and successors; Hubert Payn, his wife Eustachia and sons Rainald and Odo, concede their moiety of the land: 1139.

De eodem

DOMINVS ODO de Montinneio donat ecclesie sancti Michaelis et monachis eiusdem monasterii terram quę est iusta Pirosholdri pro anima sua. et pro anima Agnetis uxoris sue. et pro animabus antecessorum suorum et successorum. concedentibus uxore sua et filiis: ab incarnatione domini annus .m.xxx.viiii. Hubertus Paganus concedit supradicte medietatem eiusdem terre quę sua erat in elemosina pro anima sua et pro anima uxoris sue. et antecessorum. et successorum. [fol. 99v] Concedentibus uxore sua Eustachia. et filiis suis Rainaldo et Odone. Ad hęc dona: affuerunt hi. Bernardus sacerdos. Odo. Burnellus. Gacio de Castello-romano. Odo. de Loisuilla. Haimericus de Merlaio. Gaufridus. Tenpledoia. Rainaldus Cochin. Simon de Laboesche. Bochardus. Boguet. Ricanus. Herueus de Monsorel. Freelinus. Osbernus mediatorius. Garnerius. Albertus. Hęc elemosine fuit data in tempore quo Clemens sacerdos. et Briencius prior erat apud Gohereium.
[1 line blank]

Printed: *Cartulaire de l'Abbayette*, no. 12, from B.N. lat. 5430A, p. 154, where it is noted: 'Ce papier ne paroit etre que copié et même defectueuse. Semble etre de Goheri'.

96

Charter of Theobald de Dangeau (Eure-et-Loir, cant. Brou), granting, with the consent of his wife Hildeburg and son Bernard, to the priory of Gohory the tolls in all his land lying in the monks's lordship: *c.* 1131–49.

Item de eodem

Notum sit cunctis presentibus atque futuris quod ego Tebaldus de Daniol concessu uxoris mee Hildeburgis et filii mei Bernardi. concedo Deo et sancto Michaeli eiusque monachis pedagium per totam terram meam de dominio ipsorum:· ut libere et quiete teneant absque calumpnia. Si quis autem huic mee donationi uoluerit contraire:· eidem archangelo cogatur rationem de hoc reddere. in extremo examine. Huius rei testes sunt. Odo de Daniol. Albaldus presbiter. Gaufredus de Cantemerla. Hugo. Guinneleu. Odo. Brisart. Paganus de Nemore. Radulfus. Longis. Walterius. de Loisuilla. Guillelmus de Moncels.

97

Notification of the restitution by Simon de Bailleul, sworn on the relic of St Aubert on St Michael's altar, of the rights of their parishioners in Vieuvy (Mayenne, cant. Gorron); these had been usurped by Simon and his predecessors, for whom absolution is sought from, and granted by, Abbot Bernard and the monks: before 8 May 1149.

[fol. 100r] *Carta de Veteri Villa*

IN NOMINE PATRIS ET FILII ET SPIRITVS SANCTI AMEN. Simon de Ballolio parrochianos de Veteriuilla quos iniuste aliquociens per uim a sancto Victurio subtraxerat. se numquam ulterius id facturum super altare sancti Michaelis per brachium sancti Autberti confirmauit. Et quoniam tam antecessores sui quam ipse deliquerant:· petita absolutione pariter ab abbate Bernardo et a monachis absoluti sunt. + Simonis. de Ballolio huius carte confirmatoris. Signum [+] Guillelmi fratris eius. Signum Haimonis. de Desertinis. Hi sunt testes. Signum Olíueri. de Desertinis. Signum Gaugueeni. filii Andree de Haia. Signum Engelbaldi.

[1 line blank]

Printed: *Cart. Saint-Victeur*, no. XX, with a facsimile of the (now lost) original (PL. 6), of which the cartulary entry is an exact copy.

98

Notification concerning the grant of the fourth part of the church of Huisnes (-sur-Mer, cant. Pontorson, Manche) made by John fitz Garner de Huisnes, with the assent of Bishop Turgis of Avranches, of a moiety of his patrimony, his brother Ilger holding the other moiety; soon afterwards, John became a monk of Mont-Saint-Michel; fifteen years later his brother's sons, one a layman the other a cleric, contested his grant; through the mediation of Bishop Donoal of Alet and Abbot Robert of Saint-Sever, Abbot Bernard eventually concedes the portion of the church and associated land in return for an annual rent of 2 *solidi* in the money of Le Mans: 1131–19 August 1142.

De Ecclesia de Husnis

NOTVM sit omnibus sancte Dei ecclesie filiis quod Iohannes filius Garnerii de Husnis licentia et concessu donni Turgisi Abrincensis episcopi dedit ecclesie beati archangeli Michaelis quartam partem ecclesie de Husnis. quę sibi iure hereditatis contingebat [-bant *a.c.*]. et medietatem terre patrimonii sui quam fratre suo Ilgerio partitus fuerat. His uero omnibus expletis. Deo cor illius uisitante sumpsit habitum monachilem in hac eadem ecclesia sancti Michaelis. Postea autem [fol. 100v] cum iam per spatium quindecim annorum libere et quiete hęc omnia in pace hęc ecclesia tenuisset:· insurrexerunt duo nepotes predicti Iohannis unus clericus et alter laicus:· clamantes ecclesiam et terram. Verum Dei prouidentia qui cuncta prouidet. regit. ac disponit. florebat eo tempore in hac ecclesia Bernardus abbas uir sapientissimus ac disertissimus et nimie eloquentie, qui ita uiriliter illis restitit ac uerba et clamores eorum ad nichilum redigendo protriuit:· quod consilio amicorum suorum die festiuitatis sancti Michaelis pedibus misericordie ipsius prouoluti. pecierunt misericorditer ut illis saltem ad firmam concederet partem ęcclesię atque illam partem terre quam quiete tenebat. Illis autem diu in prece perseuerantibus. tandem consilio multorum procerum et eciam prece episcopi Donoaldi Aletensis. atque Rotberti abbatis Sancti Seueri et plurimorum aliorum qui ad festum conuenerant:· cessit abbas rigori mentis suę quo potissimum utebatur. et concessit illis partem ecclesie cum terra supradicta. ita quod uno quoque anno reddent uiginti .ii. solidos Cenomannensium huic ecclesie. Et quia uolebat abbas ut pactum ratum et firmum fieret:· precepit ut fide sua firmaret unusquisque quod hanc conuentionem inuiolabi[li]ter tenerent:· et predictos nummos incontradicendo soluerent in pace. Et hęc sunt nomina illorum. qui huic pacto interfuerunt. [fol. 101r] Alueredus de Maceio. Rannulfus de Viri. Mainus de Pollei. Rotbertus de Precorbin. Radulfus de Brei. Thomas de Sancto Pancratio. Haimo Rufus. Ilgerius de Vesce. Iohannes. Chesnel.

99

Notification concerning the grant made of rights in the church of Huisnes (Cant. Pontorson, Manche) by Ralph Manducans on becoming a monk, but Ralph son of Danzell claimed a third part, which he had mortgaged to Ralph Manducans; the claim is allowed, once the mortgage is redeemed; similarly, moved by pity for the youth's poverty and at the request of many people, Abbot Bernard reduces the terms on the mortgage of a garden, with the consent of Prior Hugh and the other monks: 1142–49.

Item de eodem

NOTVM sit omnibus tam presentibus quam futuris. quod quando Radulfus Manducans accepit monachalem habitum in ecclesia Sancti Michaelis de Monte. dedit eidem ecclesie totum illud quod in ecclesie de Ysnes possederat.

Sed Radulfus Danzelli filius dicebat quod terciam pars eiusdem sua esse debebat. quam super lx[ta]. et xi solidos Cenomannensium:˙ eidem Radulfo Manducanti esse in uadimonium. multis audientibus cognoscebat. Abbas ei concesserat. quod quando denarios reddidisset. quod iure in illam habere debebat:˙ habuisset. Sciant iterum. quatinus Radulfus Manducans de Bartholomeo. i. ortum de feudo illius iuuenis concessu eius de lx. solidis [-os *a.c.*]. super quos erat in uadimonium disgaiauerat. Sed abbas uidens pauperitatem iuuenis. misericordia motus. rogatuque multorum concessit. quod quando redderet ei uel monachis .xxx. solidos Cenomannensium. suum ortum haberet. Et hoc de toto testes fuerunt. Godefredus cantor. et Rogerius. et Hugo prior. et multi alii de monachis. et de laicis. Hugo filius Odonis. Letus Infans. Rualen clericus. et Willelmus [Pulcra-barba] [fol. 101v] et Ernulfus de Stampis. et multi alii.
[1 line blank]

100

Geoffrey fitz Godeschal relates that, with the assent of Hugh *vicomte* of Châteaudun and his wife Agnes, he granted a small portion of land at Montemont (Eure-et-Loir, cant. Brou, comm. Yèvres) to the monks, who built a mill there; Geoffrey held the moiety for his lifetime; this small holding supported his servant Airard, blind and deaf in extreme old age, who lived with the monks for several years after consenting to the grant; Geoffrey later added the grant of fishing rights and pannage. The heading of this charter identifies it as part of a group of six items (nos. 100-106), beginning with no. 102, which were written into a pancarte at the abbey (see above, pp. 42–3): *c.* 1100.

Carta de Gohere

INCIPIT HIC DOMINI SUB NOMINE CARTVLA SUMMI. Notum sit omnibus qui presentem cartulam legerint. quia ego Gaufredus filius Godescalis. pro salute anime mee quandam possessiunculam quę dicitur Montismons. sancto Michaeli archangelo dedi:˙ cum pratis. et omnibus appendiciis. In eadem quoque pessessiuncula. monachi memorati archangeli unum molendinum edificauerunt. cuius medietatem obtineo dum uiuo:˙ sed post mortem meam ut totum habeant sine retractatione concedo. Predictam ergo uillulam Airardus quidam seruus meus obtinuit qui nimia senectute defectus. uiribus quoque corporis amissis. simul et oculis cecus fuerat effectus:˙ quia quod dedi sancto Michaeli concessit libentius a monachis. eiusdem sancti Michaelis reuerenter est susceptus:˙ uixitque cum eis annis quam pluribus. Hoc autem beneficium quod sepius dicto archangelo contuli. Hugo uicecomes Castri Dunensis cum Agnete uxore sua concessit. assistentibus nobilibus uiris. qui scribuntur insequentibus signis. Adhuc enim concessi ut famulus monachorum pisces caperet in om[fol. 102r]nibus aquis meis. et porci eorum sine precio pascerentur in omnibus siluis meis. Signum Odonis camerarii. +. Signum

Guiterii. +. Signum Tebaldi filii Herbaldi. +. Signum Ansoldi filii Godescali. +. Signum Ailardi. +. Signum Radulfi Oculus Canis. +. Signum Garini filii Garini Guine. +. Signum Gaufredi Lege-docti. +. Signum Hugonis uicecomitis. +. Signum Agnetis uxoris eius. +. Signum Fromundi Cognati. +. Signum Fulcoi Magne-uille. +. Signum Pagani de Bouilce. +. Signum Gaufredi filii Godescalis. + Signum Rainoldi Securii. +. Signum Fulcoi uicecomitis.

The Gohory charters were discussed in Abbé Marquis, 'Gohory, son prieuré de Saint-Michel', *Bull. de la Soc. Dunoise*, t. v (1885–7), 257–76, which I have not been able to consult. The individual items in the Cartulary cannot be specifically identified in the general headings contained in the Inventory, Avranches 211, fol. 126r–v, though there is little doubt that the acts were all represented there. By contrast, there are no later copies of the Cartulary acts for Gohory, though several other and many later charters were copied into B. N. lat. 5430A, pp. 83–94.

101

Grant to Abbot Ranulf and the monks of his colibert Rainer by William II Gouet of Montmirail (Sarthe), conceded by his wife Eustachia and sons Hugh and William, in the presence of the monks Ralph, Ambrose, Drogo and Walter Carpenter at Gohory: *c.* 1083–85.

De eodem

Notum sit omnibus Christi fidelibus tam futuris quam presentibus quod ego Guillelmus Goit. presentis uice labentem cernens honorem. et me impluribus peccasse considerans. sed Dei omnipotentis misericordiam exobtans:· Deo ac beato archangelo Michaeli. quem principatum credimus obtinere celestem. atque Rannulfi abbati omnibusque Sancti Michaelis monachis. et eorum posteris omnibus:· Rainerium meum colibertum concedo ego et Eustachia uxor mea. filii mei Hugo. et Guillelmus. et hoc in presentia donni Radulfi. monachus Sancti Michaelis. atque Ambrosii monachus. et Drogonis. et Gauterii carpentarii. qui morabantur apud Goherium. Hi autem sunt:· huius rei testes. Hugo Godescal qui cultellum quo donum istud Radulfo monacho datum est:· plicuit. Hilgotus Brunellus. Radulfus Brunellus. Hugo clericus Brunellus. [fol. 102v] Gaufredus prepositus. Rainaldus maior. Gaufredus Burel. Rainaldus Paganus. Quicumque igitur demoniaca fraude seducti. hoc donum aliquando aliquomodo sancti Michaeli auferre uoluerint. nisi malam intentionem dimiserint. cum Iuda et Dathan. et Abiran quos uiuos deglutiuit terra. in inferno eternis suppliciis deputentur:· et perpetuo puniantur. Fiat. Fiat. Fiat. amen.

102

Quitclaim for the priory of Gohory by Ralph Oculus Canis, who concedes the grants of his brother Walter; among his concessions are fifteen cottars' holdings which reappear as the subject of a further restitution in no. **103**: 1097.

De eodem

IN NOMINE SANCTE ET INDIVIDVE TRINITATIS PATRIS ET FILII ET SPIRITVS SANCTI anno dominice incarnationis .m°. xc°. vii°. Indictione .v. Ego Radulfus Oculus-canis domini intimante clementia amicus et socius fraternitatis monachorum beati archangeli Michaelis. donum quod frater meus Gauterius Oculus canis apud uillam Goherium Deo et sancto archanglo et eius monachis pro anime sue redemptione concessit . xx[ti]. quidem aripennos terre in dominico ad quadraginta hospites concessi:· insuper quindecim hospites similiter in dominico in hoc quod tenent. quos prius calumpniaueram. et quicquid proficui in predicta terra et in cimiterio facere uoluerint monachi. concedo ut faciant libere et absolute. Concedo eis etiam unam carrucatam terre quam et frater meus concessit. similiter in dominico. et medietatem tocius alcius terre quę ad predictam uillam id est Goherium attinet similiter in dominico. Hęc omnia pro anima mea et pro omnibus pa[fol. 103r]rentibus meis omni penitus eliminata calumpnia concedo. et ut hoc in perpetuum ratum permaneat:· ecce hoc signo sancte crucis +. manu mea inpresso:· corroboro. testibus his adhibitis. Guillelmus de Melesuilla. +. Martino de Melesuilla. et Garnerio eiusdem uille preposito.

103

Notification by Mangis, prior of Gohory, of a plea held before Hugh, *vicomte* de Châteaudun, concerning misappropriation of priory property by Ralph Oculus Canis; seven cottars' holdings usurped by Ralph are restored, and seven more are to be quitclaimed: 1099.

De eodem

ANNO ab incarnatione domini .M. nonagesimo nono ego Mangisus Sancti Michaelis monachus. tenens obedientiam Goheri. placitaui in Castro Dunensi coram Hugone capel. atque sua uxore Comitissa nomine. contra Radulfum Oculum canis. In quo placito. rato iudicio:· adquisiui ab eo .vii. hospites et dimidium. quos sancto Michaeli abstulerat. et .vii. alios et dimidium promisit quietos facere. Huius rei:· isti fuerunt testes ex parte sancti Michaelis. Hugo uicecomes de Castri Dunensi [dunensi de castro *a.c.*] et femina eius Comitissa nomine. Hugo Godescal. et Godescal frater suus. Ansolt. filius Godescal. Gaufredus de Partei. Albertus infans. Rainaldus decanus sancte Marie.

Ex parte Radulfi. Odo Borrel. Gaufredus Lege-doctus. Girardus de Montfolet. Rotbertus Lege-doctus. Guit'. Hugo Niger. Fulcoin de Menbrelora.

104

Grant of tolls by Eustachia, wife of William II Goet of Montmirail, and Nivelon [de Fréteval]: probably *c.* 1080–85.

Item de eodem

EGO Eustachia uxor Guillelmi Goit annuo Deo sanctoque Michaeli eiusque monachis pedagium de dominio eorum per totam terram meam. teste

Rotberto monacho. Adam Burnello. Similiter Niuelon concessit pedagium dominio nostro per totam terram suam. huius concessi[fol. 103v]onis sunt hii testes. Hugo Godescal. Albertus presbiter.

105

Quitclaim for the priory of Gohory by Ralph Oculus Canis with the consent of his son Warner: *c.* 1100.

De eodem

Notum sit cunctis presentibus siue uenturis quod ego Radulfus Oculus-canis ingrediens faciem uniuerse carnis coniugis meę concessu filiique mei Garnerii reddidi Deo sanctoque Michaeli eiusque monachis uicariam de Goheri quam super eos calumpniabar. Cuius rei fuerunt hii testes Genimia nepos eiusdem Radulfi. Albaldus presbiter. Rotbertus monachus.

106

Quitclaim for the priory of Gohory by Odo Godeschal, at the request of his brothers Hugh and Godeschal and of his wife Agnes and the monk Robert: *c.* 1100.

Item de eodem

EGO ODO Godescal rogatu et requisitione fratrum meorum Hugonis uidelicet. et Godescal. coniugisque meę Agnetis. et donni Rotberti monachi concedo Deo sanctoque Michaeli uicariam de itineribus terre illorum quam super eos calumpniabar. Cui concessioni interfuit Gradulfus dapifer Odonis. Turpinus prepositus monachorum.
[1 line blank]

107

Quitclaim and confirmation of his father-in-law Gausbert Gastevin's grants at Créans (Sarthe, comm. Clermont-Créans) by Hugh Chalibot and his wife Ermensendis, who had felt that the original grant had not been legally made; accord having been reached, the monk Hubert, procurator at Créans, makes a counter-gift to them of ten pounds of the pennies of Angers; in the presence of the Countess [Eremburg, countess of Maine and, by marriage, of Anjou, d. 1126]: 14 April 1109 – 15 January 1126.

De Criant

IN NOMINE PATRIS ET FILII ET SPIRITVS SANCTI AMEN. Ego Hugo Chalibot uolo ut notum fiat et autentico scripto firmetur tam presentibus quam futuris. quod accidit michi possidere quandam terram iure hereditario uxoris mee in Andegauensi pago in loco qui dicitur Criant. in quo loco est ecclesia sancti Petri cum appen[fol. 104r]diciis suis. quam pater uxoris mee nomine Gausbertus Gasteuin dedit sancto Michaeli et monachis eius:ʼ cum una carrucata terre. Sed quia ipsa donatio ut michi uidebatur non fuit facta legitime:ʼ calumpniauimus eam tam ego quam uxor mea nomine Ermensendis.

Vnde ipsi monachi concordiam nobiscum fecerunt: dante donno Huberto monacho eiusdem loci procuratore nobis decem libris denariorum Andegauensium. Concessimus igitur et concedimus ipsam donationem sicut fecit eam Gausbertus antecessor noster. et sicut scriptum habetur in cartis eorum. Concedimus etiam eis habere totum quod uenit uel offertur ad altare prefate ecclesie: et constituere presbiterium in eadem ecclesia secundum eorum dispositionem. Et ut hec donatio firmiter omni tempore teneatur. coram Comitissa concedente et hoc confirmante hęc omnia concessimus: et manu propria confirmauimus. Si quis igitur huic donationi siue nostre confirmationi aliquam calumpniam ingesserit: sit maledictus cum Iuda traditore Domini. et non sit particeps in regno Dei. Huius rei sunt testes. Rogerius presbiter. Gaufredus de Raimefort. Fromundus Chalibot. Gaufredus de Cleers dapifer comitis. Erchenbaudus Vlrici filius. Gaufredus des Bans. Gaufredus Dori. Gauzo Dori. Gaufredus priuignus eius. Harduinus [fol. 104v] Aloin. Gaufredus de Tessei gener eius. Hugo de Clermont. Rotbertus Puilleta. Drogo Goscelin. Guillelmus. le metteer de Criant. Alfredus carpentarius. Bernerius famulus monachorum. Bernardus filius Hildiardis.
[1 line blank]

Printed: Guilloreau, *Chartes de Créans*, no. III. and IV, pp. 9–11.
Copies in B.N. lat. 5430A, pp. 101–2.

108

Notification by Henry I of England that he has given the abbey 12 librates of land in Budleigh, Devon, in exchange for the churches of Wargrave and Cholsey, Berkshire, which he has given in free alms to Reading Abbey: at Perriers-sur-Andelle, after Henry left England on 11 June 1123 and before Abbot Roger's resignation on 16 October 1123.

De Budelel

HENRICVS REX Anglorum. archiepiscopis. comitibus. baronibus. et omnibus fidelibus suis tocius Anglie: salutem. Sciatis me dedisse et concessisse ęcclesię Sancti Michaelis de Periculo Maris. et monachis ibidem Deo seruientibus duodecim libratas terre in Deneuesira [*sic*] in manerio meo de Budelega in escambio duarum ęcclesiarum suarum de Walegraua. et de Calsia quas dedi et concessi ęcclesie de Radinguis in elemosina. Et uolo et firmiter precipio. ut teneant ita bene et in pace. et honorifice. et quiete. sicut umquam melius et honorificentius et quietius tenuerunt ecclesias predictas. Test' Iohanne episcopo Luxcu'. et Gaufredo [-ti *a.c.*] cancellario. et Comite [-mes *a.c.*] Willelmo de Warenna. et Guillelmo de Tancaruilla. et Gaufredo de Glintone. et Guillelmo de Ponte-archarum. et Thome de Sancto Iohanne. Apud Pirarios super Andelam.

Calendared: *RRAN* ii, no. 1418, and Round, *CDF*, from the Cartulary. A different version of the same act was preserved in a Reading cartulary, printed in *RRAN* ii, no. clxxiii, pp. 350–1. See **Appendix i.4** below.

109

Notification of a quitclaim by which Philip de Carteret restores to Abbot Bernard and the monks the tithe of the church of Saint-Ouen in Jersey, and gives an acre of land for a grange: 1135–May 1149.

De ecclesia sancti Audoeni in Gersoio.

[fol. 105r] NOTVM sit omnibus tam futuris quam presentibus quod Philippus de Cartrait reddit Deo sanctoque Michaeli. et Bernardo abbati. et conuentui sancte ecclesie decimam sancti Audoeni in Gersoi: liberam et quietam ab omni calumpnia. et in auena. et in stramine. et in omnibus querelis: donauit itaque sancto archangelo unam acram terre ad libitum monachorum ad suam grangiam faciendam atque decimam cum gerendam. Testes sunt huius donationis qui aderant. domina Lucia. Iordanus. Rotbertus. Henricus. milites de Barneuilla. Guillemus de Tracei. Radulfus de Fulquereuilla. monachus. et Iohannes de Molinellis monachus. Odo capellanus de Braei. Rannulfus presbiter de Carterei. Stephanus prepositus. Rotbertus de Tosel. Turlant de Gersoi. et Aaliz filia Philippi.
[1 line blank]

Cartulaire de Jersey, no. 34, 'collationné à une copie ancienne sur papier existant aux Archives de La Manche.', is the charter version, which begins: 'Ego Philippus de Carteret reddo'. It ends: '...decimam congerendam. Testes sunt huius redditionis et donationis domina Lucia, Aaliz filia mea, Jordan', Robert' et Henricus de Barneville, Guillelmus de Tracei, Radulfus de Fulquerevilla et Johannes de Molinellis monachi. Odo capellanus de Braei ... de Gersoi.'.

Calendared, Round, *CDF*, no. 726, from the Cartulary.

110

Grant of the isle of Guetehou by Restald, former shipmaster of Robert I of Normandy, on fulfilling a longstanding desire to become a monk: see above, no. 33.

De Ketheho

EGO Restaldus nauclerus quondam Rotberti Normannię comitis. diuina inspiratione permotus: monachilem habitum diu ualdeque desideratum tandem suscepi. Quod factum iam dictus princeps piissimus Rotbertus gratanter accipiens. quandam paruam insulam quę uulgo Keteou uocatur perpetuo michi possidendam contradidit. Hanc autem insulam cum omnibus quę adquisita [fol. 105v] sunt a me in ea aut possidentur: post mortem meam do sancto Michaeli et fratribus sibi seruientibus iure hereditario possidenda. ea uidelicet conditione ut factus particeps omnium elemosinarum ac beneficiorum quę ipsi faciunt. ascribi et annumerari sim dignus eorum frater atque socius in perhenni seculo.
[1 line blank]

Printed: *Cartulaire de Jersey*, no. 148, from the Cartulary.

111

Grant, for the salvation of his parents, his son Josselin and his brother Walter, of the revenues of a salt-pan (*patella*) in the castelry of Dinan (Côtes-d'Amor) by Robert the steward, son of Ascelin in return for the right to become a monk of the house should he choose, or, if he should die first, to be given the funeral rites of a monk of the house; his wife Orueal attests the grant, made on St Michael's altar two days before the feast of St Michael (i.e. 27 September): 1135–49.

NOTVM sit omnibus presentibus et futuris. quod ego Rotbertus pincerna filius Ascelini do et concedo Deo sanctoque Michaeli archangelo monachisque ipsius loci in Monte uidelicet Tumba pro salute patris mei. et matris mee. filiique mei Goscelini fratrisque mei Gauterii. et pro remedio anime mee. omnem meam consuetudinem quam iure hereditario tenebam in Dinam castello. uidelicet Patellam. et omnia quę propriis usibus monachorum empta fuerint. ut a modo quiete habeant et possideant. tali pacto atque conditione ut si monachilem habitum suscipere uoluero: cum honore et gaudio me suscipient. Si uero me quod absit mori contigerit absque monachorum ordine. ubicumque finis michi euenerit corpus meum ad Montem Sancti Michaelis afferent ipsius loci monachi. et de me facient seruicium: sicut pro uno quolibet illorum. Hoc donum posuit super altare perendie ante Sancti Michaelis [fol. 106r] festum. Hanc cartam scripsit Gislebertus iuuenis. Isti sunt testes. Rogerius monachus. Petrus monachus. et Rotbertus et uxor sua Oruueal [+]. et Guillelmus [Malpennei]. Ex parte abbatis Henricus de Sancto Petro. Thomas de Lesels. Gaufredus de Bacilleio. et Demorant.

B.N. fr. 22325, p. 722, copied 'a copy of the twelfth century', perhaps the same original or quasi-original copied by Beauchesne (Arch. dépt. de la Manche, 6 J 70, M22), which had the same suprascript material as in the Cartulary. In another copy, B.N. lat. 10072, no. 76, Lechaudé d'Anisy noted that: 'la paleographie de cet acte est d'un beau caractère', and that the same hand copied the charter of Rainald fitz Hugh, no. **81** above. Calendared in Round, *CDF*, no. 732.

112

Convention with the bishop of Bayeux concerning four churches in the Bessin at Bretteville, Domjean, Evrecy and Esquay, for which the monks render one pound each of wax, incense and pepper at Christmas and Easter: after the grant of Notre-Dame d'Esquay in 1086 (see no. **67**).

De ecclesiis que site sunt in Baiocasino pago

NOTVM SIT tam presenti generationi quam future posteritati. quod nos scilicet monachi Sancti Michaelis archangeli conuentionem quandam cum episcopo Baiocasino fecimus. uidelicet ut singulis annis demus ei unam tabulam cerę. unam quoque libram incensi. aliamque piperis in natiuitate Domini. Similique modo in sancto Pascha alteram cerę tabulam. alteramque incensi libram ac piperis. Hoc ergo pro quattuor ecclesiis quę sue diocesi subiacent. id est

Briteuille. Donni Iohannis. Eurecei. atque Eschail ecclesia soluimus:˙ eas ex integro possidentes. et quicquid iuris episcopi in ipsis ecclesiis presbiteris. et laicis erat:˙ deinceps absque calumpnii causatione possidentes.
[1 line blank]

113

Notification of the grant of all the tithes and half of his land at Montdaigne, made on the altar of St Michael with the relic of St Aubert, by Ralph de Pincey (Manches, hamlet in comm. Argouges) and his son John, on the day that Ralph became a monk: 1131–49.

De decima de Pinceio

SCIANT tam presentes quam futuri quatinus eo die quo habitum monachi suscepit Radulfus de Pinceio [fol. 106v] inspirante Deo a quo bona cuncta procedunt ipse et filius eius Iohannes per brachium sancti Autberti super altare sancti Michaelis donum suum ponentes dederunt Deo et monachis Sancti Michaelis de Monte totam decimam suam. et dimidiam terram suam de Mondaineio. Signum Radulfum de Pinceio. Signum Iohannis. filii eius. +.
[1 line blank]

Cited in B.N. lat. 5430A, p. 242, as from a twelfth-century parchment amongst 'titres meslez trouvez a l'Oiseliere'.

114

Notification of the restitution and grant, made on the relic of St Aubert on the altar of St. Michael, by Helias Boterat and his two eldest sons of land, mills and tithes in the parish of Saint-Broladre, and whatever hereditary rights he has in the church, as previously granted by his father and ancestors; in addition Helias granted an acre of meadow for the soul of his father: *c.* 1135–49.

De sancto Broeladrio

HAEC sunt dona patris sui et antecessorum suorum quę Helyas Boterat confirmauit. quando quedam eorum que diu detinuerat super altare sancti Michaelis per brachium sancti Autberti ipse et duo filii maiores natu Deo et monachis sancti Michaelis reddidit. terram de Longis Sulcis. et de Curtis Sulcis. et decimam molendinii sui. et uinee quę prius uirgultum fuerat. et terram de Torpol:˙ et duodecim acras terre quę iunguntur culture sancti Michaelis ad sanctum Broeladrium. et tres maisuras in eadem uilla. et quecumque iure hereditario in ecclesia eiusdem uille sibi contingebant. Hęc reddidit:˙ et pro anima patris sui unam acram prati dedit.

115

Record of losses sustained by the abbey: i) usurpations by King William (I of England, 1066–87) in the Channel Islands, of the isles of Sark and Aurigny and Erm, as well as the tithe and episcopal laws of a moiety of Guernsey, all grants of his father Robert I (no. **5**); in the Avranchin (the vill of Céaux, a market at La Croix-Avranchin, the bourg of Beuvron and fair at Saint-James), the Bessin (the church of Sainte-Marie de La Poterie), and the land of Bernard, father of Abbot Hildebert at Rouilly; ii) the usurpations of the brothers Thomas and Roger de Saint-Jean in the forest of Bevais, Genêts and the honour of Saint-Pair, *ante* 1120; iii) after William's death in 1087, the usurpations of Hilgerius in the honour of Genêts in the time of Abbots Ranulf (c. 1058–86) and Roger (1086–1106).

De perditis huius ecclesiae

MEDIETATEM insule Guerneroi dedit sancto Michaeli co[fol. 107r]mes Rotbertus et omnem decimam ecclesiarum eiusdem insule. et omnes eciam ecclesias. et totum melagium. et omnes leges episcopales. et insulam quę dicitur Serc. et Alrene. et Erm. Ex his rebus abstulit nobis Willelmus rex Serc. et Alrene. et Erm. Et de medietate prefate insule abstulit nobis decimam et melagium. et omnes leges episcopales. Abstulit eciam nobis uillam quę uocatur Cels. quam dedit sancto Michaeli Nigellus senex quando monachus effectus est. et medietatem aquę. Pro cuius rei concessu dedit prefato Guillelmo centum. et L^{ta}. libras quas accepit Radulfus camerarius. Abstulit etiam nobis forum de Cruce. et feriam et theloneum. Abstulit eciam nobis burgum de Beuron. et feriam quę nunc est apud Sanctum Iacobum. et omnem moltam de Abrincatensi pago. Et in Holmo abstulit nobis unam domum. Et in Baiocis Sanctam Mariam de Poteria. et terram quattuor boum. Et in tempore eius perdidimus in ualle de Rodhuil terram Bernardi patris Heldeberti abbatis. et unum molendinum. et unam piscatoriam. et prata. et linguam Ballenę. et dextram alam.

Item

AD nemus Biuie occupauit Thomas de proprio ecclesie mansionem Guillelmi Nigri. et aliam mansionem quę fuit Dublelli fo[fol. 108r]restarii. et totum nemus consumpsit ad edificationem castri sui. et burgensium suorum. ~~Preterea detinet uiginti solidos quos pater suus Radulfus reddebat per singulos annos pro medietate sancti Iohannis quę sine prebenda Lanberti aurifabri.~~

~~In Poterello occupauit mansionem Wathonis quę seruiebat cum equo. et ferebat malas fratrum.~~

~~In Drageio abstulit filio Nigelli presbiteri uineam suam et nostre ecclesie terragium uinee. et de uineis~~ trium rusticorum aufert ecclesie terragium. scilicet de uinea Durandi et fratrum suorum. et similiter de uinea Goii.

In Genitio assumpsit ~~terram Morini pistoris~~. et mansionem Thetboldi. et mansionem Warenberti. Preter hęc omnia habet aduocationes suas ab hominibus ecclesie quas enumerare longum est de frumento. et de uino. de aduena. de sale. de pepere. cepe etiam non desunt.

In honore Sancti Paterni occupauit Thomas istas terras. Terram Willelmi de Grandeuilla. terram Adelelmi. terram Rotberti filii Iuonis. terram Delfai. terram Willelmi de Alneio. terram Scollandi de Ichilum. terram Mauroardi similiter de Ichilum. terram Rotberti Ad-pede. terram Hugonis de Lacherneilla. maximam partem terre Thomas. de Leysels. molendinum cementariorum. terram Delteil.

Quadraginta quattuor quartarios frumenti et plus accipit Thomas ab hominibus Sancti Michaelis in illa honore per aduocationem et per uim.

Similiter Rogerius de Sancto [fol. 108r] Iohanne occupauit istas terras. terram Willelmi Maisnet. terram Rotberti Cornart. terram Rainaldi coqui. et aduocationes et rectitudines similiter tenet iniuste.

[G *-om.*]uillelmus Patric occupauit maximam terram in abbatiam in parroechie sancti Vrsini. et unum molendinum fecit per uim.

[2 lines blank]

HAEC perdidit Sanctus Michael in Genitio post mortem Willelmi gloriossimi regis. Hugo camerarius tenet de Radulfo Bloieth masuram Guillelmi Ad-pelles. de qua Sanctus Michael solebat habere quinque solidos. Adhuc tenet Hugo masuram Rainerii Oculum uerderii. et masuram Gauterii molendinarii. et masuram Riculfi filii Frię. de istis retinet Hugo camerarius consuetudinem. In uinea Thome sunt sex masure quę solebant esse consuetudinarie. Adhuc tenet terram Alcherii. de qua Sanctus Michael perdidit modo consuetudinem. Fecit etiam unam domum in terra Riculfi Calui. Rotbertus filius Morini habet masuram Garnerii. et duas masuras Radulfi filii Huldebout. et masuram Riculfi iuuenis. et domum Gaufredi Pihan sicarii Sancti Michaelis et consuetudinem domus Gosberti. De istis masuris tollit Rotbertus Sancto Michaeli consuetudinem. et de tribus hospitibus quos habet in terra Miarnout. de quibus debemus habere consuetudinem. Adhuc [fol. 108v] tollit Sancto Michaeli terram de Bella-uilla. et terram Rotberti Belim. et terram Leterii. et terram Estur. De burgensi Radulfi filii Rohes: non habet Sanctus Michael consuetudinem. Willelmus Calcebou tenet in Genicio masuram Riculfi. et masuram Rotberti filii Harduini. et masuram Brocart. et in Tesseio: masuram Willelmi Picoth. terra Vasselot debet esse in dominico Sancti Michaelis. Viam furni superioris ostupauit Gislebertus. et tollit Sancto Michaeli masuram Garini Liborelli: Gislebertus Abrincarum tollit Sancto Michaeli domum Herberti filii Duuię. et unum cameram quę solebat reddere .ii. solidos et unam partem terre iuxta monasterium quę solebat reddere duodecim denarios. Hodierna tenet iniuste de Alano de Sancto Petro domum Morini fratris Fulcuini. et domum Radulfi Panion. domus Hugonis Calui quam Vlgerius tenet de preside: debet esse in dominico Sancti Michaelis: domus Willelmus Sescorce quam tenet de Thescelino: debet esse Sancti Michaelis: domus Rotberti inter eas quam tenet de preside: debet esse Sancti Michaelis: Preses tenet iuxta domum Osmundi Raherii duas masuras. de quibus Sanctus Michael perdit consuetudinem: domus Mali-infantis est Sancti Michaelis: Drogo lauendarius reliquit Sancto Michaeli terram et domos suas quas habuit pro pannis lauandis quando fuit monachus. et modo non habemus: domus filii Stephani debet esse Sancti

Michaelis. domus Ligerii debet esse consuetudinaria. Domus [fol. 109r] Anfredi Harde-crusta est consuetudinaria: terram Rogerii Rufi. et vii^{tem}. burgenses in Genicio: tollit Othoe Sancti Michaele: domus Radulfi Artur quam tenet de Willelmo Peurel: debet esse consuetudinaria: terra Huldin quam Gaufridus tenet: debet esse Sancti Michaelis. terram Gauterii filii Richardi: tollit Gaufredus Sancto Michaeli. et terram Clementis: Femina Rogerii tollit Sancto Michaeli terram Rainaldi Pichenot: Hugo filius Adelardi habet terram Radulfi filii Riculfi. quę est consuetudinaria. et terram Garini filii Hultru qui fuit rusticus Sancti Michaelis: Rainaldus de Aurea Valle tenet iniuste domum Rogerii Garzel: Gauterius filius Osmundi tollit Sancto Michaeli domum Eurardi quę est consuetudinaria: duę masure Garini debent esse consuetudinarie: terra Guillemi molendinarii quam Rotbertus presbiter tollit: est consuetudinaria: domus ubi Gauterius filius Osmundi stat: est consuetudinaria: Preses habet terram Mainardi Circel de dominico Sancti Michaelis: Femina Ernaudi filii Harduini tenet iniuste unam domum francam: de iardino Thome non habet Sanctus Michael seruicium: Elemosinarius clamat domum Heruelini. et domum Gisleberti filii Guntart: quę sunt consuetudinariæ: Ligerius tenet duas domos de quibus tollit consuetudinem. scilicet domum Osberni marescali. et domum uaiferaui sui.

De terra Osberni marescali tenet Thescelinus .vi. acras. et femina Rotberti de Moncels .iii. de quibus Sanctus [fol. 109v] Michael perdit consuetudinem: acram terre quam Herueus tenebat de Sancto Michaele dedit femina prepositi cuidam suo homini: Ligerius tollit Sancto Michaeli unam acram terre et dimidiam: Gauterius filius Osmundi .iiii^{or}.x Willelmus .xx. acras de terra Drogonis lauendarii. et de dominico: tres acras: Hugo filius Adelardi: tenet duodecim acras. Galterius gener Huberti tenet unam acram quam Tison dedit ei de dominico Sancti Michaelis: quia fuit ad nuptias suas. Willelmus Morini unam acram: totus Mons Corin est dominicus Sancti Michaelis. excepta uinea Rotberti. et terra Petri. et terra Rogerii Rufi. et terra Riuallonis: Terra de Merdilleio a iardino Hugonis usque ad terram Gauterii filii Hilberti: est tota Sancti Michaelis. Willemus Calcebou tenet .vi. acras de terra Riculfi filii Duin. quattuor ad molendinum Eurardi. et duas in clauso Duin: Tota terra inter duas aquas est de dominico Sancti Michaelis excepto prato Roberti. Willelmus Morini tenet .i. acram super inclusam de prato et terra. Ansgot habet unam acram de dominico Sancti Michaelis. Vlgerius tenet unam acram super bedium uiuarii. Ermenaudis. et femina Guillelmi et filius Alberici tollunt nobis vi. acras. Othoe tollit nobis uiginti acras de terra Rogerii Rufi. et vii. domus: Et Gaufredus filius Iuelini uiginti .ii. acras de terra Gauterii filii Richardi. et de terra Huldini: Riculfus filius Ermenfridi. et Radulfus filius Richardi. [fol. 110r] et Rainaldus filius Huberti tenent de preside .xxx.iii. acras de terra Hugonis Calui. quę debet esse dominica Sancti Michaelis sicut decima Drageii. quia terra et decima fuit data Lanberto aurifabro cum Hugone Caluo. Medietatem Romilleii habet Rotbertus Morini. quę erat dominica Sancti

Michaelis: Totus Romilleius debet esse sancti Michaelis exceptis duabus acris quas Robertus ibi habet. et terra Petri. et terra Radulfi de Moncel. et campo Sancte Mariae. Hugo filius Adelardi tenet decem acras. de terra Garini filii Heltru. qui fuit rusticus sancti Michaelis. Rotbertus Morini cepit ad Goolt de terra rusticorum Sancti Michaelis et fecit unum pratum. Quinque domos. et iiii[or]. salinas tollit Valquelinus Sancto Michaeli ad Poterelle: de terr[e *a.c.*]a Gognol cuiusdam rustici Sancti Michaelis: tres uirgas de terra Gois: dimidiam acram de terra Durant. dimidiam acram. Adhuc tollit Sancto Michaeli. terram Calui. quam Gauterius tenebat de terra Gois Sotel .ii. acras in landa de terra Hugonis. unam uirgam de terra Huberti Lamort .i. uirgam: de terra filiorum Drogonis sacerdotis: i. acra: et terram Gosberti et Drogonis sui fratris qui fuit monachus Sancti Michaelis. Omnes isti fuerunt rustici sancti Michaelis. Radulfus de Sancto Iohanne tollit Sancto Michaeli .iiii[or]. salinas. et terram Serlonis: Terram Hugonis Calide Auris dedit Drogo Niello sacerdoti francam quę erat consuetudinaria.

[2 lines blank]

[fol. 110v] HAEC sunt quę subtraxit Hilgerius de dominio Sancti Michaelis tempore domni Rannulfi abbatis. atque Rogerii abbatis. Terram scilicet Asselini prepositi. Domum Normanni Torte-rote. ista est consuetudinaria. Ortum Fulcuini. similiter ista. Ortum Stephani. similiter ista. Terram Gilduini unde perdimus seruicium. Terram Iohannis Heri: ista est consuetudinaria. Terram Benedicti. et ista similiter. Terram Hilberti. similiter ista. Terram Seburgis. similter ista. Terram Letheline. similiter ista. Terram Radulfi. similiter ista. Terram Ingelbaldi. similiter ista. Terram Garini Hernal de ista perdimus seruicium. Terram Hardradi. consuetudinaria. Terram Restaldi. ista seruit. Terram Hilberti Bonum[a]. consuetudinaria. Pratum Guidonis. consuetudinaria. Terram Hoellis de Husnis. de ista perdimus seruitium. Terram Rogerii carpentarii. de ista[i *a.c.*] similiter. Terram Iohannis de ista similiter. Terram Rainaldi Dan et de ista. Domum Fulcuini Loritel. censoria est. Terram Herulfi ista seruit. Terram Anfredi Hunnart. consuetudinaria. Terram Escorne Bolenc [consuetudinaria]: Molendinum unum fecit in dominico Sancti Incure. Terram Baldri. seruit. Terram Hugonis Fessart. seruit. Terram Odelini ista seruit. Domum Sesuualdi. similter. Est aliud malum quod facit in Ardeuone quod nemo hominum est ausus habere nec panem. nec uinum. nec carnem. propter suam credituram [fol. 111r] quia per uiolentiam autfert illis omnia. Ista omnia Hilgerius suo ingenio rapuit de dominio Sancti Michaelis. Quę omnia Radulfus filius eius post eum possidere uult atque habere perpetuo.

[a] perhaps *boniun*

The paragraph relating to Jersey was printed in *Cartulaire de Jersey*, no. 152, pp. 230–1, from the Cartulary.

116

Notification of a quitclaim by Peter de Saint-Hilaire-du-Harscouet concerning abbey property in La Croix-Avranchin (Manche, cant. Saint-James), which he had seized violently and long held unjustly despite several sentences of excommunication; sworn on the altar of St Michael on the relic of St Aubert, the oath was kept whilst Henry I was alive, but broken when he died; the first quitclaim having been made involuntarily, Peter subsequently has a change of heart and willingly reconfirms the quitclaim: 1135–40.

Secunda carta de Cruce

QVONIAM temporum uolubilitate multa obliuioni traduntur nisi aut scripto aut fideli memorie commendata fuerint:· dignum duximus ut quę nostris facta sunt temporibus successioni nostre presens pagina insinuet. Petrus igitur de Sancto Hylario qui diu uillam quę Crux dicitur calumpniauerat. aliquociens uero sasiuerat. depredauerat:· hinc a monachis Sancti Michaelis quibus hanc uiolentiam intulerat frequenter excommunicatus. sed tandem diuina ut estimo inspiratione compunctus. cum suis baronibus ex hac calumpnia immo tirannide satis facturus montem sancti Michaelis aduenit. Iurauit etenim super altare sancti Michaelis et super brachium sancti Autberti se hanc calumpniam omnino dimisurum. neque ulterius se uel aliquem heredum suorum in ea seu membris eius uille aliquid clamaturum. Hoc iurisurandum idemtidem fecerat rege adhuc Henrico uiuente. quod post mortem eius uiolauit:· quia se magis coactum quam spontaneum id fecisse protestabatur. et ideo quod prius [fol. 111v] inuitus:· postea fecit uoluntarius. Iurauit cum eo:· Turgisus de Taneia. Carpentarius suus miles. Pro hac dimissione et confirmatione. dederunt ei monachi Petro scilicet decem libras Cenomannensium. Hii fuerunt testes ex parte monachorum. Rualen Calcebos. Hugo Testa. Rotbertus de Monasterio. Tancredus. Ernulfus de Stampis. Lucas filius eius. Letus Infans. Rotbertus Macerot. Guillelmus Pulcra barba. Bernerius frater eius. Nicholas filius Omenes. Rotbertus. rusticus. et multi alii.
[2 lines blank]

117

Salomon fitz Grento grants a tithe held from St Michael; he also leaves the revenues of his land to the abbey after his death, on condition that the monks receive him and his wife into their prayers and accept his son William as a monk; apparently unfinished act, lacking any validation clauses: date unknown, possibly the time of Abbot Ranulf or shortly afterwards (cf. **App. ii.4**), *c.* 1080–1100.

NOTVM sit omnibus quod ego Salomon Grentonis filius do decimam quam teneo de Sancto Michaele ab Anthernut Deo ac sancto Michaeli cum omnibus suis redditibus qui ad ecclesiam pertinent:· et post obitum meum omnem ipsam terram cum omnibus suis consuetudinibus quam de sancto Michaele et abbate similiter teneo. Deo et eidem beato archangelo derelinquo:· a monachis

suis possidendam iure hereditario. tali interposita conditione: ut me in orationibus suis recipiant cum uxore mea. et filium meum Guillelmum ad monasticum habitum suscipiant.
[2 lines blank]

118

Restitution by Eudo fitz Geoffrey and his mother Hebrea of land in Marais-de-Dol (Ille-et-Vilaine) granted by his father Geoffrey when he became a monk: Eudo attested no. 20 above, *c.* 1107–30 and probably *c.* 1109.

[fol. 112r] NOVERIT cunctorum noticia fidelium. quod ego Eudo filius Gaufredi una cum matre mea Ebrea reddo Deo et sancto Michaeli suisque monachis terram medietarie de Maresco. quam bone recordationis pater meus Gaufredus sancto Michaeli dedit: dum ipsis cenobii monachis monachus factus se sociauit. Hanc autem non aliter. sed ita reddo sancto Michaeli. sicut predictus pater meus eam habebat ipsa die qua factus monachus cum ea se ipsum Deo ac sancto Michaeli tradidit. Signum ipsius Eudonis. Signum Eudonis auunculus eius. Signum Hebree matris eius. Signum Mangisi. Signum Rotberti filii Morquethen. Signum Mainardi monetarii. Signum Hilgerii prepositi.

119

Notification by William Goion that he relinquishes all claim to a tithe belonging to Saint-Meloir, for which the monks give him 100 *solidi* in the money of Rennes, and for as long as he lives they will give him 10 *solidi*; lacks final validation clauses: *c.* 1084–1100.

EGO Willelmus Goion notum uolo fieri cunctis hoc scriptum legentibus et audientibus quod illam partem decime monasterii sancti Meler quam diu contra monachos sancti Michaelis calumpniaueram et inde placita plurima feceram. linquo et trado prefatis monachis concedente herede meo. et omnibus parentibus meis et amicis. ut perpetue eam sine calumpnia habeant. teneant. et possideant. Ipsi autem monachi pro hoc dant michi centum solidos nunmorum Redonensium. et quandiu uixero dabunt michi .x. solidos.

APPENDICES

I. MATERIAL RELATED TO THE CONTENTS OF THE CARTULARY

1a

BL Royal 13 A xxiii, fol. 96r, annals of Mont-Saint-Michel composed *c.* 1035–39 mentioning the (forged) bull of John XIII and diploma of Lothar (no. 1, pp. 000).

Anno dominicae incarnationis .DCCC.LXX.VI; Rollo cum Normanni Gallis appulit.

Anno .DCCCCC.XII; Baptizatus est idem Rollo cum suis.

Anno .DCCCC.XL.III; peremptus est Willelmus [name struck through in green] filius Rollonis.

Anno .DCCCC.LX.V; auctoratum est sacro scripto tam a domno Papa Iohanne quam a Lothario francorum rege. ut monasterium montis Sancti Michaelis perpetualiter insigniatur ordine monachili; utque nullus nomine uel officio abbatis fungatur ibi. nisi quem idem monachi de suis elegerint praeesse sibi.

Anno .DCCCC.XC.VI. Richardus primus obiit.

Anno .M.XX.III. Inchoatum est hoc nouum monasterium a Richardo secundo comite et Hildeberto abbate. qui abbas ipso anno obiit.

Anno .M.XXV. Obiit Richardus secundus.

Anno .M.XXVII. Obiit Ricardus tercius. Et Mangisus episcopus.

Anno .M.XXX.III. suscepit Suppo abbatiam Montis.

anno .M.XXX.V. Obiit comes Robertus.

1b

B. N. lat. 14832, fol. 178v [inserts after the PERPENDANT paragraph in no. 1].

IN DECRETIS GREGORII PAPE

Nulli fas est uel uelle uel posse transgredi apostolice sedis decreta, nec eius dispositionis ministerium quod omnium oportet sequi caritatem. Sit ergo ruine sue dolore prostratus, quisquis uoluerit apostolicis contraire decretis. Nec locum deinceps inter sacerdotes habeat, sed extorris a sancto ministerio fiat. Nec de eius iudicio atque sententia quisquam deinceps curam habeat; quam iam dampnatus a sancta apostolica ecclesia eiusque auctoritate et propria inobedientia atque presumptione a quoquam esse non dubitatur. Qui maioris excommunicationis deiectione exigendus est cui sancte ecclesie commissa fuerit disciplina? Qui non solum prelate sancte ecclesie iussionibus parere debuit; sed eciam aliis ne preterirent insinuare. Sit ergo alienus a diuinis et pontificalibus officiis, quisquis noluerit obedire apostolicis preceptis. [Extr, Gregory IV, *Diuinis praeceptis*, ed. Jaffé, 2579, cited in Gratien, P.I. D. XX c.5 (Friedburg 1, col. 101]

GREGORIO MARINIANO EPISCOPO RAUENNE [Fol. 178v–179r]

Defuncto uero abbate non extraneus nisi de eadem congregatione quem sibi propria uoluntate congregatio elegerit; et qui electus fuerit, sine dolo uel uenalitate aliqua ordinetur. Quod si aptam inter se personam nequiuerint inuenire, sollerter de aliis monasteriis sibi similiter eligant ordinandum. Qui non ab aliis eligitur, nisi ab illis quibus debet preteresse. Neque uenienti abbati quecumque persona qualibet ocasione in suo monasterio preponatur, nisi forte exstantibus (quod absit) criminibus, que sacri canones punire monstrantur. Pariter autem custodiendum est ut, inuito eiusdem monasterii abbate, ad ordinanda alia monasteria uel ad sacros ordines uel clericatus, officium tolli exinde monachi non debeant. [Gregory IV, letter xv to Marinian bishop of Ravenna (Jaffé, 1504)]

2

B. N. lat. 5430A, pp. 107–8, version of the charter of Josbert Gastevin [cf. nos. **36**, **107**]: 1109–16.

Notum sit omnibus qui presentem cartulam legerint quia Ego Josbertus cognomento Gasteuin pro remedio anime mee ac parentum meorum do Sancto Michaeli duas uastas Ecclesias scilicet dimidias cum omnibus reditibus sibi pertinentibus in uilla que dicitur Creant super flumen Ledum, et medietatem omnium decimarum mearum ubique michi pertinentium, et medietatem unius piscatorie, insuper omnem terram que sita est inter duos riuos ubi site sunt predicte ecclesie. hoc est terra ad unam carrucam, quod si ibi defuerit iuxta uoluntatem monachorum perficiam totam carrucam. preterea de tria arpenta prati, hanc conuentionem taliter factam, ut anima patris mei Josleni, et matris mee Haduise sint participes fraternitatis Sancti Michaelis et si ego monachus fieri uoluero. a monachis eiusdem loci non repudiabor hec conuentia facta est et in capitulo Sancti Michaelis coram omnibus monachis, arte et ingenio Rainaldi monachi nostri Signum Josberti Gasteuin, Signum Erchembaldi filii Rulrici Signum (108) Pagani filii eius, Signum Isabel Signum Girardi de la Barorda Signum Harduini

3

B. N. lat. 5430A, p. 100, copy of an 'original sans datte ny scel', charter of Fulk IV of Anjou, authentic version of no. **62**: 8 May 1082–1098 (the year in which Geoffrey I de Mayenne died), probably 5 May 1096–1098, in the time of Geoffrey le Jeune de Mayenne, bishop of Angers, and before Rainald III de Châteaugontier left for Jerusalem in 1098.

In nomine sancte et indiuidue trinitatis patris et filii et spiritus sancti amen presenti et uenture posteritati notificamus quod Fulcho Angegauensium comes uenerabilis filio suo Gaufredo cognomento Martello, fauente Deo sancteque ecclesie Sancti Michaelis archangeli de Periculo Maris, domnoque Rogerio eiusdem loci abbatis pro gloria uite celestis adipiscenda, dedit in elemosina uinagium quod capere solebat de septem arpennis. et tribus quartariis uinearum quae apud Andegauum urbem ecclesia prefata antiquitus possiderabat in eadem uero urbe Andegaui concessit unum hominem in domo Sancti Michaelis manentem ab omni obsidione et tailla liberum et quietum et in suburbio Turonense urbis similiter duos hospites, unum qui uineas Sancti Michaeli, alterum uero qui domum et uinum custodit. Concessit etiam quod terre uel uinee, et quocunque monachi Sancti Michaelis tenent in Turonensi uel Andegauensi pago innanno non capiant pro quolibet foris facto siue in Normannia seu altera prouincia sua supradicta autem elemosina abbas Rogerius, et qui eum ipso erant fratres comiti et filio suo xxx lib. Andegau' monete in caritate et memoria dederunt, ut uero hac carta rata perenniter permaneat idem comes, eiusque filius, ceterique huic rei interfuerunt uiuifice crucis Signum subter impresserunt. Signum Fulconis comitis Signum filii Gauffredi Signum Girardi de Sancto Albino abbate Signum Gauffredi de Meduana Signum Raginaldi de Castro Gunterii. actum est hoc Andegauis multis uidentibus et audientibus. (Printed in Guilloreau, *Chartes de Créans*, no. II, p. 9.)

4

B.L. Egerton 3031 (*Cartulary of Reading Abbey*, ed. B. Kemp. vol. 2, no. 771, pp. 72–3); letter of Abbot Roger and his monks to Bishop Roger of Salisbury asking him to confirm to Reading Abbey the churches of Wargarve and Cholsey in Bekshire which the monks have given in exchange for 12 librates of land in Budleigh, Devon, which Henry I has given them; cf. no. **108**: probably latter half of 1123 (cf. *Cart. Reading*, i, 3 and note, p. 39).

Reuerendo domino et patri R[ogerio] Saresb[eriensi] episcopo gratia Dei strenuo regni Anglie prouisori frater Rogerius abbas Sancti Michaelis de periculo maris et conuentus fratrum eiusdem loci, deuotum cum oratione seruitium. Ecclesias de Chealseia et de Wellegraua, quas in episcopatu uestro habuimus, pro salute domini nostri regis Henrici concedimus et donamus in elemosinam fratribus in monasterio Radingensi Deo seruientibus, et per uos tanquam per episcopum eas Radingensi ecclesie iure donari deposcimus. Ecclesias itaque supradictas terras cum decimis et terris et omnibus ad ipsas more antiquo pertinentibus date et confirmate Radingensi ecclesie, uobis a Deo commisse. Precamur insuper ut xii libratas terre quas dominus noster rex Henricus in Buddeleia donauit nobis uestra liberalitate assignari nostre ecclesie citius faciatis. Valete.

5

Arch. dépt. de Calvados F 5276, *premier cahier*, copy by Gaston de Beausse, of Arch. dépt, de Manche, H 14998, 'original parchemin, sans trace de scellements, h. 0^{m}.230 x l. 0^{m}. 385' (also copied in B. N. lat. 5430a, pp. 260–1); quitclaim by John son of Thomas and his brothers, in the presence of Abbot Bernard and the whole convent, of the claim on a daily share in the provisions offered to St Michael earlier renounced by their uncle, following a vicious campaign against the abbey, described in no. **83**; Abbot Bernard takes pity on their poverty and grants them part of his annual wheat render, and one loaf daily: 1142.

Omnibus in hoc loco qui Tumba dicitur domino nostro Jesu Christo sanctoque archangelo Michaeli deuote// famulantibus sit in propatulo dominum Johannem filium Thome cum fratribus suis coram Domno abate (*sic*)// Bernardo et omni cumuentu in capitulo dimisise (*sic*) omnia illa que de Sancti Michaelis altare se debere heredi//tario jure parentum habere dicebat. Videlicet omne genus annone et leguminis quod a fidelibus populis Sancti// Michaelis archangeli sufragia deposcentibus deferrebatur. et in oblatione oferebatur et omnes uolucres et// pisces qui eodem modo oferebantur et medietatem tocius lanificii et linificii necnon et scopationes denariorum// et cere quod antea nusquam auditum fuerat. Donnus abas (*sic*) Bernardus audiens tam nefandam interrogationem ei diem// differendi constituit. Johannes autem uidens et sciens nulla ratione se posse differere judicio inito cum filio et accepto// omnia quiete dimisit ac dimissione super quatuor euangelia numquam resipiscendum se subjuramento constrinsit,// quod et omnes fratres sui similiter fecerunt. Donnus uero abbas Bernardus eorum uidens inopiam illorum misertus, uno// quoque anno octo annone quartaria de orreo suo eis, et cotidie unum panem qualem habent monachi concessit, hujus// paueti et huius cumcordie fuerunt testes. Ex parte abatis. Ricardus de Haia, Jordan Tasson, Guillelmus de Similiaco. et// de horum procerum militibus quorum nomina non est necesse referre, fuere multi. Ex familia uero abatis: Gaufredus//Cenomannensis, Richardus de Fonteneto, Radulfus Eme Panem, Ricardus Pulcher et alii quamplures. Ex parte// autem Johannis et fratrum ejus: Riuallonus Calcebof. Hernulfus de Stampis. Robert Macelot. Hugo de Monasterio. SansWanlo.// Heraldus Bonus Vinum. Robertus filius Radulfi de Monasterio et multi alii quos enumerare lungum est. Facta sunt autem hec// anno ab incarnatione domini millesimo centesimo quadragesimo secundo, regnante piissimo rege Stephano in Anglia,// in Rothomagensi cathedra presidente Donno Hugone archipresule. In Abrincatensi uero sede donno Ricardo presule.

6

B. N. fr. 22357, p. 783 (cf. B. N. lat. 5430a, p. 209) another version of no. **58**: 1135–49.

Notum sit omnibus tam presentibus quam futuris Gaufredum Galterii filium in capitulo Sancti Michaelis in presentia domni abbatis totiusque conuentus uenisse, et omnia illa que in ecclesia S. Melorii clamabat, uidelicet in decima, in tractu decime, in reclamatione agnorum, in purificationibus bastardorum, et in aliis rebus supradicte ecclesie pertinentibus omnibus qui ibi aderant audientibus omnino reliquisse. Hoc etiam a se ipso, suisque posteris, esse tenendum super textum euangeliorum jurejurando coram domno abbate totque conuentu firmiter stabilisse, teste Riualen Chascebou, Willelmo Pulcra-barba, Vitali Leienfant, Sauhale, aliisque quam pluribus et ex parte sua affuit Ginguene Albi filius, nos uero ut hec memorie tenerentur cirographo consignauimus.

7

Copy by G. Beauchesne, Arch. dépt. de La Manche, 6 J 70, M 11, from an original formerly at Saint-Lô, 'une copie de quelques années postérieures'; the phrases in curly brackets are supplied from B. N. fr. 22325, p. 719; grant by Trihan de Saint-Broladre and his wife and son: cf. nos. **21**, **56** and **89**: 1075

In nomine Patris et Filii et Spiritus Sancti. Amen. Anno // ab incarnatione domini MLXXV, indictione xiii. Ego Trehan de Sancto Broaladrio concessi et dedi Deo et Sancto Michaeli// de Monte et monachis ipsius loci pro salute mea et heredes meorum et pro animabus patris et matris mee et omnis antecessorum// meorum totam decimam quam habebam in Sancto Broaladro, et s[epultu]ram et quicquid in eadem ecclesie iure hereditario possidebat.// Dedi etiam duodecim acras terre et decimam de meo molendino et de meo pomario. Idem ego Trehen cernens appropinquare // michi finem vitae accepi monachiles pannos a monachis Sancti Michaelis et tunc etiam dedi terram de Curtis Sulcis // de Burbadrie et {omnem partem meam de Longis} Sulcis et totam terram de Torpol quae juncta est culture Sancti Michaelis et masuras Juuenis {in cimiterio} Sancti Broaladri que in meo dominio erat. Has meas donationes // Gaufridus filius meus et uxor mea Adelina concesserunt Deo et Sancto Michaeli perpetualiter absque ulla calumpnia possidendam.// Notum sit etiam omnibus quod donationem primam quam feci de decima et sepultura et de omni re quam in {illa ecclesia} habebam con//cessit Johannes Riuallonis filius proprius dominus meus, sed et Euenus qui tunc archiepiscopus erat hoc concessit. Hujus res testes sunt // Alui filius Moruu qui signum crucis subter impressit. + Signum Maini Calui* + Signum Euueni {bastardi} + Ego quoque Trehan signum crucis feci + et filio meo Gaufrido firmari feci + // ex nostra parte isti sunt testes. Hugo cubicularius abbatis. Hugonis signum. Ligerius filius Ermenulfi + Morinus de Sessun +.

* So BN fr. 22325; Beauchesne is difficult to read here but appears to have: Mainilcatu
Printed in Morice, *Preuves*, ii, col. 441.

8

B. N. Coll. Moreau 36, 141 (*ex chart.* B. N. 5430A); another version of no. **65**, charter of William fitz Hugh de Sillé-le-Guillaume (Sarthe): 1087.

Notum sit omnibus uiuentibus atque uicturis Guillelmus filius Hugonis de Silliaco gratia Dei sanctique Michaelis archangeli hoc impetrante ob omnium suorum remissionem delictorum suorumque predecessorum omnium et successorum et ob fraternitatem et orationes monachorum predicti archangeli nec non et unius honesti equi concessisse eisdem monachis omnes consuetudines terre sue, id est eos perpetue absoluit ab omnibus consuetudinibus que solebant ei dari, ab eisdem monachis scilicet de theloneo et aliis redditibus que pertinent ad similia negotia acceptores huius doni fuerunt Radulfus monachus atque Andreas cum quodam uiridi ramo spine. actum est hoc tempore Guillelmi anglorum regis et Hoelli Cenomannensis presulis atque Huberti uicecomitis et Gauffredi de Mehena. Oldeburga uero mater prefati Guillelmi hoc domum concessit loco suorum etiam filiorum absentium et ita effecta est particeps orationum predictorum monachorum. testes autem sunt rei istius Guillelmus de Vernaico. Amelinus forestarius. Beradus de Silliaco. Guarinus Rotgeri filius. Radulfus de Doleid. Herbertus de Orta. Theobaldus capellanus. Drogo de Sancto Christophoro. Fulco Droart. Fulconius de Plessiaco. Robertus Coignart. Rad[] filius Goscelini de Monte Sauoneir. Fulconus [...] Gualterius Constant filius. Galterus de Curte Aleru. Ex parte monachorum sunt teste. Gaufridus de Hispania. Rotbertus de Sancto Medardo. Johannes famulus eorum qui hoc auferre uel contradicere aussus fuerit cum Juda traditore Domini maledictus sit.

II. MATERIAL OMITTED BY THE CARTULARY

1

Guillotel, *Actes des ducs de Bretagne*, no. 6, redaction 1, charter-notification relating grants by Conan I of Brittany at Villamée (Ille-et-Vilaine, cant. Louvigné-du-Désert), Passillé (Ille-et-Vilaine, cant. Fougères, comm. Parigné), Lillèle and Ville-Perdue (Ille-et-Vilaine, cant. Louvigné-du-Désert, comm. Villamée): the basic grant described is undoubtedly genuine, though an authentic text of the original grant is only subliminally present; the most flagrant anachronisms are indicated in the text: 28 July 990.

In nomine Domini. Haec cartula indicat atque conseruat quod dedit atque obtulit Conan Britannorum princeps pro Deo et pro uita aeterna adquirenda anime senioris sui, et sue anime atque coniugis anime et patris matrisque anime et fratrum sororumve nec non ceterorum quibus velle collesit villas tres, quas Main nepos archiepiscopi tenebat de eo < en pheuu > eo tempore: villam Amois et villam Passilei et uillam Islel, quas permisit domino suo dare atque offerre sicut uellet uoluit dare summo archangelo Michaeli pro Deo et pro uita aeterna anime sue predictorumque animabus et villam Perduht et masuram unam positam inter villam Amois et villam Perduht quam Rorges Gozleni filius nepos fratris Hugonis Cinomanis similiter tenebat < en pheuu > sicut predictus uir < et sic date sunt he ville sancto Michaeli a supradicto domino cum territorio de ipsis villis et si aliquis de his habitantibus infra istas villas homicidium fecerit aut effusionem sanguinis aut latrocinium aut preterierit hostem aut equitatum, sit bonum principis Michaelis et monachorum suorum, sed si aliquis de foris homicidium fecerit super habitantes aut ipsi super alios, sit comitis bannum, aut raptum aut incendium fortunam aut siluaticas bestias captas, aut sit celatum, sit comitis bannum et de seruitio Redonis ciuitatis erunt tailla, auxilium, reservata reddent et insuper ipsa lege et ipso servitio quo serviunt Redonenses habitatores tali ratione seruient hii qui in his villis habitauerint, excepto quod nominatim hic legitur.> Hoc factum fuit in monasterio sancti Sansonis Doli in die festiuitatis eius et in probatione huius cartule Mainardus prepositus et Heroardus decanus fuerunt legatores huius facti apud predictum comitem, missi a Mainardo abbate et a ceteris monachis, et hec ratio firmata fuit sedente comite in una cripta sancti Sansonis Doli V kalendas augusti, luna II, anno ab incarnatione domini DCCCC LXXXX. Hec cartula scripta fuit in Redonica urbe in vigilia sancti Laurentii die sabbati, die tricesima a festiuitate predicti Sansonis, coram multis testibus qui viderunt et audierunt. Clemens presbiter t. Arufus abbas Sancti Saluatoris t. Signum Conani. Signum Gosfredi Conani filii. Main archiepiscopus t. Constantius episcopus t. Rodaldus episcopus t. Drehtcandrus episcopus t. Ugo t. Nannetensis episcopus. Auriscandus episcopus t. Oratius episcopus Cornugalliae t. Retualatrus episcopus t. Deotbaldus episcopus Redonensis t. Hi nouem episcopi iussu Conano illorum domino testes sunt huius cartule. Guruedem laicus t. Fraterque eius Arscot laicus t. Main laicus t. Rorges laicus t. Brient laicus t. Iungeneu laicus t. Ratfredus vicharius t. Doniert laicus t. Adam laicus t. Guezenoc laicus t. Arluinus abbas t. Salomon abbas t.

2

Grant by Hugh III of Maine of three mills on the river Sarthe in the *faubourg* of Le Mans: 1000–1015. Printed from the original in *Cartulaire de Saint-Victeur*, no. II, with partial facsiile.

In nomine sanctæ et indiuidue Trinitatis, Patris et Filii et Spiritus Sancti.

Diuina præcepta patenter ammonent terrenis bonis lucrari cælestia. Quapropter ego Hugo, Cinomannensis comes, notum uolo esse omnibus sanctæ Dei Æcclesie fidelibus, tam presentibus quam futuris, et precipue successoribus meis, quoniam, sub huius noticiæ testamento, tres molendinos Sancto Michaeli de Monte periculosi maris, pro remedio animæ meæ, et patris matrisque necnon filiorum, perpetualiter habendos trado, per assensum et uoluntatem Hugonis, filii Herbrannis, qui eos de meo beneficio tenebat.

Sunt autem predicti molendini in suburbio Cinomannensis ciuitatis super Sartam fluuium siti.

Ea tamen lege illos concedo ut annis singulis, in festiuitate sancti Iohannis Baptistæ, de illis census tres solidos soluatur. Si quis autem contra hoc scriptum insurgere uoluerit, cum Iuda traditore Domini Datan et Abiron, Anna et Cahypha, dampnationem accipiant.

V̇t autem huius nostræ donacionis auctoritas uerius credatur et diligentius conseruetur per omnia. manu propria subterfirmauimus.

(column 1) Herbertus frater comitis. Hugo. Albericus. Hugolinus. (column 2) Rotscelinus. Fulco Franciscus. Goslenus. Ernoldus (column 3) Hugo decanus. Hubertus clericus. Fulcuinus cancelarius. Mainardus cantor. Rainaldus. (column 4) Rainaldus. Turstinus. Goscelinus. Mainardus.

3

Charter by which Robert I of Normandy renounces all the rights claimed by his ancestors: 1027–33. Printed as Fauroux, no. 65, from a nineteenth-century copy by Ch.-E. Lambert of one of two twelfth-century redactions which survived until 1944 at Saint-Lô. Cf. no. **5**.

In nomine sanctæ et indiuidue Trinitatis, Patris et Filii et Spiritus Sancti. Ego Rotbertus comes, filius magni Richardi, gratia Dei dux et princeps Normannorum reddo Sancto Michaeli altare suum cum toto monasterio quod predecessores mei sibi actenus uindicauerunt. Reddo autem illud tali conditione ut quæcumque a fidelibus populis ibi Deo et Sancto Michaeli fuerint oblata, monachi ibidem Deo seruientes omnino habeant, teneant et possideant in loci utilitate et ulterius ueniat in custodia clericorum aut laicorum, nisi abbatis et monachorum. Et hoc facio pro remedio animarum parentum meorum, patris et matris, fratrum et sororum et meæ. Si quis autem aliquando successorum meorum, instinctu diaboli commotus, hoc decretum uiolare uel aliorsum uertere presumpserit, in diem magni iudicii, Deo et Sancto Michaelis rationem reddere cogatur. Et ut hoc inconuulsum permaneat et omnibus seculis notum, manu proprio subterfirmo, fidelium quoque nostrorum testimoniis confirmare iussimus.

+ Ego Rotbertus, gratia Dei Normannorum dux, hoc signum crucis faciens, manu propria hanc donationis cartulam confirmo, fidelium quoque nostrorum testimonio et auctoritate subter confirmare iussimus, quorum nomina hæc sunt:

+ Hugo Baiocensis episcopus. + Herbertus Luesuicacensis episcopus. + Hugo Abrincatensis episcopus. + Iohannes Fiscanensis abba. + Gislebertus filius Godefredi comitis. + Anschitillus Baiocacensis uicecomes. + Hugo uicecomes filius Turstingi. + Richardus de Crolei. + Rodulfus Taison et frater eius Ernis. + Osbertus filius Herfasti. + Nigellus uicecomes. Fulco filius Girardi. + Rabel. + Vuilelmus filius Turstingi et alii quam plures. + Suppo monachus. + Iozelinus monachus.

4

Arch. dépt. de Calvados F 5276, *premier cahier*, copy by G. de Beausse of: 'Original parchemin haut. O^{m}. 215 x larg. O^{m}. 425, régle au dos à la point sèche, Arch. dépt. Manche H.'. The monks appoint Rivallon I de Dol-Combour as custodian and defender of their rights at Pontorson; in return they grant fraternity to Rivallon, his wife and their sons, and, for the corporal and spiritual salvation of Rivalllon, they undertake also daily to feed one poor man: 1040–65.

Nouerit tam presens generatio quam futura posteritas nos scilicet Sancti archangeli Michaelis monachos cum Riuallono nobilissimo procerum Brittaniae hujusmodi pactum conuentionis inisse: In primis societatem nostram illi// tribuimus participemque ac consortem omnis beneficii esse constituimus quodcumque Deo cooperante in jejuniis uigiliis, orationibus atque elemosinis// perfecerimus. Deinde speciale adjungimus ut per singulas ebdomadas unam pro ipso missam dicamus. Aliud quoque privile//gium adicimus quod pauperem unum pro ejusdem domni Riualloni tam corporis quam anime salute, cotidie reficimus.// Haec autem omnia, sicut ipsi sic et suae uxori ac filiis exhibemus. Vir enim iste nobilissimus, magna cura // ac diligentia res Sancti Michahelis custodire ac defensare se promittit penitus precipueque locum quem Pontem Ursi vocamus // suo. tutamine atque fiducia aedificare coepimus.

5

B. N. lat. 14832 fol. 183v–184r (early thirteenth-century hand) Convention between Abbot Ranulf (d. 9 December 1084/5) and John, bishop of Avranches; a slightly altered version of the manuscript text was printed in J. Petit, *Theodori Cantuarientiis archiepiscopi Paenitentiale* (1677), pp. 664–6, and reprinted. in Migne *P.L.*, t. 147, col. 265–8; discussed by J. Lemarignier, *Etude sur les privilèges d'exemption*, pp. 156–9: 1061.

Anno ab incarnatione domini millesimo LX.I, Rannulfus abbas montis S. Michaelis, uir cautus in regimine tam cleri et populi quam in monachilis ordinis, conuenit Iohannem uenerabilem Abrincarum pontificem super quibusdam grauaminibus que fiebant a ministris episcopalibus frequentissime super clerum et populum Montis. Cogebantur enim uenire Abrincas ad respondendum de quacunque accusatione contra Christianitatem, nec excusare poterat eos mare insurgens, nec Britonum insidie, quia preueniri ac preuideri poterant, et ita sepe in forisfacta et emendationes episcopales incidebant, et sepe iuramentis fatigabantur. Propter predicta sibi habenda in Monte. obtulit abbas episcopo de suo competentur per singulos annos, scilicet unam pelliciam grisiam, que tam nobilem et tam sullimem personam deceret cum gratia recipere; et abbatem Montis honorifice dare. Et tres libras incensi. et tres libras piperis. et sex tabulis cere. de .ix. ponderibus. et tres cereos in purificatione S. Marie. Vnum scilicet albe cere unius ponderis; ad manus episcopi; duos alterius cere unius ponderis ad decani et thesaurarii manus. Episcopus uero prefatus, ut erat animo et genere nobilis, petitioni abbatis annuit, et archidiaconum suum in Monte eum fecit: Ita tamen ut quod bene non faceret, uel non posset, episcopus corrigeret Abrincis [et -added later] ecclesiastico iuditio terminaret; De coniugiis autem illicitis, si qui legales testes procederent, apud episcopum audirentur, et per sacramentum ipsorum lege dissolueretur, quod contra legem presumptum erat; De criminalibus culpis uenirent ad iuditium et sententiam episcopi penitentes, confessi, uel conuicti coram suo archidiacono; [et *added later*] excumunicati ab episcopo ad satisfactionem et eius absolutionem uenirent; Iuditium [184r] ferri igniti et aque feruentis Abrincis portabitur a Muntanis. Pr[esbiter]i ipsi si lapsi in culpam degradationis forte inuenirentur, quia ad episcopum pertinet ordinatio, ad eius iudicium pertinet degradatio; suspensio uero officii pro leuioribus culpis in abbatis iuditium est ad correptionem. Talis inter episcopum et abbatem de uilla Montis facta est conuentio.

In monasterio uero Sancti Michaeli in abbatem, et monachos, et xii canonicos totum ius episcopale retinuit episcopus. In monasterio habet officium facere dedicationis: uesperas precedentis diei cantabit, et missam in die dedicationis, et quicquid interim offeretur ad altare, episcopi est; et quod offertur ad manus eius, capellanorum suorum, et ipse et omnes qui cum eo uenerint, habundanter et honorifice debent procurari. Et equi. aqua dulcis. et cetera necessaria de monasterio inueniri. Eo die debet esse presto pellicia prefata episcopi. Et cera et piper et incensum. cerei tres ad purificationem Sancte Marie. Etiam si episcopus defuerit, abbas cum duobus de canonicis bis in anno debet esse ad synodum, nisi licentia episcopi remanserit, et sacerdotes Montis. Quotiens etiam grauiores cause emerserint episcopo, mandabit abbati et uocabit eum et uenire debet, nisi ineuitabilem et legalem excusationem pretenderit. Nec communicabit excumunicato episcopi scienter nec excumunicabit nominatim aliquem parrochianem episcopi extra Montem consistentem inconsulto episcopo. Monachi v^{ta} feria Pentecostes. uenient Abrincas cum capite Sancti Auberti ad ecclesiam Sancti Andre, in qua ipse sedit episcopus, com [*sic*] processione magno tam clericorum quam laicorum omnium qui domos tenent: et denariatas cere matrici ecclesie debent, ut sedi episcopali, de qua recipiunt consilium animarum, et abbas per se, uel per decanum suum, oleum et crisma, ad erogandum presbiteris ad christianitatem faciendam. Canonici omnes sub episcopo priore sunt et canonicas, id est prebendas, cum uacue fuerint, distribuere debet sicut dignum decreuerit. Beatus enim Aubertus, cui diuino munere Mons ille collatus est, eos instituit. et de suo episcopio, ecclesie quam construxit, duas uillas, Icium scilicet et Genecium ad usum suum et illorum contulit.

6

Arch. dépt. de Calvados F 5276, *premier cahier*, copy by G. de Beausse of: 'Arch. dépt. Manche H [15173 *added in pencil*] orig. parch. 0^m.220 x 0^m.155 règle au dos à la pointe seche'; also copied in B. N. lat. 10072, no. 110 (1060–66); cf. no. 117: Abbot Ranulf makes a series of conventions: 1058–83/5.

Hic scribitur quoddam pactum inter Rannulfum abbatem et Guatzonem // de quodam filio suo pro quo accepit ab abbate vi libras denariorum et // ipse abbas debet habere partem tertiam cuiusdam aecclesie quam ipse optinet// filius. Interim vero jussu abbatis docebitur ad litteras usque dum possit ordinari presbiter postea auxilio eius ordinabitur eandem autem ecclesiam si voluerit tenere ad misericordiam abbatis tenebit, ita ut nullus alius po//terit habere quamdiu voluerit habere cum sua tertia parte. Haec testatur// Rainaldus filius Brientii et Hugo de Brichevilla et Ricardus Gravararius Vuidm[u]ndus filius Hardret. Abbas Rannulfus accipit in vadimonium septi//mam p[artem] cuiusdam molendini quam uxor Rotberti habet pro sex libris de//nariorum usque ad decem annos si vero tunc non redditi fuerint semper tenebit// usque dum reddantur. Huius conventionis sunt testes Rainaldus filius Brientii.// Ricardus. Rannulfus. Mainardus. Gaufridus. Unfridus. Guatszo.//

Vuidmundus sacerdos et Guillelmus eius frater vendiderunt unam domum abbati Rannulfo .xl. solidis. Isdem Vuidmundus vendidit medietatem aecclesie .iii. libris et .x. solidis. quam tenet abbati, Rainaldo filio Brientii fidejussore et Ricardo Gravarario// teste et Mainardo et Unfrido de Holchineo et Gauffrido Trenchart.// Abbas accepit in vademonium partem molendini Hugonis Sapientis pro .iiii. libris usque ad septem annos et est terminus in introitu Augusti// tali conventione quod si ad terminum non reddentur semper tenebit abbas// usque dum reddantur, plege Vuatszone et Rainaldo filio Brienni [sic]// Osmundus filius Grenti dimittit in vadimonium partem cuiusdam molendini // sui Rannulfo abbati pro centum solidis usque ad .xii. annos eadem conventione et// termino quo et aliud vadimonium, plege Rainaldo filio Brienni et // Vuatszone. De eodem molendino Vuatszo partem suam dimittit in vadi//monium pro .c. solidis eadem conventione et termino usque ad decem annos, plege Osmun//do et Rainaldo filio Brienni. Harum omnium conventionum sunt testes Rannulfus// Tison, Hugo prepositus Otbertus cocus Guillelmus Niger.

7

Arch. dépt. de Calvados F 5276, *premier cahier*, copy by G. de Beausse of a now-lost 'original. 0^m.165 x 0^m.190, sans trace de scelleur' in the Arch. dépt. de La Manche: grant by William de Tracy, on becoming a monk of the abbey, of land at Montpincon (Manche, cant. Cerisy-la-Salle), La Lucerne (cant. La Haye-Pesnel), Champrépus (cant. Villedieu), Saint-Vigor-des-Monts (cant.

Tessy) and Argouges (cant. Saint-James-de-Beuvron) (calendared in Round, *CDF*, no. 719): 1110.

In nomine Patris et Filii et Spiritus Sanctus. Amen.// Notum sit omnibus tam presentibus quam futuris, quod ego Guillelmus de Traceio, pro magnitudine delictorum // meorum et pro salvatione et remedio anime mee et animarum antecessorum meorum, apud Montem // Sancti Michaelis monachalem habitem Sancti Benedicti, Deo favente et conventu ecclesie concedente, suscepi. Et // propter hoc decimam molendinorum de Monpinzon et decimam nemoris de Lucerna et cujusdam molendini qui // in villa erat et decimam de molendino de Campo Repus et decimam molendinorum meorum apud Sanctum // Vigorem et ecclesiam de Argogis cum tota decima et decimam molendini ipsius ville, Deo et Sancto Michaeli et monachis eiusdem ecclesie concessi. Huius rei ex parte ipsius Guillelmi de Traceio testes fuerunt Turgisus // episcopus Abrincensis. Othoer de Solegneio. Radulfus de Neuilla. Radulfus Barbort. Ex parte vero monachorum. Rogerius // Bec de Fert. Gislebertus Bella Caliga. Guillelmus de Brichevilla. Signum Guillelmi de Traceio. Signum Rohes uxoris sue. Signum Torgisi filii sui. Signum Henrici filii sui. Signum Gieve sororis sue. Actum anno ab incarnatione domini MCX. Tempore Turgisi episcopi Abrincensis, qui hoc donum concessit.

8

Arch. dépt. de La Manche, 6 J 70, M1, copy by Geneviève Beauchesne of a now lost original charter given by Hugh fitz Ranulf for the Mont's priory of Saint-Broladre: 1096–1139, probably *c.* 1131.

Cyrographum
Inter cetera sancte operationis studia precipua laude predicatur primoque loco habetur elemosina//unde Dominus: Date inquit elemosinas et omnia munda sunt vobis et propheta sicut aqua ignem ita elemosi//na extinguit peccatum his ex hujusmodi hortamentis incitatus ego [Hugo] Ranulfi filius// anime mee curam gerens de jure hereditario meo do Deo et Beato Michaeli ar//changelo et in ejus servitio mancipatis monachis quamdam masuram apud sanctum Broa//ladrum juxta Pontem Ansgoti et tantum de virideria mea quantum die una falcatores // x falcare poterunt annis singulis in omnium successura posteritate. Quod meum donum // liberi mei Will. et Thomas quibus natu prioribus hereditatem meam diviseram atque dimiseram. // tres et fratres eorum juniores concesserunt et super altar sancti Michaelis posuerunt. Monachi vero // pro Dei amore et elemosina quam in eadem villa a meis antecessoribus habebant et pro hoc // meo beneficio libente et honorifice monachicum habitum mihi largiti sunt. Hujus mee dona//cionis testes sunt hi Guido filius Ranulfi, Helyas Boterat, Willelmus Cantapia Ansgerius filius Dauid et frater ejus Gaufredus sacerdos Robertus Latro Hugo Brito et de meis hominibus multi alii // Ex parte vero monachorum Willelmus de Braeio

Hugo filius Odonis Rualendus Calcebos Briendus // Chesnel Robertus de Monasterio et multi alii.

9

B. N. lat. 5430a, pp. 270–1: memorandum concerning the way in which the chamberlain Roger came to lose the land he held, justly and unjustly, from the abbey; after an unsuccessful career as a mercenary had reduced him to poverty he sought reconciliation with the abbot, but following the death of Henry I of England in 1135 he joined the partisans of Stephen who attacked the church's land and he died excommunicate: after 1138.

De Rogerio camerario, memorie litterarum tradere dignum duximus qua ratione ipse perdiderit ea que in ecclesia siue juste siue injuste habebat, cum enim Domnus Bernardus Beccensis monachus ad ecclesiam S. Michaelis regendam uenisset et a uenerabili pontifice Turgiso Abrincatensi consecratus fuisset, continuo prefatus Rotgerius eumdem requisiuit, ut sibi ea que jure hereditario contingebant, redderet quo respondente quesiuit ab eo que essent. dixit hujusmodi se habiturum liberationes duos panes uidelicet dimidium sextarium uini duos denarios et candelas in magnis festiuitatibus pigmentum ad natale domini xx.s, totidem ad Pascha preter frequentia dona que ab abbatis se recipere solere dicebat, prebendam uero duobus equis sufficiente, hec predicta singulis diebus accipiebat super quibus consulto capitulo et fidelibus suis abbas hec omnia sibi concessit. Ipse autem deinceps cum potentia est pluribus amicorum suorum eundem abbatem requisiuit, ut redderet ei clauem denariorum ecclesie, tam de altari quam de cunctis redditibus ecclesie. Ita ut eo nesciente non liceret abbati dare 5s. et ut omnes tam monachi quam laici eidem responderent et suo consilio mitterentur forinsecus ad obedientias et laici reciperent firmas; que cum abbas audisset, non mediocriter indignans, respondit quod seruitium pro tantis insigniis ipse deberet, qui respondit eidem abbati, lectulum preparaturum deinde discalciaturum cui abbas fertur tale dedisse responsum. Sicut pes pedi gradiendo est necessarius, ita sis in discalciando utilis et propinquus, hec superflua que dicitis uobis abnego tamen diem rectitudinis constituere uobis non recuso. quem ipse omnino respuens, omnia sua que habebat et habere querebat quod reliquit, et cum quanto conamine potuit. In Brittaniam ad guerram faciendam se recepit, quo per tempus moram non paruam faciens et nichil aut parum proficiens, nimia paupertate districtus reditum quesiuit, et uix ab abbate inuenit relictis tamen omnibus superfluis calumpniis tunc demum hominium suum fecit, et super sanctuariam ecclesie jurauit in uita abbatis se nunquam ea predicta clamaturum. Sed post mortem Regis Anglie sacramentum irritum fecit Britanniam cum omni supellectili petiit, unde multa mala non solum per se, uerum etiam dux factus inimicorum qui tunc temporis nimia auiditate Normanniam infestabunt terre et hominibus ecclesie irrogauit. quo in malitia perseuerante cum et asinum qui pauperibus Dei aquam deferret, cepisset ilico domini et archangeli Michaelis sagitta percussus nec diutius uiuens sine absolutione excommunicationis ecclesie est defunctus, et iccirco sicut nunc usque apparet super terram iacet inhumatus. hac occasione predictus Rotgerus testimonio terre marisque prescripta perdidit.

10

Arch. dépt. de Calvados F 5276, *premier cahier*, copy by G. de Beausse, from Arch. de la Manche non classé (unsealed original, chirograph, $0^{m}.128$ x $0^{m}.150$): grant by Peter fitz Desirée on becoming a monk, of all his inheritance in Guernsey, with the assent of his wife Osanna of the Isles and daughter Orenga: 1131–49, probably after *c.* 1135.

Notum sit tam presentibus quam futuris in tempore domini Bernardi abbatis // ecclesie Sancti Michaelis de Monte. Petrum filium Desiderie factam fuisse mo//nachum in eadem ecclesia dando ibidem omnem hereditatem suam. Et hoc fecit // consensu Osanne uxoris sue de insulis et filie ipsorum Orenge nomine. Qui predictus Petrus cum predicta uxore et filia posuit donum hujus rei // super altare Sancti Michaelis per brachium Sancti Autberti. Et ob hoc ipse abbas et conuentus monachorum concesserunt jam dicti Petri uxori et filie // in Guerneleio accram et dimidiam terre ubi domus Petri sita erat. tres uir//gas terre unde reddebat tres bussellos frumenti Et juxta illam accram// unam terre uel plus aliquantulum. Et agram unam de Follaia. Et ob hoc dati sunt Orenge quinque solidi Rotomagensium.

Ex parte monachorum testes fu//erunt. Rualenth Calcebos. Gislebertus Daufin. Hugo cum Testei. Ex parte // Orenge. Osmundus de Curia. Ricardus filius Osanne.

Printed in *Cartulaire de Jersey*, no. 117, pp. 186–7; copy in B.N. lat. 10072, no. 31; calendared in Round, *CDF*, no. 727.

11

Cartulaire de Jersey no. 9, pp. 13–15, printed from the original then in the Archives de La Manche. Bull of Eugenius III confirming to the abbey, at the request of Abbot Geoffrey, its possessions and taking it under the protection of St Peter: 15 December 1150.

Eugenius Episcopus servus servorum Dei dilectis filiis Gaufrido abbati ecclesie Sancti Michaelis de periculo maris ejusque fratribus tam presentibus quam futuris regularem vitam professis in perpetuam. Pie postulatio voluntatis effectu debet prosequenter compleri ut devotionis sinceritas laudabiliter enitescat et utilitas postulata vires indubitanter assumat. Quocirca dilecti in Domino filii vestris justis postulationibus clementer annuimus et prefatum monasterium in quo divino mancipati estis obsequio sub beati Petri et nostra protectione suscipimus et presentis scripti privilegio communimus statuentes ut quascumque possessiones quecumque bona eadem ecclesia in presentiarum juste et legitime possidet aut in futurum concessione pontificum largitione regum vel principum oblatione fidelium seu aliis justis modis, Deo propitio, poterit adipisci, firma vobis vestrisque successoribus et illibata permaneant. In quibus hec propriis duximus exprimenda vocabulis villam que vocatur Geneceium cum ecclesia ipsius ville et cum pertinenciis suis, ecclesiam de Ardevon cum ipsa villa et pertinenciis suis; villam que Crux dicitur cum pertinenciis suis, capellam Hamelini cum pertinenciis suis; ecclesiam Sancti Paterni cum villa ipsa et pertinenciis suis, ecclesiam de Fulcheravilla cum ipsa villa et pertinenciis suis, villam de Eventor, villam Sancti Clementis in Gerseio cum pertinenciis suis; quicquid habetis in insula que vocatur Guernerey; ecclesiam de Quarterai cum pertinenciis suis; villam que vocatur Domnus Johannes cum ecclesia ejusdem ville et pertinenciis suis; villam que dicitur Brethevilla cum ecclesia ipsius ville et pertinenciis suis; villam que dicitur Verson cum pertinenciis suis, ecclesiam de Evreceyo cum pertinenciis suis, ecclesiam que dicitur Villamers cum ecclesia ipsius et pertinenciis suis: ecclesiam de Livare cum pertinenciis suis Villarenton[a], ecclesiam de Montanai cum pertinenciis suis, ecclesiam Sancti Victurii in suburbio Cenomanis, cum burgo ipsius suburbii et pertinenciis suis; in eodem suburbio ecclesiam Sancti Johannis cum pertinenciis suis, villam que dicitur Gohere cum ecclesia ejus et pertinenciis suis; villam que dicitur Poleium de feodo Odonis Borelli cum ecclesia ipsius et pertinenciis suis, villam que dicitur Mont-Rouault cum pertinenciis suis; ecclesiam Sancti Broeladii cum pertinenciis suis; ecclesiam Sancti Melorii cum pertinenciis suis; ecclesiam Sancti Michaelis de Cornubia cum pertinenciis suis, villam que dicitur Otritonia cum pertinenciis suis; Wiscumbam, Basingas, Bodelai, Estoleiam cum pertinenciis suis; ecclesiam de Meretoch cum pertinenciis suis; obeunte vero te nunc ejusdem loci abbate vel tuorum quolibet successorum nullus in predicta ecclesia qualibet surreptionis astutia seu violentia preponatur nisi quem fratres communi consensu vel pars fratrum consilii sanioris secundum Dei timorem et beati Benedicti regulam previderint eligendum,[b] salva Abrincensis episcopi canonica justicia. Decernimus ergo ut nulli omnino hominum liceat prefatum monasterium temere perturbare aut ejus possessiones auferre vel ablatas retinere, minuere, seu aliquibus vexationibus fatigare, sed omnia integra conserventur eorum pro quorum gubernatione ac sustentacione concessa sunt usibus omnimodis profutura, salva apostolice sedis auctoritate et diocesanorum episcoporum canonica justitia. Si qua igitur in futurum ecclesiastica secularisve persona hanc nostre constitutionis paginam sciens contra eam temere venire temptaverit, secundo terciove commonita nisi presumptionem suam satisfactione congrua emendaverit potestatis honorisque sui dignitate careat et a sacratissimo corpore et sanguine Dei et Domini Redemptoris nostri Jhesu Christi aliena fiat atque in extremo examine districte ultioni subjaceat. Cunctis autem eidem ecclesie justa servantibus sit pax Domini nostri Jesu Christi quatenus et hic fructum bone actionis percipiant et apud districtum judicem premia eterne pacis inveniant, Amen. Datum Ferentini per manum Maximini Sancte Romane ecclesie scriptoris decimo octavo kalendas Januarii indictione decima quarta, incarnationis dominice anno millesimo centesimo quinquagesimo pontificatus vero domini Eugenii pape tercii anno sexto.

[a] - *sic*. Compare the text of the 1155 bull of Adrian IV (printed *ibid.*, no. 10, p. 17): ...ecclesiam de Liuare cum pertinenciis suis; ecclesiam de Montenai cum pertinenciis suis; Villarenton cum pertinenciis suis.... Also, the bull of Alexander III of 1179, in Delisle, *Torigni*, ii, p. 317: ... Villarentoniam, cum molendinis, silvis et pertinentiis suis
[b] - Rule of St Benedict, cap. LXIV.

12

B. N. lat. 10072, nos. 19 and 20, from a manuscript formerly Bibliothèque d'Avranches, no. 81, *Homeliae diuersae SS PP pia euangelia per annum*, copied by Lechaudé d'Anisy. These are not Mont-Saint-Michel charters but they were of interest to the monks for their relation to Cartulary, no. **57**: '*au dernier folio se trouve deux chartes de donation faite a l'eglise d'Aletense* [Saint-Malo]': *c.* 1090–1110/11.

[no. 19] Notum sit tam futuris quam presenti generationi hanc scripturam legenti vel audienti. Robertum filium Bresel de Morhenno pro salute anime sue et filii sui Hingandi atque uxoris sue E. et omnium parentum suorum in elemosinam perpetuam Beato Petro Alete atque ejus episcopo nomine Benedicto qui tunc ecclesiam Aletensem regebat, ejusque episcopis successoribus dedisse quadam terram juxta prefate urbis portam sanctique Servacii cimiterium sitam qum hereditario jure a vicario nomine Wigono libere tenebat. Eo videlicet tenore ut ipse ipsiusque successores omnium supradicte ecclesie beneficiorum in perpetuum particeps permaneat cunctis que episcopatus illius ecclesiarum dedicationibus ejus memoria perennis fiat et quando ad finem pervenerit ejus corpus pro ... (corpus) pro alterius crimine inumatum non existat quod ne tempporum [*sic*] prolixitate seu successorum liuore corrumpi ualeat scripti memorie commendauimus. Hujus rei sunt testes ipse Benedictus episcopus qui de manu Roberti hanc elemosinam suscepit fratresque ipsius Eudo uidelicet monachus et Wihenocus Boistardus presbiter, Euenus presbiter de Dinam, Symon et Lucas capellani Hamo presbiter de Ploermo. Willelmus de Molbraio Judicael Taluayn Tanel medicus. Vt igitur hoc donum inconuulsum magisque et firmatum existat, ipse Robertus ejusque filius Hingandus hic signa manibus propriis fecerunt. + Signum Roberti. Signum Hingandi quicumque itaque hanc elemosinam infringere vel auferre predicte ecclesie temptaverit a liminibus sancte Dei ecclesie separatus sit; nisi ad emendationem canonicam venerit.

[there follows an act in the MS now illegible because of the binding]
'*au revers du folio 114 se trouve la copie de la charte suivante:*'

[no. 20] [1098] Notum sit tam presentibus quam futuris hominibus quam emendationem fuerit Guegonis vicarius Herbrandi filius super infractura ecclesia beati Peteri Aletensis quam in diebus sancte quadragesime infra ipsam ecclesiam facere presumptis anno ab incarnationis Domini Jesu MXCVIIJ cum itaque in subsequenturi etate divino judicio gravi plaga in capite [...] vulneratus et nori inde timens votans et obn ... per nuncios deprecans presulem prefate ecclesie Benedicti nomine qui tunc forte apud Sanctum Maclovium de Insula morabatur ut ad se visitandum veniret et super tanti sacrilegii crimine quod in Deum et in predictam ecclesiam exercuerat emendationem suam reciperet. Cum in primis venire contempnerat tandem ad eum venit. Plorans igitur peccatum suum ab eo et a presbiteris secum astantibus confessionem canonicum suscepit sub ea conditione ut omnia que in predicta ecclesia rapuerat et pauperibus abstulerat in proximo redderet et anima non ferret nisi cum consilio et licentia episcopi. Concessit enim totam terram liberam absque aliqua calumpnia in perpetuum quam prius dederat Rotbertus Breseli filius in elemosinam episcopo Benedicto et omnibus successoribus sibi episcopis. Iuuesticus episcopum de hoc per virgam ejus pastoralem Preter hoc etiam dedit ipse Guegonus et frater ejus Haimo ecclesie S Petro et episcopis ejus in elemosinam perpetuam duas partes omnes prefate terre quas in manu sua tenebant. Dedit quoque episcopo in elemosinam ipse Guegonus duas partes decime carruce sue. Concessit etiam fieri cymiterium de una corda juxta ecclesiam in terra sua.

Super his itaque omnibus sunt hii testes. Benedictus episcopus qui hoc donum suscepit. Walterius monachus ... Rotbertus clericus episcopi filius Johannis Hingant. Hugo presbiter. Guillelmus presbiter. Menfinnec presbiter. Anschetil presbiter. Kemmarrochus presbiter. Hingant presbiter. Blou Bastardus. Guillelmus filius Jungomani. Languevinus filius Kemmaroci. Lungumarus filius Halanaii . Berhauch prepositus. Lungomarus filius Eveni. Paganus filius Konaudi. Mat ... et uxor ejus. Euenus filius Judicael. Guillelmus ... quicumque qui hoc donum abstulerit ...[*le surplus est coupé par le reliur du ms*].

III. NOTES ON PERSONS OCCURRING IN THE CARTULARY

The following notes are not intended to cover all people occurring in the charters of the Cartulary, or to be exhaustive about those they do concern. The intention is primarily to offer information that will add to an appreciation of the charters, especially where this helps to elucidate the complex links between these people, which are rarely made explicit in the charters themselves. Further information may be found in K. S. B. Keats-Rohan, *Domesday People: A Prosopography of Persons Occurring in English Documents 1066–1166 I, Domesday Book*, Woodbridge, 1999, and *Domesday Descendants: ... II, Pipe Rolls to Cartae Baronum*, Woodbridge, 2002, and L. C. Loyd, *The Origins of Some Anglo-Norman Families*, Harleian Society Publications vol. 103 (Leeds, 1951), hereafter abbreviated to *Dom. People*, *Dom. Desc.* and Loyd, respectively. Most references in the Notes are to works cited in full in the Bibliography. The principal abbreviations used here are: Ord. Vit., reference to Orderic Vitalis, *Ecclesiastical History*, ed. M. Chibnall, and Delisle, *Torigni*, reference to L. Delisle's edition of the *Chronicle of Robert of Torigny...*, both cited in the Bibliography, *MSHAB*, *Mémoires de la Société d'Histoire et d'Archéologie de Bretagne*, and *Les évêques*, *Les évêques normandes du XIe siècle*, ed. P. Bouet and F. Neveux (Caen, 1995).

Regular reference is made to a number of manuscript sources from Mont-Saint-Michel. These are:

1. The Register of Robert of Torigny is the text that begins on the verso left blank at the end of the Cartulary, Avranches 210, fol. 112v. It was printed by Delisle in the second volume of his edition of Robert's Chronicle. Reference here is to Delisle's edition.
2. The Inventory, made in 1326, is a list of the abbey muniments found in Bib. mun. Avranches 211. See Introduction, pp. 40–43, and Table 1.
3. The Mont had two principal necrologies in its Chapter Book, now Bib. mun. Avranches 214. These are the Necrology (Avranches 214, part II, pp. 109–199, for monks and laymen in confraternity with Mont-Saint-Michel) and the Martyrology-Necrology (Avranches 214, part 1, pp. 6–196, for professed monks of the Mont, plus certain select others). References here to these texts are in summary form. An edition of both is being prepared for publication in a separate volume, where full commentary will be provided. There was also an Obituary, a fifteenth-century text now part of Avranches 215. The entries in this are fuller than in the necrologies and so they are sometimes cited in these Notes in preference to the summary entries in the necrologies. For an overview of all three texts see K. S. B. Keats-Rohan, 'Testimonies of The Living Dead: The Necrology and Martyrology-Necrology in the Chapter Book of Mont-Saint-Michel, Avranches Bibliothèque Municipale, MS 214', in *The Durham Liber Vitae*, ed. D. and L. Rollason, M. Harvey and A. Piper (2004).

Additional Sources cited in abbreviated form

Cartulaire dunois de Marmoutier, ed. Mabille, Châteaudun 1874

Cartulaire manceau de Marmoutier, ed. E. Laurain, Laval 1911

Cartulaire de l'abbaye de Saint-Denis de Nogent-le-Rotrou, ed. abbé Métais, Vannes 1895

Cartulaire de Saint-Père de Chartres, ed. B. Guérard, Paris 1840

Cartulaires de l'abbaye Saint-Serge et Saint-Bach d'Angers, ed. Y. Chauvin, 2 vols, Angers 1997

Chartes du prieuré de la Sainte-Trinité de Fougères, A. de La Borderie and Delabigne Villeneuve, *Bull. arch. de l'assoc. bretonne*, 1851, 178–99, 236–50

Cartulaire de l'abbaye de la Sainte-Trinité de Tiron, ed. L. Merlet, Chartres 1883

Vital l'Ermite prédicateur ... fondateur de l'abbaye normande de Savigny, J. van Moolenbroek, Revue de l'Avranchin 68 (1991), pp. 257–322, Éditions de textes

Heads of Religious Houses in England and Wales, 940–1216, The, D. Knowles, C. N. L. Brooke and V. London, Cambridge, 1972

Complete Peerage, new edn. by V. Gibbs, H. A. Doubleday, H. H. White and Lord Howard of Walden, 13 vols, London 1910–1959

Histoire Féodale des Marais, Territoire et Église de Dol. Enquête par Tourbe, ordonnée par Henri II, roi d'Angleterre, ed. Jean Allenou, Paris 1917

Dictionnaire historique, topographique et biographique de la Mayenne, A. Angot, 4. vols., Laval 1900–1909.

[1]

The *Historia* is a composite of two different texts. It was re-used as the introduction to the later, now lost, cartulary of Pierre Le Roy. The older text, *Revelatio*, was used as a lectionary for the feast of the Dedication of St Michael's Basilica on 16 October and therefore survives in numerous copies, including a tenth-century copy now part of MS Avranches 211. A critical edition is being prepared by Pierre Bouet, who has suggested that the text was written *c.* 820. See Pierre Bouet, 'La *Reuelatio* et les origines du culte à Saint Michel sur le Mont Tombe', forthcoming in F. Bougard, ed., *Culte et pèlerinages à saint Michel en Occident. Les trois Monts dédiés à l'archange* (2003). The second text in the *Historia* is part of a longer compilation of texts written in the eleventh century. Like all Norman historiography of the time, it followed the account of early Norman history provided by Dudo of St Quentin in his *De moribus et actis primorum Normanniae ducum* (ed. Jules Lair, Caen, 1865). [An important surviving manuscript of Dudo's work, now Berlin, Deutsche Staatsbibliothek 1854, was written in the mid-eleventh century at Mont-Saint-Michel for use at Fécamp.] A portion describing how hidden relics of St Aubert were found and translated to the abbey church, and subsequent miracles associated with them, is omitted. The second work contains a forged bull of John XIII with a forged diploma of King Lothar. The importance of these texts in establishing a history of Mont-Saint-Michel is considerable, but they cannot be taken at face value. The very complex issues raised by these texts (especially the Lothar diploma) have been treated in outline in the Introduction, section II.b. Further discussion will appear in a separate book currently in preparation, which will contain editions of the abbey necrologies.

Richard I of Normandy succeeded his father William I Longsword after the latter's assassination in 942. He survived a troubled minority and lived until 996. A shadowy figure of whom little is known, though he presided over the initial stage of the a major revival of the Norman Church and founded the collegiate church of Sainte-Trinité at Fécamp in 990 (replaced by a community of monks in 1001). His first marriage to Emma, daughter of

Hugh of Paris, was childless. Father by his Scandinavian second wife Gunnor of his successor Richard II, Robert, archbishop of Rouen (989–1037), Hadvisa, wife of Count Geoffrey of Brittany, and Emma, wife of Æthelred II and Cnut, kings of England. He was also father of natural sons Robert, count of Avranches (nos. **31** and **60**), William, count of Eu, and Godfrey, count of Brionne. Remembered as *Richardus primus dux Normannorum* in the abbey Martyrology-Necrology on 21 November.

Lothar, son of Louis IV Outremer, king of Francia from 954 until 985.

John XIII, pope from 1 October 965 until 6 September 972. John XII (16 December 955–14 May 964) was originally named Octavian.

[2–3]

Richard II (996–1026) of Normandy, son of Richard I and Gunnor, was remembered for no. **2** in the abbey's Obituary, MS Avranches 215, fol. 168r, on 23 July: *Obiit Ricardus II comes Norm- qui dona aui patris et matris suorum huic monasterio facta confirmauit ac insuper baronias de Sancto Paterno donauit de Ardeuone et de Geneceyo.* References to 'grants' by William I Longsword of Normandy should not be taken at face value. Such 'grants' are normally the means by which ancient, usually pre-Norman, property was restored to the Carolingian abbeys of Normandy. The same is true here of Richard I, since there are no traces of authentic grants by Richard I. Richard II's influence at the abbey was real and important. According to the chronicler William of Jumièges (ed. Houts, ii, pp. 28–9), he had married his wife, Judith of Rennes, there shortly before 1000. After his father-in-law Geoffrey's death in 1009, when his sister became regent for her son Alan III, Richard marked the new influence of his family in the region by forcing the retirement of Abbot Mainard II, on grounds of age (no. **52**). He suggested that the monks elect in his place Hildebert, a virtuous monk, 'in the flower of youth', known to him personally. As no. **2** shows, Abbot Hildebert I's (1009–1017) father Bernard was a landholder in the Cotentin. (no. **115** shows that this property was lost in the time of William the Conqueror.) The earliest annals of the abbey (London, BL Royal 13 A xxiii, fol. 96r, edited here as **Appendix i.1a**) do not mention any Norman ruler before Richard II in connexion with the abbey. Of Richard it is noted that he patronized the rebuilding of the abbey in collaboration with Hildebert II, who died in 1023. The entry describes the re-building as begun – *inchoatum* – in 1023, but it clearly refers to a longer process of collaboration between Richard (who abdicated in 1025 and died in 1026) and Hildebert II, probably starting with the latter's accession in 1017, soon after Richard's mother Gunnor had become an important benefactor of the abbey (no. **3**). This charter and the next were attested by Richard's eldest son and initial successor Richard III, whose early death shortly after his succession is usually attributed to his brother and successor Robert (see no. **5**), whose sign follows his in the witness list. No. **3** was given after the death of Richard II's first wife Judith in 1017 and is attested by his second wife Papia mother of Mauger, archbishop of Rouen, and two daughters who married respectively Gilbert d'Auffay and Ranulf fitz Ansquetil, *vicomte* of Bayeux (no. 7) (Orderic Vitalis, iii, 86, 252; *Torigni*, i, p. 34). Papia's brothers Osbern and 'Hunfred' attest no. **2**. Two charters of Richard II show that Osbern and his brother Anfred, probably the same as 'Hunfredus', became monks of Saint-Wandrille before Richard's retirement in 1026 (Fauroux, 46 and 46 *bis*). Richard was remembered in the abbey's Martyrology-Necrology, Avranches 214, part 1, p. 116, on 6 August: *Richardus comes tercius Normannorum.*

Robert, archbishop of Rouen (989–1037), son of Richard I and Gunnor, combined his ecclesiastical career with that of a layman. As count of Evreux he married a woman named Herlève and had issue three sons, Richard, later count of Evreux, Ralph and William (Ord. Vit. iii, 84). He was remembered on 16 March in the Martyrology-Necrology.

The count Robert who usurped abbey property in the Avranchin (the alleged grants of William Longsword) was Robert, count of Avranches, donor of no. **31**, an illegitimate son of Richard I.

Hugh, bishop of Bayeux (d. 1049) was son of Count Ralph d'Ivry and brother or half-brother of John, bishop of Avranches (later archbishop of Rouen). He was the son of Ralph's first marriage to Eremburga (Robert of Torigny, interpolation in *William of Jumièges*, ii, 174 and note). His sister Emma married Osbern son of Herfast, a nephew of Countess Gunnor, and was mother of William fitz Osbern (k. 1071), an intimate of William II of Normandy whom he accompanied to England in 1066. Osbern attested no. **2** and William attested nos. **43** and **11**. Hugh's considerable property eventually passed to the issue of his two sisters, with some, according to Orderic Vitalis, going to his daughter Albreda, wife of Albert de Cravant (Ord. Vit., iii, 122, 244), and her heirs the Lovels of Ivry. See Véronique Gazeau, 'Le patrimoine d'Hugues de Bayeux (c. 1011–1049), in *Les évêques normandes du XIe siècle* (Caen, 1995), pp. 139–47.

Maugis was appointed bishop of Avranches in 1022, filling a vacancy that had existed since his predecessor Norgod become a monk of the abbey in 1017. His name is invariably written *Mangisus* in Mont documents. He was remembered in the Martyrology-Necrology, p. 122, on 17 August, and in the later Obituary, fol. 167v.

Niel I *uicecomes*, lord of Saint-Sauveur, attested nos. **5** and **10**; his son Niel II attested nos. **5** and **43**.

Turstin *uicecomes* was ancestor of the vicomtes of Avranches, earls of Chester. Lucien Musset, 'Les origines et le patrimoine de l'abbaye de Saint-Sever', in *La Normandie bénédictine au temps du Guillaume le Conquérant*, ed. J. Daoust (Lille, 1967), pp. 357–367; Keats-Rohan, in *Medieval Prosopography* 14.1 (1992), 23–30. He also attested nos. **5** and **8**. Turstin was *vicomte* of the Hiémois before his temporary disgrace in 1046, when he permitted Henry I of France to enter Normandy. In one of a series of acts intended to increase ducal authority in western Normandy, following the revolts of the western *vicomtes* in 1046, William of Normandy gave one of his kinswomen in marriage to Turstin's son Richard Goz, *vicomte* of the Avranchin (no. 70), and thus Hugh of Avranches (no. 74), later earl of Chester, was a kinsman of William the Conqueror.

[4]

The witnesses were: Robert, archbishop of Rouen (989–1037), Hugh, bishop of Coutances (c. 989–1025), Hugh, bishop of Sées (*ante c.* 1017), Roger, bishop of Lisieux (c. 985–1021), Norgod, bishop of Avranches (990–1022), Abbot Hildebert of Mont-Saint-Michel, (1009–1017), Abbot William [de Volpiano] of Fécamp (1001–1031), Abbot Robert Uspac of Jumièges (1000–1015). For Count Robert, see no. **31** below. Gunnor's charter was subsequently confirmed by her son Richard II between 1022 and 1026 (no. **2**). She was remembered for both charters in the abbey Martyrology-Necrology, as well as in the later Obituary, Avranches 215, fol. 159r, vi Id. Jan. (8 January): *Obiit Gonnor comitissa Norm- qui nobis dedit Breteuillam et Domnum Iohannem et firmari fecit.* Both Bretteville and Domjean became priories of the abbey. Although they had lost this status by the mid-fourteenth century (Dubois, 'Dépendances', *Mill. mon.*, i, 638), the Inventory of 1326 listed the muniments of Bretteville on fol. 133v; those of Domjean followed on fol. 134v.

Roger of Lisieux is mentioned as a man of great virtue by Orderic Vitalis (ii, 26). Hugh, bishop of Sées is otherwise unknown. Norgod of Avranches became a monk of Mont-Saint-Michel in 1017. He was remembered in the Martyrology-Necrology on 14 October: *Norgodus episcopus Abrincatensis et postea monachus huius loci.* Pierre Bouet and Monique Dosdat, 'Les évêques normandes de 985 à 1150', in *Les évêques normands du XIe siècle* (Caen, 1995), pp. 19–37. The *vicomte* Ansquetil was probably Ansquetil of Bayeux, whose son Ranulf occurs in no. 7.

[5]

Robert I of Normandy, son of Richard II and Judith, succeeded his elder brother Richard III in 1027. He died at Nicaea during a pilgrimage in 1035, leaving his seven-year-old son William II as his heir. He was remembered in the Martyrology-Necrology on 2 July (Avranches 214, part 1, p. 97): *Robertus dux Normannorum quartus.*

Niel I *vicomte*, son of Roger, was *vicomte* of the Cotentin and seigneur of Saint-Sauveur-le-Vicomte (Manche). His son Niel II (also nos. **6** and **43**) was disgraced in 1047 for his part in the revolt against William II and briefly fled to Brittany (Jumièges, i, 120; Ord. Vit. iv, 82). He reappears *c.* 1060, though he was never influential thereafter. By his wife Adela, sister of Richard, William and Baldwin I de Reviers (Fauroux, *Recueil*, no. 147) and a relative of William de Vernon, he was father of Niel, Roger, and two sons named William. Their three daughters were named Emma, Bilelda (Bilihildis) and Matilda (Delisle, *Saint-Sauveur*, *pièces just.*, no. 31, pp. 34–5). The name

Bilelda/Bilihildis perhaps originated in a marriage between her grandfather Niel I and a daughter of Robert count of Avranches and his first wife Bilihild. Cf. L. Delisle, *Histoire de Saint-Sauveur-le-Vicomte*, Valognes, 1867; K. S. B. Keats-Rohan, 'Aspects of the genealogies of Robert of Torigny revisited', *Nottingham Medieval Studies* 1993, and 'Les Bilihildis du Maine', in *Onomastique et Parenté*; cf. Robert Bearman, *Charters of the Redvers Family and the Earldom of Devon 1090–1217*, Devon and Cornwall Record Society, new series, vol. 37, Exeter, 1994, 1–5.

Aimo or Haimo *vicecomes* was Haimo Dentatus, lord of Torigny-sur-Vire, Manche; see no **8**.

The *vicomte* Geoffrey Farsels is probably the same Geoffrey who attests nos. 7 and **8**. He also attested a shorter version of this charter, **Appendix ii.3** (Fauroux, 65). The Hugo *vicecomes* who attested this charter was probably the Hugo *vicecomes filius Turstingi* who attested **App. ii.3**. He was probably the Hugo de Montfort, son of Turstin de Bastembourg, who was killed *c.* 1040. Another of Turstin's sons, better known as William Bertram, attested **App. ii.3**. Hugh's son attested a charter of 1055 as *Hugonis vicecomitis de Monteforti* (Fauroux, 137).

[6]

The family of Ranulf the Moneyer, to whom Abbot Suppo alienated the count's mill at Vains, is discussed in *Complete Peerage* xii, p. 272. See also Lucien Musset, 'A-t-il existé en Normandie au XIe siècle une aristocratie d'argent?', *Annales de Normandie*, ix (1959). Ranulf had four sons, Waleran, Osbern, Richard and Conan. Waleran and his nephew John son of Richard, who made the claim on the mill described in the charter, both acquired minor tenancies-in-chief in Essex after the conquest of England in 1066. Waleran had died before *c.* 1086 and been succeeded by his son John. *Dom. People*, pp. 283–4, 446.

John, bishop of Avranches, was son of Ralph d'Ivry and Albreda and hence half-brother of Hugh, bishop of Bayeux, and nephew of Richard I of Normandy. Bishop of Avranches from 1060 to 1067, he became archbishop of Rouen in 1067, dying on 9 September 1079, when he was remembered in the abbey's Martyrology-Necrology, Avranches 214, part 1, p. 136. Author of *De officiis ecclesiasticis*, ed. R. Delamare, Paris 1923. The *factum* of 1061 by which Abbot Ranulf recognized the rights of the bishop of Avranches and the canons on the Mont is printed in **Appendix ii.5**.

Hugh, bishop of Lisieux (1049–77), son of William, count of Eu and Lesceline, brother of Robert, count of Eu. His death in July 1077 and his burial in his mother's foundation at Saint-Pierre-sur-Dives is described by Orderic Vitalis (iii, 14–20).

Robert Bertram, son of William Bertram (**Appendix ii.3**) and grandson of Turstin de Bastembourg, seigneur of Bricquebec, Calvados; occurs *c.* 1060 with his wife Susanna in a grant to Saint-Ouen de Rouen (Fauroux, 205). Cf. G. Saige, *Cartulaire de l'abbaye de Fontenay le Marmion*, Monaco 1885.

Richard *vicecomes* of the Avranchin was son of Turstin Goz, *vicomte* of the Hiémois (nos. **2**, **4**). He was father of Hugh d'Avranches, earl of Chester from 1069–1101 (no. **74**). L. Musset, 'Actes Inédits du xie Siècle, I: Les plus anciennes Chartes du Prieuré de Saint-Gabriel (Calvados)', *Bulletin de la Société des Antiquaires de Normandie* 52 (1952–54), 124–29; Keats-Rohan, 'Prosopography of Post-Conquest England', 23–30.

Geoffrey, bishop of Coutances (1049–1093), from Montbrai, Manche, arr. Saint-Lô. According to Orderic Vitalis (ii, 266), Robert de Mowbray, earl of Northumberland, was his nephew; he was probaby therefore a brother of the Roger de Mowbray mentioned as a prominent layman by Orderic (iv, 278). According to the *De Statu*, a source produced at Coutances in the early twelfth century, he had a brother Malger, and was a relative of Niel de Saint-Sauveur, vicomte of the Cotentin (*Gall. Christ.* xi, Inst., cols. 218–19, 222). Malger bought the bishopric for his brother, leading to an accusation of simony against Geoffrey at the Council of Reims in 1049. In the end, Pope Leo IX accepted the validity of Geoffrey's consecration. He fought at the battle of Hastings, and thereafter acquired extensive estates in England, especially in the south and west. He pursued a cross-Channel career, which saw him effective in English administration whilst rebuilding both his cathedral and the organisation of his Norman see. He died at Coutances on 2 February 1093. See J. Le Patourel, 'Geoffrey of Montbray, Bishop of Coutances, 1049–1093', *EHR* 59 (1944).

Ranulf *vicecomes* was the Ranulf son of Ansquetil of no. 7, *vicomte* of Bayeux. He married a daughter of Richard II (or III, according to Robert of Torigny, Delisle, *Torigni*, i, p. 34) of Normandy, by whom he had issue a son Ranulf. The younger Ranulf married a daughter of Richard fitz Turstin, *vicomte* of Avranches; their son Ranulf (no. 77) succeeded his cousin Richard as earl of Chester in 1120. See *Complete Peerage* iii, pp. 164–70.

Niel fitz Niel was Niel II of the Cotentin (no. **5**).

Robert de Vieuxpont (Eure) attested other charters of William the Conqueror (Bates, *RRAN*, nos. 29(II) and 264). He is mentioned by Orderic Vitalis (ii, p. 308) as a 'brave veteran' sent by William to the aid of John de La Flèche in Maine *c.* 1077/81.

Ralph the chamberlain, father of Ralph and William de Tancarville (nos. **16**, **108**), attested charters throughout William's reign. He first occurs as William's tutor in a charter of *c.* 1050 confirming his endowment of the priory of Saint-Georges de Boscherville (Fauroux, 197). He occurs in Caen charters as a fee-holder near Caen, and as lord of Mirville in a charter of Jumièges (Bates, *RRAN*, nos. 59, 164.

[7]

This act was written onto the parchment containing a grant of Robert I of Normandy (no. **5**). William II of Normandy succeeded his father Robert in 1035 as a minor. King of England from 1066 until his death in 1087, he was father of William II and Henry I of England and Robert II of Normandy. He was remembered simply in the abbey Martyrology-Necrology, MS Avranches 214, p. 136, on 9 September: *Guillelmus rex Anglorum. et dux Normannorum.* Depredations of abbey property ascribed to William are listed in no. **115**.

Ranulf fitz Ansquetil, *vicomte* of Bayeux: see no. **6**.

Hatuuardus rex is William's cousin Edward the Confessor, king of England from 1042 to 1066. He was donor, before his accession, of no. **10**.

Roger (de Beaumont), son of Humphrey de Vielles also attested no. **9**: q.v. Humphrey and his son were *vicomtes* at Rouen; founders and benefactors of two abbeys at Préaux.

Geoffrey *vicomte*, probably the Geoffrey Farsels who attested no. **5**. Also attests no. **8**.

[8]

Ralph and his brother Erneis were members of the Taisson family from Anjou, founders of the abbey of Fontenay. They occur together as witnesses to Robert I's charter, **Appendix ii.3**. Jordan Taisson attested **Appendix i.5** in 1142. See *Gallia Christiana* xi, Inst. cols. 63–4.

Mauger, archbishop of Rouen from 1037 until 1055, son of Richard II and his second wife Papia. Educated at the abbey of Fécamp and a noted biblical exegete, he proved an unsatisfactory archbishop, given to despoiling his church. He was deeply implicated in the revolt of 1046–7 against William II of Normandy. A controversial career was ended by his deposition at the council of Lisieux in 1055. Pierre Bouet and Monique Dosdat, 'Les évêques normandes de 985 à 1150', in *Les évêques normands du XIe siècle* (Caen, 1995), pp. 19–20.

Gilbert Crispin was castellan of Tillières in the Norman Vexin. See *Miraculum de nobili genere Crispinorum*, ed. J.-P. Migne, PL 150, cols. 735–744. This gives the sons of Gilbert I Crispin as Gilbert II, William I (d. 1074), and Robert, who died in Constantinople *c.* 1072 (col. 738). The family were major benefactors of the abbey of Bec.

Haimo *uicecomes* (also no. **5**) was Haimo Dentatus, lord of Torigny-sur-Vire, Manche (Wace, *Roman de Rou*, ed. H. Andresen, 2 vols. Heilbronn, 1877–79, 2: 192). He was killed fighting for the rebels at Val-ès-Dunes in 1047, for which his family lost control of Torigny. His son and grandson, Haimo and Robert fitz Haimo, became landholders in Kent after 1066: *Dom. People*, p. 242; *Dom. Desc.*, pp. 902–3.

The benefice of Hugh Paisfolet at Saint-Marcouf (Manche, cant. Montebourg) is mentioned *c.* 1082 (Fauroux, no. 234). An Osbern Paisforer was later found among the tenants of Bishop Odo of Bayeux in Kent; *Dom. People*, p. 317.

Guy, son of Count Rainald, was a nephew of Robert I of Normandy and cousin of William. Younger son of Rainald, count of Burgundy and Adeliz, daughter of Richard II of Normandy, he had been educated with the young William and other noble boys, including Roger de Beaumont, Roger de Montgomery and William fitz Osbern. He did not share their conspicuous and lifelong loyalty to William and revolted against him in 1047, for which he lost his Norman possessions. In an act of 1075 his mother gave the castle of *Homme* (now L'Isle-Marie) in the Cotentin to the abbey of Caen, relating that she had bought it from her brother Robert I but it had been unjustly usurped by Guy, who gave it to Niel, *vicomte* of the Cotentin (*Actes caennaises*, no. 21). His niece Sibil, daughter of his elder brother, William Tête-Hardi, count of Burgundy (d. 1087), married Eudes Borel, duke of Burgundy (d. 1102). Their granddaughter Clemence of Ponthieu was wife of Juhel I de Mayenne (see no. **38**), whose sister Matilda-Felicia was wife of their son, Hugh II, duke of Burgundy (d. 1143). William Tête-Hardi was father of Guy de Vienne, who became Pope Calixtus II in 1124. Ord. Vit. vi, 210.

[9]

William Pichenot was father of Richard Pichenot, as appears from the latter's attestation of a Troarn charter of 1109 (B. N. lat. 10086, fol. 84). There is a hamlet called Le Piquenot to the north-west of Pontaubault. A claim was later made against the tithe of Perrelle in Guernsey by William priest of Ivetot, his brother Alan and Alan's son Richard, the subject of an accord in 1157 (Delisle, *Torigni*, no. IV, pp. 263–4). A Rainald Pichenot occurs in no. **115**.

William of Normandy's confirmation was attested by the most senior men in Normandy. Archbishop Malger of Rouen (no. **8**) was the son of Richard II of Normandy and his second wife Papia, and nephew of his predecessor, Robert, as archbishop.

Roger de Bellomonte (Beaumont-le-Roger, Eure), was a son of Humphrey de Vielles. Around 1050 he was *vicomte* of Rouen. He married Adelina, sister and heiress of Hugh, count of Meulan. He became a monk at the abbey of Préaux, founded by his father, in 1094, when his heir in his extensive holdings in Normany, France and England was his son Robert, count of Meulan, first earl of Leicester. Father also of Henry, first earl of Warwick, and Albreda, abbess of Saint-Léger de Préaux. See *Complete Peerage* vii, 522ff and xii pt. 2, 357ff.

Roger de Montgomery was one of the duke's closest confidantes. His daughter Matilda was the first wife of William's brother, Robert count of Mortain (nos. **12**, **15**). *Dom. Peop.*, p. 399.

The family of Ralph de Saint-John reappears in nos. **16** and **87**. Ralph occurs in nos. **67**, **70**, **73**.

Ilger of Ardevon, brother of Tescelin, is to be identified with the Hilger who appears in no. **115**, a record of the property usurped by abbey tenants and servants in the late eleventh century. The monks complained that his son Ralph treated the usurpations as his heritance. Ilger, operative in the time of abbots Rannulf and Roger (*c.* 1060–1106), was particularly rapacious. He was the abbey servant who attested nos. **12** and **79** as *Ilger prepositus*, an office he evidently abused.

Rainald de Granville: cf. no. **16**.

[10]

The charter has been thoroughly discussed by Simon Keynes, 'The Æthelings in Normandy', *Anglo-Norman Studies* xiii (1991), 190–4, who shows that the charter is genuine, despite its apparent improbabilities, and suggests identifications for the places mentioned. During the reign of his half-brother Harthacanute Edward was in exile at the court of Robert I of Normandy, where he was recognized as the rightful king of England. See also E. van Houts, 'The political relations between Normandy and England according to the *Gesta Normannorum Ducum*', in *Les Mutations socio-culturelles au tournant des XIe–XIIe siècles. Etudes Anselmiennes (IV session)* (1984), ed. Raymonde Foreville, pp. 85–98.

Rabel attested a number of Robert I's charters (Fauroux nos. 65, 69 and 76); one of his officers (*ibid.*, p. 61), perhaps head of the fleet sent to attack Brittany in 1033 (Ord. Vit., in William of Jumièges, ii, p. 78).

[11–12]

Robert, count of Mortain, was son of Herluin de Conteville and his wife Herlève, mother by a previous alliance of William the Conqueror. He was twice married. His first wife Matilda, daughter of Roger de Montgomery, died *c.* 1082. His second wife Almodis survived him at his death in 1094. She was probably a kinswoman of Robert's son-in-law William de Toulouse. None of Robert's children by Almodis appear to have survived childhood. His heir was the son of his first marriage, William, who forfeited his honour for his support of Robert II of Normandy against Henry I of England at Tinchebray in 1106. He also left three daughters by his first wife, Agnes, wife of André I de Vitré, Denise, wife of Guy III of Laval, and Emma, wife of Count William of Toulouse. Robert died *c.* 1094/5. A count Robert was remembered in the Necrology on 6 November; Robert of Mortain was remembered at Mortain Abbey on 8 December (*Rec. Hist. Gaule. Fr.*, t. 23, p. 583). See K. S. B. Keats-Rohan, 'The prosopography of post-Conquest England: four case studies', *Medieval Prosopography* 14.1 (1993), 30–46; B. Golding, 'Robert of Mortain', *Anglo-Norman Studies*, xiii (1991), 119–144. J. Pouëssel, 'Les structures militaires du comté de Mortain xi et xii siècles', *Revue de l'Avranchin*, lviii (1981), 11–74, 81–156. Robert acquired his dominant position in Cornwall and the south-west only after the withdrawal from England in 1069 of the Breton Count Brien, brother of Count Alan Rufus, cousins and close allies of William the Conqueror in 1066 (*Dom. People*, p. 48). In his detailed discussion of no. **11**, a forgery, David Bates (*RRAN*, no. 213) suggests that it is underpinned with the substance of a genuine grant, which he dates to *c.* 1070, regarding the grantor as more likely to have been Robert of Mortain than his predecessor in Cornwall, Count Brien. However, it is noteworthy that the monks remembered in their Martyrology-Necrology, on 14 February, a Count Brien who can only be Robert's predecessor in Cornwall. Brien will certainly have been accepted into confraternity by the monks but no record survives of the donation that he will have made in return. The fourteenth-century *Cartulary of St Michael's Mount* (ed. P. Hull, no. 5), which claims a version of Robert's part of this charter as the foundation charter, includes a grant by Alan III of Richmond of rent from the fair of Merther Sithny for the soul of his uncle Count Brien.

Ranulf Avenel of Les Biards was mentioned as a benefactor of the abbey in a charter of his son (no. **76**).

Robert's tenant Turstin was his sheriff in Cornwall in 1086 (*Dom. People*, p. 435). Warin, ancestor of the Eytons, was a tenant of Robert's father-in-law Roger of Montgomery in 1086 (*Dom. People*, p. 461).

Richard fitz Turold was a tenant of Robert of Mortain in Cornwall and elsewhere in 1086 (*Dom. People*, pp. 364–5). Ancestor of the Cardinham family. See I. N. Soulsby, 'Richard fitz Turold, lord of Penhallam in Cornwall', *Medieval Archaeology* 20 (1976).

[13]

See further in the register of Robert of Torigny, printed in Delisle, *Torigni*, ii, nos. XXXVII, LVII.

[14]

At least three women named Asa occur in the abbey's necrology, MS Avranches 214, two of them together on p. 113, *xii kal Feb.* (21 January), and p. 183, *iiii kal. Nov.* (29 October).

[15]

The family of Chambernon later established itself in Devon as tenants of the Tracy lords of Totnes (cf. **App. ii.7**), the lords of Okehampton (descendants of Robert fitz William of Avranches, nos. **16**, **71**, **72**), and the earls of Gloucester. Loyd 26; *Dom. Desc.* pp. 377–8.

[16]

Thomas de Saint-Jean-le-Thomas, son of Ralph, and his brothers Roger and John, were favourites of Henry I of England, who established them on lands in Oxfordshire. Thomas of St John died without issue before 1129 and was succeeded by his brother Roger. Roger's son Robert appears among the knights of Mont-Saint-Michel in 1154. See *Complete Peerage* xi, pp. 340ff. John died between 1149 and 1153 and was remembered as a benefactor of the abbey in the Obituary, Avranches 215, fol. 170r, vi Id. Oct. (10 October): *Obiit Iohannes de Sancto Iohanne...*

Roger II, monk of Jumièges, appointed abbot by Henry I in 1106. Under pressure from Henry, he resigned on 16 October 1123, returning to Jumièges where he died on 2 April 1124. The charter text gives him a nephew, or other kinsman (*nepos*), Ralph de Port.

Richard de Méré, a Cluniac monk, was appointed by Henry I to succeed Roger II as abbot after the latter's resignation in October 1123. His abbatiate was a disaster since he set out to exploit the wealth of the abbey to his own advantage. The monks eventually complained to Henry I, around 1128. Richard was deposed at a meeting at Domfront by the papal legate Matthew bishop of Albano and relegated to his monastery of Saint Pancras of Lewes (Dufief, 'La vie monastique..', *Mill. mon.* i, pp. 91–2). Richard was probably a member of the Bohun family, from Saint-Georges de Bohun in the Cotentin. A branch of this family was established in Sussex in the early twelfth century by the marriage of Muriel, daughter of Richard de Méré, son of Humphrey de Bohun (*Dom. People*, pp. 359–60, *Dom. Desc.*, p. 331).

Ralph Malregard, mentioned here as having mortgaged land to Ralph de Port, a kinsman (*nepos*) of Abbot Roger II, when he went to Apulia, was possibly the son of the Ralph Malregard who attested no. **67** in 1086.

Some of the depredations restored in this accord are mentioned in no. **115**, headed *De perditis huius ecclesie*, where, amongst other things, Thomas is stated to have usurped the land of William de Granville (probably father of the Roger de Granville mentioned in this charter; cf. Rainald de Granville, who attested no. **9**), Robert fitz Ivo, Thomas de Lezeaux and a manse of Dublell the forester. Roger of Saint-John is there given as usurper of the land of Rainald *coquus*. Thomas is also mentioned as withholding rent of 20 *solidi* his father Ralph had owed on a moiety of Saint-Jean, which had been the prebend of Lambert *aurifaber*.

Robert de La Haye-du-Puits (d. *c.* 1150) was lord of Halnaker, Sussex. *Dom. Desc.* pp. 496–7. Founder of Boxgrove priory.

William de Tancarville (d. 1129) was chamberlain of Normandy. His wife was Matilda d'Arques of Folkestone, Kent. *Dom. Desc.*, p. 729. He was a son of Ralph the Chamberlain (no. **6**).

William *pincerna* de Albini (Aubigny, Manche) was father of William, earl of Arundel, husband of Henry I's widow Adelicia of Louvain. *Dom. Desc.*, p. 273; *Comp. Peer.* i, pp. 230–9.

William Brito was also known as William de Albini Brito. He was son of Main de Sain-Aubin-d'Aubigné (Ille-et-Vilaine), donor of no. **64**. *Dom. Desc.*, pp. 271–2.

Robert d'Avranches was son of William fitz Wimund (no. **73**) and donor of nos. **71** and **72**.

Gilbert d'Avranches was father of Lescelina, wife of Otuel de Subligny. His heirs were her son Harscoit de Subligny, founder of the abbey of Lucerne (1143), and his issue Gilbert of Avranches (d. 1169) and Lescelina, wife of Fulk Paynel. *Dom. Desc.*, p. 262.

Otuel de Subligny was also father of Richard, bishop ofAvranches (d. 24 April 1142). He was grandfather of Henry II's favourite, John de Subligny (founder, *c.* 1160, with Ruelland de Houlme [nos. **74** and **75**], of the abbey of Montmorel), whose son Harscoit acquired the seigneurie of Dol-Combour by marriage to Iseldis, eldest daughter and heiress of John II of Dol. *Dom. Desc.*, pp. 725–6 (Harscoit and Johannes de Suligny). Both Gilbert d'Avranches and his son-in-law Otuel feature in no. **115**, a list of losses suffered by the abbey. Also attested the grant in 1110 by William de Tracy, **App. ii.7**.

Hugh Talemascha occurs on the 1129/30 Pipe Roll in Oxfordshire where he and his family held land of the St John family, He became a monk of Gloucester early in the reign of Henry II. *Dom. Desc.*, p. 1123.

An Alan de Sancto Petro was named as a vavassor of the abbey at Donville (Manche, cant. Granville) in 1172 (Delisle, *Torigni*, ii, p. 300). A certain Hodierna is mentioned in no. **115** as holding unjustly from Alan de Sancto Petro the houses of Morin brother of Fulcuin and Ralph Panion.

Gilbert and Philip de Monte, sons of John of St John's sister Alice, occur c. 1100 (*Dom. Desc.*, p. 594).

[17]

Son of Geoffrey count of Rennes and Hadvisa, daughter of Richard I of Normandy, Alan III of Brittany succeeded his father as a minor in 1008. He was active by 1027 when he embarked on a vigorous campaign in northern Poitou in defence of Herbert I of Maine, whom Alan's kinsman Geoffrey Martel of Anjou was holding prisoner (*Actus pont. Cenomannis*, pp. 355–60; Latouche, *Maine*, 22–5). The Angevin attempts to control Maine were contrary to Breton interests, but the extraordinary vigour of the campaign suggests that Alan and Herbert were probably related; Keats-Rohan, '"Un vassal sans histoire": Count Hugh II (fl. 955–992) and the Origins of Angevin Overlordship in Maine', *Family Trees*, 189–210. At the conclusion of this campaign, *c.* 1029, Alan married Bertha, daughter of Odo II of Blois, by whom he had issue his son and successor Conan II (d. 1066), and a daughter Hadvise (d. 1072), whose husband Hoel of Cornouailles eventually succeeded her brother in her right (their grandson was Conan III, no. **63**). Alan's hope that God might grant him a son, expressed in this charter, is perhaps an indication that his new wife was pregnant, or that she had recently given birth to their first child, a daughter. Around the same time, 1029, Alan was campaigning against his Norman cousin Robert I in a bid to retain as Breton land in the Avranchin lying between the rivers Couesnon and Sélune. He ultimately lost the struggle, as he recognized in a peace brokered by his uncle Archbishop Robert of Rouen at Mont-Saint-Michel in 1033 (William of

Jumièges, ii, pp. 56–8, 78). Alan was killed in 1040 during a disturbed period when he was one of the regents for the young William II of Normandy (Ord. Vit. iii, pp. 87–8). He was remembered for this charter in the monks' Obituary, MS Avranches 215, fol. 169v, i Kal. Oct. (1 October): *Obiit Alanus dux Brit[annie] qui nobis dedit Montrouaut cum pertinentiis et confirmauit donum Gaufridi patris sui.* His father was remembered on fol. 172r, xi Kal. Nov. (22 October): *Gaufredus comes Brit[annie] qui dedit quod [habemus] in Pollet*, i.e. Pays d'Alet. Geoffrey's grants formed the basis for the priory of Saint-Meloir-des-Ondes.

Alan's brother Eudo (d. 1079), later styled count, was an ally of Geoffrey Martel of Anjou against William of Normandy in 1055. His wife Agnes, known also as Oruen, was probably an Angevin. (On the links between Bretons and Anjou at this time, see J.-P. Brunterc'h, 'Puissance temporelle et pouvoir diocésain des évêques de Nantes entre 936 1t 1049', *MSHAB.*, lxi (1984), 29–82.) Eudo was loyal to his brother throughout his reign and succeeded him as regent for Alan's infant son Conan II (1040–66). During his years as regent he tried to advance the interests of his own family, ultimately engaging in a power struggle with Conan when the latter's minority ended *c.* 1055/6. Eudo was finally defeated in 1057, but the loyalty of both his eldest son Geoffrey I Boterel and his nephew Geoffrey Grenonat, count of Rennes (1066–84), a natural son of Alan III, remained dubious until their respective deaths, in revolt, in 1093 and 1084. Eudo was father of a large number of sons, both legitimate and illegitimate, many of whom subsequently settled in England, in and after 1066. The lordship established at Richmond by his son Alan Rufus (d. 1093) was one of the most important tenancies-in-chief of the Conquest period. It passed successively to Alan's brothers Alan Niger and Stephen. Another brother, Brien, was probably the Count Brien remembered in the abbey Martyrology-Necrology on 14 February. He had held the land of Robert of Mortain before his withdrawal from England soon after 1069, land that became the basis of the priory of St Michael's Mount. Cf. the account of his nephew Alan of Richmond in *The Cartulary of St Michael's Mount*, p. 6, no. 5. *Dom. People*, p. 48. Eudo was succeeded in Brittany first by his son Geoffrey I Boterel (killed at Dol on 24 September 1093), whose son Conan died at the siege of Nicaea in 1097 (Ord. Vit. v, 54, 58), and secondly by his son Stephen, also lord of Richmond after 1098. Geoffrey and his brothers occur in no. 42. H. Guillotel, 'Les origines de Guingamp', *MSHAB*, 56 (1979), 93–4; id., 'La place de Châteaubriant dans l'essor des châtellenies bretonnes (xie–xiie siècles)', *MSHAB*, 66 (1989), 18–19.

Alan's tenant Guy bore a name that was unusual in this part of north-western France at this time; it was much more common in the region of Anjou and southern Maine. Possibly (as Hubert Guillotel has suggested to me) Guy was the man who gave no. 47, on behalf of his wife and her sons Hugh (de Sillé), Gauzlin and Herbran (de Pirmil), the donors of no. 30. The church mentioned in Guy's charter has proved difficult to identify conclusively, but may have been at Saint-Berthevin-la-Tannière, which was much closer to the border between Maine and Brittany than to Sillé-le-Guillaume, near Le Mans, where Hugh and his descendants were seigneurs. Angevin documents relating to the abbey of Sainte-Trinité de Vendôme reveal that the fief of Saint-Saturnin in Anjou, originally given by Fulk Nerra to Orric, had later been given to Gauzlin, a knight of Maine, and after his death, to a Breton, Eudo son of Melian. Eudo returned to Brittany and the fief was granted by Fulk and subsequently by Geoffrey Martel of Anjou to Gauzlin's brother Herbran de Pirmil. Herbran forfeited the fief before *c.* 1046, when he supported Hugh IV of Maine against Geoffrey Martel. The same documents show that Herbran de Pirmil was uncle of William (fitz Hugh) de Sillé and his brother Hubert (*Cart. Sainte-Trinité de Vendôme*, nos. LXVI–VII). His brother Gauzlin is perhaps to be identifed with the Gauzlin Mansel who attested an early charter of Alan III of Brittany for Saint-Florent de Saumur (Guillotel, *Actes*, no. 13, *c.* 1013–22; Morice, *Preuves*i, col. 381–2). Pirmil lay within the seigneurie of Laval in Maine, established by *c.* 1040. Gauzlin's stepfather Guy was perhaps a kinsman or lineal ancestor of the long line of seigneurs of Laval named Guy, the first of whom was active *c.* 1020 to *c.* 1060.

Junguené archbishop of Dol was a figure of major importance in the reign of Alan III (1008–40). He appointed his brother Rivallon as lay lord of the temporalities of his see. Their other brothers were Josselin of Dinan and Haimo II, *vicomte* of Alet. The original charter was also attested by Roiantelina, daughter of Rivallon, who was probably their mother, and her sons Hugh and Geoffrey. Roiantelina appears to have been the heiress of an extensive patrimony in north-eastern Brittany built upon land abandoned by monasteries in the early tenth century (Guillotel, 'Saint-Suliac', *MSHAB* lxxvi, 1998, 5–25). She or her husband Haimo may have been a sibling of Archbishop Main, through whom succession to the diocese was transmitted to their son Junguené. A charter of Alan III of *c.* 1024–21 February 1034 relates how Roiantelina *vicecomitissa* had established a small community of ten nuns at Chavagne, but, unable to support them there, had asked that they could become part of the new abbey of Saint-Georges de Rennes, currently under construction, under Abbess Adela, the count's sister (*Cart. Saint-Georges de Rennes*, ed. P. de La Bigne Villeneuve, no. XII, pp. 108–9; Guillotel, *Actes*, no. 29). A Roiantelina was remembered in the abbey Necrology on 3 June; Abbess Adela was remembered on 4 March. See Guillotel, 'Des vicomtes d'Alet aux vicomtes de Poudouvre', *Société d'histoire et d'archéologie de l'arrondissement de Saint-Malo, Annales* 1988, 208–15; *Histoire Féodale de Dol*, pp. 38–41.

Budic count of Nantes, descendant of Alan Barbetorte of Brittany (d. 952) and a natural son of Count Judicael, accepted the authority of Alan III, count of Rennes and duke of Brittany, *c.* 1030. His half-sister Judith married Alan Canhiart count of Cornouaille *c.* 1026. Her son Hoël, count of Cornouaille and Nantes, married Havise, daughter of Alan III, who succeeded her brother Conan II in 1066. They were parents of Alan IV Fergant, father of Conan III (no. **63**). Conan's heiress was his daughter Bertha, remembered in the Necrology on 1 December. Her son Conan IV (d. 1171) was remembered on 20 February.

Hervé of Acigné, fl. *c.* 1032–60, was Hervé fitz Goranton de Vitré, a family displaced at Vitré during the eleventh century by the family of Rivallon *le vicaire*. Goranton attested no. **23.** Benefactor of the abbey of Saint-Florent de Saumur, to which he, his wife Cecilia, son Goranton and son-in-law Rivallon, made a grant in the time of Abbot Sigo (Morice, *Preuves*, i, col. 493). M. Brand'honneur, 'Les Goranton-Hervé de Vitré aux XI, XII et XIII siècles', *MSHAB*, lxx (1993) 65–87.

Cario was Cario son of Caradoc, brother of Crescand, who later became tutor to Alan's son Conan II. He was named among Conan's fifty barons in a charter given at Tours *c.* 1050 (Morice, *Preuves*, i, cols. 405–6, 408–9; Guillotel, *Actes*, pp. 195–8, no. 54; Keats-Rohan, 'La lutte pour le pouvoir...', *MSHAB*, lxviii (1991), 45–69). He and his brother attested a charter of Conan's mother Bertha of 1058 (Morice, *Preuves*, i, col. 408).

Alvus son of the *vicomte* Bernard was the first of a line of *vicomtes* of Poher, according to ideas proposed by Hubert Guillotel (reported in Joëlle Quaghebeur, *La Cornouaille du IXe au XIIe siècle* (2nd edn., Rennes, 2002), pp. 379 ff., esp. note 175, p. 384), who has suggested a marriage between his family and Hadvisa, daughter of Rivallon I of Dol. The *vicomte* Rivallon who attested no. **42**, a grant by the bishop of Tréguier, in 1086 may have been a descendant of such a union.

[18]

Rivallon I of Dol-Combour, son of Haimo I *vicomte* of Alet and Roiantelina, youngest surviving brother of Archbishop Junguené of Dol (from 1010 to *circa* 1040). Rivallon was lord of Combour and doyen of the temporalities of the see of Dol. He notoriously supported William of Normandy during the Norman invasion of Brittany in 1064, probably in return for the land of Céaux, later the subject of a dispute between John of Dol, Ralph I of Fougères and Saint-Florent (*Chartes Normandes de l'Abbaye de Saint-Florent de Saumur*, ed. Marchegay, 16–18; discussed in K. S. B. Keats-Rohan, 'William the Conqueror and the Breton contingent in the non-Norman Conquest 1066–1086', *Anglo-Norman Studies*, xiii (1991), 157–72), but was reconciled on his deathbed with Conan II, shortly before Conan left for his fatal campaign in Anjou late in 1066. By his wife Eremburg, daughter of Gelduin de Chartres, Rivallon was father of four sons and a daughter Hadvisa, perhaps wife of Alvus, *vicomte* of Poher, whose kin attested no. 17 (Guillotel, 'Des vicomtes d'Alet...', *Société d'histoire et d'archéologie de l'arrondissement de Saint-Malo, Annales* 1988). His sister Innoguent was mother of Brien I of Châteaubriant. Rivallon, his wife and children were received into confraternity at the abbey by the charter printed here in **Appendix ii.4**. His eldest son William fitz Rivallon chose to became a monk of Saint-Florent of Saumur rather than succeed to his father's honours. In 1070 he was elected abbot. He died in 1118 and was remembered in the abbey Martyrology-Necrology on 30 May.

The second son, John, succeeded their father, but he too, after the death of his wife Godehildis, sister of Ralph I of Fougères, eventually became a monk of Saint-Florent. He died as archbishop-elect of Dol in 1093. He was remembered in the Martyrology-Necrology on 27 January.

The third son, St Gelduin, was a canon of the cathedral of Dol. In August 1076 he was elected bishop of Dol and despatched to Rome to seek the approval of Gregory VII. Gregory refused to ratify his appointment. Gelduin died at Saint-Père de Chartres on his way home (*De S. Gilduino canonico Dolensi in Britannia*, in *Acta Sanctorum, Januarii*, II, 790–93).

Absent from this charter is the youngest son, Geoffrey fitz Rivallon, who was named in two charters relating his father's establishment and endowment of a priory of Sainte-Trinité at Combour, later given to Marmoutier (Morice, *Preuves* i, 425; Guillotel, *Actes*, nos. 57, 65). Just a few years later Rivallon was dead and his three eldest and extremely pious sons began to issue a number of charters for monasteries. None of them ever made a grant for the soul of their brother Geoffrey, as would have been expected had he predeceased them. The last act of Rivallon for Combour priory before his death does not contain Geoffrey's name among those of his other children (*Actes*, no. 66), but this was probably a scribal oversight since the death of a child is not mentioned. Only two of Rivallon's other three sons, William and Gelduin, signed the act. Perhaps Geoffrey was absent when this act was done and later became estranged from his family. If so, he may be identifiable as the man who attested several charters of Robert of Mortain and who acquired, probably by marriage, the lordship of Lévaré and Saint-Berthevin-la-Tannière in Mayenne (no. **41**); his heirs were the Gorron family who were major benefactors of the abbey priory of L'Abbayette in the twelfth and thirteeth centuries. *Cart. de l'Abbayette*, nos. 10, 20

The present charter confirms the evidence of Rivallon's last charter for Sainte-Trinité, which shows that had been reconciled to duke Conan II shortly before his death, some time between his treacherous support of the Normans in mid 1064 and Conan's own death on 11 December 1066, discussed in Guillotel, 'Châteaubriant', 22–3 and printed in Guillotel, *Actes*, no. 66. As Broussillon (*Cart. de L'Abbayette*, no. 5) noted, in the copy found in lat. 5430a that this charter is included with charters of Saint-Broladre, though other copies place it with acts of L'Abbayette. Hubert Guillotel, 'Combour: proto-histoire d'une seigneurie', pp. 269–298, esp. p. 275.

Maino fitz Trehen attested a charter of John I fitz Rivallon of Dol granting the church of Pleine-Fougères to Saint-Florent de Saumur (Arch.

dépt. Maine-et-Loire, H 3713, fol. 69v–70r; Marchegay, *Livre noir de Saint-Florent de Saumur*, Archives d'Anjou I, no. 141).

William fitz Ursoën was the donor of no. **20**.

Hato and his brother made gifts to the priory of Saint-Pern, near Ploasme, on the same day as Josselin of Dinan and his brother Rivallon of Dol (Archives départementales d'Ille-et-Villaine, IF 510). Hato de Miniac attested a charter of 1086 for Saint-Florent given by John fitz Rivallon of Dol (Arch. dépt. Maine-et-Loire H 3713, fol. 86v–87r).

Walter fitz Ricoli and two of his sons William and Geoffrey attested a charter of William fitz Rivallon, abbot of Saint-Florent, concerning the church of Lanrigan (Livre Blanc de Saint-Florent, Arch. dépt. Maine-et-Loir, H 3713, fol. 70r); in another charter relating to the same he attested with Rivallon fitz Gurgar (fol. 87r) and attested Rivallon's charter for Sainte-Trinité de Combour (Guillotel, *Actes*, no. 66).

[19]

A Rivallon fitz Walter attested a charter of Haimo *botellarius* for Saint-Florent de Saumur, B. N. Lat. nov. acq. 1930, fol. 71v–72r.

[20]

William fitz Irsoi was mentioned in a later inquest into the fiefs of the see of Dol as William fitz Ursoën of Cherrueix, a man of John I fitz Rivallon of Dol. In one entry we are told John gave him the moiety of the mill of Olivet for the service of feeding his dogs: *Histoire Féodale ... de Dol*, pp. 32–3 and note 7, pp. 48–9. He was a witness to no. **18**, a charter of William fitz Rivallon. For William's heir Hugh fitz Ranulf, see **App. ii.8**.

Gelduin II of Dol, was son of John fitz Rivallon (d. 1093) and heir of his elder brother Rivallon; killed during a raid on Mont-Saint-Michel in 1137 (Ord. Vit. vi, 492), when he was succeeded by his son John; had a stormy relationship withWilliam l'Ismaélite of Tinteniac, whose daughter Noga he married. Noga was sister of Donoal, bishop of Alet (no. **49**), a former monk of Mont-Saint-Michel and abbot of Saint-Melaine (d. 1142), who was remembered on 19 August in the Martyrology-Necrology. See Guillotel, 'Combour', 281–3. Gelduin's daughter Hadvise married Robert fitz William of Avranches, donor of no. **72**. His sister was wife of Geoffrey II Boterel, a grandson of Eudo, brother of Alan III (nos. **17** and **23**).

Gelduin fitz Haimo held the fee near Combour called Montsorel; ancestor of the seigneurs of Landal. Perhaps a son of Haimo III of Alet and a collateral of Gelduin II of Dol (see nos. **17** and **18**). Founder in 1137, with his wife Adelaide and sons John and Haimon, of the Cistercian abbey of La Vieuville, a cell of Savigny, a few miles south-east of Dol (Morice, *Preuves*, i, col. 575–6; Paris, B. N. Coll. Baluze 47, fols. 208ff.). His brother Gervaise went on the first Crusade (Ord. Vit., v, 58). Guillotel, 'Des vicomtes d'Alet'.

Eudo fitz Geoffrey, kinsman of Rivallon of Dol, occurs as the donor of no. **118**.

Eudo Gobio occurs *c.* 1130 with his sons Wigan and Oliver as witnesses to a grant to Combour priory attested by Gelduin II of Dol (B. N. lat. 5441/3, p.437, no. 2; cf. Morice, *Preuves* i, 525–6). Oliver Gobion later restored land held unjustly at Saint-Meloir to Mont-Saint-Michel, attested by Guy fitz Ranulf (Morice, *Preuves*, i, col. 579.

The father of Geoffrey fitz Junguené (*Gingonei*) was possibly son of Geoffrey fitz Ansketil, father by his wife Judith of Junguené, Wigan and Rivallon (Morice, *Preuves* i, col. 463). There are no firm indications that Geoffrey fitz Ansquetil was brother of Giro fitz Ansquetil of Châteaugiron, whose wife was a sister of Rivallon of Dol's wife Eremburg. He mortgaged land in the parish of Carfenton, Dol, to Saint-Florent-de-Saumur in 1082 (Morice, *Preuves*, i, 389–90). He also had land at Mezvoit, in Dol, which suggests that he was part of an extended kingroup that included the lords of Dol (Guillotel, 'Combour: proto-histoire d'une seigneurie'). His knight (*miles*) Ralph de Ponte Leutmar gave a charter for Saint-Florent attested by Eudo fitz Geoffrey and William Goion (no. **119**) (Arch. Maine-et-Loire H3713, fol. 89v).

Eudo fitz Baderon, son of Baderon fitz Caradoc of Laboussac, near Dol. Baderon acquired the honour of Monmouth after 1066 and had been succeeded there by his son William by 1086. See H. Guillotel, 'Une famille bretonne aux services du Conquérant: les Baderon', *Droit privé et institutions régionales: Etudes historiques offertes à Jean Yver* (1976), 361–6. *Dom. People*, 484; *Dom. Desc.*, pp. 591–2.

A notification of William fitz Rivallon, abbot of Saint-Florent (1070–1118), concerning the church of Liffré, was attested by William *puer*, son of William fitz Hervé, and Brien son of Alvus (de Martigné-Ferchaud); Morice, *Preuves*, i, cols. 474–5.

[**21** and **56**]

First of three items dealing with the gift of Trehan fitz Brien of Saint-Broladre of 12 acres of land and the tithes of a mill over the period 1075–1081. The land was named in a charter dated 1075 which is not in the cartulary but is printed here as **Appendix i.** 7. From the place-names, particularly that of the land called *Torpol*, we can see the link between Trehan's charters and a subsequent challenge to his grant which resulted in a restitution charter given by Baldwin son of Homenes (no. **89**), whose father Homenes attested Trehan's charters. Trehan's gifts were authorized by his son Geoffrey, who may be the father mentioned in the charter of Helias Boterat (no. **114**) confirming this grant. Saint-Broladre was the only parish of the diocese of Dol held by Mont-Saint-Michel (cf. Dubois, 'Dépendances', *Mill. mon.*, i, p. 644).

[22]

Guethenoc, or Guihenoc, was *vicomte* of Rennes by 1008; ancestor of later *vicomtes* of Porhoët and of the Rohan family. He was one of the witnesses to the charter of Conan I of Brittany in 990 (**Appendix ii.1**). See Hubert Guillotel, 'De la vicomté de Rennes à la vicomté du Porhoët', *MSHAB* lxxiii (1995), 5–23. The grants were located in the diocese of Saint-Malo, where the abbey had a priory at Saint-Meloir-des-Ondes. However, as the Inventory, fol. 125v, shows, the property was subsequently allocated to the priory of Treverez (Locmikael), in the diocese of Quimper.

Amongst the Breton names in this family, the Frankish name Josselin, or Gauzlin, of Guethenoc's eldest son is remarkable. One of Conan's tenants named in the 990 charter was Rorgo son of Gauzlin, explicitly described as the son of Hugh of Maine's brother, which means his father was a son of Hugh I of Maine and a brother of Hugh II, who died soon after this charter was given. The names of Rorgo and Junguené following closely upon each other in the witness list gives pause for thought. Junguené's parents are known to have been Haimo *vicomte* of Alet and Roiantelina, a Breton noblewoman thought to have been an heiress of Archbishop Wichohen, of whom Main is the first known successor. Main's successor Archbishop Junguené was brother of Josselin, ancestor of the seigneurs of Dinan, who bore the same Rorgonide name as Rorgo's father and Guethenoc's son. Another brother was their father Haimo's successor as *vicomte* in Alet, Haimo II, who was father of Main, bishop of Rennes (no. **40**). Their youngest brother, Rivallon of Dol, was a benefactor of the Mont as were three of his sons, including the youngest, Geoffrey, who also bore a Rorgonide name (nos. **18**, **41**, **44**, **App. ii. 2**). The appearance of the Rorgonide name Gauzlin/Josselin in Breton families with otherwise marked Breton onomastic is a strong indicator of marriage alliances. Conceivably, the mothers of Guethenoc of Porhoët and of Roiantelina, mother of Archbishop Junguené and his brother Haimo II d'Alet, were two daughters of Gauzlin, son of Hugh I of Maine. The close connexion of Gauzlin's family with north-east Brittany, clearly entrenched by 990, leads to the further suggestion that his own marriage was in the same area. His wife may have been a kinswoman of Count Berengar of Rennes, grandfather of Conan I. The names of Berengar and his son Juhel are themselves indicative of the interrelationships that developed between Frankish nobles and their Breton counterparts in the ninth century. Berengar was the name of two Mont monks under Mainard I or II who had died before 1000/04 (Gremont and Donnat, *Mill. mon.* i, p. 783).

The witness Gausbert *abba* also bore a Rorgonide name. At this date an abbot Gausbert was a leading figure in the reform or re-establishment of a number of monasteries, including Saint-Julien de Tours. He took over Saint-Pierre de la Couture at the request of Hugh III of Maine (nos. **27**, **35**, **Appendix ii.2**), as appears from a charter, corrupt in its present form, which was attested by the count's brother Fulcoin and Bishop Seifrid of Le Mans (see no. **26**); Latouche, *Le comté de Maine*, pièce just. no. 3, pp. 162–164, cf. p. 138 and note 7. Gauzbert was *consanguineus* of Odo I of Blois; he was also abbot of the houses founded by Odo or his sister Emma at Bourgueil, and at Maillezais, the Poitevin abbey to which Hugh III made the gift of the relics of St Rigomer; Guy M. Oury, 'La Reconstruction Monastique dans l'Ouest: L'Abbé Gauzbert de Saint-Julien de Tours (v. 990–1007)', *Revue Mabillon* 1964, 69–124. Gausbert died on 27 September 1007; he was remembered at Mont-Saint-Michel a month earlier, on 28 August.

[23]

Alan III of Brittany married Bertha, daughter of Odo II of Blois, *c.* 1029, after a successful campaign against Geoffrey of Anjou waged in defence of Herbert I of Maine. He acts here at the behest of Almodus, the only identifiable abbot of Mont-Saint-Michel to have been a Manceau (Le Roy, *Les curieuses recherches*, p. 111). Almod was a monk of the abbey *c.* 1000/1004 (Gremont and Donnat, *Mill. mon.* i, p. 783). He was elected abbot by his community after the death of Abbot Theoderic, an unpopular outsider from the circle of William of Volpiano. Almod was forced out by Robert I of Normandy and sent as abbot to Cerisy in 1032, where he died the following year. He was remembered in the Martyrology-Necrology, together with Abbot Theoderic, on 17 May. A lay Almod occurs in the abbey necrology on 2 August.

Junguené archbishop of Dol (1008–c.1039), brother of Rivallon of Dol-Combour (no. **18**): Guillotel, 'Des vicomtes d'Alet aux vicomtes de Poudouvre', *Soc. hist. arch. de l'arrond. de Saint-Malo, Annales* 1988, 208–15 .

Warin, bishop of Rennes between 1032 and 1038 (**App. ii.1**), was ancestor of several seigneurial families. See Jean-Claude Meuret, 'Familles seigneuriales aux confins Anjou-Bretagne', *MSHAB* lxx, 1993, pp. 199–201.

Budic count of Nantes, great-grandson of Alan Barbetorte (d. 952), formerly the chief rival of Alan III in Brittany who submitted to Alan in 1030. He died in 1038, leaving two sons, Mathias and Budic. Also attested no. **17**.

Josselin *vicomte*. Josselin of Porhoët, fl. 1032–65, eldest son of Guihenoc, donor of no. **22**.

Ralph *Anglicus*, lord of Gaël and Montfort, son of an Englishwoman; he was a wealthy landholder in England, where as Ralph the Staller, he was a favourite of Edward the Confessor. He became earl of East Anglia in 1066–7 and held the office until his death c.1069. See *Complete Peerage* ix, 568ff.

Rivallon *uicarius* of Marcillé. Founder, with his wife Junargande, of Marcillé, a priory of Marmoutier, attested by his sons Tristan and Geoffrey (Morice, *Preuves* i, col. 386). His great-grandson André I of Vitré (son of Robert I, who attested no. **40**) would marry Agnes, daughter of Robert, count of Mortain (nos. **11–12**), and acquire with her land in Cornwall (*Dom. People*, p. 151.

Gorenton was member of the Goranton-Hervé family whom Rivallon of Marcillé's descendants displaced as lords of Vitré. Father of Hervé d'Acigné who attested no. **17**. See M. Brand'honneur, 'Les Goranton-Hervé de Vitré aux XI, XII et XIII siècles', *MSHAB*, lxx (1993) 65–87.

[24]

Gradeloc, originator of this gift of a church in Poilley, may have been the *Gradalonus* remembered in the abbey Necrology on 1 May. His son Ansger was probably the Ansger who gave land in Saint-Brice-en-Cogles to Saint-Florent de Saumur (Arch. dépt. Maine-et-Loire, H 3713, fol. 65v), with the consent of his sons Corbin, Ranulf and Hervé. Corbin's sons Ilger and Gradelon later confirmed the gift. He also occurs as Ansger *vicarius* [of Cogles] in no. **40**, and also in no. **66**. A Hervé de Cogles was married to Jueta (Judith), sister of Warin bishop of Rennes (Morice, *Preuves*, i, 353).

[25]

The site of Saint-Victeur, on the banks of the river Sarthe just outside the walls of Le Mans, had existed since the eariest Christian era in Le Mans. Evidenced as a *monasterium* in the Carolingian period, it was the burial place of St Victeur, apostle of Le Mans and several early bishops, according to the *Actus pontificum Cenomannis*. Both Saint-Victeur and the neighbouring monastery of Saint-Julien were destroyed during the Norse raids of the mid ninth century. Saint-Julien was restored by Abbot Gausbert (no. **22**) in the late tenth century, when the site of Saint-Victeur was in lay hands. The date of the restoration of Saint-Victeur, and the extent to which it was a functioning *monasterium c.* 1040, is unknown, but thereafter it was rapidly developed as one of Mont-Saint-Michel's principal priories outside the Avranchin. At the date of the Cartulary the priory controlled the neighbouring parish church of Saint-Jean-de-la-Cheverie, and acquired soon afterwards the church of Etival. The presbytery of the church of Domfront-en-Champagne (cant. Conlie, Sarthe) was already a source of dispute with the neighbouring abbey of the abbey of Beaulieu, founded by Berard de Sillé (note to no. **65**), before it was mentioned in the bull of Alexander III (1176); *Cart. Saint-Victeur*, nos. 10, 22, 24.

This was a substantial and significant donation, completing work that Drogo and his wife had already begun. Broussillon printed in *Cartulaire de Saint-Victeur*, no. 8, a list of rents due on thirty dwellings that Drogo and Hersendis had given to Mont-Saint-Michel. A grant with permission to build more such dwellings was made in no. **48**. Drogo, father of Rainald, is probably to be identified with Drogo son of Milo who attested Hugh III's grant of Voivres to Mont-Saint-Michel in 1014 (no. **35**). Milo attested charters of Hugh III before 1000 (*Cartulaire de Saint-Pierre-de-la-Cour*, nos. 1–2). By fulfilling Drogo's own plans, Rainald became the founder of one of the Mont's most important priories, Saint-Victeur-au-Mans (no. **25**). Monks of the Mont may already have been living in the city, since Rainald's charter described Saint-Victeur, located in a suburb of the city, as *monasterium*, home to a small number of monks. After Drogo's death, Rainald and his mother Hersendis respected his wishes by the grant of Saint-Victeur and an endowment of land and revenues in and around Le Mans. The grant was enacted at Mont-Saint-Michel in 1040 in the presence of Abbot Suppo. The name Hersendis reappears in the charter relating the gift of one Odo, a citizen of Le Mans, and his wife Hersendis, also in the time of Abbot Suppo (no. **29**). This Hersendis may have been a daughter of the first. Conceivably, Odo was the son of that name of Ralph *vicomte* of Le Mans whose grant, like Odo's, related to vines. Rainald's charter survived in three recensions, one of which was interpolated by the monks and supplied, anachronistically, with the same witnesses as no. **35**, one of whom was Drogo fitz Milo. The Grodulf who occurs among the witnesses in the Cartulary version can be identified as the canon Gradulf who occurs in the Cartulary of Saint-Vincent du Mans as the uncle of Rainald and Herbert of La Suze, whose father was named as Drogo in charters of Saint-Pierre-de-la-Couture (*Cart. de Saint-Vincent au Mans*, no. 392; *Cart. de Saint-Pierre-de-la-Couture*, no. XII). Other charters of Saint-Vincent show that Rainald had a son Drogo, and that his brother Herbert's son was named Milo. Herbert's daughter Hersendis eventually took the fief of La Suze to her husband Robert II of Sablé (*Cart. Saint-Vincent*, 77, 137).

[26]

This striking and important charter was the foundation charter for the abbey's priory of Villarenton, which was known as L'Abbayette (*Abbaciola*) by the time the Inventory was written. Villarenton and its associated estates had been the part of the abbey's patrimony before the Norse raids in the region, which occurred between the mid-ninth century and the mid tenth. Ivo fitz Fulcoin is known only from this act, which provides a good deal of information about his family. The phrase *antecessores mei* refers to Ivo's lineal ancestors, though whether in the paternal or maternal line is unclear. Although the word *cognati* can apply equally to kinsmen in the paternal as well as the maternal (agnatic and cognatic) lines, it seems likely that it refers to kinsman in the maternal line, since Ivo names his sisters and two of his maternal uncles – before the twelfth century *avunculus* always means maternal uncle and is not confused with *patruus*, 'paternal uncle'. The apparent dominance of his maternal kin in this charter suggests that the land granted had initially been dower of his (defunct) mother expected to pass to his sisters. Neither Ivo nor his sisters were married at the time of this charter. His mother was a sister of Bishop Seifrid (whom Ivo calls *avunculus*), none of whose descendants held land in this region.

All the founders and principal benefactors of the abbey's principal priories before 1050 were high-status laymen, normally counts: Counts Conan and Geoffrey of Brittany, Hugh III of Maine, Countess Gunnor of

Normandy, Richard II of Normandy and Robert, count of Avranches. The later Inventory, muddled though it often is, attempts to begin the list of the muniments of each priory with the earliest grant by a high-status donor, who is usually named. The list of the muniments of L'Abbayette begin with Ivo's charter, but he himself is not named. Compare the case of Fulk IV of Anjou whom the Inventory never named, though both the forged and the genuine version of his charter are mentioned among the muniments of Saint-Victeur. His son Geoffrey IV le Bel is given pride of place in the entry for Le Mans (Saint-Victeur), though this should have gone to Hugh III of Maine, who instead - and mistakenly - shares the honours with Conan I of Brittany under Villamée. Ivo gives no overt indication of his status in his charter; he does not use a title or claim to be acting as the heir of his father. Ivo's charter contains two anomalies in the validation and dating clauses which suggest that he was indeed a high-status nobleman. The first anomaly is the phrase *manu propria subter firmauimus* in the validation clause. Ivo has used the singular form throughout, nowhere using a first person plural form that might suggest he is associating the maternal kin he names in his action. His independence of action is emphasized by the singularity of *manu propria*, 'with my own hand'. This usage is paralleled in the Mont charters only in the charters given by counts Alan III of Brittany (no. **23** but not **17**) and Hugh of Maine (the Norman counts used the first person singular throughout). It is also used by Guethenoc (no. **22**), but he clearly associates his wife and sons with his act of corroboration. The closest parallel is the charter of Hugh III of Maine which follows this one in cartulary (no. **27**), where we read: *manu propria subter firmare studuimus*. In another of Hugh III's charters, not in the Cartulary but printed here in **Appendix ii.2**, the usage exactly reflects Ivo's charter in using the first person singular throughout, but using the validation phrase *manu propria subter firmauimus*. The second anomaly in Ivo's charter is the phrase *Actum castro Fraternensi iii idibus Octobris*. The word *actum* occurs 23 times in the Cartulary, always, as here, in a dating-clause, but only in one other case is the location of the actor mentioned. The other case is the act by which Richard II of Normandy dismissed Abbot Mainard II, dated at Rouen (no. **52**). The place mentioned here is Le Fresnay-sur-Sarthe, which next occurs in documents as the site of a castle held by Hubert, *vicomte* of Le Mans, in the 1070s. Such evidence as there is points to Hugh III as the creator of a number of castellanies whose castellans were loyal to him and his son Herbert Wake-Dog. Their heirs normally became the hereditary seigneurs of these castelries. Ivo does not call upon a lord to corroborate his grant, suggesting perhaps that he has sufficient authority to act in his own right. A facsimile of the original of this charter was published by Broussillon and clearly shows the monogram of Count Hugh III of Maine, under which is a list of witnesses headed by *vicomte* Ralph. This might indicate that Ivo had indeed sought the corroboration of Hugh III, as we should expect. It may be that the *manu propria* phrase was never written in full (the facsimile shows that more could have been written on the line in which it appears). Compare the charter of Guy (no. **47**), which is closely related in time to this one and may even have been given on the same day. Guy, a man of considerably lesser status whose rights derived solely through his wife, acts with his wife and stepsons and so uses both the first person plural and *manibus propriis* in his validation clause, which concludes: *subter firmauiumus dominoque meo Hugoni atque episcopo ceterisque principibus domini mei firmandam tradidimus.*

It is likely that Ivo's father was Fulcoin, son of Hugh II of Maine, who is well-evidenced in several documents (in none of which is he ever styled *comes* or given any other title). Fulcoin appeared with Hugh II and his brother Hugh (III) in a charter of 967 given by Gerald canon of St-Julien-de-Tours (*Fragments des chartes de Saint-Julien-de-Tours*, no. 21). Fulcoin, brother of Hugh (III) count of Maine, was already dead when was mentioned by William Fier-à-Bras in a charter for Saint-Maixent dè Poitou, in 992 (*Chartes et documents pour servir à l'histoire de l'abbaye de Saint-Maixent*, ed. A. Richard, 2 vols, Poitiers, 1887, i, no. LXI, p. 78). Count Hugh (II) and his sons Hugh and Fulcoin consented to a charter for Saint-Julien-de-Tours by Bishop Seifrid in 971. *Fragments des chartes*, no. 23. The witness list of that charter is directly comparable with Ivo's charter; it was attested by Ysaac *leuita*, William *diaconus*, Hubert *subdiaconus*, Suthard *puer et subdiaconus*, Ralph *uicecomes*, Ivo [de Bellême], and Mainard, among others. It is unfortunate that, because the charter focuses upon maternal kin and does not explicitly call upon any higher authority to validate the gift, Ivo had no need to allege such relationship with the counts of Maine as he might have had, whether familial or other, thereby depriving us of valuable information. The fact that he did not claim such a relationship does not mean, or even imply, that it did not exist. Once again, the Cartulary offers a parallel, in the charter of Count Robert [of Avranches] (nos. **31**, **60**), which used the first person singular throughout and explicitly sought the confirmation of Richard II. Nowhere does Robert indicate his kinship with his lord, Richard II, though there is good evidence from André de Fleury's Life of Abbot Gauzlin that he was a natural son of Richard I and that his sons were Richard II's nephews. (It is very likely that Ivo's sister Bilihildis became the first wife of this Count Robert, whose charter for the abbey reveals that she was dead by 1014.) There are vague hints that Ivo was related in the maternal line to the vicomtes of Le Mans, the first being that his charter was given at Le Fresnay, certainly linked to the *vicomtes* by *c.* 1070 and not far from their stronghold at Beaumont-sur-Sarthe. Another is that the only other known reference to this region at about this time is the statement of the *Actus pontificum Cennomanensium* (pp. 350–2, and note 1, p. 352) that Bishop Mainard of Le Mans (*c.* 955–71) gave to his canons, the land and parishes of Courgenard, from his own inheritance, and the vill and church of La Dorée. There are indications that one of the ancestors of the *vicomtes* of Le Mans was named Ivo and that the name passed by marriage into the Bellême family. Avesgaud (no. **35**), successor of his uncle Bishop Seifrid, was son of Ivo de Bellême. In a charter for Saint-Victeur of the mid-eleventh century, Geoffrey Payn de Sevillé granted tithes at Domfront-en-Champagne (cant. Conlie, Sarthe) and confirmed what the monks had held from his ancestors at Domfront. The act was conceded by his children Fulcoius, Hugo and Ermengarde, and his wife Eremburg, a possible descendant of Ivo fitz Fulcoin's sister Eremburg. Geoffrey's charter was also attested by his mother Emma and witnesses including Ivo, Fulco and Fulcoius of Domfront (*Cart. S.-Victeur*, no. 10). Cf. note **[65]** on Berard de Sillé. See Keats-Rohan, 'Two studies in North French prosopography : 1. Ivo fitz Fulcoin, the counts of Maine, the lords of Bellême and the foundation of L'Abbayette', *JMH* 20, 1994, 3–25; id. 'Politique et parentèle: les comtes, vicomtes et évêques du Maine *c.* 950–1050', *Francia* 26.1 (1996), 13–30; 'Observations upon the earliest seigneuries in Maine', in *Mélanges ... Chédeville*, Rennes 1998, 361–373.

[27]

Hugh III of Maine was an important benefactor of the Mont, not only in his own grants but also in his authorization of those of his vassals (nos. **26**, **28**, **47**). This was probably the earliest of the three charters Hugh gave for the Mont; the second, granting three mills on the Sarthe at Le Mans (**Appendix ii.2** below), mentions his issue ('filiorum'), and refers to his vassal Hugh fitz Herbran (no. **30**). Both probably belong to the time of Mainard II (991–1009). The latest was the grant of Voivres in 1014 (no. **35**). Hugh's father Herbran is very likely to have been the first husband of Raimburgis, whose second husband Guy sold parts of a church in her inheritance to the abbey before the death of Bishop Seifrid, *c.* 1004 (no. **47**), with the assent of his wife and stepsons Hugh, Herbran and Gauzlin. Guy's stepson Hugh's charter (no. **30**) is datable to between 1009 and 1017. Hugh III occurs in the abbey Necrology on 28 October. He was the son of Hugh II of Maine (*c.* 955–c.991) and brother of Fulcoin and a much younger brother Herbert Bacon (see under no. **35** below). His heir at his death *c.* 1016 was his son Herbert Wake-Dog. The Hugonide counts of Maine descended from a count Roger who took over after the death of Count Berengar *c.* 898, displacing a line of Rorgonide counts of whom the last was a Count Gauzlin. Roger's heir by his wife Rothilde, a daughter of Charles the Bald, was Hugh I of Maine, whose sister was the first wife of Hugh the Great of Paris. Hugh I appears to have made peace with the Rorgonides by marrying a daughter of Count Gauzlin. One recension of a charter for Mont-Saint-Michel (**App. ii.1**) shows that Hugh II of Maine had a nephew Rorgo son of Gauzlin who was tenant of Conan I of Brittany at Ville-Perdue (Ille-et-Vilaine, cant. Louvigné-du-Désert, comm. Villamée). Rorgo seems to have founded a dynasty 10 kilometres to the south-west at Saint-Brice-en-Cogles, where a family in which Breton onomastic alternated with the name Rorgo was well-established by the late eleventh century (cf. under no. **22** above). It is also overwhelmingly likely that Richilde mother of

Theobald le Tricheur, count of Chartres and lord of Tours, was sister of Hugh I of Maine. Theobald's grandson Odo II was father of Bertha, wife successively of Alan III of Brittany (nos. **17**, **23**) and Hugh IV of Maine, and Theobald, whose first wife was Hugh IV's sister Gersendis. Keats-Rohan, '*Un vassal sans histoire*'? Count Hugh II (fl. 955–992) and the Origins of Angevin Overlordship in Maine', in *Family Trees*, pp. 189–210; id., 'Politique et parentèle: les comtes, vicomtes et évêques du Maine *c.* 950–1050', *Francia* 26.1 (1996), 13–30; id., 'Les Bilihildis du Maine', *Onomastique et parenté*, pp. 60–1.

Hugh Dublel's grant of land at Tuffé and Montdublel to Saint-Vincent was approved by Hugh III *c.* 1012–16 (Métais, *Chartes vendomois*, no. 31).

[28]

Ralph *vicomte* of Le Mans, brother (possibly nephew) of Mainard bishop of Le Mans *c.* 950–69/70 and Hildeburg, mother of Seifrid bishop of Le Mans (nos. **26**, **47**). He was succeeded soon after 1000 by his son Ralph. Father of several other sons, including Odo and Geoffrey, first castellan of Sablé. See Keats-Rohan, 'Politique et parentèle: les comtes, vicomtes et évêques du Maine c.950–1050', *Francia* 26.1 (1996), 13–30;. The name Godehilda occurs in the abbey Necrology on 16 November.

[29]

The Cartulary is the sole source of this and the previous charter. Possibly the Hersendis of this charter was related to the mother of Rainald of no. **25**. Odo's grant of 5 arpents of vines echoes the grant of vineyards by Ralph *vicomte* of Le Mans, donor of no. **28**. Possibly he was the same as Ralph's son Odo, evidenced in a charter of his brother Geoffrey de Sablé (*Cartulaire de Saint-Pierre-de-la- Couture*, no. 4).

[30]

The location of *Centrannis* cannot be satisfactorily established. The Abbé Angot's argument (in his *Dictionnaire ... de Mayenne*) for associating it with the church that later gave its name to Saint-Berthevin-la-Tannière is inherently indemonstrable and does not deserve the unqualified acceptance it has acquired. His reasoning concerns the location of Saint-Berthevin in a plateau of the val d'Ernée surrounded by water-courses, reflecting the derivation of *Centrannis* from Latin *inter amnis*. Unfortunately, there are many places where such reasoning could be applied with equal validity. There is a clear break between the two charters relating to *Centrannis* and the later grant of the church of Saint-Berthevin, reflected both in the Cartulary and in the later Inventory. The register of the muniments of the priory of L'Abbayette at Villarenton, in the Inventory, fol. 118r, list acts pertaining to Saint-Berthevin and also the acts relating to *Centrannis*. This act is closely linked to no. **47**; either or both are indicated in the inventory as *Littera ecclesie Centrannis quod debemus habere duas partes in eadem et tamen emimus quicquid habemus in* *eadem*. The church is never mentioned in papal confirmations of the twelfth century onward, though Saint-Berthevin is mentioned. The grant of the church of Saint-Berthevin (no. **38**) from the inheritance of a certain Robert alleges that previous holders had sold their rights in the time of Geoffrey I de Mayenne. This cannot refer to the donors of this charter and no. **47**. If Angot's identification is correct, it shows that the monks lost control of the church of *Centrannis* soon after this sale and the church soon found its way back to lay control. Though this not impossible, the status of Guy's stepsons as major figures in the history of Maine in the mid-eleventh century and the fact that they continued, as seigneurs of Sillé-le-Guillaume, to be benefactors of the abbey, is not good evidence for Angot's thesis.

The donors of this charter and no. **47** can be identified as ancestors of the seigneurs of Sillé-le-Guillaume (Sarthe), who were benefactors of the abbey (no. **65**). Hugh and his brothers had consented to the sale of rights in the church of *Centrannis* once held by their mother Raimburgis's parents to Mont-Saint-Michel, possibly on the same occasion that Ivo fitz Fulcoin restored Villarenton (nos. **47** and **26**).

Hugh's brother Herbran occurs in two acts of La Couture given between 1009 and 1045. Herbran is mentioned several times in the *Actus pontificum Cenomannis in urbe degentium*, ed. Busson et Ledru, Le Mans 1902. He supported Herbert I of Maine against Bishop Avesgaud and, as Herbrand of Pirmil, he was given the fee of Saint-Saturnin previously held by his brother Gauzlin Mansel from Fulk Nerra of Anjou. He gave land there to the abbey of Ronceray, with the assent of his son Hugh and wife Richildis. It is also mentioned in a charter-notice of Sainte-Trinité de Vendôme (*Cart.*, no. LXVII), attested by Herbran's *nepotes* William de Sillé and his brother Hubert. He forfeited it *c.* 1045 when a Manceau revolt, led by Bishop Gervaise, in support of Hugh IV against his uncle and guardian Herbert Bacon and the Angevin count Geoffrey Martel, found him on the same side as the bishop (*Cart. Sainte-Trinité deVendôme*, no. LXVI). Hugh son of Herbran assented to Hugh III's grant of three mills on the Sarthe in Le Mans to Saint-Victeur in a charter that does not appear in the Cartulary (*Cart. Saint-Victeur*, no. 3, **Appendix ii.2** below). The occurrence is too early to be associated with the son of Hugh's brother, so there is a strong chance that it reveals the name of Hugh's father. On his brothers Herbran and Gauzlin see further the discussion under **17**] above.

Hugh son of Hugh was, as Hugh seigneur of Sillé (fl. 1050–70), regarded by the author of the *Actus pontificum Cenommanensis* (p. 378) as one of the great men of the region. Around 1069 he was an opponent of the pro-Norman bishop of Le Mans, Arnold, whom he captured during the bishop's attack on his castle, though he soon released him. He was an opponent of Geoffrey I de Mayenne during the period that followed. His son and successor William, who occurs in the 1080s, probably gave his name to Sillé-le-Guillaume (no. **65**).

[31 and 60]

Count Robert was an illegitimate son of Richard I of Normandy. His principal holdings were in the county of Avranches, though he is also thought of as a precursor of Robert count of Mortain on account of his holdings in the castellany of Mortain, which were detailed in no. **2**, a charter of Richard II. See D. C. Douglas, 'The earliest Norman counts', *EHR* 61 (1964), 129–56; C. Potts, 'The earliest Norman counts revisted: the lords of Mortain', *Journal of the Haskins Society* iv, 1992, 23–35.

His son Richard joined a plot against Richard II, for which he and his brothers had forfeited their father's county by 1027, when it had been given to their cousin William Werlenc, son of Richard I of Normandy's son Malger count of Corbeil. See André de Fleury, *Vie de Gauzlin abbé de Fleury*, ed. R. H. Bautier and G. Labory, (Paris, 1969), §16, pp. 48–9 and notes; Gremont and Donnat, 'Fleury, le Mont Saint-Michel et l'Angleterre', *Mill. mon.* i, 787–93.

His first wife Bilihildis was doubtless the sister of another benefactor, Ivo fitz Fulcoin of Maine (no. **26**). The name recurs as that of one of the daughters of Niel II of the Cotentin, whose wife Adela was a sister of Richard de Vernon-Redvers. Bilihildis was the name of the ancestress of Rorgonide counts of Maine; it occurs four times in the abbey's necrology, ms. Avranches 214, pp. 155–6, 158, 180. Cf. Keats-Rohan, 'Bilihildis', in *Onomastique et parenté.*

[32]

Son of Fouquier de Valensole, a Provençale noble who was forced into exile at Mâcon a few years after Maiol's birth *c.* 910. Maiol's early career was as a regular cleric, canon and archdeacon of Saint-Vincent-de-Mâcon. On the point of being offered the archdiocese of Besançon, he became a *conversus* at Cluny, *c.* 940/4. Fourth abbot of Cluny, which he ruled from 954 until his death in 994, though he had a co-adjutor from 986. He was canonised within a few years of his death.

The significance of the charter as a celebration of Benedictinism at the Mont is highlighted by the use of the word *monachi* only in relation to Mont-Saint-Michel and combined with the condition relating to the Rule of St Benedict – *ut quam diu ipsi monachi secundam regulam sancti Benedicti regulariter uixerint*. The witness-list is predominantly if not entirely composed of Cluniac monks. Four of them are well-evidenced in other charters of Cluny. The deacon Vivian and the priest Achedeus both attest a charter of Abbot Maiol at Cluny on 11 November 978; Achedeus attested a similar charter in September 965, Vivian and Achedeus attested a charter of 12 November 981/11 November 982; Achedeus wrote a number of charters as *uice cancellarius* in 982 (*Recueil ... Cluny*, nos. 1460, 1186, 1574, 1017, 1618–20). The priest Otger also occurs in a number of charters, often as scribe, from March 966 to the end of August 972 (*Ibid*., nos. 1198, 1258, 1292,

1301, 1320). Randuin, the scribe of the current charter, occurs as scribe of a charter of December 978 (*Ibid.*, no. 1455). K. S. B. Keats-Rohan, 'Une chartre de l'abbé Mayeul de Cluny et la Réforme du Mont Saint-Michel', *Société de l'Histoire de Normandie*, 2000.

The monks of Mont-Saint-Michel maintained a small vineyard at Le Mortier, as revealed by a confirmation of Fulk IV of Anjou, **App. i.3**, and by a later charter of Robert de Torigny, permitting the grant of vines to Marmoutier by Durand Burel, a Manceaux holding of the Mont's fee in return for Marmoutier's confirmation of the abbey's vines at Le Mortier (Delisle, *Torigni*, ii, no. XLIX, pp. 326–7). They formed a three-way confraternity with the monks of Cluny and Vézelay in 1172, under Abbot Robert de Torigny (Delisle, *Torigni*, ii, pp. 41, 294–5).

[33]

A monk Restoldus was remembered in the abbey Martyrology-Necrology on 22 May (p. 75).

[34]

The first charter for the Mont's priory of Gohory. Around 1020 Hildiardis grandmother of Geoffrey *vicomte* of Châteaudun made a gift to Saint-Père de Chartres attested by one Hubert and his son Godeschal, Odo and Hubert Brunel, Ralph *legis-doctus* (nos. **100**, **103**), and an earlier Bernard de Buslo (Bullou) (*Cartulaire de Saint-Père de Chartres*, ed. B. Guérard, Paris 1840, i, p. 117); cf. no 100. See Christian Settipani, 'Les comtes d'Anjou et leurs alliances aux X et XI siècles', in Keats-Rohan ed., *Family Trees* (1997), 254–266, and id., 'Les vicomtes de Châteaudun et leur alliés', *Prosopon* 10 (1999). Geoffrey fitz Godeschal subsequently occurs granting land at Montemont when his servant Airard becomes a monk (no. **100**).

Warner *Oculus Canis* attested a grant to Marmoutiers by Emelina de Châteaudun *c.* 1040 (*Cartulaire dunois de Marmoutier*, ed. Mabille, Châteaudun 1874, no. 35, p. 33). Walter *Oculus Canis*'s grant was confirmed in 1097 by his brother Ralph (no. **102**), whose reluctance to accept the grant continued after that date (nos. **103**, **105**).

Ralph *Oculus Canis*, father of Warner (no. **105**), attested a grant by Hugh *vicomte* de Châteaudun (d. 1094) to Marmoutier abbey's priory of Saint-Leonard de Bellême in the late eleventh century. Hugh's grant was conceded by his brother Geoffrey, count of Perche, and Robert (ib., no 150, pp. 138–9).

Gerard Brunel gave land to Marmoutier in 1071 with the consent of his wife Ermengard and sons Hilgod, Hugh and Adam (*Cart. Dunois*, no. CXXXIV); he also gave to Saint-Père de Chartres (*Cart.*, pp. 504–5), *c.* 1092–1120, the moiety of Saint-Leobin de Brou, with the consent of his wife Habelina and sons Helgod, Ralph, Adam and Hugh, and the assent of William II Gouet and Eustachia.

Matthias or Matthew prior of Mont-Saint-Michel under Abbot Roger I, was brother of Geoffrey Ridel, a servant of Henry I of England who married a natural daughter of Hugh, *vicomte* of Avranches and earl of Chester (no. **74**) (*Dom. People*, pp. 230–1; Ord. Vit., vi, 316; *Heads of Religious Houses*, 60). He was consecrated abbot of Peterborough a year before his death on 20 October 1103. He was remembered in the Martyrology-Necrology.

[35]

Important charter showing the emergence of the seigneuries in Maine. Hugh III's charter is attested by the ancestors of the senior Manceaux barons, Hamelin of Château-du-Loir, father of Bishop Gervaise of Le Mans, successor of Bishop Avesgaud (*Cartulaire de Château-du-Loir*, ed. Vallée, Arch. hist du Maine, t 6, Le Mans 1906), and Haimo de Mayenne, father of Geoffrey and Hugh (nos. **38**, **62**, **65**) both of whom were probably related to Hugh III.

Avesgaud was son of Ivo de Bellême and an opponent of Hugh III.

Drogo fitz Milo was probably the Drogo whose wife Hersendis and son Rainald granted the monastery of Saint-Victeur to the abbey after his death, *c.* 1040, in fulfillment of his wishes (no. **25**), attested by Grodulf. Around 1070 Canon Gradulf (of Saint-Julien) and his two nephews, Rainald de La Suze and his brother Herbert, made a grant to Saint-Vincent du Mans, attested by Rainald's son Drogo. Herbert was a benefactor of Saint-Aubin, to which he gave the church of Saint-Pierre-des-Ormes with the assent of his mother Hersend and brother Rainald (*Cart. Saint-Aubin* ii, no. DCXXX).

The count's brother, Herbert Bacon, was briefly an unpopular regent for his great-nephew Hugh IV. He was eventually deposed and despatched to a monastery by Bishop Gervaise of Le Mans (*Actus pontificum Cenomannis*, p. 365). The abbey necrology remembers a Count Herbert on 8 September (ms Avranches 214, p. 169, *vi kal. Sept.*). This was possibly either Herbert I Wake-Dog or Herbert Bacon, but cf. Latouche, *Maine*, note 4, p. 26. Also *ibid.*, pp. 22–30, 56–69; Keats-Rohan, 'Politique et parentèle: les comtes, vicomtes et évêques du Maine *c.* 950–1050', *Francia* 26.1 (1996), 13–30; id., 'Observations upon the earliest castellanies in Maine', in *Mondes de l'Ouest et villes du Monde. Mélanges en l'honneur d'André Chédeville*, Rennes 1998, 361–373.

[36]

Another version of Josbert's charter is given in **Appendix i.2**. In no. 107 Hugh Chalibot, husband of Josbert's daughter and heiress, renewed the grant in a charter which remedied a defect they perceived in the original donation.

Archembald fitz Ulric *de Bresis* occurs as husband of Isabelle, sister of Sulpice de Chaumont-Amboise, in two acts of Saint-Serge, Angers, in 1109 and 1116, *Cartulaires de l'abbaye Saint-Serge et Saint-Bach d'Angers*, ed. Y. Chauvin, 2 vols, Angers 1997, i, nos. 225, 234, 295. The charters associate him closely with the family of Jean de La Flèche, son-in-law of Herbert I of Maine and father of Count Helias of Maine (d. 1110), who was father of Countess Eremburg (no. **107**).

[38]

38, **39** and **41** relate to the gift of churches by laymen. The lay ownership of churches was an abuse that was increasingly the subject of lay benefactions to monasteries in the later eleventh and early twelfth centuries. See Guillotel, 'Combour: proto-histoire d'une seigneurie', in *Family Trees*, pp. 269–298. Some of the earlier charters also show the monks attempting to acquire churches in lay control, nos. **25**, **30**, **47**. The problem continued into the time of Robert of Torigny: see A. Dufief, 'Vie monastique au Mont pendant le XIIe siècle', *Mill. mon.* i, pp. 113–116.

This is the first grant of the church of Saint-Berthevin-la-Tannière. It was mentioned again in 1128, when Guy bishop of Le Mans noted its restoration to the abbey after a period during which it had been deserted (no. **45**), a probable reference to the effects of war in the region. A dispute over patronage of the church between the abbey and the bishop of Le Mans was resolved in the abbey's favour *c.* 1180, when Bishop William de Passavant conceded the abbey's claim, despite its defects: *Cart. de l'Abbayette*, no. 15. There is no compelling evidence to accept Angot's identification of this church with that of *Centrannis* (nos. **30**, **47**).

Nothing is known of Robert, grantor of the churches of Saint-Victeur de Levaré and Saint-Berthevin, nor of any link between him and Geoffrey fitz Rivallon, donor of the church of Lévaré whose de Gorron successors held Levaré and Saint-Berthevin-la-Tannière from the seigneurs of Mayenne (nos. **41**, **45**) and were major benefactors of the priory of L'Abbayette (*Cart. de L'Abbayette*, nos. 20, 29–33). A link involving inheritance, probably through females, is nevertheless very likely. Robert speaks of his inheritance, where Geoffrey speaks of his right – *mei iuris*. Geoffrey had probably derived his right through his marriage to Robert's heiress.

Hugh de Mayenne was a younger brother of Geoffrey I de Mayenne (no. **65**) who appears to have usurped the seigneurie after the death of his brother in 1098. His nephew Walter, son of Geoffrey I and successor of an elder brother Hamelin d. *c.* 1099, father of Hamelin (no. **39**) and Juhel I (no. **45**), occurs as seigneur soon after 1100 until 1116. Hugh was father by his wife Beatrice of Geoffrey de Mayenne, bishop of Angers from 1095 until his deposition in 1100/01, when he became a monk of Cluny (O. Guillot, *Le comte d'Anjou*, i, pp. 256, 259, 272–4).

Robert fitz Pavonis, or Robert Le Paon, occurs as clerk of Bishop Hildebert of Le Mans (1096–1125) in 1120 (*Patrologia Latina*, t. 171, col. 314). In that year Robert Pavo, clerk, granted rights in the church of Parigné to the priory of Marmoutier at Mayenne (*Cart. manceau de Marmoutier*, ii, Mayenne nos. XII, XX, pp. 11, 18–19).

[39]

One of the few acts confirmed by Geoffrey I de Mayenne's short-lived grandson Hamelin fitz Walter de Mayenne. He was succeeded by his brother Juhel (no. **45**) *c.* 1120. Another brother, Geoffrey, husband of Filquergardis de La Suze, made a gift for his soul to Saint-Serge in 1130 (Chauvin, *Cartulaire de Saint-Serge* i, no. 328). Their sister Hersende was wife of Ralph de Gorron, heir of Geoffrey fitz Rivallon (nos. **41**, **45**).

The charter is interesting for its claim that Robert and his father were restoring to the abbey what had been its property in the distant past, *antiquitus*, and which had been lost a fair time ago, *aliquanto tempore.* Unfortunately, the agents of this depredation are lost in the ambiguous phrase *malignorum culpa*, which could mean almost anything. Compare the clear statement in Ivo fitz Fulcoin's charter (no. **26**) that the land he restored had been lost during the Norse invasions – *irruente Normannorum infestatione* – and the charter of Alan III who accuses Abbot Almod's predecessors of careless guardianship of the earlier grants of his father, Geoffrey, *incuriam antecessorum abbatum uel monachorum* (no. **24**). The loss probably was at a considerable remove in time because the church of Saint-Denis had been alienated to lay control and had become part of the patrimony of the donor's family. Late in the twelfth century Robert de Landivy granted the chapel of St. Thomas de la Censive to the abbey. The chapel subsequently acquired the revenues of Saint-Denis (*Cart. de l'Abbayette*, nos. 22, 28).

Robert de Saint-Denis attested no. **46**. On Saint-Denis see Angot, *Dictionnaire de la Mayenne*, iii, p. 537.

[40]

Bishop Main of Rennes was son of Haimo II of Alet and nephew of Archbishop Junguené, himself nephew and successor of Archbishop Main (Guillotel, 'Des vicomtes d'Alet'). In this act he concedes to Mont-Saint-Michel the churches of Villamée and Poilley, once subject to his church of St Pierre de Rennes. The vills of Villamée and other adjacent lands were originally given to the abbey by Conan I of Brittany in 990, when the tenant there was Main, *nepos* of Archbishop Main. (**App. ii.1**). Bishop Main was a collateral descendent of this Main.

Main II of Fougères was the seigneur to which Villamée and Poilley were subject by this date. Main I's son Alfred, father of Main II, was probably the one who laid the foundations for the family's rise, which began when his son Main II controlled the new seigneurie of Fougères. Alfred attested several charters of Alan III early in his reign, in the company of Rivallon *le vicaire* and his son Triscan (Guillotel, *Actes*, nos. 10, 13, 19). One of these acts, no. 10, for Marmoutier, he attested in the company of Heldebert I abbot of Mont-Saint-Michel, Mainard abbot of Redon and former abbot of the Mont, and Haimo, *magister* of Alan III, i.e. Haimo I of Alet, father of Rivallon of Dol and Archbishop Junguené. No. 13 is perhaps significant in that Alfred is the last witness, preceded by Goslin Mansel, i.e. the Manceau, from Maine. This Goslin was Gauzlin of Pirmil, one of three brothers mentioned in their step-father Guy's charter for the Mont (nos. **47**, **30**). H. Guillotel has plausibly suggested, in an unpublished paper read to the Sociéte d'archéologie et d'histoire de Bretagne, that Main II of Fougères's wife Adelaide was from Maine and that she introduced the names Ralph and Godehildis into his family; cf. no. **28**, grant by Ralph of Le Mans and his wife Godehildis). At the time of Main's death, *c.* 1064, his sons Juhel (who died in infancy) and Ralph were still minors. He was also father of Godehildis, wife of John I fitz Rivallon of Dol (nos. **18**, **44**). His successor Ralph I of Fougères (d. 1124) was probably the person of that name remembered on 19 September in the Martyrology-Necrology.

After the death of Main of Fougères, Rainer and Hubert sons of Hermeniot sold a portion of land to Marmoutier (Morice, *Preuves* i, col. 405). Hervé son of Hermeniot attested charters in the time of Ralph I of Fougères. Another of Hermeniot's sons, Pinel, gave his name to a family holding land of Fougères at Saint-Sauveur-des-Landes. See no. **57**.

The charter is important evidence for political turbulence in Brittany at that date, since it reveals that two of the witnesses, Hugh brother of Geoffrey and Roscelin fitz Robert de Marcillé, had recently been confined respectively in a neck-yoke or manacles (*boia*) and in chains as prisoners of Robert de Vitré. The incident relates to a war between Robert de Vitré and Brien de Châteaubriant (whose mother Innoguent was a sister of Archbishop Junguené), which itself was related to the struggle between Conan II of Brittany and his uncle Eudo. See J.-P. Brunterc'h, 'Puissance temporelle et pouvoir diocésain des évêques de Nantes entre 936 et 1049', *MSHAB*, t. LXI, 1984, pp. 60–70; H. Guillotel, 'La place de Châteaubriant dans l'essor des châtellenies bretonnes (xi–xii siècles), *MSHAB*, t. LXVI, 1989, pp. 11–18; K. S. B. Keats-Rohan, 'Crime et châtiment à la manière du XIe siècle?: note sur une charte bretonne de l'abbaye du Mont-Saint-Michel', *MSHAB*, 72 (1995) 25–30. Quite why Robert de Vitré should figure in this charter, relating as it does to property far from his own, is not evident. Robert was grandson of Rivallon *vicarius* and son of Triscan. According to the often unreliable Breton historian Pierre Le Baud, Triscan married Innoguent, daughter of Alfred of Fougères. There is almost no surviving record of Triscan's career, but a close family link between his son Robert and the family of Fougères is plausible and would certainly account for Robert's appearance among the witnesses to this charter.

[41]

Geoffrey fitz Rivallon is perhaps the same as Geoffrey, youngest son of Rivallon of Dol (see no. **18** above). He may have been raised by the seigneur of Fougères (John fitz Rivallon married Godehildis sister of Ralph I de Fougères). By 1082 or shortly thereafter Geoffrey was in the service of the count of Mortain ('Chartes du Prieuré de la Sainte-Trinité de Fougères', 192–6; Arch. dépt. d'Ille-et-Vilaine, IF 517, no. 33; *Regesta* i, nos. 145, 204–5.) Rivallon of Dol had supported the Normans in 1064 (see above, no. **18**). Main II of Fougères had recognized Norman overlordship of his land beyond the Sélune as early as 1050 (Fauroux, *Recueil*, nos. 160–62). In 1082 Robert of Mortain is evidenced in charge of the castle of Gorron, probably recently built by the Normans, who had built a castle at Ambrières in 1055 before their conquest of Maine (J. Boussard, 'Le comté de Mortain', *Le Moyen Age*, 58 (1952), 273–276). Both these castles lay in the territory of the seigneur of Mayenne, who may have been related to the counts of Maine. Geoffrey's descendants were surnamed de Gorron from their service in the ward of this castle, but their landholdings were further west, in the val d'Ernée, where they later built a castle at Saint-Berthevin-la-Tannière. This was the area in which Ivo fitz Fulcoin had made his restitution to the abbey *c.* 1000 (no. **26**) and one that was dominated by 1100 by the seigneurs of Mayenne, the counts of Mortain and the seigneurs of Fougères. There is no datable trace of Geoffrey after 1100. Between 1100 and 1106 William count of Mortain seems to have lost the support of many of the Bretons and Manceaux who had worked for his father in the castles ofAmbrières and Gorron because of a war he waged against Walter of Mayenne. Walter tried to obtain peace by arranging a consanguineous marriage between William and his daughter, but Hildebert of Le Mans forbade the match (Bossuet, ed., *Recueil des historiens de la France*, t. 15, p. 317; discussed in Keats-Rohan, 'The prosopography of post-Conquest England: four case studies', *Medieval Prosopography* 14.1 (1993), 1–52). It was probably this war that occasioned the damage referred to in no. **45**, a charter of William de Gorron. William of Mortain was captured at Tinchebrai in 1106, when Walter of Mayenne was also captured and imprisoned at the castle of Fougères. Rivallon fitz Geoffrey made a grant to Marmoutier that he had ratified by the imprisoned Walter at Fougères (*Cartulaire Manceau de Marmoutiers*, ed. E. Laurain, 1903, t. II, 5–6). This Rivallon was the Ruallo de Gorron who attested Savigny charters of Hamelin de L'Ecluse, his wife Adelaide, son Hamelin and brother Ernald (Mayenne, cant. Gorron, comm. Brécé) together with William son of Ralph de Gorron, *c.* 1116/20 (Van Moolenbroek, *Savigny*, nos. 15, 15a). Ralph de Gorron was married to Walter of Mayenne's daughter Hersendis. Their sons William and Henry occur as benefactors of Mont-Saint-Michel in 1128 (no. **45**). The Ralph who appears as the first witness to this charter was conceivably Geoffrey's heir Ralph de Gorron. Hamelin was perhaps Hamelin de l'Ecluse.

Alfred Bozart was son of Bozart de Castellario (cf. Hamelin de Castelario, no. **40**), a tenant of Ralph I de Fougères who attested, with Harscoet son of Bosard, an early grant of Ralph to Savigny (Moolenbroek, *Vital l'Ermite prédicateur*, App., Savigny charter no. 12). Named from Le Châtellier, (Ille-et-Vilaine) near Fougères.

Geoffrey de Colombiers was probably from Colombiers-le-Plessis, near Gorron. Around 1181 Pope Lucius gave judgement for the monks against Adam de Columberiis who had clained rights in the church of Lévaré and at Montenay (*Cart. de L'Abbayette*, no. 16). A later Geoffrey de Colombiers attested a charter of William de Gorron for Savigny (Arch. de Mayenne, H38, no. 94.

[42]

The westernmost possession of the abbey, the location of this grant was the modern *lieu-dit* of Le Moustier in Elliant, cant. Rosporden, dépt. Finistère, in the county of Cornouailles, diocese of Quimper. The priory was known as Treverez and Locmikael in medieval times and occurs under both names in various papal confirmations. This grant was misplaced among the muniments of Gohory priory in the Inventory, fol. 126v; the list for the priory of Treverez on fol. 125v includes *Litera de Plestim de compositione inter nos et rectorem ecclesie de Plestim ratione capelle de Naugarae* and *Litera pro decima de Hyrglas contra inuasores ipsius decime*. The donor, bishop of the newly created see of Tréguier in northern Brittany, will have been a nobleman of Cornouaille by birth, according to Joëlle Quaghebeur, *La Cornouaille du IXe au XIIe siècle* (2nd edn., Rennes, 2002), p. 382. Saint-Pabuel is perhaps modern Saint-Pabu, comm. cant. Ploudalmezeau, Finistère.

Between the death of Alan III of Brittany in 1040 and the grant of Conan III in 1116 (no. **63**) there were no grants to the abbey involving the rulers of Brittany, Hoel count of Cornouaille, duke from 1066 until 1084 in right of his wife, sister of Conan II, and his son Alan IV (1084 to *c.* 1115). The monks seem nonetheless to have had the support of the rival collateral line formed by the heirs of Alan III's brother Count Eudo (nos. **17** and **23**), probably because of the close links between Count Geoffrey Boterel I and the lords of Dol (nos. **18**, **44**, **App. ii.4**). In 1098 Stephen son of Count Eudo, brother of Alan III of Brittany (see no. **17**), succeeded his brothers Alan I Rufus (d. 1093) and Alan II Niger (d. 1098) as lord of the honour of Richmond in England. Their eldest brother Geoffrey Boterel (d. 1093) had stayed in Brittany, to which another brother, Brien, returned in 1069. Count Brien had been a major landholder in Cornwall before his retirement late in 1069, when the county was given to Robert, count of Mortain (see under no. **11** above). Both Geoffrey (died 24 August 1093) and his brother Brien (died on a 14 February after 1086) were remembered in the monks's Martyrology-Necrology. Stephen's eldest son was Geoffrey II Boterel (d. 1148), who married a daughter of John fitz Rivallon of Dol-Combour (d. 1093); he occurs in 1141 as a supporter of the Empress Matilda during the English civil war. His rival was his brother Alan III, lord of Richmond, benefactor of the abbey's priory of St Michael's Mount and firm supporter of King Stephen. Alan was the first husband of Conan III's daughter and heiress Bertha and father of Conan IV. Bertha's mother was a natural daughter of Henry I, benefactor of the abbey and father of the

Empress (no. **108**). Both Bertha and Conan IV occur in the Martyrology-Necrology. H. Guillotel, 'Les origines de Guingamp', *MSHAB*, 56 (1979); Dom A. Wilmart, 'Alain le Roux et Alain le Noir', *Annales de Bretagne*, 38 (1929), 576–595; K. S. B. Keats-Rohan, 'The Bretons and Normans of England 1066–1154: the family, the fief, and the feudal monarchy', *Nottingham Mediaeval Studies* 36 (1992), 42–78.

Rivallon *vicecomes* was probably the *vicomte* of Poher, possibly a son of Hadvisa, daughter of Rivallon I of Dol (see no. **17**).

Ruald son of Guegon/Wigan was perhaps a relative of Rivallon of Poher and allied also to the family of Hennebont; see Joëlle Quaghebeur, *La Cornouaille du IXe au XIIe siècle* (2nd edn., Rennes, 2002), p. 383. He occurs as witness in a notification concerning Marmoutier abbey's priory of Lamballe in 1084 (*Ancien Evéchés*, IV, pp. 300–1).

[43]

This item occurs in the Inventory, fol. 123v, under Saint-Germain-sur-Ay as *Carta Nielli de Sancta Columba cum consuetudinibus a G. Normanorum ducis confirmata*.

Niel the priest was very probably a relative of Niel of Saint-Sauveur, *vicomte* of the Cotentin, who attests the confirmation by William II of Normandy. A son of a Niel the priest is mentioned in no. **115** as having usurped abbey property at Dragey (cant. Sartilly, Manche).

Archbishop Maurilius: the obit of *Maurilius archiepiscopus Rothom-* is given on 11 July in MS Avranches 214, p. 101. His death on 9 August 1067 was described by Orderic Vitalis (ii, 198).

William fitz Osbern, son of Countess Gunnor's nephew Osbern fitz Herfast (no. **2**), intimate of William II of Normandy. After the conquest of England he acquired extensive lands in the south-west of England in the old earldom of Wessex. He was killed in battle against the Flemings in 1071, leaving a son Roger whose reduction to the earldom of Hereford led to his revolt in 1075. A junior, much reduced, line was established by Roger's son Rainald in Herefordshire. Father also of William (no. **69**), who succeeded him at Breteuil and Pacy in Normandy, and of Emma, wife of Ralph II de Montfort-Gael, son of Ralph I *Anglicus* who attested no. **23**. *Dom. People*, pp. 487–8; *Dom. Desc*, pp. 233, 878.

William de Vauville (comm. cant. Beaumont-Hague, Manche), member of a family holding land from the seigneurie of Saint-Sauveur. He was a tenant of the bishop of Coutances in Devon after 1066. The family occurs as benefactors of the abbey of Montebourg, Paris BN lat. 10087, nos. 506–8, p. 157.

[44]

There is a hill at Bernoui called Le Petit-Mont-Saint-Michel.

John was the second son and successor of Rivallon I of Dol-Combour (see no. **18**). Father, by Godehildis of Fougères, of Gelduin II of Dol-Combour and of a daughter who married Geoffrey II Boterel (cf. no. **42**), a great-nephew of Alan III of Brittany. He became a monk of Saint-Florent de Saumur, of which his brother William was abbot, *c.* 1084, leaving his seigneurie to his son Rivallon II. Before 1095 Rivallon II was dead and had been succeeded by his brother Gelduin (nos. **20**, **54**). At the death of Even archbishop of Dol in 1096 John became archbishop-elect, a position briefly occupied in August–September 1076 by his brother Gelduin fitz Rivallon (no. **18**), whose appointment the pope had refused to ratify. He died on his way to Rome to receive his pallium. Guillotel, 'Des vicomtes d'Alet', 205–6.

Hugh Taon was probably the son of Rainfred and Adelaide. He gave land at Ros-sur-Couësnon to Saint-Florent de Saumur (Arch. dépt. Maine-et-Loire, H. 3713, fol. 76v). The names Rainfred and Adelaide both occur in the necrology, ms Avranches 214, Rainfred on 18 February, p. 113, and, on 14 August, Adelaide, p. 160. Hugo Taon and Haimeric fitz Geoffrey attested the charter by which by Count Geoffrey Boterel (no. **42**), then living in Dol, founded a priory of Marmoutier at Lamballe (*Anciens Evéchés de Bretagne*, IV, p. 300). Geoffrey fitz Haimeric or Aimeric was one of the *filii Aimerici* who held Cherrueix of the archbishops of Dol. Two of them, Geoffrey and his brother Alan, were the ancestors of families (Boterel and de Lanvallay) established both in Brittany and in England; Keats-Rohan, 'Wigan the Marshal and other Bretons in Orderic Vitalis's *Ecclesiastical History*', *JMH* 20, 1994, 35–6.

For the *nepotes* of Trehan fitz Brien, benefactor of the priory of Saint-Broladre, see nos. **21** and **56**.

Baderon was the son of Caradoc of Laboussac. He succeeded his brother Wihenoc as lord of the honour of Monmouth in Wales. The brothers were co-founders of a priory established there as a cell of Saint-Florent de Saumur, of which John's brother was abbot; H. Guillotel, 'Une famille bretonne aux services du Conquérant: les Baderon', *Droit privé et institutions régionales: Etudes historiques offertes à Jean Yver* (1976), 361–6.

Warin de Maidreio, named from Moidrey (Manche, cant. Pontorson).

[45]

On the devastation mentioned in this charter, the result of a war between William, count of Mortain, and the seigneurs of Mayenne, see notes to no. **41**. The original grant of the church of Saint-Berthevin-la-Tannière had been made by Robert *c.* 1100 (no. **38**).

Guy d'Etampes, bishop of Le Mans from 1126 until his death on 7 February 1135.

William and Henry de Gorron were the sons of Ralph fitz Geoffrey fitz Rivallon de Gorron (no. **41**) and Hersende, daughter of Walter de Mayenne (no. **38**).

Jordan was their sister's husband. Jordan and Salomon sons of Maurice, known both as de Mayenne and de Gorron, an intimate of Juhel de Mayenne, occur in Mayenne and Fougères charters from *c.* 1128 to 1160 (eg. *Cart. manceau de Marmoutier* ii, p. 439).

The children of William de Gorron and Matilda were probably very young in 1128. Their heir was their son Gilo, father of another William. Gilo was mentioned in the bull of Alexander III in 1179; he was remembered on 31 March in the abbey Necrology. The family were benefactors of the Mont's priory of L'Abbayette and the abbey of Savigny (*Cart. de L'Abbayette*, nos. 20, 21, 29–33; Paris, Arch. nationales L 693, nos. 385–7). William and Henry also had brothers Ralph and Ivo.

Geoffrey de Gorron, who was appointed abbot of the important monastery of St Albans by Henry I in 1119, was probably their uncle (*Gesta Abbatum Sancti Albani* , ed. H. T. Riley, Rolls Series 1867–9, i. 73). He was accompanied to England by a number of relatives, including Ivo, and a nephew Robert who also became abbot at St Albans. William de Gorron and Juhel de Mayenne were among the prisoners taken by Henry II at Dol in 1173.

Juhel de Mayenne, son of Walter, was grandson of Geoffrey I de Mayenne (no. **65**), and brother of Hamelin (no. **39**). His wife Clemence was a daughter of William de Bellême count of Alençon and Ela of Burgundy (Torigny, Interpolation in William of Jumièges, ii, 266). Their son Geoffrey cannot have been more than a child at this date.

Heluin de Montenay was the donor of no. **46**.

Osmund Pisce, son of Hugh, was the ancestor of the seigneurs of Vautortes, a fief of Mayenne (B.N. lat. 14822, p. 454). He was father by Juliana of Saint-Hilaire-des-Landes of Hugh II of Vautortes and Ingeran (Arch. dépt. de la Mayenne, H 33, pp. 44–50, 108–9).

Harscoit and Roger de Maidreio were named from Moidrey (Manche, cant. Pontorson). In 1155 Alfred de Maidreio became a monk of the abbey, to which he gave 5 solidi of Le Mans per annum in the marsh of Ardevon (Delisle, *Torigni*, ii, p. 250).

William of Ambrières was son of Arraud fitz Hugh of Ambrières, as appears from a charter for the priory of Marmoutiers at Mayenne (*Cart. manceau*, ii, Mayenne no. VIII).

Geoffrey IV Le Bel of Anjou, son of Fulk V, king of Jerusalem by right of his second wife from 1129, was count of Maine as heir of his mother Countess Eremburg (d. 1126) (no. **107**), daughter and heiress of Count Helias of Maine (d. 1110).

[46]

Montenay, cant. Ernée, was a fief of the seigneurie of Mayenne. William de Montenay occurs in 1150 when Geoffrey de Mayenne confirmed to Savigny land in Châtillon-sur-Colmont once part of William's fee (Arch. de la Mayenne, H 35, p. 519). See Angot, *Dictionnaire de la Mayenne*, iii, p. 77.

Robert de Saint-Denis; see no. **39**.

[47]

Several previous commentaries on this charter have failed to understand the relationships expressed within it (cf. Dubois, 'Les dépendances', *Mill. mon.* i, p. 642; Potts, *Monastic Revival*, pp. 92–3). The donor of the charter, Guy, sells, at the abbot's request, his rights in two parts of the church of *Centrannis*. He explains that the rights were held by his *antecessor* and his wife, to whose dower they pertained, who had mortgaged them to the monks. After their deaths, the rights had reverted to Guy. This couple were clearly not Guy's parents and his rights not hereditary (unlike modern commentators, he does not make either claim). The word *antecessor* was used of their father-in-law by men giving charters disposing of the property inherited by their wives, which is the case here (numerous examples could be adduced, eg. Hugh Chalibot's charter, no. **107**; see Keats-Rohan, '*Antecessor noster*', *Prosopon* 2, May 1995). Guy needs the authorization also of his step-sons, Hugh, Gauzlin and Herbran, the sons of his wife Rainburgis's first marriage, because they share her inherited right in the property, which Guy himself enjoys only *iure uxoris*. Hugh and his brothers gave a separate charter selling the same two parts some fifteen years later (no. **30**). Hugh was the great-grandfather of a later benefactor of the abbey, William de Sillé (no. **65**).

Guy's identity is a matter for speculation. His wife's children were the ancestors of the seigneurs of Sillé-le-Guillaume and Pirmil; see no. **30** above. The name Raimburgis occurs more than once in the abbey's necrology; cf. MS Avranches 214, p. 153, where the names occurs for the Kalends of July (1 July) between Emma and Gisla, and on V Nones (3 July) with Flaaudus *miles* and Ermenildis.

The witness list is directly comparable with that for no. **26**, both acts possibly belonging to the same occasion. Isaac attested an act of Count Hugh for La Couture of *c.* 990, as did Drogo son of William, Hubert and Bishop Seifrid of Le Mans (*Cart. St-Pierre-de-la-Couture*, no. 6). The Hugh fitz Herbran mentioned in a charter of Hugh III (**Appendix ii.2**) was probably Guy's predecessor (see nos. **26** and **30**).

[48]

Geoffrey le Bel acts for Saint-Victeur as successor, through his mother Eremburg (d. 1126), of the counts of Maine. Pipin provost of Anjou also occurs as Pipin of Tours. Peter *Calopin* was probably a relative of Hugh Chalopin (no. **107**). Cf. *Cartulaire de Saint-Victeur*, no. 8, for rents due from dwellings *c.* 1040.

[49]

Geoffrey's father William Goion occurs in nos. **57** and **119** as a benefactor of the abbey who subsequently found himself in the position of usurper forced to make restitution. Geoffrey's grant and restitution see him, his father and other forebears absolved from excommunication. His heir was a niece

Dameta, wife of Adam de Hereford, who later confirmed the gifts of her grandfather William and her uncles Robert and Geoffrey Goion (Morice, *Preuves*, i, 643; Inventory, fol. 125r), authorized by her lord Rolland de Dinan. Their fee was La Roche-Goion, afterwards called the castellany of Matignon, in Lamballe. Cf. ibid., 455, 562, 579, 602, 623.

Donoald, bishop of Alet, was son of William l'Ismaélite of Tinteniac, and brother of Noga, wife of Gelduin fitz John of Dol (nos. **54**, **20**). A former monk of Mont-Saint-Michel, he became abbot of Saint-Melaine de Rennes in 1116, and bishop of Alet in 1120. He died in 1142, and was remembered in the Mont Martyrology-Necrology on 19 August. Guillotel, 'Les évêques d'Alet du IX au milieu du XII siècle', *Soc. hist. arch. de l'arrondissement de Saint-Malo, Année 1979, 251–66.*

William Pontel; cf. the Pointel or Ponitel brothers of Geoffrey Caorces (no. **59**)

[50]

Escirard husband of Hildiardis [Hildegarde] is probably the nephew of Robert fitz Haimo; see below, no. **67**. A number of subsequent charters were listed in the Inventory of 1326 under the heading *Bala[ant] et Capella Hamelin* (fol. 116v). One of them was a grant by Oliva, daughter of Jordan fitz Alan (no. **76**).

[51]

Robert de Lapenty was a tenant of Ralph I de Fougères at Romagné, cant. Fougères. Charters for Savigny show that as well as Hamelin he had a son Philip (Bib. mun. Flers 22, no. 20; B. N. lat. nov. acq. 1002, p. 15). Attested a confirmation charter for Savigny as a vassal of the count of Mortain in 1113 (van Moolenbroek, no. 11). Pouëssel, 'Fiefs de Mortain', 89–90 (his identification of the location of *Lentilleis* is erroneous).

Richard de *Tuschueio* attested a grant to Savigny by Philip fitz Milo de Louvigné *c.* 1114 (van Moolenbroek, *Vital...Savigny*, no. 13, pp. 279–80). The grant was made in her house at Notre-Dame-du-Touchet (cant. Mortain) where Clarice, Philip's mother, lay dying. See also, Pouëssel, 'Fiefs de Mortain', 118–20.

[52]

Mainard II, abbot of Mont-Saint-Michel from 991 until 1009. Prior of the abbey under his predecessor Mainard I (**Appendix ii.1**). Resigned as abbot in 1009 and retired to Redon of which he had previously been appointed abbot by Geoffrey, duke of Brittany (d. 1008), according to a chronicle of Redon preserved at Mont-Saint-Michel: 'Eodem tempore sub Gaufrido, Conani filio, Mainardus abbas Rothoniense monasterium et abbatiam sancti Michaelis de Periculo maris optime rexit sed, Rothoniense vivens, dimisit', *Annales de Saint-Sauveur de Redon*, ed. Ph. Labbe, *Nova bibliotheca manuscriptorum*, t. 1

(Paris, 1675), p. 250; *PL* 202, col. 1326B. These annals are preserved in a fifteenth-century copy in a Mont manuscript, Avranches 213, fol. 178. See Hubert Guillotel, 'Le premier siècle du pouvoir ducal breton', in *Actes du 103e Congrès national des Sociétés Savantes, Nancy-Metz 1977, Section de philologie et d'histoire jusqu'à 1610* (Paris, 1979), p. 83. Described at Redon as *Vir magnae vitae et sanctitatis*, allegedly still alive in 1025 (*Cartulaire de Redon*, ed. A. de Courson, Appendix, pp. 425–6).

[53]

Geoffrey fitz Oliver de Dinan (d. 1123); great-nephew of Rivallon of Dol, whose brother Josselin (no. **23**) was Oliver's father. See Michael Jones, *The Family of Dinan in England in the Middle Ages*, Dinan 1987.

Wiguen *miles* was probably the Guiguen *uicarius Aletensium ciuitatis* who was one of the donors of no. **57**.

[54]

This grant is probably the earlier of the two grants by Clamarhoc. The reference to the son of John of Dol is probably to his eldest son, Rivallon II, who succeeded as a minor and had died by 1096. William fitz Harscoit occurs in a charter of Saint-Florent de Saumur (Arch. dépt. Maine-et-Loire, H. 3713, fol. 76v) claiming land in Mezvoit in Dol from John fitz Rivallon. He gave Hingand and Baderon de Laboussac (no. **44**) as pledges.

[55]

Alan fitz Aimeric; brother of Geoffrey (no. **44**).

Walter was named from Montrouault, Rossell from a now-lost village named Saint-Georges, John from Moidrey and Enard from Montitier. Demorand de Monte was presumably named from Mont-Saint-Michel itself.

Brien was named from Chesnaye-au-Bouteiller, fief of the butlers of Dol. He and his brother John occur in no. **68**.

[56]

(cf. **21**) A series of early grants to the priory of Saint-Broladre, based on grants made by Trihan fitz Brien of Saint-Broladre, a vassal of John of Dol (no. **44**). The churches mentioned are probably the churches of St Peter and St Broladre mentioned in no. **19**. See also no. **114**.

[57]

The Dol inquest of 1181 stated that what Mont-Saint-Michel held in the *voyerie* of the pays d'Alet was part of the domaine of the archbishop of Dol (Duine, *Histoire ...de Dol*, pp. 41–3). Wigan (Guegon) *uicarius* son of Herhad and brother of Haimo contested the grant of his vassal Robert fitz Bresel de Ploierno to the church of Alet, for which he did penance in 1098 (Morice, *Preuves*, i, cols. 491–2, 497); *Gall. Christ*. xiv, 999. Wigan of Alet was conceivably the man recruited as his marshal by Henry I. Granted land in Cornwall, he was married to Juliana Pantulf and with her acquired land in Warwickshire. He became *vicomte* of Exmes and was given the ward of the castles of Gorron and Ambrières before 1135. Keats-Rohan, 'Two studies in North French prosopography: 2. Wigan the Marshal and other Bretons in Orderic Vitalis's *Ecclesiastical History*', *JMH* 20, 1994, 26–30.

Flaaldus was the seneschal of the archbishop of Dol. His son Alan was one of the first Bretons to be promoted in England by the new king Henry I in 1100: J. H. Round, 'The origin of the Stewarts', in *Studies in Peerage and Family History*, London 1901, pp. 115–31.

Pinel was a tenant of Ralph of Fougères (also an English landholder), and son of Hermeniot fitz Duiseth (no. **40**); Arch. dépt. Ille-et-Vilaine, IF 543, nos. iii, vii, xiii. He gave the mill of Tronchet to the priory of Sainte-Trinité de Fougères (*Chartes... Fougères*, no. XI). Father of William and Hamelin, who were the first of Pinel's descendants to take his name as a surname. The family were lords of Chaudeboeuf in Saint-Sauveur-des-Landes, a major fief of the barony of Fougères.

[58]

Ruallend Calcebos, father of William, was one of the abbey's lay administrators. In 1155 he restored land he had usurped at Beauvoir, Montitier and Genêts (Delisle, *Torigni*, ii, p. 242). William occurs as a fee-holder of the abbey in 1172, holding of the fee of Badelun (? Baderon) and of his own father (ibid., pp. 299–300). A Geoffrey Calcebuef occurs in the late-eleventh century at Tremblay in the Breton seigneurie of Fougères in a Saint-Florent charter attested also by Harscoit *vicecomes* de Saint-James and Alfred son of Rorgo; Arch. dépt. Maine-et-Loire, H3515, iv.

[59]

John and Walter Chaorcin, uncles of Hervé de Tremigon, who gave tithes of Chastillies to the priory of Combour *c.* 1150 (Morice, *Preuves*, i, col. 642).

[60]

See no. **[31]**, above.

[61]

The witnesses were from Moidrey (Manche, cant. Pontorson), Meigné (Manche, cant. Ducey, comm. Crollon), Boucey (Manche, cant. Pontorson), Dameigné (Manche, comm. Curey, cant. Pontorson), and Curey (Manche, cant. Pontorson). The son of Richolin de Boucey was donor of no. **93**.

[62]

A forged version of a genuine charter (printed in **Appendix i. 3** and discussed below) relating to abbey property in Anjou and the Touraine. It has been discussed by Olivier Guillot, *Le comte d'Anjou et son entourage*, t. 2, <C 26>,

p. 307: 'La notice a été fabriqué en utilisant de manière maladroite l'une des clauses d'une donation authentique faite par Foulques le Réchin à l'abbaye, et certains seulement des personnages qui y sont cités ... Mais ici, la notice est datée d'une manière qui condamne l'acte: en l'an 1090 "au premier jour de l'Avent", l'évêque d'Angers n'était pas Renaud mais Geoffroy (de Tours). Le nom du prétendu évêque Renaud est cité pourtant à deux reprises, une fois dans le corps de la notice, tout près de la date, une autre à l'endroit des souscriptions. De plus, et ceci écarte l'hypothèse d'une simple erreur de date, la souscription de Marbode "maître école" est incompatible avec la présence de l'évêque Renaud: Marbode, devenu évêque de Rennes,a cessé d'être maître-école dès 1096 (Ch. Urseau, *Introd.* au *Cartul. noir de Saint-Maurice*, p. xlvi), tandis que Renaud n'a été ordonné évêque d'Angers que le 12 janvier 1102 (*Annales de Saint-Aubin*, *Rec. d'ann. angev. et vend.*, p. 6). On voit mal pour quelles raisons bizarres cet acte diffus a été fabriqué. Ce fut peut-être pour mettre les possessions angevines et tourangelles du Mont-Saint-Michel à l'abri de la représaille comtale lors de quelque différend entre la Normandie et l'Anjou. La chose n'est guère concevable que jusqu'en 1144, cf. *Annales de Saint-Aubin*, *Rec. d'ann. angev. et vend.*, pp. 10–11'. Perhaps forged during 1150. See Introduction, pp. 38–9, above.

[63]

Conan III of Brittany (1114/5–48) was son of Alan IV Fergant and grandson of Hadvise, sister of Conan II (d. 1066) and daughter of Alan III (nos. **17**, **23**). He married Matilda, a natural daughter of Henry I, by whom he left a daughter and heiress Bertha, wife first of Alan III of Richmond (grandson of Alan III's brother Count Eudo) and secondly of Eudo, *vicomte* of Porhoët. His sister Hadvisa was divorced from Baldwin VII of Flanders before this charter was given. On Conan see H. Guillotel, 'Administration et finances ducales sous le règne de Conan III', *MSHAB* lxviii, 1991, 19–43. This charter occurs among the muniments of Saint-Meloir in the Inventory, fol. 125r, attributed to Count Alan.

Brice bishop of Nantes died 30 October 1140.

Geoffrey I de La Guerche was son of Silvester, bishop of Rennes and a great-grandson of Theobald, bishop of Rennes (**Appendix ii.1**). He acquired a tenancy-in-chief in England in marriage with Alfeva, daughter of Leofwin, but returned to La Guerche in 1093. Charters show he had a son Hervé (Morice, *Preuves*, i, col. 529). The seigneurie of La Guerche was held by his brother William. *Dom. People*, p. 226. J.-C. Meuret, 'Familles seigneuriales aux confins Anjou-Bretagne', *MSHAB*, lxx (1993), 91ff.

Simon II fitz Bernard of La Roche-Bernard (Morbihan), founder of Monton priory (*Cartulaire de Notre-Dame de Monton...dioc. Nantes*, ed. Ct. Paul de Berthou, 1903). His wife was a sister of Josselin de Porhoët (descendant of the donor of no. **22**)

Oliver, son of Brien, seigneur de Varades (Loire-Atlantique) in the county of Nantes, was father by his wife Agnes Dangerosa of six sons, including his heir Brien and Peter, a canon of Tours, and a daughter Margaret, wife of Geoffrey d'Ancenis (d. *c.* 1147); Morice, *Preuves* i, col. 542; Paris B. N. lat. 5441/3, p. 326, no. 3)

[64]

Main was a son of Ralph Largus of Gahard (Morice, *Preuves*, i, 408; *Cartulaire de Saint-Aubin d'Angers*, ii, no. 677, pp. 171–5; Arch. dépt. d'Ille-et-Vilaine, IF 529, Gahard III). His wife Adelaide was daughter of Humphrey de Bohun. Their son William, known in England as de Albini Brito, was a favourite of Henry I, who married him to an important Lincolnshire heiress before 1129 (*Dom. Desc.*, pp. 271–22). The *Liber vitae* of Thorney Abbey, BL Additional MS 40,000, fol. 2r, provides important information on the family: *Main pater Willelmi de Albinico. Adelisa. Hunfredus de Buun avunculus eius. Hos colligimus in anniversario quem faciemus pro animabus patrum et matrum nostrorum. Willelmus de Albinico. Cecilia uxor eius* [granddaughter and heiress of Robert de Tosny, lord of Belvoir, Leicestershire]. *Filii eius Willelmus. Rogerus. Matildis filia eius. Istis concedimus fraternitatem loci.*

The brothers Euen de Albini, Helias de Albini and Geoffrey de Chauvigné, occur as tenants of their cousin William II de Albini Brito in England (*Dom. Desc.*, pp. 270–1, 392).

Main de Saint-Germain was probably a nephew of the donor, one of whose many brothers was Euen de Saint-Germain (B. N. lat. 5441.3, pp. 295–6).

[65]

The abbey holdings in the fief of Sillé-le-Guillaume at this date are unidentifiable (did they include the parts of the church of *Centrannis* sold in nos. 30 and 47?). William, son of Hugh of Sillé and Oldeburga, was grandson of Hugh de Sillé and Reine (no. 30). His father opposed Geoffrey de Mayenne as regent of Maine in 1070, by when the influence of his family was well established in the county (*Actus pont. Cenom.*, p. 378). William gave his name to Sillé-le-Guillaume. Father of Hugh (fl. 1090/1140) and William. His descendant was remembered in the Obituary, Avranches 215, 169r, on 17 Sept.: *Guill. de Silliaco miles de quo habemus pictanciam.*

Berard de Sillé founded the church of Beaulieu in Le Mans in 1121 with his sons Hugh, Richard, Matthew *canonicus*, Hubert and Simon (B. N. Coll. Baluze 38, fol. 275r). Laurain, *Généalogies féodales*, regarded Berard as a brother of William. He also suggested that Albert de Sillé, husband of Eremburg and father of Hugh, William, Richildis and Eremburg (*Cart. Saint-Vincent*, no. 269) was another of the sons of Oldeburga. *Inventaire des titres de l'abbaye de Beaulieu du Mans (1124–1413)*, ed. L. Froger, Archives historique du Maine vii (Le Mans, 1907). Beaulieu was located a short distance to the west of the abbey's priory of Saint-Victeur, which by 1170 was disputing rights in the church of Domfront-en-Champagne with Beaulieu. Domfront lies about 15km south-east of Sillé-le-Guillaume. Land there was given *c.* 1060 to the priory by Geoffrey Payn de Sevillé, his wife Eremburg and sons Fulcoius and Hugh (*Cart. Saint-Victeur*, no. 10).

Hoel, bishop of Le Mans from 1081 until 1096.

Hubert *uicecomes* of Le Mans was the great-grandson of the *uicecomes* Ralph and his wife Godehildis who made a gift to the abbey in no. **28**. His father Ralph (son of Ralph, son of Ralph) was dead by 1067. Hubert married Ermengarde, daughter of William, count of Nevers, a niece of Robert the Burgundian, lord of Sablé. He died *c.* 1095 leaving four sons, his successor Ralph, Hubert, William and Denis, and a daughter Godehildis (*Cart. St-Aubin d'Angers*, no. DCC.) Famous as a determined opponent of the Normans in Maine.

[66]

The charter of Ranulf de Poilley can be dated by its witness Stephen fitz Ivo, who occurs in a document of Sainte-Trinité de Fougères in the time of Ralph I of Fougères (c. 1066–1124) ('Chartes du prieuré de La Sainte-Trinité de Fougères', pp. 248–50). Ranulf was perhaps one of the sons of Ansger, donor of no. **24**, whose sons Corbin, Ranulf and Hervé are mentioned in documents of Saint-Florent de Saumur of the mid-eleventh century (Arch. dépt. Maine-et-Loire H 3713, fol. 65v).

[67]

In a charter for Sées (Arch. dépt. de l'Orne, H938, fol. 34) mention is made of a sale of land at *Vado Calvonis* by Escirard, nephew of Robert fitz Hamon. Perhaps this man should be identified with Escirard husband of Hildiardis de la Chapelle-Hamelin, near Saint-James, a benefactor of Mont-Saint-Michel (no. **50**). Robert fitz Hamon, the donor of this charter, was later a monk of the abbey, as appears from no. **16**, involving members of the Saint-John family.

The family of Ralph de Saint-Jean-le-Thomas occurs frequently in the cartulary (see no. **16**). They were among the west Normans who profited from the favour of Henry I.

[68]

John Caisnel and his brother Brien (no. **55**) were named from Chesnaye-au-Bouteiller, fief of the butlers of Dol. John and his son Philip attested the grant by Prima (no. **91**).

The monk Robert *Legatus* was remembered in the Martyrology-Necrology on 11 October.

The monk Richard de Musca would later be elected abbot in succession to Abbot Geoffrey, provoking a conflict with Henry of Normandy. See Introduction, p. 000.

The monk Geoffrey *Episcopus*, or Levesque, was perhaps the Geoffrey elected to succeed Abbot Bernard the night the latter died, on 8 May 1141. He was from a local family. Richard, surnamed *Episcopus*, archdeacon of Coutances, who held the fee farm of *Estreis* (lost place in the southern Cotentin) from the abbey, occurs in 1157 (Delisle, *Torigni*, ii, pp. 239–40).

[69]

Mont-Saint-Michel treated the memory of Duke Robert II Curthose more kindly than any other Norman house, despite the fact that he once (1091) besieged his brother, the future King Henry I, on the Mont and had subsequently ended his life in Henry's prison on 11 February 1134 (Orderic Vitalis, iv, pp. 118–20, 148, 164, 220–226, 250; vi, pp. 98, 280). The monks remembered both Robert (11 February) and his wife Sibil of Conversano (18 March) in their Martyrology-Necrology.

William de Breteuil was son of William fitz Osbern (nos. **11**, **43**). He succeeded to his father's Norman honour of Breteuil in 1071. He died in January 1103 leaving no issue by his wife Adeline, daughter of Hugh II de Montfort (Ord. Vit. vi, 40).

[70]

Robert bishop of Sées *c.* 1070 - *c.* 1081 (also witnessed no. **90**) was a son of Hubert de Ryes (Calvados, arr. Bayeux) (no. **90**), from a family notably loyal to William II of Normandy (Ord. Vit. ii, 254). His brothers Eudo Dapifer and Adam were among those whom followed the duke to England after 1066 (*Dom. Peop*, pp. 123, 194).

Roger de Montgomery, Roger de Beaumont: see no. **9**.

Richard *proconsul*, Richard Goz, *vicomte* of Avranches (no. **6**), father of Earl Hugh of Chester (no. **74**).

Turgis de Tracy's son William was a benefactor of the abbey. See **Appendix ii.7**.

[**71** and **72**]

Robert fitz William fitz Wimund Cufel; his wife Hadvise, as is clear from the *Pipe Roll 30 Henry I*, p. 155, was daughter of Gelduin fitz John of Dol (cf. no. **54**) and hence granddaughter of John fitz Rivallon of Dol, nos. **18**, **44**). Robert was lord of the Devonshire honour of Okehampton through the marriage of a daughter of Baldwin de Meules (uncle of the wife of Ralph de Fougères) to William fitz Wimund (*Complete Peerage*, iii, pp. 308–9, 317). The Cartulary gives her name as Matilda. Her second husband was Ranulf Avenel (cf. no. **76**), by whom she was mother of Ranulf Avenel junior. Robert's sister married William Paynel, grandson of the William Paynel of no. **90** (Delisle, *Torigni*, ii, no. 42, pp. 254–5). The grants of William fitz Wimund and Ranulf Avenel were later disputed by Fulk Paynel and resolved in an accord of 1157 (*ibid.*, no. 41, pp. 254–5). Robert fitz William was a supporter of the Empress

Matilda during the English civil war. Before its end in 1154, his daughter and heiress Matilda had been married to the Empress's half brother Robert fitz Roy, who was lord of Okehampton in her right by 1166.

This charter was mistakenly attributed to Robert I of Normandy in the Inventory, fol. 128v.

[73]

William and his family were clearly tenants of Avranches cathedral, but this charter is interesting because William fitz Wimund reveals that his grant was made at the suggestion of his friends, three canons of the cathedral, including John, master of what was then an important school. Both bishops John (died in 1070 as archbishop of Rouen) and Michael were outstanding intellectuals. Lanfranc, later monk and abbot of Bec and then archbishop of Canterbury, studied for a while at Avranches. The abbey had an important monastic school, but there was no link with the cathedral school. Strikingly, Mont-Saint-Michel remembered neither Lanfranc nor his successor Anselm in its necrologies, though both were widely remembered within Normandy and beyond.

Bertram de Verdun (also no. 77) from Verdun, a fief in par. Vessey, Manche, cant. Pontorson; a minor landholder in Buckinghamshire in 1086 (*Dom. People*, p. 168). He was a royal servant in Yorkshire under William II, *c.* 1099–1100. He gave the church of Bosworth, Leicestershire, to St Mary's, York. Cf. Dugdale, *Monasticon Anglicanum*, rev. edn., i, 241; W. Farrer, *Early Yorkshire Charters*, i, 274 and note 11. His heir was his son Norman.

[74 and 75]

Ruallend de Hulme, *sororius* (brother-in-law) of Gilbert de Champeaux, appears in the register of Robert of Torigny (printed in Delisle, ii, 242) restoring land he had usurped at Beauvoir and Montitier and in the fee of Peter fitz Desideria (cf. **App. ii. 10**). Around 1160 he co-founded, with John de Subligny (cf. notes for no. **16**), the abbey of Montmorel. *Cartulaire de l'abbaye de Mont-Morel (Cartulaire du Manche)*, ed. M. Dubosc (Saint-Lô, 1878).

Gilbert occurs in an accord, dated 1155, between Robert of Torigny on the one hand and Gilbert de Champeaux and his wife's brother Ruallen fitz Hugh de Houlme on the other, concerning the land of Beaufeugeray, which was recognized as part of the parish of Saint-Planchers (cant. Granville, Manche). He had been excommunicate for almost two years and had then made a restitution *per brachium Sancti Auberti* (Delisle, *Torigni*, ii, pp. 240, 261–2).

Turpis Infans was mentioned in an accord between Robert de Torigny and Ruallend de Genêts as a kinsman (*cognatus*) of Ruallend (ib., 287) .

Hugh *comes*, i.e. Hugh *vicomte* of Avranches, earl of Chester in England, one of the greatest of the Domesday magnates (*Dom. Peop.*, pp. 258–9). He died in 1106 and was succeeded by his son Richard, who died childless in the

White Ship disaster of 1120. His heir then was his nephew Ranulf, *vicomte* of Bayeux (d. *c.* 1129) (no. 77). *Complete Peerage*, iii, pp. 164–70.

Hervé de Champeaux, a royal servant who occurs in Domesday Book as Hervé *Legatus*, was a tenant of Ilbert de Lascy in Yorkshire in 1086 (*Dom. Peop.*, p. 255).

Richard de *Leises*, or *Lesellis* i.e. Lezeaux, brother of Thomas (nos. **16**, **78**, **82**, **115**).

Osbern Escolland: also no. 77. A reference to the fee of Scolland in Yquelon occurs in no. **116**.

[76]

Ranulf Avenel was son of Ranulf Avenel and Matilda, daughter of Baldwin de Meulles and widow of William fitz Wimund of Avranches (no. **71**); *Complete Peerage*, iii, pp. 308–9, 317. His family held the fief of Les Biards from the counts of Mortain.

Jordan, son of Alan, son of Flaad (no. **57**) was steward to the archbishop of Dol. In 1130 he and his wife Maria made a grant of the church of Le Fresnay to the church of Dol (B. N. fr. 22319, p. 104). Father of Alan and Robert. A charter of Alan's daughter Oliva, wife first of Robert de Saint-John, concerning La Chapelle-Hamelin (no. **50**), was listed in the Inventory, fol. 116v.

[77 and **78**]

The Ducey family are best evidenced as holders of one of the Mortain fiefs of Fougères, benefactors of Savigny. William de Ducey was succeded by his *nepta* (probably granddaughter) Matilda, wife of William de Heuchon (Bib. mun. Flers 22, nos. 55, 58 and 125, pp. 85–8, 97–9).

Thomas de Lezeaux (Manche, ham. comm. Bouillon) (also nos. **82**, **111**), brother of Richard (no. **75**), occurs in acts of Robert de Torigny (Delisle, *Torigni*, ii, pp. 239–45.

Ranulf I, earl of Chester, was nephew and eventual heir of Hugh, earl of Chester, vicomte of Avranches (no. **74**). Son of Ranulf II of Bayeux, himself son of Ranulf fitz Ansketil (no. 7) and Adelisa, daughter of Richard II of Normandy, and a sister of Earl Hugh of Chester. He died *c.* 1129 leaving a son Ranulf II.

A family named from Macey were tenants of the earls of Chester in England. Hamo and Ruallon de Macé owed a third of one knight's service to the abbey in 1172 (Delisle, *Torigni*, ii, 299). *Dom. Peop.*, p. 242; *Dom. Desc.*, p. 561.

Harscoit de Tani occurs in England as the husband of Matilda, daughter and heiress of Roger, a knight of John fitz Waleran of Vains (*Veim*) (see no. **6**) above. Their son Graelandus occurs in 1166. This Gradelon was probably father or brother of Harscoit. Named from Tanis, cant. Pontorson. *Dom.*

Desc., p. 730. Eudo de Tanie held two vavassors of Mont-Saint-Michel in 1172 (Delisle, *Torigni*, ii, p. 299).

Richard Cardon occurs in no. **93** as *nepos* of Richard fitz Richolin de Boucey.

[79–80]

These two documents follow each other without a break in the manuscript. The first is the later of the two, belonging to the latter part of Ranulf's abbacy (as indicated by the witnesses). In it one Niel concedes a carrucate called *Plemmunt* (perhaps Pleinmont) in Guernsey that had formerly been granted by his brother Hugh.

No. **79** is interesting for the appearance of two of the canons of Mont-Saint-Michel among the winesses. See also no. **82**.

In the second, and earlier, charter Bishop Hugh of Avranches (1028–1059/60) recognizes that that he holds the tithes of half Guernsey together with one (unnnamed) carrucate for his life as the grant of Abbot Suppo. Little is known of Bishop Hugh, but he seems to have been responsible for the major part of the building of Avranches Cathedral. He consecrated John of Ravenna as abbot of Fécamp, at the request of Robert II. It was during his time that Lanfranc studied and taught in the cathedral school at Avranches, according to Lanfranc's biographer Miles Crispin (Bouet and Dosdat, in *Les évêques normandes*, pp. 22–3). Hugh was remembered in the abbey Martyrology-Necrology on 5 April.

[82]

Humphrey and Malger de Carteret were tenants of Robert of Mortain in south-west England in 1086 (*Dom. People*, p. 180). Drogo son of Malger de Carteret was a major tenant of Geoffrey, bishop of Coutances in the honour of Barnstaple in 1086 (*Dom. People*, p. 180); his heir in 1166 was Philip de Carteret (*Dom. Desc.*, p. 387), son of Rainald.

Philip de Carteret was an important tenant of the (de Redvers) earls of Devon in 1166. His relations with the abbey improved with the advent of Robert de Torigny, who was his kinsman, *cognatus*, according to an item in Robert's register for 1156 (printed in Delisle, *Torigni*, ii, pp. 243–4). He made a gift to Mont-Saint-Michel on 5 January 1167 (o.s.), with the assent of his wife Nichola, son Rainald and nephew William (Delisle, *Torigni*, ii, pp. 289–90). *Dom. Desc.*, p. 387.

Richard I de Méré, a member of the Bohun family from the Cotentin, monk of Cluny at its priory of St Pancras of Lewes, in Sussex, abbot of Mont-Saint-Michel from 1126/7 until he was deposed, following the monks' opposition to him, around April 1130. He died on 12 January 1131 at St Pancras. His homonym Richard de Méré, son of Humphrey I de Bohun, held a single manor in Somerset in 1086. His daughter Muriel married Savaric fitz Cana, a younger son of Ralph V, *vicomte* of Le Mans (who was grandson of the donor of no. **28**), who was given an important Sussex fief *c.* 1090 (*Dom. Desc.*, p. 876).

[83]

William Bellebarbe was doubtless the abbey servant William Pulcra barba. Berner Pulcra Barba attested an act of 1159 in which Luke and Matthew, sons of Henry the chamberlain, made a quitclaim with the consent of their paternal uncle, Prior Rannulf (Delisle, *Torigni*, ii, p. 257, no. 44).

An Arnulf fitz Adrald de Stampis (Etampes, Yvelines) occurs in a charter for Longpont (*Cart.*, no. CCCXVIII), in 1100.

[84]

Osbern's son subsequently disputed the grant of a *masura* made by his father on becoming a monk, claiming that the grant had been made without his consent. The dispute was settled in 1157 when Abbot Robert of Torigny paid 30 *solidi* of Le Mans to Osbern fitz Osbern (Delisle, *Torigni*, ii, p. 248), attested by *Grauerench de Ebreceio vicecomes*. In 1166 Robert d'Evrecy held one fee of the bishop of Worcester. The family occur as benefactors of Aulnay during the twefth century. One of them was Thomas d'Evrecy, son of William Graverenc (B. N. lat. 9215, no. 20).

[85]

Ranulf de Colleville was probably of the same family as the Walter who attested the charter of Robert fitz Haimo (no. **67**). Several Colleville families were English landholders, holding fees of Percy, Bigod and the earls of Devon. *Dom. Desc.*, pp. 407–8.

Ernald de Montit- was from Montitier (Manche, cant. Pontorson, comm. Huisnes).

[86]

Estolleia was listed among the abbey's holdings in the diocese of Exeter in the bull of Alexander III of 1179 or 1181 (Delisle, *Torigni*, ii, p. 318). A later grant, by Ralph Blondel, was kept among the charters of the priory of Saint-Pair (MS Avranches 211, fol. 122r); the family perhaps came from Blondellière, a hamlet of Saint-Jean-des-Champs, one of the abbey's churches attached to the lordship of Saint-Pair (Manche, cant. Granville).

Ralph and William de Beauvoir (Manche, cant. Pontorson): Thomas de Beauvoir was a knight of the abbey in the Avranchin in 1172 (Delisle, *Torigni*, ii, p. 299).

[87]

Gelduin d'Aucey occurs in the abbey's 1172 declaration of fiefs as a vavassor in the Avranchin, owing service with sword and lance (Delisle, *Torigni*, ii, p. 300). His condition that his name appear in the abbey's memorial book may have been met; a layman Gelduin appears once in the Necrology, on 10 August.

This is the only reference to Stephen of Blois, king of England from 1135 to 1154, in the main Cartulary. In **Appendix i.5** an act of Abbot Bernard is dated AD 1142, *regnante piissimo rege Stephano in Anglia*. Stephen usurped the throne from his cousin Matilda, daughter and designated heiress of Henry I, wife of Geoffrey, count of Anjou and mother of the future Henry II of England. In the only brief campaign he fought against Matilda and Geoffrey in Normandy in 1138, his partisans mounted an attack on the abbey of Mont-Saint-Michel, causing extensive damage (cf. no. **83** and **App. ii.9**). He was defeated by Matilda's army at the battle of Lincoln on 2 February 1141 and held as her prisoner until 1 November 1142. He is the only king of England from William I to Henry III not to have been remembered in the abbey Martyrology-Necrology. His wife, Matilda, countess of Boulogne, is the only queen to have been entered in the Necrology rather than the Martyrology-Necrology (3 May).

The mark of Rainald of St John occurs in no. **90** as prior of Saint-Broladre.

[88]

Robert de Grentais and Richard his son attested an act of Abbot Robert in 1165 (Delisle, *Torigni*, ii, pp. 244–5).

[89]

A *Homenisius* occurs in the abbey necrology, MS Avranches 214, p. 111, *ii id. Feb.* (12 February).

Baldwin was the son of the Homenes who attested the charters of Trehan fitz Brien granting land to the priory of Saint-Broladre (no. **21**).

Juhel de Maresco (Marais-de-Dol), occurs in England with Jordan son of Alan fitz Flaald of Dol (no. **76**) in 1129/30, *Pipe Roll 31 Henry I*, p. 11.

Gelduin Taun cf. no. **44**.

[90]

William Paynel, from a family associated with Moutiers-Hubert, Calvados, arr. Lisieux, cant. Livarot, and Hambye, Manche, arr. Coutances, cant. Gavray (Loyd, 77). In 1086 Ralph Paynel (d. 1118/24), perhaps a brother of William, was a Domesday tenant-in-chief in Yorkshire and elsewhere. See Clay, *EYC* vi, 1 ff. This important charter contains a detailed statement of the obligations of William and his men towards the abbot of Mont-Saint-Michel as lord of the fee William has been given in marriage by King William. In 1172 Fulk Paynel held one knight's fee of the abbey at Briqueville; Delisle, *Torigni*, ii, p. 299. Fulk was a grandson of William fitz Wimund of Avranches (nos. **72**, **73**) and nephew of Ranulf Avenel (no. **76**) whose grants to the abbey he disputed; the claim was the subject of a lengthy negotiation with Abbot Robert de Torigny and an accord of 1157 (*ibid.*, no. 41, pp. 254–5).

Michael bishop of Avranches 1068–1096.

Robert bishop of Sées *c.* 1071/2–1081/2, son of Hubert de Ryes.

Roger de Montgomery, Roger de Beaumont, Richard *proconsulis* (*vicomte* of Avranches), Turgis de Tracei and Geoffrey de Sai all attested no. **70**.

Hubert de Ryes, father of Eudo Dapifer, both important followers of William the Conqueror, and Robert bishop of Sées.

Humphrey de Bohun, from Saint-Georges de Bohon in the Cotentin. A branch of this family was established in Sussex in the early twelfth century by the marriage of Muriel, daughter of Richard de Méré, son of Humphrey de Bohun (*Dom. People*, pp. 359–60, *Dom. Desc.*, p. 331). Cf. no. **64**, a charter of Main d'Aubigny-Saint-Germain, whose wife was a daughter of Humphrey de Bohun.

Hubert de Port-en-Bessin occurs as a minor English landholder after 1066 (*Dom. People*, p. 257).

[91]

The charter is listed among the muniments of the priory of Saint-Meloir in MS Avranches 211, fol. 125r. Cf. the return of the abbey's fees in 1172 which refers to William de *Vastinneio*, vavassor in Grainville, who holds of the fee of Prima – *de feudo Prime*, Delisle, *Torigni*, ii, p. 301. In the time of Abbot Robert of Torigny a knight named Alan maintained a chapel in Saint-Meloir to the detriment of the parish church controlled by the monks. Cited before an episcopal tribunal at Avranches, Alan remained obdurate and was excommunicated. See A. Dufief, in *Mill. mon.* i, pp. 115–116, citing B. N. lat. 5430A, p. 205, and nov. acq. fr. 21821, p. 247.

[92]

Gilbert de Champeaux, cf. no. **75**.

William de Bree (variants, *Brae*, *Brahe*), named from Bree (Manche, ham. comm. Tanis, cant. Pontsorson). He became a monk of the abbey in 1157 (Delisle, *Torigni*, ii., p. 253). Another William de Bree was a knight of the abbey in 1172 (ibid., pp. 298, 302). The Inventory lists acts of a knight William de Brae concerning sale of property in Bretteville (fol. 133v).

[93]

Cf. Richolinus de Boceio (Bucey) in no. **61**.

Richard Cardo, nephew of Richard fitz Richolin, attested no. **87**. He was a warrantor for a grant made by Alan, priest of Boucey, when his nephew Ralph became a monk in 1155 (Delisle, *Torigni*, ii, p. 238, no. 5). A charter of Peter de Saint-Hilaire (no. **96**) for the Marmoutier priory at Sacey was attested by Geoffrey fitz Michael, his sons Jordan and Peter, and William fitz Michael (B. N. lat. 5441.2, pp. 167–8).

A Haimeric Cardo, a tenant of Ralph I de Fougères, held land in Saint-Sauveur-des-Landes in marriage with his wife, a daughter of Ralph de Vendelles (Arch. dépt. Ille-et-Vilaine, IF 542, no. XIII).

William de Sacey, son of Hugh fitz Rorgo de Sacey, brother of Robert and of Basilia, wife of Ansger, second cousin of Peter de Saint-Hilaire (no. **116**), all of them benefactors of the priory of Marmoutier at Sacey (B. N. Coll. Baluze 77, fol. 66, no. 86; B. N. lat. 5441.2, pp. 159–60).

William d'Archis, a kinsman of Abbot Bernard; cf Arques's family, tenants in Yorkshire.

[94]

Odo *Potarius* attested William II Gouet's charter founding Saint-Gilles de Châteigniers, *c.* 1117 (*Cart. de Tiron*, 1883, no. XII)). He is perhaps to be identified with the chamberlain Odo who attested Geoffrey fitz Godeschal's grant of land at Montemont (no. **100**). For the grant of rights in the church of Montemont by Walter *Oculus Canis*, conveyed in the house of Geoffrey Godeschal at Châteaudun, see no. **34**.

[95]

Odo (Eudes) de Vallières (d. *c.* 1140) was the second husband of Agnes, daughter and coheiress of Ganelon II of Montigny-le-Ganelon (Eure-et-Loir, cant. Cloyes-sur-le-Loir), whose sister Adelaide (or their widowed mother, cf. *Cart. Dunois*, no. lxi and *Cart. Trinité de Vendôme*, no. CCCXXX) married Hamelin, brother of Nivelon de Fréteval and Agnes Comitissa, wife of Hugh de Châteaudun (nos. **100**, **103**). He and Agnes had issue Rahier, Hugh, Eudes, Eustachia, Jacqueline, Hildearde and Galiena (*Cart. Tiron*, i, note p. 22).

Eustachia's husband Hubert Pagan was presumably the son of Odo Potarius (no. **94**).

[96]

Theobald de Dangeau attested the foundation charter of Saint-Giles de Châteignières given by William Gouet and Eustachia *c.* 1117 as a cell of Tiron (ref. as under no. **94** above). Around 1150 he confirmed the gift of William de Monthou to Nogent-le-Rotrou, with the assent of his wife Hildeburg, son Bernard and daughter Oda. It was also attested by Odo Brisart and Payn de Bosco, i.e. de Nemore (*Cartulaire de l'abbaye de Saint-Denis de Nogent*, ed. abbé Métais, Vannes 1895, no. XVI, pp. 53–4).

Odo Brisart was a brother of Guihel and Rotroc fitz Rainald Brisard, who occur in a charter dated *c.* 1080–1100 and attested by the sons of Gerard Brunel (no. **34**) (*Cart. Dunois de Marmoutier*, no. CXLI).

Payn de Nemore or de Bosco gave land in Saint-Maxime to Tiron (*Cart. Tiron*, i, p. 72). His wife Mathilde was secondly the wife of Hugh d'Alluyes.

[97]

Simon de Bailleul was son of Warin de Bailleul and brother of Ralph and William. All were benefactors of Savigny abbey, for which their grants were authorized by Juhel of Mayenne (Arch. dépt. de la Mayenne H 38, no. 1; H 35, pp. 160–1; Van Moolenbroek, no. 14, p. 281). Named from Bailleul, in Hercé, cant. Gorron, Mayenne.

Simon de Bailleul confirmed a grant to Savigny by William fitz Urse de Désertines (cant. Landivy, Mayenne) *c.* 1130 (Van Moolenbroek, no. 36, pp. 312–314).

[98]

Bishop Donoald was a former monk of Mont-Saint-Michel; see **49** above.

[99]

A *Letus Infans* (also no. **116**), witnessed a charter of Rivallon fitz Geoffrey de Gorron in 1106 (*Cart. manceau de Marmoutier* ii, Mayenne no. VII, pp. 5–6).

[100]

Around 1020 Hildiardis grandmother of Geoffrey vicomte of Châteaudun made a gift to Saint-Père de Chartres attested by one Hubert and his son Godeschal, Odo and Hubert Brunel, Ralph *Legis doctus*; cf. no. **34**. In 1100 Geoffrey *Legis doctus* (also no. **103**), his wife Helvisa and their issue Robert, Ralph, Ivo, Gervaise, Geoffrey, Godeschal, Lucia and Olimpias, were one of several people making quitclaims in respect of a much disputed mill belong to Saint-Père de Chartres's priory of Saint-Leobin de Châteaudun at Brou (B. N. lat. 10101, fol. 52v); Helvise and her sons occur in *Cart. Dunois*, no. CLXVIII (c. 1116–36). Geoffrey and his brother Robert attested the foundation of Oisème, priory of Tiron, by Ansold fitz Godeschal (*Cart. Tiron*, i, p. 149).

Vicomte Hugh had married Agnes or Comitissa, sister of Nivelon fitz Fulcher of Fréteval by 1097 (*Cart. Saint-Père de Chartres*, p. 428). They gave a charter for Saint-Leonard de Bellême attested by Ralph Oculus canis, Fulcoius de Membrolles and Ansold de Camolo (Arch. dépt. de l'Orne, H 2152).

Payn de La Bouèche attested a charter of 1116 recorded a settlement by William II Gouet and his wife Eustachia (*Cart. Dunois*, no. XCV).

[101]

William II Gouet (d. *c.* 1120) of Montmirail (Sarthe, cant. Mamers), son of William I and Matilda d'Alluye, secondly the wife of Geoffrey de Mayenne (nos. **38**, **62**, **65**), *Cart. manceau de Marmoutier*, i, pp. 117–9. His wife Eustachia and his sister's son Nivelon de Fréteval (fl. 1087–1122) were donors of no. **104**. On the family see K. Thompson, 'The Formation of the County of Perche: the Rise and Fall of the Gouet Family', in Keats-Rohan ed., *Family Trees*. The Necrology has entries for two women named Eustachia, on 16 May (ms Avranches 214, p. 142) and 10 December (p. 186).

William and his wife Eustachia were benefactors of the priory of Gohory (nos. **101**, **104**). Their charters were attested by members of the Godeschal and Brunel families, also benefactors of Gohory (nos. **34**, **100**, **106**) whose grants were confirmed by the vicomtes of Châteaudun (nos. **34**, **100**, **103**). The *vicomtes* of the time, the late-eleventh century, were descended from Hildegarde, a possible granddaughter of Hugh I of Maine who appears to have been heiress in her issue to the county of Mortagne or Perche (see Christian Settipani, 'Les comtes d'Anjou et leurs alliances aux X et XI siècles', in Keats-Rohan, ed., *Family Trees* (1997), 254–266, and id., 'Les vicomtes de Châteaudun et leur alliés', *Onomastique et Parenté*, pp. 256–8). The Gouets had acquired their holding at Perche-Gouet at the expense of the vicomtes, who had been gravely weakened by a bloody feud with the *vidames* of Chartres in the 1030s. The names of William, his father William, and his sister Hildeburg, suggest a link with the kinsmen (*cognati*) named in the charter of Ivo fitz Fulcoin (no. **26**). Ivo's mother Rothais was sister of Bishop Seifrid of Le Mans, whose niece Hildeburg de Bellême married Hamelin, first seigneur of Château-du-Loir. Around 1070, William Gouet and his sister Hildeburg claimed jurisdiction in Château-du-Loir against Gervaise de Château-du-Loir, who was nephew of Bishop Gervaise of Le Mans, grandson of Hamelin de Château-du-Loir and his wife Hildeburg, niece of Bishop Seifrid, and father of an heiress Mathilde, wife of Count Helias of Maine and mother of Countess Eremburg (no. **107**). *Cart. manceau de Marmoutier*, i, pp. 117–9; cf. Keats-Rohan, 'Politique et parentèle: les comtes, vicomtes et évêques du Maine *c.* 950–1050', *Francia* 26.1 (1996), 13–30, demonstrating that Hildeburg was a *Leitname* of Bishop Seifrid's family.

[102]

Ralph *Oculus Canis*, brother of Walter; also nos. **103** and **105**; see no. **34.**

[103]

Mangis, or Maugis, prior of Gohory in 1099 was perhaps the monk of that name recorded in the Martyrology-Necrology on 1 September (p. 130).

Comitissa, otherwise called Agnes, daughter of Fulcher de Fréteval and Hildeburg, sister of William II Gouet (no. **101**).

Odo Borrel of Courtalain (Eure-et-Loir, cant. Cloyes), occurs *c.* 1073–89 with Azzo Borrel, son of Praxedis, and *c.* 1064–73 contesting land held in right of his wife Elisindis (*Cart dunois*, nos. CCCIV and CXXXVII). According to a notification of around 1140 by Bishop Jocelyn (de Lèves) of Chartres recorded in B. N. lat. 5430a, pp. 89–90, from the *Livre Blanc* but absent in the first Cartulary, Odo Borrel gave Le Poislay to Mont-Saint-Michel, in the time of Bishop Ivo of Chartres (1092–1115), a grant now confirmed by his grandson Odo, with the assent of his wife Bertha and brother Hugh: *Odo Borellus in presentia nostra confessus est quidquid frater noster Richerius archid[iaconus] de dono et feodo patris sui et suo apud Poleium tenuerat ab auo suo Odone seniore ecclesia Sancti Michaelis de Periculo Maris per manum predecessoris nostri beati memorie Yvonis ... et fratrem suum Hugonem et Bertam uxorem hoc concedentes in manu nostra pepigit.*

Robert *Legis doctus* was a brother of Geoffrey (no. **100**) (*Cart. dunois*, no. CLVI, pp. 146–7). Around 1116/36 a Helvisa *Legis docta*, with her sons Robert, Ivo *clericus*, Geoffrey de Montiniaco, Bodetus and a daughter known as Burda, confirmed to Marmoutier the church and tithe of Saint-Jean de Aubevoie (*Cart. dunois*, no. CLXVII, pp. 158–9).

Fulcoin de Membrolles, cf. *Cart. Nogent-le-Rotrou*, no. vii, pp. 24–13; *Cart. Tiron*, p. 138.

[104]

The donors were the wife of William Gouet II and his sister's son, Nivelon de Fréteval. See no. **101**.

[105]

Warner *Oculus Canis* gave rents on vines near Châteaudun to Tiron with the consent of his mother Comitissa and his wife Loremera (*Cart Tiron*, i, p. 177).

[107]

See no. **36**. The Countess Eremburg was daughter and heiress of Count Helias of Maine and his first wife Mathilde de Château-du-Loir. She married Fulk V of Anjou in 1106, after the death of his elder brother on 19 May 1106 and before the death of his father Fulk IV on 14 April 1109. She died on 15 February 1126. Eremburg and her son Helias were remembered at Ronceray on 15 January (B. N. Collection Anjou-Touraine 12.2, p. 213). Her husband subsequently married Melisende, heiress of Baldwin II of Jerusalem.

Geoffrey de Clefs, dapifer or seneschal of Fulk V of Anjou, and Fromond Chalibot occur in *Cart. St.-Aubin d'Angers*, nos. CCCLI, DCCLIII, DCCCXLIX.

[108]

See further **Appendix i.4**. Henry I of England (1100–1135), son of William I the Conqueror and brother and heir of William II (1087–1100). Founder of Reading Abbey, where his heart was buried in 1135. His first wife Matilda of Scotland (d. 1118) was remembered in the Martyrology-Necrology on 1 May, Henry himself on 1 December.

Geoffrey the Chancellor: Geoffrey Rufus, chancellor from 1123 until his appointment as bishop of Durham in 1133. He died on 6 May 1141 (*Dom. Desc.*, p. 827).

William II, earl Warenne: son of William de Warenne (d. 1088). He died in 1138 and was buried at Lewes priory (*Dom. Desc.*, pp. 239–40).

William de Tancarville: son of Ralph de Tancarville (no. **6**), chamberlain of Normandy (d. 1082). Financial officer in Normandy under Henry I. He died in 1129 and was succeeded by his son Rabel (*Dom. Desc.*, p. 729).

Geoffrey I de Clinton: from a family originating at Saint-Pierre-de-Semilly, near Saint-Lô. Notable royal servant under Henry I in whose service he made a fortune. Founder of the castle and abbey of Kenilworth in Warwickshire, and also a benefactor of the abbey of Savigny. In disgrace by 1129/20 (*Dom. Desc.*, p. 403).

William de Pont-de-l'Arche: sheriff under Henry I, to whom he was notably loyal. He died in 1143 (*Dom. Desc.*, p. 644).

[109]

Cf. no. **82**.

[110]

Same as no. **33**.

[111]

Cf. nos. **18** and **61**. Robert's wife Oruueal was perhaps a member of the Dinan family, descended from Josselin de Dinan (see no. **53** above). An Oreal occurs once in the Necrology, on 12 December (ms Avranches 214, p. 187).

[113]

Ralph de Pincey held the fief of Montdaigne. The grants of Geoffrey de Pincey were confirmed to the abbey's priory at Pontorson by Peter de Saint-Hilaire (MS Avranches 211, fol. 116v).

[114]

Helias Boterat was the successor of Geoffrey son of Trehan fitz Brien of Saint-Broladre (nos. **21**, **56**). His grant confirms that of his father and is certainly related to the original grant by Trehan. Chronologically, Trehan cannot have been his father, so he was probably son of Geoffrey.

[115]

This dense list of usurpations of abbey property shows the significance of the many charters of restitution that feature in the Cartulary, as well as the principal charters of donation. Many of the depredations in the Channel Islands and the Cotentin ascribed to William I of England occur as grants in charters of his father Robert (no. **5**) and of his grandfather Richard II (no. **2**). The depradations of the brothers Thomas and Roger de Saint-Jean-le-Thomas were the subject of a chirograph of *c.* 1121–5, no. **16**. Ilger *prepositus* of Ardevon attested nos. **9**, **12** and **79**.

[116]

Peter of Saint-Hilaire-du-Harscouët (fl. 1135–57) was one of the sons of the *vicomte* Harscoit fitz Eudo of Saint-Hilaire (fl. 1094–1130), also known as de Saint-James. Important information of the early history of the family is found in charters for the Marmoutiers priory of Sacey, in the Avranchin, B. N. lat. 5441(2), pp. 159–60, where we learn that Harscoit was the nephew of Robert *vicomte* de *Bodiaco* (Boucey), whose grandson Ansger married a daughter of Hugh fitz Rorgo of Sacey. Peter's numerous charters for Savigny abbey show him married to a woman named Assaillita and father of Harscoit, James, Henry and Philip (B. N. nov. acq. lat. 1002, pp. 20, 25, 28; Bib. mun. Flers 22, nos. 24, 52, 103). His father Harscoit usurped the abbey's property at La Croix Avranchin in the late eleventh century. Abbot Roger appealed to Urban II, who instructed Turgis bishop of Avranches to deal with the culprit. Harscoit failed to appear before Turgis and two other bishops, Roland of Dol and Marbod of Rennes, on 13 May 1095 and was the subject of a second papal instruction, by Calixtus II, to Bishop Turgis in 1119 concerning his usurpation of land at La Croix-Avranchin, Villiers and Balland (Dufief, 'Vie monastique', *Mill. mon.* i, 86, 89). Peter's charter is a renunciation of any right claimed in La Croix. He had clearly followed firmly in his father's footsteps since he refers to the several excommunications pronounced upon him. Charters of a Peter de Saint-Hilaire are listed for the priory of Pontorson in MS Avranches 211, fol. 116v. *Dom. Desc.*, pp. 689–90.

Peter's *cognatus* Carpentarius attested one of his charters for Sacey, B. N. lat. 5441.2, pp. 166–7.

[117]

Possibly Salomon's son William, who became a monk of the abbey with this grant, was the William son of Salomon who was prior of Saint-Victeur au Mans in 1135/43 (*Cart. Saint-Victeur*, no. XIX). The obscure phrase *ab anthernut* is either a corruption of a word indicating a specific type of tenure or merely a corruption of *et abbate*, as suggested by the subsequent phrase *de sancto Michaele et abbate similiter teneo*. Possibly it is a corrupt locative form, referring to the abbey's church of Saint-Michel-des-Loups (comm. Sartilly), in the diocese of Avranches, *Abrincatis*, though the earliest reference to this as an abbey holding was the bull of Adrian IV, given in February 1156 (Dubois, 'Dépendances', p. 628). A clue to the donor's identity is perhaps afforded by the grants made to Abbot Ranulf in the item printed in **App. ii.4**, one of which was Osmund fitz Grento's demise of the moiety of an unidentified mill to Abbot Ranulf. The participants in this item were all from the Avranchin, from an area north of Avranches between Briqueville (Manche, comm. Granville) and Hocquigny (Manche, comm. La Haye Pesnel). The abbey's church of Saint-Michel-des-Loups was in this region. The Necrology contains several Salomons, and two Grentos, one a monk (ms Avranches 214, p. 146, 6 May) and one a layman (p. 138, 4 May).

[118]

The grant by Eudo, son of Geoffrey and Hebrea, of land in the Marais de Dol links him to an entry in an inquest of 1181 relating to the temporalities of the see of Dol which refers to the fee of Eudo fitz Geoffrey given by Archbishop Junguené to his bastard brother Salomon, ancestor of the du Guesclin family: *Histoire Féodale de Dol*, pp. 40–1 and note 43. His father Geoffrey was probably the Geoffrey son of Salomon whom Count Eudo, brother of Alan III of Brittany, permitted to build a castle at *Nulliaco*, possibly Noyal-sur-Seiche (Morice, *Preuves* i, 398). If so, then he was a relative of his lord John fitz Rivallon of Dol, a nephew of Archbishop Junguené (see under no. **17** above).

[119]

There are signs of haste in the copying of this act. It lacks validation clauses and fails to specify the conditions of the grant of 10 *solidi* to be made to William for as long as he lives. William also occurs in no. **57**. See notes for no. **49** above.

[Appendix i.2]

See no. **36** above.

[Appendix i.3]

The vineyards mentioned in this charter lay in the parish of Saint-Sylvain-d'Anjou, Maine-et-Loire, as shown by later charters for the priory of Créans and at Mortier in the Touraine (see no. **32**). Dubois, 'Dépendances', *Mill. mon.*, i, p. 640.

Fulk IV le Réchin, count of Anjou 1065–1109, father of Geoffrey Martel, who predeceased him on 19 May 1106, and of Fulk V.

Abbot Gerard II of Saint-Aubin d'Angers died in 1109. He was remembered in the Necrology on 9 January.

For Geoffrey I de Mayenne (d. 1098) and his nephew, Geoffrey, bishop of Angers, see nos. **38** and **65** above.

Rainald III de Château-Gontier held an important castle built by Fulk III Nerra of Anjou. Neighbour and ally of Robert I de Sablé, whose daughter he married. He left with Robert with the second army (*profectio secunda*) of the First Crusade on or after 27 March 1098. He died at Jerusalem leaving issue Adelard, his successor, Rainald, Anselm, Matthew and Laurentia (*Cart. Saint-Aubin*, nos. DCLXXVII–DCLXXXII).

[Appendix i.4]

Abbot Roger's letter to Roger bishop of Salisbury was written before Henry I left England on 11 June 1123, leaving Bishop Roger as regent, but before Roger's resignation of the abbacy on 16 October 1123. He returned to Jumièges, where he died on 2 April 1124.

Roger of Salisbury was originally a priest at Avranches. He became a favoured servant of Henry I of England, who entrusted him with the reform of English administrative practices. He acted as regent more than once. Bishop of Salisbury from 29 September until his death on 11 December 1139. He had a concubine, Matilda of Ramsbury, and placed both illegitimate sons and nephews in senior ecclesiastical positions in England. See E. J. Kealey, *Roger of Salisbury* (1972).

[Appendix i.5]

This act and no. **83**, to which it is the sequel, are among those showing the severe problems faced by the abbey during the early years of the struggle between Stephen and Matilda for control of England and Normandy. Jordan Taisson, a witness to this act, was the son-in-law and successor of Roger II de Saint-Sauveur, *vicomte* of the Cotentin. Appointed justiciar by Stephen and initially successful in maintaining order, Roger was ambushed and savagely murdered by partisans of Matilda in 1138 (Ord. Vit. vi, pp. 494, 512–514). This and no. **87** are the only two acts of the abbey which mention King Stephen. Both belong to this year, 1142, which had started with Stephen as Matilda's prisoner. He was released on 1 November.

[Appendix.ii.1]

Conan I of Britany, killed 27 June 992 at the second battle of Conquereuil. André Chédeville, 'Un millénaire: la bataille de Conquereuil (1992), *MSHAB* lxx, 1993, 365–84, shows that he was twice married. His second marriage, *c.* 970, was important to his politics of unifying Brittany under his sole rule since it was to Ermengarde, daughter of Geoffrey Grisegonelle of Anjou, who had ambitions over the region ruled by Conan of Rennes's rivals, the counts of Nantes. He was father of Geoffrey I of Brittany and Judith, wife of Richard II of Normandy. He was possibly also a close kinsman of Hugh II of Maine and his son Hugh III. Conan's grandson Alan III of Brittany was also major benefactor of the Mont (nos. **17**, **23**, **24**). Conan and his daughter Judith, wife of Richard II of Normandy, were remembered in the abbey's Martyrology-Necrology. According to the much later Obituary, MS Avranches 215, fol. 165, he was buried at the Mont: *Obiit Iudita comitissa Norma. Conanus dux Britann- qui iacet in capella Sancti Martini in ista ecclesia.*

Geoffrey, son of Conan, ruled Brittany from 992 until his death on pilgrimage *c.* 1008. By his wife Hadvise, sister of his brother-in-law Richard II of Normandy, he was father of Alan III and count Eudo (no. **17**). It was probably he who, as reformer of Breton monasteries, appointed Mainard II of Mont-Saint-Michel to the abbacy of Redon.

Arufus, or Radulfus, abbot of Saint-Sauveur de Redon, became bishop of Alet soon after the date of this charter.

Main archbishop of Dol was mentioned in the abbey Necrology on 26 June. He was succeeded in the early eleventh century by Junguené, son of Haimo I of Alet and Roiantelina of Dol (see no. **18**), who attested this act as a layman. He was probably a nephew of Main. Junguené's own nephew, Main, bishop of Rennes (no. **40**), later augmented this act by the grant of the church at Villamée.

It has been suggested that the bishop of Cornouaille adopted Horatius as a surname upon his appointment to his see and that he was otherwise known as Gulhoet, abbot of Landévennec: Joëlle Quaghebeur, *La Cornouaille du IXe au XIIe siècle* (2nd edn., Rennes, 2002), pp. 88–9.

Orscand le Grand bishop of Vannes was father of a son Rudalt and a daughter Guigoedon who married Benoît, bishop and count of Cornouaille (d. 1019). She was mother of Alan Canhiart (d. 1058), count of Cornouaille, whose son Hoel (d. 1084) became ruler of Brittany in right of his wife Hadvisa, sister and heiress of Conan II.

Theobald bishop of Rennes was father of three sons by two marriages, Walter, later bishop of Rennes, Mainguené de La Guerche and Triscan, abbot of Saint-Melaine de Rennes by *c.* 1020. Walter's son Warin was his successor in the see of Rennes which he occupied between 1032 and 1038. Theobald's great-grandson Geoffrey de La Guerche attested no. **63**.

Conan's tenant Rorgo son of Gauzlin, a nephew of Hugh II of Maine (see no. **27** above), was the probable ancestor of a family who occur 10km south-west of Ville-Perdue at Saint-Brice-en-Cogles. Aluered, Hugh and Juhel occur as seigneurs at Saint-Brice, then called Pruniers, in a charter of Saint-Florent de Saumur of the late eleventh century, attested by Harscoit *vicomte*, B. N. nouv. acq. lat. 1930, fol. lxxi. Juhel fils de Rorgo occurs in the boundary clause of a charter for Savigny *c.* 1120–29, Bibl. mun. de Flers, ms. 22, no. 7, p. 11ff. Basilia, daughter of Hugh son of Rorgo, married Ansger son of Ralph, from a family established at Sacey, near Pontorson. Anger's collateral relatives, descendants of a brother of his grandfather, were *vicomtes* of Boucey and seigneurs of Saint-James or Saint-Hilaire (see no. **116** above).

The monks sent by Mainard I to Conan can perhaps be identified as the prior, later Abbot Mainard II, and the dean Heriward or Heruard, a celebrated scribe of the abbey active until *c.* 1015 (Alexander, *Norman Illumination*).

Some time before 1040, two later redactions of this act were supplied with a new witness list including Archbishop Junguené, Warin, bishop of Rennes, Triscan abbot of Saint-Melaine, Rivallon and Triscan his son (Guillotel, 'Actes', pp. 29–30). A charter of Alan III of Brittany for Marmoutier, given between 1009 and 1017, was attested by Abbot Hildebert I of Mont-Saint-Michel (d. 1017), Mainard abbot of Redon (Mainard II of the Mont until his deposition in 1009, no. **52**), Rivallon *vicarius* – father of Triscan, ancestor of the lords of Vitré – and Warin, bishop of Rennes. Another of Alan's charters, dated 1013, was attested by Archbishop Junguené, Warin bishop of Rennes, Rivallon *vicarius* and Triscan (ib., no. 13; see also no. **23**). Triscan's son Robert de Marcillé attested the charter of Main bishop of Rennes which was the sequel to this grant (no. **40**).

[Appendix ii.2]

Hugh III of Maine's youngest (?half-) brother Herbert Bacon, was briefly regent for his great nephew Hugh IV (c. 1035–45), before he was forced to abdicate and end his days in a monastery. Hugh III's only known issue is his son and successor Herbert I, surnamed Wake-Dog, who succeeded him *c.* 1015.

Hugolin, Goscelin, Mainard and Hubert *clericus* occur among the witnesses to the charter of Ivo fitz Fulcoin (no. **26**). Hubert *clericus* and Rainald *capellanus* attested Hugh III's grant of Voivres (no. **35**); Goscelin, Hubert, Alberic and Rotselin *clericus* attested Hugh's grant of vines (no. **27**).

[Appendix ii.3]

John of Ravenna, a monk of Saint-Bénigne de Dijon under William of Volpiano and his successor as abbot of Fécamp in 1027/8. Briefly abbot also of Saint-Bénigne, 1052–4. He died on 22 February 1078.

Gilbert son of Count Godfrey was the grandson of Richard I of Normandy. One of the guardians of Robert's young son and heir, William, he was assassinated early in 1041 (William of Jumièges, ii, p. 94).

The monk Suppo was appointed abbot of Mont-Saint-Michel before the end of 1033. Following problems with the monks, in 1048 he left the abbey, without first formally resigning the abbacy, and returned to the abbey of Fruttaria, of which he had been abbot since *c.* 1042.

Hugh and William were sons of Turstin de Bastembourg, ancestors respectively of the lords of Montfort-sur-Risle and the Bertram family. Hugh also attested the long version of this charter, no. **5**. On the family, see D. C. Douglas ed., *The Domesday Monachorum of Christ Church, Canterbury* (1944).

[Appendix ii.4]

Rivallon I of Dol (d. 1065/6), father by his wife Eremburgis of Chartres, of William and Gelduin fitz Rivallon (no. **18**), John fitz Rivallon (no. **44**) and Geoffrey fitz Rivallon (no. **41**). See no. **18** above. Only his son William, abbot of Saint-Florent de Saumur from 1070 until 1118, can be securely identified in the abbey necrologies.

[Appendix ii.6]

See no. **117** above.

[Appendix ii.7]

William de Tracy, father of Turgis, was probably son of the Turgis de Tracy who attested no. **91**. Probably named from the fief of Tracy in Neuville, Calvados, arr. and cant. Vire (Loyd, *Anglo-Norman Families*, p. 106). His grant, on becoming a monk of the abbey, was of land at Montpinchon (Manche, cant. Cerisy-la-Salle), La Lucerne (cant. La Haye-Pesnel), Champrépus (cant. Villedieu), Saint-Vigor-des-Monts (cant. Tessy) and

Argouges (cant. Saint-James-de-Beuvron). By 1139 his son Henry, a supporter of King Stephen, had become lord of the honour of Barnstaple, in Devon (*Gesta Stephani*, ed. K. R. Potter and R. H. C. Davis, Oxford, 1976,pp. 82–4, 210–12, 222); *Dom. Desc.*, p. 743.

[Appendix ii.8]

Hugh fitz Ranulf attested no. **20**. All the witnesses occur in charters of time of Abbot Bernard (nos. **114, 58, 68, 83, 84, 86, 87, 89, 91**). The William de Braeio who attested for the monks was perhaps either the William de Brae *prefectus* who attested an item in Robert of Torigny's register concerning the grant made by another William de Brae on becoming a monk in 1157, or that William himself (Delisle, *Torigni*, ii, p. 253).

[Appendix ii.10]

The names of Peter's wife and daughter occur together in the abbey's Necrology on 5 February. This grant, of Peter's inheritance in Guernsey, was entered as *Carta Petri filii Desiderie* in the Inventory, fol. 136r. In 1155 Rualend Calcebuf demised to the abbey what he had of the land of Peter son of Desirée, apparently in the region of Genêts (Delisle, *Torigni*, ii, p. 242).

[Appendix ii.11]

Bernard Pignatelli, abbot of the Cistercian abbey of SS Vincenzo and Anastasio outside Rome, elected pope as Eugenius III on 15 February 1145. Pupil and friend of Abbot Bernard of Clairvaux who greatly influenced his reforming programme, the two were responsible for initiating the ill-fated Second Crusade of 1147. He died on 8 July 1153. This bull is the clearest indication that the Cartulary was written before it was given on 15 December 1150. It would certainly have found an important place in the text if it had reached the abbey before the Cartulary was written or completed.

[Appendix ii.12]

See Hubert Guillotel, 'Du rôle des cimetières en Bretagne dans le renouveau du XIe et de la première moitié du XIIe siècle', *Mémoires de la Société d'Histoire et d'Archéologie de Bretagne* t. LII (1972–4), 1–22.

SELECT BIBLIOGRAPHY

Manuscripts

Bibliothèque municipale d'Avranches
- ms 210
- ms 211
- ms 213
- ms 214
- ms 215

Paris, Bibliothèque nationale
- ms fr. 18947 (Dom Hynes)
- ms fr. 18950 (Dom Le Roy)
- ms fr. 22325 (Dom Briant)
- ms fr. 22357
- ms lat. 5440A
- ms lat. 9215, no. 59
- ms lat. 10072(Lechaudé d'Anisy)
- ms lat. 14832, fols. 179r–181r
- ms lat. 17723
- ms nouv. acq. lat. 1674, fol.4

(A partial modern copy of the Cartulary, ms nouv. acq. lat. 1024, has not been consulted.)

London, British Library, Additional Charter 66980 and MS Royal 13 A xxiii.

Archives départementales de Calvados, F5276, *premier cahier*, copies by Gaston de Beausse of charters surviving until 1944 at Saint-Lô.

Archives départementales de La Manche, 6 J 70, copies by Geneviève Beauchesne of charters formerly in the archives and destroyed in 1944.

Printed Sources

General

Henri Omont, *Catalogue général des manuscrits des bibilothèques publiques de la France* t. x, 1–125, manuscrits de la bibliothèque d'Avranches, Paris 1889, based upon *Catalogue général des manuscrits des bibliothèques publiques des départements*, 7 vols, Paris 1849–85, t. iv, 427–562.

Millénaire monastique du Mont-Saint-Michel, 5 vols, Paris 1967–2001 [hereafter *Mill. mon.*], *i. Histoire et vie monastiques de l'abbaye* (ed. J. Laporte); *ii. Vie montoise et rayonnement intellectuel* (ed. R. Foreville); *iii. Culte de Saint Michel et pélerinages au Mont* (ed. M. Baudot); *iv. Sources et bibliographie générale*, by Michel Nortier, 2nd edition revisions by Henri Decaens; *v. Études archéologiques* (ed. M. Nortier)

1. Manuscript Production at Mont-Saint-Michel

J. J. G. Alexander, *Norman Illumination at Mont-Saint-Michel, 966–1100*, Oxford 1970

— 'A Romanesque copy from Mont Saint-Michel of an initial in the Corbie Psalter', *Mill. mon. ii*, 239–244

François Avril, 'La décoration des manuscrits du Mont-Saint-Michel, xi–xii siècles', *Mill. mon.*, ii, 203–238

— 'Notes sur quelques manuscrits bénédictins normands du XIe et XIIe siècle', *Mélanges d'Archéologie et d'Histoire de l'Ecole française de Rome*, t. 75, 1964, 514–22

A. Boinet, 'L'illustration du cartulaire du Mont-Saint-Michel', *Bibliothèque de l'Ecole des Chartes* t. lxx, 1909, 335–4, 337

M. Bourgeois-Lechartier, 'A la recherche du *Scriptorium* de l'abbaye du Mont Saint-Michel', *Mill. mon.*, ii, 171–200

F. Columbaluzier, 'Le Pontifical dit d'Avranches', *Mill. mon.* i, 383–398

Monique Dosdat, *L'enluminure romane au Mont Saint-Michel x^e–xiie siècles*, Rennes/Avranches 1991

Ursula Nilgen, 'Le *Cartulaire du Mont-Saint-Michel* et la miniature anglaise', in *Manuscrits et enluminures dans le monde normand (X^e–XVe siècles)*, ed. P. Bouet and M. Dosdat, Caen 1999

G. Nortier, 'La bibliothèque du Mont Saint-Michel', in id., *Les bibliothèques médiévales des abbayes bénédictines de Normandie. Fécamp, Le Bec, Le Mont Saint-Michel, Saint-Evroul, Lyre, Jumièges, Saint-Wandrille, Saint-Ouen*, Caen 1966 (reprinted, with same pagination, from *Revue Mabillon*, juillet–septembre 1957, pp. 135–171)

2. History of Mont-Saint-Michel and Its Region

A. Angot, *Dictionnaire historique, topographique et biographique de la Mayenne*, 4. vols., Laval 1900–1909

Mathieu Arnoux, 'Before the *Gesta Normannorum* and beyond Dudo. Some evidence on the first Norman historiography', read to the Battle Conference in 1999, forthcoming in *Anglo-Norman Studies*

D. Bates, *Normandy Before 1066*, Longmans, London/New York 1982

Geneviève Beauchesne, *Les possessions en Bretagne aux XIe et XIIe siècles des abbayes bénédictines de Touraine, d'Anjou et de Normandie*, Position des thèses...de l'Ecole des Chartes, 1935

A. Chédeville And H. Guillotel, *La Bretagne des saints et des rois Vᵉ–Xᵉ siècle*, Ouest-France, Rennes 1984

Jacques Dubois, 'Les dépendances de l'abbaye du Mont Saint-Michel et la vie monastique dans les prieurés', *Mill. mon.* i, note 1 on pp. 620–624

— 'Le martyrologue de l'abbaye du Mont-Saint-Michel', *Mill. Mon.* i, 489–99

André Dufief, 'Vie monastique au Mont pendant le XIIe siècle', *Mill. mon. i*, 121

André Dupont, *Un catalogue critique des églises et chapelles dont le patronage appartenant à l'abbaye du Mont Saint-Michel*, Saint-Lô 1979

D. Gremont and L. Donnat, 'Fleury, le Mont Saint-Michel et l'Angleterre à la fin du X et au début du XI siècle à propos du manuscrit d'Orléans, no. 127 (105), *Mill. mon.* i, 751–793

Hubert Guillotel, 'L'exode du clergé breton devant les invasions scandinaves', *Mémoires de la Société d'Histoire et d'Archéologie de Bretagne* lix, 1982, 301–316

— 'Le premier siècle du pouvoir ducal breton (936–1040), in: *Actes du 103 Congrès National des Sociétés Savantes* (Nancy-Metz, 1977) 63–84

— 'Les temps des rois VIIIᵉ - Xᵉ siècle', in A. Chédeville and H. Guillotel, *La Bretagne des saints et des rois Vᵉ - Xᵉ siècle*, Ouest-France 1984

— 'L'action de Charles le Chauve vis-à-vis la Bretagne de 843 à 852', *Mémoires de la Société d'Histoire et d'Archéologie de Bretagne* lii, 1975–6, 5–32

— 'Des vicomtes d'Alet aux vicomtes de Poudouvre', *Société d'histoire et d'archéologie de l'arrondissement de Saint-Malo, Année* 1988, 208–15

— 'Les évêques d'Alet du IX au milieu du XII siècle', *ibid.*, *Année* 1979, 251–66

— 'Combour: proto-histoire d'une seigneurie et mis en oeuvre de la reforme gregorienne', in *Family Trees and the Roots of Politics*, ed. K. S. B. Keats-Rohan, Woodbridge 1997

— 'Saint-Suliac: recontre de l'archéologie, de la diplomatique, du droit et de l'hagiographie', *Mémoires de la Société d'Histoire et d'Archéologie de Bretagne* lxxvi, 1998, 5–25

— 'Cartulaires bretons médiévaux', dans O. Guyotjeannin, L. Morelle, M. Parisse, edd. *Les cartulaires. Actes de la table ronde (Paris, décembre 1991)* Paris, Ecole des Chartes, 1993

Hubert Guillotel and André Chèdeville, *Cartulaire de l'abbaye de Saint-Sauveur de Redon* (no date, Association des Amis des Archives Historiques du diocèse de Rennes, Dol et Saint-Malo)

Guillotin De Corson, *Pouillé historique de l'archevéché de Rennes*, 6 vols, Rennes 1880–86

Jacques Hourlier, 'Le Mont Saint-Michel avant 966', *Mill. mon. MSM* i, 13–28

— 'L'abbaye du Mont Saint-Michel aux Xe et XIe siècles', *ib.*, i, 53–80

P. Hull, 'The foundation of Saint Michael's Mount, Cornwall, a priory of the abbey of Mont-Saint-Michel', in *Mill. mon. MSM*, i, 703–24

Jean Huynes, *Histoire générale de l'abbaye du Mont Saint-Michel au péril de la mer*, publié par Eugène de Robillard de Beaurepaire, 2 vols, Rouen 1872–3, ii, 232.

K. S. B. Keats-Rohan, 'Two studies in North French prosopography : 1. Ivo fitz Fulcoin, the counts of Maine, the lords of Bellême and the foundation of L'Abbayette. 2. Wigan the Marshal and other Bretons in Orderic Vitalis's *Ecclesiastical History*', *Journal of Medieval History* 20, 1994, 3–25, 25–37

— '*Un vassal sans histoire*'? Count Hugh II (fl. 955–992) and the Origins of Angevin Overlordship in Maine', in id. ed., *Family Trees and the Roots of Politics: British and French Prosopography from the Tenth to the Twelfth Century*, Woodbridge 1997, 189–210

— 'Politique et parentèle: les comtes, vicomtes et évêques du Maine c.950–1050', *Francia* 26.1 (1996), 13–30

— 'Observations upon the earliest castellanies in Maine', in *Mondes de l'Ouest et villes du Monde. Mélanges en l'honneur d'André Chédeville*, Rennes 1998, 361–373

— 'Poppa of Bayeux and her family', *The American Genealogist* 72 (1997), 187–204

— 'Les Bilihildis du Maine: Problèmes et possibilités d'une étude de l'onomastique et de la parenté de la France du nord-ouest', in *Onomastique et parenté*, ed. Christian Settipani and K. S. B. Keats-Rohan (Prosopographica et Genealogica 3, Oxford, 2000), 57–68

— 'L'histoire secrète d'un sanctuaire célèbre: la reformation du Mont-Saint-Michel d'après l'analyse de son cartulaire et de ses nécrologes', in *Culte et pèlerinages à saint Michel en Occident. Les trois Monts dédiés à l'archange*, ed. P. Bouet, George Otranto, Andre Vauchez, Coll. de l'Ecole français de Rome 316, Rome 2003

— 'Francs, scandinaves ou normands? Aperçus sur les premiers moines des monastères normands', forthcoming in *Les Fondations scandinaves et les débuts du duché de Normandie: Colloque de Cerisy-la-Salle, septembre 2002*, ed. Pierre Bauduin and Claude Lorren

S. Keynes, 'The Aethelings in Normandy', *Anglo-Norman Studies* xiii, 1991, 190–94

J. Laporte, 'L'abbaye du Mont Saint-Michel aux Xe et XIe siècles', *Mill. mon.*, i, 53–80

Robert Latouche, *Histoire du comté du Maine pendant le X et le XI siècle*, Bibliothèque de l'Ecole des Hautes Etudes CLXXXIII, Paris 1910

Abbé M. Lelagard, 'Saint Aubert', in *Millénaire monastique du Mont-Saint-Michel*, 2 vols, Paris 1967–93 [hereafter *Mill. mon.*], t. i, 29–52

J. F. Lemarignier, *Etude sur les privilèges d'exemption et de juridiction ecclésiastique des abbayes normandes depuis les origines jusqu'en 1140*, Paris 1937, 156–160, 264–66

Thomas Le Roy, *Les curieuses recherches du Mont Saint-Saint par Dom Thomas Le Roy*, published by Eugène de Robillard de Beaurepaire, Caen 1878

Gérard Louise, *La seigneurie de Bellême X–XII siècles* (Le Pays Bas-Normand 83 Année, nos. 199 and 200 1990, nos 201–202 1991)

Guy M. Oury, 'La Reconstruction Monastique dans l'Ouest: L'Abbé Gauzbert de Saint-Julien de Tours (v. 990–1007)', *Revue Mabillon* 1964, 69–124

Paul Peyron, *Recherches sur le culte de saint Michel au diocèse de Quimper et de Léon*, Rennes, 1896

Cassandra Potts, *Monastic Revival and Regional Identity in Early Normandy*, Woodbridge, 1997, 81–104.

Joëlle Quaghebeur, *La Cornouaille du IXe au XIIe siècle*, 2nd edn., Rennes, 2000

Michel Reulos, 'L'organisation et l'administration de l'abbaye à partir de l'Abbé Pierre Le Roi jusqu'à l'application du Concordat', *Mill. mon.* i, 191–209

E. Searle, *Predatory Kinship and the Creation of Norman Power 840–1066*, Berkeley and Los Angeles 1989

Christian Settipani, 'Les comtes d'Anjou et leurs alliances aux X et XI siècles', in Keats-Rohan ed., *Family Trees* (1997), 254–266

— 'Les vicomtes de Châteaudun et leur alliés', in *Onomastique et parenté*, ed. K. S. B. Keats-Rohan and Christian Settipani (Prosopographica et Genealogica 3, Oxford, 2000), 247–61

Nicolas Simonnet, 'La fondation du Mont-Saint-Michel d'après la *Revelatio ecclesiæ sancti Michælis*', *Annales de Bretagne et des pays de l'Ouest, t. 106, Année 1999*

Emily Zack Tabuteau, *Transfers of Property in Eleventh-Century Norman Law* (University of North Carolina Press, 1988)

Elisabeth M. C. Van Houts, 'Historiography and Hagiography at Saint-Wandrille: The *Inventio et Miracula Sancti Vulfranni*', *Anglo-Norman Studies* xii (1990) 233–51, here, p. 251

3. Chronicles and Charter Collections for Mont-Saint-Michel and Its Region

Actus pontificum Cenomannis in urbe degentium, ed. G. Busson et A. Ledru, Le Mans 1902 (*Arch. hist. du Maine* t. 2)

Anciens évêchés de Bretagne, ed. J. Geslin De Bourgogne and A. De Barthélemy, 6 vols. (St-Brieuc and Paris, 1855–79)

David Bates, *Regesta Regum Anglo-Normannorum. The Acta of William I (1066–1087)*, Oxford 1998

Pierre Bouet, 'La *Reuelatio* et les origines du culte à Saint Michel sur le Mont Tombe', in P. Brouet, G. Otranto, A. Vauchez, eds, *Culte et pèlerinages à saint Michel en Occident. Les trois Monts dédiés à l'archange* (Rome 2003)

B. de Broussillon, ed., *Cartulaire de Saint-Michel-de-l'Abbayette*, Paris 1894

B. de Broussillon, ed., *Cartulaire de Saint-Victeur au Mans*, Paris 1895

Cartulaire du Jersey. Recueil de documents concernant l'histoire de l'ile conservés aux archives de la Manche. Edition Société Jersiaise (vol. 23), Jersey 1918–20,

L. Delisle, *Histoire de Saint-Sauveur-le-Vicomte, suivi de pièces justificatives*, Valognes, 1867

L. Delisle, 'Charte Normande de 1088', *Société de l'Histoire de France*, Paris, 1886. Exh., *Millénaire*, no. 123

Marie Fauroux, ed., *Recueil des actes des ducs de Normandie (911–1066)*, Société des Antiquaires de Normandie t. 36, Caen, 1961

L. Guilloreau, *Chartes d'Otterton,* Ligugé, Vienne 1909

L. Guilloreau, *Chartes de Créans, prieuré dépendant de l'abbaye du Mont Saint-Michel (xi–xviii siècle)*, in *Annales Fléchoises*, 1909

H. Guillotel, *Les Actes des Ducs de Bretagne (944–1148)* (Thèse pour le Doctorat en Droit, Juillet, 1973, Paris)

Jacques Hourlier, 'Les sources écrites de l'histoire montoise anterieure à 966', *Mill. mon.*, ii, 121–132

Peter L. Hull, ed., *The Cartulary of St Michael's Mount*, Devon and Cornwall Record Society, N.S. 5 (1962 for 1958)

L. R. and L. Hulmet, 'Monographie sur la paroisse de la Chapelle-Hamelin', *Revue de l'Avranchin*, Année 95, t. 54, June 1977, 149–57

V. Hunger, *Histoire de Verson*, 1908

Inventio et miracula Sancti Vulfranni, ed. Dom J. Laporte, Société Hist. Norm. *Mélanges*, t. xiv, 1938

William of Jumièges *The* Gesta Normannorum Ducum *of William of Jumièges, Orderic Vitalis and Robert of Torigni*, ed. E. M. C. Van Houts, 2 vols, Oxford 1992–5

K. S. B. Keats-Rohan, 'Crime et châtiment à la manière du XIe siècle?: note sur une charte bretonne de l'abbaye du Mont-Saint-Michel', *Mémoires de la Société d'Histoire et d'Archéologie de Bretagne*, 72 (1995) 25–30

— 'Bibliothèque municipale d'Avranches, 210: Cartulary of Mont-Saint-Michel', *Anglo-Norman Studies* xxi (1999), 95–112

— 'Une charte de l'Abbé Mayeul de Cluny et la Réforme de l'abbaye de Mont-Saint-Michel', in *La Normandie autour de l'an mil*, ed. F. de Beaurepaire, J.-P. Chaline (Société de l'Histoire de Normandie, 2000), 159–70

— 'Testimonies of The Living Dead: The Necrology and Martyrology-Necrology in the Chapter Book of Mont-Saint-Michel, Avranches Bibliothèque Municipale, MS 214', in *The Durham Liber Vitae*, ed. D. and L. Rollason, M. Harvey and A. Piper (2004), 165–90

Jean Laporte, 'Les obituaires du Mont Saint-Michel', *Mill. mon.* i, 725–41

Lechaudé D'Anisy, *Grand rôles des Echiquiers de Normandie*, in *Mémoires de la Société des antiquaires de Normandie*, t. 15, Paris, 1845

Abbé Marquis, 'Gohory, son prieuré de Saint-Michel', *Bull. de la Soc. Dunoise*, t. v, 1885–7, 257–76

Hyacinthe Morice, *Histoire ecclésiastique et civile de Bretagne: Preuves* t.1, Paris, 1742

Orderic Vitalis, *The Ecclesiastical History of Orderic Vitalis*, ed. M. Chibnall, 6 vols., Oxford 1969–80

William of Poitiers, *The* Gesta Willelmi *of William of Poitiers*, ed. R. H. C. Davis and M. Chibnall, Oxford 1998

Regesta Regum Anglo-Normannorum, i, ed. H. W. C. Davis, ii, ed. C. Johnson and H. A. Cronne, iii, ed. H. A. Cronne and R. H. C. Davis, Oxford, 1913–1968; see also under Bates, above.

J. H. Round, ed., *Calendar of Documents preserved in France, illustrative of the history of Great Britain and Ireland*, vol. I (Public Record Office, 1899)

William de Saint-Pair, *Li romanz del Munt Saint-Michiel par Guillaume de Saint-Pair*, ed. Francisque-Michel, Caen 1856 (*Mémoires de la Société des Antiquaires de Normandie*, t. xx), includes a study of the author by Eugène De Beaurepaire; also edited by Paul Redlich, *Le Roman du Mont Saint-Michel*, Marburg 1894, and by Graham Birrell in an unpublished doctoral thesis, Aberdeen 1978. On the text see G. Birrell, *Romania* 100, 1978, 260–70; R. Herval, 'Un moine jongleur au Mont Saint-Michel: Guillaume de Saint-Pair', *Mill. mon.* ii, 383–96.

Dudo De Saint-Quentin, *De moribus et actis primorum Normanniae ducum*, publié par Jules Lair, Caen, 1865, (Mémoires de la Société des Antiquaires de Normandie, t. 23); *Dudo of St Quentin: History of the Normans*, trans. Eric Christiansen, Woodbridge 1998.

Robert De Torigny, *Chronique de Robert de Torigni ... suivie de divers opuscules historiques de cet auteur*, ed. L. Delisle, 2 vols, Rouen 1872–3. See also his *Interpolations* in William of Jumièges, above.

GENERAL INDEX

Numbers refer to pages, except those in bold which refer to item numbers in the edition. Entries under Saint are listed in alphabetical order irrespective of the spelling of 'saint'. The modern *département* name is given after a French place-name. The compiler was the author.

INDEX NOMINA

Latin personal and place names occurring in the Cartulary and in the Appendices are indexed here. Numbers refer to the charter numbers in the edition. Personal names are given in the nominative.